WHITE TEACHERS / DIVERSE CLASSROOMS

Creating Inclusive Schools, Building on Students' Diversity, and Providing True Educational Equity

Edited by

Julie G. Landsman and *Chance W. Lewis*

SECOND EDITION

1996–2011 15TH ANNIVERSARY

Sty us
PUBLISHING, LLC.

STERLING, VIRGINIA

Sty/us

Published by Stylus Publishing, LLC
22883 Quicksilver Drive
Sterling, Virginia 20166-2102

Library of Congress Cataloging-in-Publication-Data
White teachers, diverse classrooms : creating inclusive
schools, building on students' diversity, and providing true
educational equity / edited by Julie Landsman and Chance
W. Lewis.—2nd ed.
    p. cm.
Includes bibliographical references and index.
ISBN 978-1-57922-595-7 (cloth : alk. paper)
ISBN 978-1-57922-596-4 (pbk. : alk. paper)
ISBN 978-1-57922-597-1 (library networkable e-edition)
ISBN 978-1-57922-598-8 (consumer e-edition)
1. Multicultural education—United States.
2. Minorities—Education—United States.   3. Race
awareness—Study and teaching—United States.
4. Teachers, White—United States.   5. Multiculturalism—
United States.   I. Landsman, Julie. II. Lewis, Chance W.
(Chance Wayne), 1972–
LC1099.3.W48   2010
370.1170973—dc22
                                                    2010045363

13-digit ISBN: 978-1-57922-595-7 (cloth)
13-digit ISBN: 978-1-57922-596-4 (paper)
13-digit ISBN: 978-1-57922-597-1 (library networkable
e-edition)
13-digit ISBN: 978-1-57922-598-8 (consumer e-edition)

Printed in the United States of America

All first editions printed on acid free paper
that meets the American National Standards Institute
Z39-48 Standard.

Bulk Purchases

Quantity discounts are available for use in
workshops and for staff development.
Call 1-800-232-0223

Second Edition, 2011

10   9   8   7   6

Becoming Joey

Paul C. Gorski

José's ten.
Looks six by size,
twenty in the eyes.

Down
the school-morning street
he ambles along
dotted lines of busses and cars
that spit exhaust like expletives,
disturbing his meditation
on a few final moments of peace.

He is frail but upright.
Hand-me-downs hang
from his slenderness,
patched and stained.
Soles flop beneath battered shoes,
worn through but hanging on,
if only by a lace.

He pauses in the schoolyard
where white kids laugh and scurry
unaware of this, his battle;
of this, his burden;
of these, his borderlands.
Behind him: cracked sidewalks
and frosty nights
sweetened by the warmth of belonging.
Before him: manicured playgrounds,
heated classrooms,
and enthusiastic lessons about a world
that doesn't see him.

Still, he moves forward,
what feels in his stomach
a regressive sort of forward.

And he straightens his shirt,
tries dusting off the stains of ancestry.
And he clears his throat,
tries spitting out his Mexican voice.
And, becoming Joey, he crosses into school.

CONTENTS

PART FOUR: CREATING CLASSROOMS FOR EQUITY, ACTIVISM, AND SOCIAL JUSTICE

POEMS

A CALL TO ACTION AND SELF-REFLECTION FOR WHITE TEACHERS IN DIVERSE CLASSROOMS

Julie G. Landsman and Chance W. Lewis

I t is with great pleasure that we bring out a new, enlarged, and more encompassing edition of *White Teachers/Diverse Classrooms*. Over the past four years, since the first edition of this book was published, we have received positive feedback from teachers, professors, and community workers across the country. When we visited classrooms and conference halls they requested that we include chapters that expand on the cultures and issues of students covered in the text. Thus, we have added seven chapters that include suggestions for working with immigrant, Latino, Asian, and Native American students. While you cannot make generalizations about one single cultural group, there are some ideas and insights that can help us position ourselves in relation to cultures, communities, practices, and perceptions when we teach in our increasingly diverse classrooms. This new edition expands on specific ideas for students from minority backgrounds in addition to African American students who were the emphasis in the first edition. Unfortunately, the need for this information is as great today as it was four years ago. We hope you enjoy and can use the practical approaches in this second edition.

In retrospect, the title of Gloria Ladson-Billings's chapter would have been most appropriate for the entire book: " 'Yes, But How Do We Do It?'"

There is plenty of research for public consumption (journal articles, policy briefs, and books) and some inaccessible jargon focused on the simple fact that students of color are not achieving at the same rates academically as their White classmates in public school systems across the United States. While this information is critical to know, to understand, and to be concerned about, there is a pressing need for practical and concrete ideas to help "turn the tide" academically for all students of color.

W. E. B. DuBois noted in his groundbreaking book *The Souls of Black Folk* that the problem of America is because of the color line. If this is the case, then we are deplorably behind in addressing issues of education for students of color, since DuBois identified this problem over a century ago. What makes us so reluctant to grapple with this issue? Some believe it is White people's unwillingness to talk about racism, much less work on changing methods and curriculum. Others say the issue is already being addressed; we just have to give it more time. Some refuse to admit there is a problem at all, unless it resides solely in the Black, Latino, Asian, or Native American communities. We, the editors of this book, believe that much of the work must be done within the community and the racial group that does most of the educating: the White teachers, administrators, counselors, and social workers of our students. We also believe that real change requires deep reflecting, re-evaluating, and continually revisiting our actions and responses to students and their families.

We hope this book provides practical help in the day-to-day interactions that occur in our classrooms and hallways across the country: be it in college, teaching certification programs, or elementary and secondary schools. A plethora of research and testimony show the gap between test scores, grades, and college entrance rates of students of color and White students across the country. To further fuel the debate, the continuing emphasis on No Child Left Behind and Race to the Top legislation has caused considerable debate and discussion about standardized tests and what they actually indicate. All this is on the table at this moment in our educational history.

We, the editors, believe now is the time to have the uncomfortable talks, the continuing dialogue, the community work, and the self-reflection necessary to truly understand and change the situation for those students who are being failed by our public educational institutions and assessment standards. We felt this way four years ago and feel it with even more intensity today. Now is the time to look at practices and results of those practices with the blunt and critical lens of urgency and concern. We hope this book gives its readers pause. We also hope it energizes White teachers to look at their classrooms, reflect on their interactions with students of color and even their school building policies, and opt for true change and equity.

We continue to find that while all children of color experience difficulty and systematic racism in this country, African Americans have received more than a fair share of negative media attention. Parts of the original edition were devoted to their education and to what needs to be addressed to close the opportunity gap between African American students and all others. We have kept many of these chapters in this new edition. We also believe that Latino, Native American, and Asian students suffer from stereotyping, generalizations, and invisibility in our schools and colleges. This edition devotes new chapters to addressing their unique situations. For many of these students the suggestions, ideas, theories, and pedagogies include ways for teachers to reach all students, including those who are poor—be they White or of color. These new chapters include ideas for good teaching across the board. Thus, we hope the chapters in this edition address a general outlook regarding education as a whole and advocate for important changes for all students in the United States. Everyone can benefit from the truth of history, of knowledge, and of best practices. This book explores issues of race and culture in education, yet also presents theory and pedagogy for teachers in any environment.

We are also great believers in the power of stories to tell important truths and inscribe wisdom. Autobiography and memoirs are interspersed throughout this book to bring home to readers, on a visceral level, what we really mean when we speak of low expectations or invisibility within the curriculum. We need such stories to remind us of the human costs of our educational failures, our systematic indifference. Poems go even more deeply into the moment. We open and close this book with a poem to give the reader pause, to take time with that individual moment. We hope you take those moments. We hope you reflect on your own background and perceptions to locate the intersections you experience and create that can build bridges to your students.

Part One, entitled "Foundations of Our Work: Recognizing Power, Privilege, and Perspectives," includes Julie Landsman's chapter entitled "Being White: Invisible Privileges of a New England Prep School Girl." In this opening chapter, Landsman calls on the work of Peggy McIntosh, Thandeka, W. E. B. DuBois, and Barack Obama (whom she referenced in the original edition four years ago) to clarify what it means to be White in this country and how this affects everything we do and how we live. She concludes with some suggestions for exploring this further in groups and in communities. She emphasizes that this is ongoing, and that with each new group of students we start over, creating new "ways in" to cultures that are not our own.

In chapter 2, "Reflections on Education: A Two-Way Journey," Kalia Yang gives us the benefit of her story. She describes her own experience coming to the United States and her invitation to learn from her White teachers. Aaron Rudolph Miller Hokanson co-writes the chapter and tells the story of his own White upbringing and how his education influenced the way he teaches today. The combination of these straightforward accounts poignantly demonstrates what our jobs and our work is all about.

Part Two, "Culturally Relevant Teachers: Foundations and Personal Engagement," includes nine chapters by practitioners working in classrooms in both universities and public schools. In her chapter, " 'Yes, But How Do We Do It?' " Ladson-Billings breaks down what it means to teach students of color effectively and how to apply this to the classroom in a practical, doable manner. Ladson-Billings gives clear and passionate, well-researched and well-documented suggestions that work effectively for all students in our schools. Robert Simmons's chapter 4, "The Empty Desk in the Third Row," captures an experience he had with a student in his inner-city classroom. He calls us back to the basic impulses and passion we each feel about teaching and about children. H. Richard Milner explores the theories of multicultural education and best practices in chapter 5, "But Good Intentions Are Not Enough." He gives us the vital overview we need to understand what has been happening in our schools and some ways to rethink how we look at teaching, history, and integration of subject matter into our curriculum for students of many cultures.

Paul Gorski asks us to go further than the "Heroes and Holidays" approach to multicultural education in chapter 6, "The Unintentional Undermining of Multicultural Education." He challenges us to look at the system behind the system. How are we contributing to our students' lack of achievement when we are silent in the face of racist curricula or generalizations by our colleagues? How do we change our work from education to educational activism? Gorski provides some important questions and suggested responses in his piece. Stephen Hancock's chapter 7, "White Women's Work," addresses White women and their role in the school systems as they exist today. Hancock gives voices to White women teachers to explore what they believe are critical factors for their success in diverse classrooms. This chapter also explores avenues that encourage, empower, and enlighten White women to become more effective in diverse classrooms. In "When Truth and Joy Are at Stake," Julie Landsman uses her 30 years as a Minneapolis teacher to talk about how to build trust, not only among students each hour, but also between a White teacher and her students who are primarily Black. Practical activities, curriculum interweaving, and a firm structure provide the basis for her exploration into effective diverse classrooms.

In chapter 9, "Color Blindness, Unconscious Bias, and Student Achievement in Suburban Schools," Justin Grinage observes what happens to and what is said about students of color in the high school where he teaches and reveals his own story of being the only African American teacher in a large suburban high school. It is an article full of the practical, down-to-earth reality of schools today. Justin insists that teachers explore their own perceptions and assumptions about race and culture and gives some suggestions for doing just that. In their chapter, "Tips for School Principals and Teachers," Dorothy Garrison-Wade and Chance W. Lewis provide a research-based article stating ways administrators can address the achievement gap. This chapter, after hearing the voices of African American students, provides practical recommendations to administrators and other educational professionals working with African American students. In chapter 11, "How Can Service-Learning Increase the Academic Achievement of Urban African American Students?" Verna Cornelia Price gives us a passionate and well researched way of providing the important connection to students, their parents, and their communities. African American students need to experience a connection to their real world in their schools. Dr. Price helps us construct a vibrant and important method for doing this.

In Part Three, "Knowing Who Is in the Classroom: How White Teachers Can Ensure All Children Achieve," Stephanie Flores-Koulish addresses the needs of students who may not fit any existing category. She uses her situation as a Columbian adoptee into a mixed-race family to explore the complexities of identity for students who are adopted or simply of mixed parentage. Flores-Koulish uses her story to illustrate how racial and cultural stereotypes are simplistic and harmful to students. Beverly Klug's chapter, "Daring to Teach: Challenging the Western Narrative of American Indians in the Classroom," gives us an overview of historical consequences of the way American Indians have been treated in this country. She explores how these consequences play out in the public school classrooms. She also describes some examples of cultural mismatches between White teachers and mainstream education and Native children. These cultural mismatches include expectations for behavior and academic work. Professor Joseph White, in an interview with Julie Landsman, provides a clear, thoughtful voice about teaching young Black men. He calls on his years of experience and research into Black psychology to give the reader practical, compassionate, and vivid ideas for reaching young Black boys in our classrooms.

In their chapter entitled "Black/African Families: Coming of Age in Predominately White Communities," Val Middleton, Kieran Coleman, and Chance Lewis explore the unique challenges of educating Black students in a predominately White setting. These authors uncover the experiences of Black students and their families in their attempt to adjust in this setting. "Understanding Korean American Students: Facts, Not Myth," by Ok-Hee Lee, describes the history of Korean students, the stereotypes of Asian students, and ways to make these students feel visible in the classroom. She deconstructs the myth of the "ideal minority" and gives us a rich collection of ideas on how to think about students in new ways. Carolyn Holbrook, in her autobiographical piece entitled "Low Expectations Are the Worst Form of Racism" intimately explores the troubling experiences of a Black single mother and teacher raising her children in a system that rarely expects as much from her bright, eager sons and daughters as it does from their White friends. She shows us the life of one woman trying to advocate for her own and others' children, the damage of generalization and unconscious racist actions and reactions, and some ways to avoid these pitfalls. In chapter 18, "How Educators Can Support the High Expectations for Education That Exist in the Latino Family and Student Community," Jennifer Godinez emphasizes the persistence and desire of Latino families to provide higher education for their children. She uses her own story to highlight her parents' reverence for education and the ways teachers can build upon these expectations with their students. It is a chapter that encourages all of us to focus on Latinos, the fastest growing demographic in our student population, and the gifts and aspirations they contribute to our schools and communities.

Verna Cornelia Price's chapter "I Don't Understand Why My African American Students Are Not Achieving" clearly and concisely spells out exactly why we have an educational gap in America and what needs to be done about it. With copious research and systematic explanation and recommendations, she makes it abundantly clear where we have gone wrong and how to make things right. She is direct, unflinching, and brings us her academic and psychological grasp of the subject in an accessible and powerful way. Bruce Douglas, Esrom Pitre, and Chance W. Lewis address a specific situation in their chapter entitled "African American Male Student-Athletes and White Teachers' Classroom Interactions." These authors reveal how African American student-athletes are not held to the same academic standards as their classmates as long as they perform well in their designated school sports teams. The findings from this chapter will make us take a closer look at the potential damage we are doing to African American student-athletes.

In Part Four, "Creating Classrooms for Equity, Activism, and Social Justice," three chapters provide ways to tap into activism in our students and their families and communities to move beyond equality and toward equity. William Perez, Susana Munoz, Cynthia Alcantar, and Nancy Guarneros, who collectively wrote chapter 21, "Educators Supporting DREAMERS: Becoming an Undocumented Student Ally," present us with vivid anecdotes, extensive research, and action studies that show the difficulties undocumented students face, their position in the larger Latino community, and what teachers can do to advocate for them. These educators have a wealth of information and common sense suggestions for actively encouraging students and supporting the DREAM Act. Sharon Ishii-Jordan speaks from her perspective as a teacher educator. She is clear and unequivocal in her article "Preparing Teachers to Develop Inclusive Communities," about what is needed to truly bring about equity in education and what part teachers can play in this. Finally, Bridgie A. Ford urges us to connect to the communities in which our students live in her chapter entitled "Culturally Responsive School-Community Partnerships: Strategy for Success." While we often pay lip service to the importance of the community, we usually do very little to reach out to the world our students come from. Through this chapter we not only understand the importance of reaching out to parents and communities but are also given examples of ways of making this connection.

Ultimately, this book is only as useful as White teachers make it. We have culled together a rich, fresh look at schools and teachers from young and old; veteran and new; teachers and professors of color; and White teachers, researchers, and professors from all over the country. In their wise words they bring us new ways of looking at ourselves in relation to education, to race, and to the practice of teaching. Unless we put their suggestions into practice, not only in the classroom but in our own private moments of reflection; in our board rooms, faculty meetings, and town hall gatherings; racism, inequity, and the achievement gap will continue to deprive the majority of our students of the right to live up to their potential. Unless we are willing to make the effort to change the way we think and act, many young people will find themselves hopeless. Put in these terms, it is imperative to challenge racist assumptions in ourselves and others, and then to put into practice new strategies and form true partnerships with parents and communities across the United States. In 10 years, the majority of our students will be of color.

Our job then, as educators and change makers, is no less important than the healthy future of our young people and our world. And lest it be forgotten, White students, as well as those of color, have a great amount to gain from equity for all. For the sake of all our children we must follow up our reading with action and our contemplation with change. The writers, teachers, and thinkers in this book give us a way.

PART ONE

FOUNDATIONS OF OUR WORK: RECOGNIZING POWER, PRIVILEGE, AND PERSPECTIVES

I

BEING WHITE

Invisible Privileges of a New England Prep School Girl

Julie G. Landsman

Oprah Winfrey was once turned away from a fancy department store in Paris. All sorts of excuses were offered afterward. Yet the fact remained, if this had been Barbra Streisand, Celine Dion, or Britney Spears, she would have been welcomed onto the premises, no matter the time of day or what was going on inside. Because she had dark skin, one of the richest Americans was excluded from this department store.

After she was named president of Brown University, Ruth Simmons went shopping at a major department store in New York. She was followed and questioned as she walked the aisles, dressed in her Ivy League tweed. There is little question that she would have been left alone if she had been a White woman. "Some things have not changed," she said, in an interview on *60 Minutes* after being named the first Black woman president of an Ivy League university.

Similar stories abound in every city, every town, and every suburb in the United States. These stories give the lie to the claim that "it is really all about class." If it were "all about class," Oprah Winfrey, Ruth Simmons, and countless other rich Black Americans would not be turned away, followed, or harassed. College professors, administrators, teachers, engineers, photographers, scientists, doctors, CEOs of corporations tell the same tale: "I was walking down the street in my suit and tie on my way to work" . . . "I was waiting for my wife to get off work in a suburb near where we live" . . . "I was driving down the street like everyone else and . . ." These statements come not from kids dressed in low riders and gold necklaces, not from T-shirted workers on a construction site at lunch hour, or from women on their way home from cleaning someone's house. The stories that reverberate across America come from upper- and middle-class African Americans, often dressed conservatively in order to protect themselves from "unreasonable search" and scrutiny. In *The Corner* (1997), by David Simon and Edward Burns, a book that documents the lives of crack addicts and others living on a single street corner in Baltimore, there is a very telling statement about a Black man who is a drug addict, yet who was at one time a rich executive and stock holder in major corporations:

> He could admit personal guilt; he knew what he'd done. Yet if that was all there was to it, why did the world treat him exactly the same when he was doing right, when he had all those jobs and all those stocks and mutual funds? Back then, all his money and standing didn't matter to the sales clerks and security guards, who would follow him around the stores. The world was no different when he drove his Mercedes—bought and paid for with Beth Steel paychecks and tech-stock dividends—and suffered through dozens of police stops and registration checks. Nor did money count when he would get dressed up and bring a date down to the harbor restaurants. His worst, most humiliating memory, was of a cool summer night when he took a girl to City Lights in Harborplace and asked if it might be possible to sit outside on the balcony. No, sorry, he was told; then they were seated at a table by the kitchen while the balcony tables stayed empty for the next two hours. A small insult, of course—nothing that could level a person in a single blow, unless that person came from Fayette Street, where every moment tells you who you are and what you were meant to be. (p. 356)

The Urgency: Understanding White Privilege

When, as Whites, we talk about the unearned privileges of white skin, we are simply trying to make the reality of our experience understood in itself. We try to name it as a racial privilege, not something that can be denied, or minimized as only affecting those of a certain class. It is important to tease out what this White privilege means before we can understand the complexities of its combination with other experiences of class or ethnicity. Only then can we work to bring true equality to all Americans. At this moment, the key to understanding a basic inequity and injustice in the United States is to acknowledge that the problem resides not in Oprah, Ruth Simmons, or the well-dressed Black man shown to the worst seat in a restaurant full of empty choice tables. The problem resides in the men and women at the doors, or those in the boardrooms, management offices, school districts, and other decision-making locations, blocking the way, or following customers in their stores, or denying places and classes, entrance and access, to men and women based solely on their Blackness or their Brownness. As a result, the privilege resides in the fact that White people can move about, can experience life, can apply to college, for loans, for jobs without being denied entrance or freedom based on their skin color—and never for a moment have to think about it.

White Resistance

It is when I ask for an acceptance of the aforementioned presence of White privilege that I encounter the most resistance. Many would like to couch the discussion of race in a litany of stories such as those I described to introduce this chapter and stop there. After all, we can easily shake our heads and feel sympathy, sorrow, or disapproval for the victims of race discrimination. And all the time, we know we would never do this: we would never deny a person a table, a choice seat, or a chance to shop if we were in charge. We can feel comfortable when the discussion rests on the misfortunes of others and does not come back to our own place in the story, having to do with our experience, responsibility, complicity, and advantages as Whites in America.

When I conduct two-day workshops for teachers, I often save the discussion of White privilege until the last hours, hoping I have built up trust and ease among the members of the group, so that they will feel free to discuss their misperceptions; their mistakes; and, ultimately, their experiences of privilege. Teachers are often willing to examine curriculum in their classrooms honestly; they are even willing to talk about relationships and biases regarding students and parents but only if this occurs in a nonthreatening atmosphere. Yet, many of these same teachers balk when it comes to examining their own advantages as White people in the world.

However, such self-scrutiny is exactly what White teachers must engage in if we are to make change in our classrooms and in institutions. This reflection is the way we will experience the significant deep transformation in the education of students in our classrooms that can lead to equal opportunity in our country. More than 90 percent of the teaching force in America is White. It is incumbent upon us to explore this area of White privilege in depth to truly counter racism in education and to provide equity for all students.

Defining White Privilege

In the opening paragraphs of his book *The Souls of Black Folks* (1903), W. E. B. DuBois articulates a basic difference between the experience of Whites and Blacks when he describes the "double consciousness" that Black Americans must possess to survive.

> After the Egyptian and Indian, the Greek and Roman, the Teuton and Mongolian, the Negro is a sort of seventh son, born with a veil, and gifted with second-sight in this American world,—a world which yields him no true self-consciousness, but only lets him see himself through the revelation of the other world. It is a peculiar sensation, this double-consciousness, this sense of always looking at one's self through the eyes of others, of measuring one's soul by the tape of a world that looks on in amused contempt and pity. One ever feels his two-ness,—an American, a Negro; two souls, two thoughts, two unreconciled strivings; two warring ideals in one dark body, whose dogged strength alone keeps it from being torn asunder. (p. 3)

Some ninety years later, Barack Obama (1996), in his book *Dreams from My Father*, describes a time when these two warring selves came together on a visit to Africa:

> And all of this while a steady procession of black faces passed before your eyes, the round faces of babies and the chipped, worn faces of the old; beautiful faces that made me understand the transformation that Asante and other black Americans claimed to have undergone after their first visit to freedom that comes from not feeling watched, the freedom of believing that your hair grows as it's supposed to grow and that your rump sways the way a rump is supposed to sway. You could see a man talking to himself as just plain crazy, or read about the criminal on the front page of the daily paper and ponder the corruption of the human heart, without having to think about whether the criminal or lunatic said something about your own fate. Here the world was black, and so you were just you; you could discover all those things that were unique to your life without living a lie or committing betrayal. (p. 284)

From these two passages one gets a view of the overarching privilege Whites have in this country: that of *single racial consciousness, single sight*. We can walk through America being who we are without an awareness of a second racial self: the self as viewed by others. If we fail, we fail as who we are, unique and flawed individuals. If we succeed, we succeed because we have accomplished what we have through hard work, as individuals with our complicated histories and qualities.

Instead of seeing double consciousness as a problem for Blacks, we must see single consciousness as a privilege of Whites in America. When we understand this single consciousness, we must work to make sure that all Americans have the chance to live as Obama (1996, p. 284) describes: "So you were just you; you could discover all those things that were unique to your life without living a lie or committing a betrayal." Although it may be true that other groups also experience a version of double consciousness, this chapter focuses on that privilege of single consciousness we have as people with white skin in order to understand and accept the reality of racism.

Acknowledging this reality, we need more concrete descriptions of how it plays out in everyday living and, ultimately, in the context of education. Additionally, to acknowledge this privilege as a reality is a strong beginning, a necessary step toward the self-reflection and examination so many of us avoid or shy away from. Peggy McIntosh, in her groundbreaking paper "White Privilege and Male Privilege: A Personal Account of Coming to See Correspondences through Work in Women's Studies," captures in very specific terms what it means to be White in the United States. She insists that we change our perspective radically, from a listing of deficits and problems of people of color to a listing of the concrete privileges and advantages Whites have based simply on the color of their skin.

McIntosh distinguishes between "earned strength and unearned power conferred systemically." She says:

> Some privileges, like the expectation that neighbors will be decent to you, or that your race will not count against you in court, should be the norm in a just society and should be considered as the entitlement of everyone. Others, like the privilege not to listen to less powerful people, distort the humanity of the holders as well as the ignored groups. Still others, like finding one's staple foods everywhere, may be a function of being a member of a numerical majority in the population. Others have to do with not having to labor under pervasive negative stereotyping and mythology. (p. 13)

In a description of one major advantage on her list, we hear both DuBois and Obama's reflective voices:

> The positive "privilege" of belonging, the feeling that one belongs within the human circle, as Native Americans say, fosters development and should not be seen as privilege for a few. It is, let us say, an entitlement none of us would have to earn; ideally it is an unearned entitlement. At present, since only a few have it, it is an unearned advantage for some. The negative "privilege" which gave me cultural permission not to take darker-skinned Others seriously can be seen as arbitrarily conferred dominance and should not be desirable for anyone. (p. 14)

From here McIntosh goes on to list fifty specific privileges we experience as Whites. This list is of those things she experiences as an insider based solely on her skin color. Those with darker skin are made to feel outsiders in their own homeland, and especially in relation to the powerful, the decision makers. For us as Whites, to accept this list is to accept our own experience as having certain advantages—in getting jobs, in getting a good education, in experiencing daily ease, in getting help with financial matters, and in simply living our daily lives, solely as a result of having white skin. Here are a few of the fifty items from McIntosh's list:

> I can if I wish arrange to be in the company of people of my race most of the time.

> If I should need to move, I can be pretty sure of renting or purchasing housing in an area which I can afford and in which I would want to live.

> I can go shopping alone most of the time, pretty well assured that I will not be followed or harassed.

> When I am told about our national heritage or about 'civilization' I am shown that people of my color made it what it is.

> I can be pretty sure that my children's teachers and employers will tolerate them if they fit school and workplace norms; my chief worries about them do not concern other's attitudes toward their race.

> I am never asked to speak for all the people of my racial group.

> My culture gives me little fear about ignoring the perspectives and powers of people of other races. (pp. 5–9)

I have taken these seven items as illustrations of McIntosh's way of helping us think in explicit terms of what advantages we have as Whites. She makes visible what has been invisible to many of us. Our schools surround us with such privileges and rear us in the assumption that such privileges are available to all Americans. We are rarely, if ever, asked to think of our skin color as relevant to our plans, our future, our daily experience. This obliviousness is in itself a privilege, our "single consciousness" again.

The Price Whites Pay

Thandeka (2000) eloquently describes the cost to us as White people living this life in her book *Learning to Be White*. When she traces White people's sense of alienation, she finds we have something she calls White shame. Time after time, in her interviews with Whites who worked for racial equality and justice, she watches as her interviewee breaks down in tears, describing some moment in childhood when that person hurt someone who was not White because he or she had been taught to do so by his or her parents.

> In the face of adult silence to racial abuse, the child learns to silence and then deny its own resonant feelings toward racially proscribed others, not because it chooses to become white, but because it wishes to remain within the community that is quite literally its life. The child thus learns, "layer by layer," to stay away from the nonwhite zones of its own desires.
>
> The internal nonwhite zone is the killing fields of desire, the place where impulses to community with persons beyond the pale are slaughtered. The child develops an antipathy toward its own forbidden feelings and to the persons who are the objects of these forbidden desires: the racial others. This developing white attitude in the child is a "means of being 'ready' and 'set'" to act in a certain way. (p. 24)

I felt this shame often as a young girl. We had moved to Texas from Connecticut so my father could become chief test pilot for Chance Vaught Aircraft. At the age of four, one warm noontime in Dallas, I used the word *nigger* in front of Leah, the woman who worked for my mother as a nurse and kitchen helper. My father had taught me that word in a rhyme that began "eeny meeny miney mo." Leah sat me down across from her and told me, looking me directly in the eye, that she was hurt by "that word," that she hoped I would not use it again. I felt awful. I had never experienced my own behavior as a way to hurt anyone so deeply. When I told my father what Leah said, he shrugged his shoulders, talked about how oversensitive she was, and told me not to worry about it. And yet I knew what hurt I was capable of causing someone I liked and respected. And it was in this moment of shame that I also learned the fallibility of my own, all-powerful father. This frightened me as well. Ever since that day I have experienced a split within myself in my connection to my father, a man I respected and also feared, and even in connection to my mother, who acquiesced in his views.

For much of my life my father used the word *nigger*, as well as other epithets to describe Italian Americans, Chinese Americans, and Latinos. Thandeka (2000, p. 127) describes this as part of my White race identity development: "The white self-image that emerges from this process will include the emotional fallout from the self-annihilating process that created it: the breakup of one's own sense of coherency, efficacy and agency as a personal center of activity."

Thandeka eventually ties in aspects of class and upbringing with the development of race identity. My father struggled all his life with his identity as a poor man from Missouri who made it into the upper-class life of wealthy Whites in Connecticut. He found himself mixing with those with the last names Lodge or Adams: "old money" names of wealth long-established, the kind of money and background he never knew as a child. My mother was from a wealthy Connecticut banking family. I was brought up in this life of wealth and privilege. Our house was a rambling one in a toney suburb. We had a tennis court, a basketball hoop, and acres of field and orchard. Three of five children, myself included, went away to boarding school. All of us attended college, graduating debt free.

When my friend Sue O'Halloran, a White Irish American woman from the south side of Chicago, introduced me to an audience at a performance of poetry in Minneapolis one evening, she said, "I thought I was White until I met Julie! Now that is *White!*" So this is a cyclical thing we inherit, a class and race confluence depending on who raises us. The ultimate cost of it all, however, is a lack of ease at the base of our experience in the world. Although we cannot name it, we feel it, haunting us, nudging us. If we have challenged our own parents, as I have all my life, we are forever alienated from those who brought us up. If we have continued to compromise with what we know is wrong in order to maintain approval of our particular White community, we feel a dis-ease we cannot name. Thus, the cost of White privilege, in all its perpetuation and reinforcement, is a split in our psyche, and in a generalized way this becomes a split in the psyche of our country.

In a most profound way, then, it is in our interest to rid our country of White privilege. When we do this, or at least spend our lives working to do this by constant reflection and change in behavior and perception, we weave our selves together. In our own way, because of what we know instinctively about White dominance and power based on skin color, we experience *our own double way of being in the world:* what we know is right conflicts with how we believe we should act as ethical human beings. We often do not "see" it or "feel" it and can rarely articulate what it is that makes us uneasy. Yet it is there.

The Psychic Benefits of Acknowledging Privilege

Since I have been thinking in this way, with truth and clarity about my privilege, both racial and economic, I have found myself feeling more and more liberated. I cannot define precisely what this liberation is all about, but I know it has to do with connecting to the world in a new way, a way that feels my whole self is allowed to participate. It has not been easy or comfortable. I often make mistakes, yet I would not trade the way I think or feel now for the comfort of ignorance of my White race and class advantages for anything. I find I have a new fearlessness. I am ready for discussions on any topic in this area of race, as well as class, gender, and sexual orientation. I have been opened up to a real world I sensed was there yet was afraid to acknowledge before reading McIntosh, Thandeka, James Banks, Sonia Nieto, Beverly Tatum—to name a few. To liberate ourselves from ignorance in this area is to liberate ourselves into the full potential of our humanity; there is no more important work.

Steps to Take: No Quick Fixes, Please

We want solutions, quick fixes, a shortcut to a place of enlightenment, or comfort. White people especially seem to think that if we just apply some rule or chart or system, we will solve the "race problem" and go on. This kind of work will not happen with one workshop or a one-week seminar. Rather, it is a process, a way of living with the world, that we can take in and make a part of our response to events and situations. Dr. Joseph White, professor emeritus at University of California Irvine, and co-author of *Black Man Emerging* (1999), describes in talks and in presentations three ways we can prepare for the process of understanding privilege and then moving beyond mere understanding to true empathy and activism. White people will never live the reality of having a darker skin in America, but we can strive to understand it. Dr. White gives us ways to acquire and act on such knowledge.

First, he says we can *engage conceptually* by reaching out intellectually.

This means we can read, go to conferences, watch television shows, and attend theatrical productions on issues of race and ethnicity. This is a lifelong task. This task is not solved by one book, or one documentary. Rather, it happens after consistent layers of exposure—the new insight from a novel, the getting inside of another person's heart and mind in a powerful film, or the portrait painted by an artist who lives in our own neighborhood; these accumulate over time to influence our very thought patterns.

That this engagement has to happen in classrooms all over the country is discussed more fully in other chapters of this book. Provocative books, poems, speakers, and history texts must be a part of our education and our students' education. And such experiences and texts, visual images and speakers, must be woven into the history, literature, math and science, music and art all during the year for all students, in schools rich in diversity and those that are all White.

Second, Professor White tells us to *engage in dialogue* with those who are not White, to meet face-to-face. Again, this is a lifelong experience and may mean that we meet, disagree, take a time-out, and come back, again and again. Real engaged dialogue may mean that we will feel anxious, uncomfortable, and weary. We will hear different perceptions of the same situation, and we will struggle to figure out where we stand. We may first want to blame others, or externalize the blame outside ourselves. But if we persist and understand the importance of this work, spending time in introspection as well as discussion, we will discover what we can do differently to change, what we need to ask for from others, and how to compromise. Finally, we will gain true empathy, an understanding of the world from another point of view.

These steps take work and patience. It is worth doing, from neighborhood meetings on crime prevention to board meetings of arts organizations to volunteer groups building houses for Habitat for Humanity. This dialogue is at the heart of addressing our privilege, and of seeing where this privilege might intersect with other privileges of gender and class, sexual orientation, or ethnicity. It is a kind of interaction that can bring us deeply into understanding what it means to live with racial single vision versus seeing with DuBois's double consciousness, and so to learn at the most basic level, what our advantage is in the United States.

In the classroom, this engagement means having touchy dialogues about race with our students. Often students want this dialogue to happen but teachers avoid such talks. They fear the possibility of anger, an outburst, anxiety, or tears. It is true that these things might happen. There is probably no more important discussion to have, whether it is because of a topic that has come up in class, an incident in school, or a remark by a student before the first bell. Young people are always trying to figure out their position in relation to others in their age group. Both White and Black students are puzzled about whether a teacher, a principal, a hall guard is racist, or just seems so. They may wish to talk about the fact that some of them get followed around in a store whereas others do not.

Students who are not White and who attend schools that are predominantly White often say that the toughest thing for them is when they are not believed when they speak of racism. It is extremely painful to them when they describe a racial incident, a slur, or an experience by a family member and the teacher or other students dismiss it as implausible or even impossible. If we are comfortable with dialogue about issues and situations that are racially charged, we can then be there to help students—White and Black, Latino and Native, Asian and Chicano—comprehend the thicket of perception and language that surrounds them all the time. My hope for the future in this area increases as I talk with students. Many who go to schools with diverse populations are breaking old patterns of racist thought, accepting different perceptions, and having the tough talks their parents and even teachers avoid or resist.

Third, Dr. White suggests that we *engage in behavioral interaction* with those of another culture than our own. Step out and into another environment. This way of interacting and stretching means being "the only" in places where most others are of a culture not your own. Dancing at a pow-wow when invited, working against violence in a neighborhood where you are a new resident, spending time in a country where you do not speak the language—all are examples of venturing outside your comfort zone. Dr. White told me of his experience in this area. At the age of seventy, he has been invited to go to a synagogue on Friday evenings. He grew up in north Minneapolis when it was gradually changing from a Jewish area to a Black area of the city. He had never attended Jewish religious services or celebrations, or observed Jewish holidays before, and now he has become interested in this religion. He is often the only Black person there.

In our classrooms, this requires providing active engagement experiences, perhaps assignments for students outside of class to go places where they are not accustomed to going because they are not in the majority. Being in a minority can enlighten us about what it might feel like to experience the world as a person of color in the United States. It gives us a sense of this double consciousness, an awareness of being who we are versus who we are observed to be, because we are "different."

I would also add a fourth category of experiences we can engage in to counter our White status, and that is to *engage in ongoing activism*. Often we sit at meetings, or on boards or in the audience at city council sessions, and talk—for hours. And then we leave and nothing changes. As White people, we can go on about our lives without acting on the issue of racism. It is one of our privileges not to have our lives made difficult by such racism and, thus, we can choose not to try to change things. We can then feel satisfied if things are simply *said*.

However, to counter this privilege, we need to act. This means the difficult work of tutoring, mentoring, running for office, opening up our classrooms for after-school discussions with students who wish to change the climate in our schools. It means working for candidates who believe in true racial and economic justice. The things we can do as activists are endless, whether in writing letters to the editor; moving into a neighborhood to help contribute to change there; or speaking out against racism in our jobs and our schools at parties.

Students can be encouraged along these lines too. They can work for the rights of children and against child labor—a situation that disproportionately affects children of color—and they can sponsor dialogues when issues come up in their school or neighborhood or job. They can join groups that work to bring change, real substantive change. A multiplicity of organizations exist now. Students can be encouraged to join these groups. They can conduct research about groups as an assignment and invite speakers from organizations they admire. I am aware that this is risky in our role as teachers. But the least we can do is venture into tricky and even dangerous territory if we are going to facilitate change.

From here, from understanding skin privilege, we can also begin to understand the privilege of class, of growing up with money and access; or the privilege of being a male, or that of being a heterosexual in a world that demonizes those who are not. As long as we do not use these experiences or situations or even disadvantages as a way to avoid discussions of racial privilege, we can use our understanding of White privilege to open up our minds to the complex interweaving of privileges and of the social capital such privileges create. The clearer and more powerful this information becomes for us, the more we cannot deny the truths we are learning. But we must see it first. Really see it. Because it is there, haunting us, as Thandeka describes, from our earliest childhood, when we noticed and took in an injustice and then were silent and buried it deep within our psyches. To learn about Whiteness is, in a sense, to learn to liberate ourselves from denial and guilt.

Final Thoughts

One evening a few years ago in Minneapolis, there was a young African American man on a panel of which I was also a member. He looked out at the primarily White audience of teachers and said, "You know, we've got to remember that White teachers were all brought up in the system too. And the system is racist and not perfect. So we can't blame them really. We just have to go ahead and ask them to learn with us."

I could feel the entire audience take a deep breath and become at ease in the room, ready for the stories, the questions, and the troubling thoughts that came afterward. It was one of the best dialogues of which I have been privileged to be a part.

Ultimately, perhaps, we can take back the word *privileged* and give it a deep and positive meaning. Maybe it will come to mean those of us are privileged who learn and work together with those who want to bring racial and economic justice into the world.

The epilogue to Thandeka's *Learning to Be White* (2000, p. 135) is an appropriate ending to this chapter, and I quote it in full here with great appreciation for her work and her hope:

> The end of this book is a beginning, a place where new conversations about money, race and God in America can commence.
> With this new beginning, loyalties need no longer be skin-keep.
> Here God's broken humanity can be healed.
> Difference will be affirmed as the grace of human engagement.
> The term *person of color* will now refer to every human being.
> Dare we dream of such a day?
> Yes.
> Let the church say Amen.

References

DuBois, W. E. B. (1903). *The souls of black folk.* New York: Bantam Books.

McIntosh, P. (1990). White privilege and male privilege: A personal account of coming to see correspondences through work in women's studies. *Independent Schools, 90*(49), 31–36.

Obama, B. (1996). *Dreams from my father.* New York: Kodansha International.

Simon, D., & Burns, E. (1997). *The corner: A year in the life of an inner city neighbor-hood*. New York: Broadway Books.

Thandeka (2000). *Learning to be white*. Continuum: New York.

White, J., & Coones, J. H. III (1999). *Black man emerging: Facing the past and seizing a future in America*. New York: W. H. Freeman.

QUESTIONS

1. What impact does White privilege have on educators who work with students of color in your school or school district? Please discuss.
2. How can educators use their privilege to learn and work together with those who want to bring racial and economic justice into the world to benefit all students?

2

REFLECTIONS ON EDUCATION

A Two-Way Journey

Kao Kalia Yang and Aaron Rudolf Miller Hokanson

Kao Kalia Yang

I was a thin six-year-old from the camps of Thailand who did not know any English beyond *A*, *B*, and *C*. Ms. Olson had glasses, dark hair, and a big belly, round as a melon beneath her stretchy cotton shirts. She was short, maybe? She read to us. Book after book, pictures melding into one another, stories in a language we didn't speak. I thought she was lovely. She was my introduction to education: this world that my mom and dad had dreamt for us.

Years later, I think back to her when I think about education. Long after my journey through the St. Paul Public Schools, through Carleton College and Columbia University, and long after the kindness and the lack thereof from many teachers I return to her image, to my first educational experience in a school.

When is the moment a child learns that a teacher cares? When is the moment a teacher learns that education comes down to the simple premise of communicating care: for our world, for ourselves, for each other?

The lone Ethiopian boy sits beneath the faraway Ethiopian sky, underneath an unrelenting sun. His mother and father look to him, and they say, "Son." The words are confused in the English of wintry cold Minnesota, where one sun cannot translate easily or fiercely into the other son.

> Buffered by the winds of Time and Distance, chasms of air and gravity,
> the stretch of earth,

We sit in the spaces we've made, the shelter of our skies:
Wind ripples across the surface of the Mighty Mississippi,
An eagle merging into a tree,
Fish swim beneath the surfaces of unnamed seas.
Book after book,
Pictures melding into one another,
Stories in a language,
We did not speak.
I thought she was lovely.

I read over his words, time and again. There is the confusion of tenses. His teacher, an English Language Learners (ELL) classroom teacher, invites me for the week. They call it a writing residency and I can do anything I want to do, but my job is to make him realize that his story is more powerful than the parts of the language he is working in, because the language of his life is more complicated than the languages we speak to one another in search of understanding. There is the frustration of almost getting it. His teacher, a White woman with a not so White last name, smiles and smiles and she gets a little angry when the high schoolers in the Minneapolis public school classroom, mostly students from Africa, laugh too loud and talk too much because they are too eager for the coming spring. I read over his words, again and again.

His mom works at Kentucky Fried Chicken in the morning and her skin, he says, turns from chocolate to dust as the day wears on. He talks about a wall I cannot picture and a sofa that he rests on that was old in the world but is new to their home, and he keeps talking about the wall.

I write on his page, "What is on this wall? Describe for me. Is the paint peeling? What color? Do you have pictures, or posters? What is on this wall? Let it tell me the pieces of your life." I want him to answer the questions for me on the page. On his page. I want us to talk. He is marveling at what is happening. He says, "Why do you care?"

I care because I feel your story. My father works in a place that drains the color of day from his skin and lets night seep into his pores, shadows under his eyes, and shadows within them. I care because a long time ago it didn't matter if I felt the story or not: what did matter was that someone cared to share, every day. Her name was Ms. Olson and she has no idea how much I remember her. I don't know how long you will remember me, but it doesn't matter because when we give each other words we are giving each other pieces of ourselves. Like hugs and smells and taste, we take the world in.

I don't write this. I don't say it. I just think it. I just feel it. I just respond to it, inside, and outside it all just becomes a look in the eye, a breath in the air. I teach because of her, Ms. Olson. And we wonder what this has to do with White teachers? Diverse classrooms?

Aaron Rudolph Miller Hokanson

I was a White kid with a bit of a belly. I grew up in Milwaukee, in the same house where my dad had grown up. My school had been my father's school. My grandmother was a volunteer in one of the first grade classrooms. There were kids from outside the neighborhood who were bussed in daily to take classes with us. Those of us who weren't bussed in were mostly White.

On drives through the city, I tried to imagine where my friends who took the bus lived. I heard about the "inner city" but I was never exposed to it. My experiences were mostly with the neighborhood, house, and school that had been my father's growing up. Many of the same people worked or lived in these places from his childhood and I felt connected through these relationships. My world and the worlds of the kids on the busses never really intersected except in school. When I went to a place I thought might be the inner city, I went to serve soup at a soup kitchen. I imagine I suspected that I might run into one of the bus riders there.

In third grade one of my friends who took the bus started a fire in a trashcan outside the school. He was immediately expelled. I wonder where he ended up? I remember it being the first time I heard about juvenile hall, but I also remember wondering about schools in the neighborhood where his parents lived (the assumptions I made as a child were as numerous as today). Banishment from our neighborhood was not something I could imagine. I could not imagine his life turning out very differently from my own, while at the same time I knew something was different. In sixth grade I became really close friends with a boy who had just arrived from Hungary. His English was weighted with an Eastern European accent. He lived in the apartment buildings that my grandma stayed in. He invited me over at some point, but I wasn't sure about how that would be possible. I remember over-hearing some other children making fun of him and me.

I remember one of my sister's friends being "allergic" to the Indian boy in her class because he smelled like the curries his family made.

I don't remember if or when the teachers cared about these students. I only remember feeling like I belonged because of the long history and the number of relationships my family had in the neighborhood and the school.

I loved my school. When teachers talked about their lives or about the things they thought were important for us to learn I not only listened, I understood.

I never lost credit for being scared to venture into the houses or neighborhoods where the people that made our classroom "diverse" came from. Yet, of the courage they showed by coming to my neighborhood I never heard, I only remember one being expelled and knowing that the boys who most often got into trouble were the Black ones. We were taught about civil rights, but it seemed as if the fact that they were bussed in was enough to solve the issues of our segregated community. It was assumed they would earn an equal education if they came to our school. However, from the first moment I was told I couldn't play with a kid because he didn't live in my neighborhood, I started imagining rather than ever really getting to know. The imbalance was always apparent, it just became less and less immediate for me.

Many years later I moved to Australia to get my teaching degree. I was in the process of applying for an extended student teaching internship. I had primarily applied to suburban schools, not too dissimilar from the one in which I had been taught. There was one school directly in the middle of government commissioned housing to which I applied and was accepted. The children were poorer, largely refugees and immigrants from around the world. A teacher from another school where I had done some work heard about this and told me horror stories about misbehaving kids.

I was scared, but I learned within minutes of being in the classroom that attention to building relationships, not only with the families and within the neighborhood, but with the students themselves made them immediately more accessible. They were honest and confident. According to official record keeping, one might suspect that no valuable learning was happening. The test scores, I am sure, were less than enviable. However, in my opinion, test scores mattered far less than the care the teachers showed toward the students, their families, each other, and the care that it engendered in the children themselves.

I quickly left teaching to pursue a Ph.D. in education. I have since come to the conclusion that our emphasis is too often on knowing or understanding the children we work with; however, it is much more important that we begin to admit what we do not and cannot ever know. It is more important to care than to understand; more important to care than to know. With a diverse classroom we often work with students who do not know the culture underlying our daily curriculum: the manners and ways of speaking that White people, particularly middle class White people, take for granted. In many classrooms the diversity is also more immediate with regard to language, culture, and everyday experiences. We aren't just bridging difference in these classrooms; we are in a space where many different worlds and lifestyles collide. Rather than open doors, more often we are told to shut the blinds.

As White teachers, we have the luxury of coasting through the world never knowing what it is like to be told you are doing something wrong without knowing why it is wrong. As White teachers, I doubt we could ever say for sure why something is unacceptable. As a White teacher in classrooms with many home cultures, I encountered many moments of frustration, many moments when the things I took for granted were not as implicit in my students' worlds or ways of doing things. However hard these moments were, I now realize that such moments are our only real windows into the everyday experience of those students who make our classrooms diverse—the frustration they feel at every turn.

I'm reminded of a moment when my co-author, Kalia, told a room full of researchers that the work they do slowly replaces the memories of her grandmother and the things that her grandmother, who spoke no English and never really understood the culture she had been forced into, taught her. What does this have to do with diverse classrooms? White teachers?

As White teachers in diverse classrooms we need to realize that the world is much bigger than what we know, or what the classroom can allow. We need to accept the reality that our students often have many teachers besides us. We need to worry less about how to "reach out" or "welcome" these students and focus more on how we care about them and the places they come from. Frustration, confusion, uncertainty, and discomfort all have a place in the diverse classroom, these experiences deserve to be privileged. We should not seek ways to alleviate these, but rather ways to put them to constructive use; we need to make them the bedrock for meaningful relationships with our students, their families, and their communities. We also need to listen when they share, and if we do not understand them sometimes, to realize the frustration our students feel almost every second that they are in school.

Kalia

Because I was the little girl who sat at the lunchroom table eating French toast sticks with her mouth open, savoring each bite and smiling, the other children mimicked and laughed at the way I ate. Long ago, tears seeped into this keyboard. The moment of disillusionment, when the adults in the office said, "In this country, you have to learn how to do things the way people here do them."

There were words, then, that I could not utter in a language I had not learned how to speak: "This is how my mother and father eat, this is how they have taught me to eat, this is how most of my people eat, this is how most of the world eats." Even now I know that what they taught me is one more thing about their lives, my life. And now it all slips from the fabric of my certainty, the heart of my being.

I am not a White teacher. I go into classrooms because of the memory of one and the promise of another.

Learning is what happens when the heart is uncomfortable with its lack of knowing. If we have the courage to reach toward another in these moments of uncertainty, we will all learn to reach out, to connect, to care.

QUESTIONS

1. The authors note: "As White teachers, we have the luxury of coasting through the world never knowing what it is like to be told you are doing something wrong without knowing why it could be wrong. As White teachers, I doubt we could ever say for sure why something is unacceptable." What can White teachers learn from this statement?

2. What are your thoughts on the following statement: "We [White teachers] need to worry less about how to 'reach out' or 'welcome' these students [students of color] and focus more on how we care about them and the places they come from?"

PART TWO

CULTURALLY RELEVANT TEACHERS: FOUNDATIONS AND PERSONAL ENGAGEMENT

3

"YES, BUT HOW DO WE DO IT?"

Practicing Culturally Relevant Pedagogy

Gloria Ladson-Billings

I n 1989, when I began documenting the practice of teachers who achieved success with African American students, I had no idea that it would create a kind of cottage industry of exemplary teachers. I began the project with the assumption that there were indeed teachers who could and did teach poor students of color to achieve high levels of academic success (Ladson-Billings, 1994). Other scholars (Foster, 1997; Mathews, 1988) verified this aspect of my work. Unfortunately, much of the work that addresses successful teaching of poor students of color is linked to the notion of the teacher as heroic isolate. Thus, stories such as those of Marva Collins (Collins & Tamarkin, 1990), Jaime Escalante (Mathews, 1988), Vivian Paley (2000), and Louanne Johnson (1992) inadvertently transmit a message of the teacher as savior and charismatic maverick without exploring the complexities of teaching and nuanced intellectual work that undergirds pedagogical practices.

In this chapter, I discuss the components of culturally relevant teaching (Ladson-Billings, 1995) and provide practical examples of how teachers might implement these components in their classrooms. I choose to provide practice-based examples to remove some of the mystery and mythology tied to theory that keep teachers from doing the work designed to support high levels of achievement for poor students of color.

But, How Do We Do It?

Almost every teacher educator devoted to issues of diversity and social justice finds himself or herself confronted by prospective and in-service teachers who quickly reject teaching for social justice by insisting that there are no practical exemplars that make such teaching possible. A semester or staff development session typically ends with teachers unsure of what they can or should do and eventually defaulting to regular routines and practices. Nothing changes in the classroom and poor students of color are no closer to experiencing the kind of education to which they are entitled.

I argue that the first problem teachers confront is believing that successful teaching for poor students of color is primarily about "what to do." Instead, I suggest that the problem is rooted in how we think—about the social contexts, about the students, about the curriculum, and about instruction. Instead of the specific lessons and activities that we select to fill the day, we must begin to understand the ways our theories and philosophies are made to manifest in the pedagogical practices and rationales we exhibit in the classroom. The following sections briefly describe the salient elements of teacher thinking that contribute to what I have termed *culturally relevant teaching*.

Social Contexts

Teaching takes place not only in classrooms. It takes place in schools and communities. It takes place in local, state, national, and global contexts that impact students regardless of whether teachers acknowledge them or not. How teachers think about those contexts creates an environment for thinking about teaching. Teachers who believe that society is fair and just believe that their students are participating on a level playing field and simply have to learn to be better competitors than other students. They also believe in a kind of social Darwinism that supports the survival of the fittest. Teachers with this outlook accept that some students will necessarily fall by the wayside and experience academic failure.

Teachers who I term *culturally relevant* assume that an asymmetrical (even antagonistic) relationship exists between poor students of color and society. Thus, their vision of their work is one of preparing students to combat inequity by being highly competent and critically conscious. While the teachers are concerned with the students who sit in their classrooms each day, they see them in relation to a continuum of struggle—past, present, and future. Thus, the AIDS crisis in Black and Brown communities, immigration laws, and affordable health care are not merely "adult" issues, but also are a part of the social context in which teachers attempt to do their work.

Being aware of the social context is not an excuse for neglecting the classroom tasks associated with helping students to learn literacy, numeracy, scientific, and social skills. Rather, it reminds teachers of the larger social purposes of their work.

The Students

Of course teachers think about their students. But *how* they think about their students is a central concern of successful teaching. In my work as a teacher educator, I regularly see prospective teachers who approach teaching with romantic notions about students. They believe that the goodwill and energy they bring to the classroom will be rewarded by enthusiastic, appreciative students, who will comply with their requests and return the love they purport to give their students. Unfortunately, real life rarely matches that ideal. Poor students of color, like all children, live complex lives that challenge teachers' best intentions. Whether teachers think of their students as needy and deficient or capable and resilient can spell the difference between pedagogy grounded in compensatory perspectives and those grounded in critical and liberatory ones.

My best examples of the first perspective come from years of observing prospective teachers enter classrooms where students fail to comply with their wishes and directives. Quickly the students are constructed as problems—"at risk," behavior problems, savages—and those constructions become self-fulfilling prophecies (Rist, 1970). Before long, the classroom is no longer a place where students are taught and expected to learn. Rather, it becomes a place where bodies are managed and maintaining order becomes the primary task. Unfortunately, many urban schools reinforce and reward this type of pedagogical response (Haberman, 1991).

Culturally relevant teachers envision their students as being filled with possibilities. They imagine that somewhere in the classroom is the next Nobel laureate (a Toni Morrison), the next neurosurgeon (a Benjamin Carson), or the next pioneer for social justice (a Fannie Lou Hamer).[1] This perspective moves the teachers from a position of sympathy ("you poor dear")[2] to one of informed empathy. This informed empathy requires the teacher to feel with the students rather than feel for them. Feeling with the students builds a sense of solidarity between the teacher and the students but does not excuse students from working hard in pursuit of excellence.

Culturally relevant teachers recognize that their students are "school dependent."[3] I use this term to suggest that some students are successful in spite of their schooling, as a result of material resources and cultural capital. If they have incompetent or uncaring teachers, their parents and families have the resources to supplement and enhance the schooling experience.

However, most poor students of color look to schools as the vehicle for social advancement and equity. They are totally dependent on the school to help them achieve a variety of goals. When the school fails to provide for those needs, these students are locked out of social and cultural benefits. For example, a number of poor students of color find themselves in classrooms with teachers who are unqualified or underqualified to teach (Ladson-Billings, 2005). More striking is that some of these children find themselves in classrooms where there is no regularly assigned teacher. Instead, the students spend entire school years with a series of substitute teachers who have no responsibility for supporting their academic success.

The Curriculum

Typically, teachers are expected to follow a prescribed curriculum that state and local administrators have approved. In many large school districts, that approved curriculum may merely be a textbook. In several poorly performing districts, that curriculum may be a script that teachers are required to recite and follow. I argue that teachers engaged in culturally relevant pedagogy must be able to deconstruct, construct, and reconstruct (Shujaa, 1994) the curriculum. *Deconstruction* refers to the ability to take apart the "official knowledge" (Apple, 2000) to expose its weaknesses, myths, distortions, and omissions. *Construction* refers to the ability to build curriculum. Similar to the work that John Dewey (1997) advocated, construction relies on the experiences and knowledge that teachers and their students bring to the classroom. *Reconstruction* requires the work of rebuilding the curriculum that was previously taken apart and examined. It is never enough to tear down. Teachers must be prepared to build up and fill in the holes that emerge when students begin to use critical analysis as they attempt to make sense of the curriculum.

The perspective of culturally relevant teachers is that the curriculum is a cultural artifact and as such is not an ideologically neutral document. Whereas the highly ideological nature of the curriculum is evident in high-profile communities where there are fights over evolution versus creation or sex education curricula that advocate safe sex versus abstinence, it is more subtle and pernicious in other curriculum documents. For example, the history curriculum reflects ethnocentric and sometimes xenophobic attitudes and regularly minimizes the faults of the United States and some European nations. Even an area such as mathematics is susceptible to ideology that leaves poor children of color receiving mathematics curricula that focus on rote memorization and algorithms whereas middle-class students have early access to algebraic thinking and more conceptually grounded approaches.

Instruction

No curriculum can teach itself. It does not matter if teachers have access to exceptional curriculum if they do not have the instructional skills to teach all students. College and university professors have the means to provide students with intellectually challenging and critical knowledge, but few professors are able to teach the wide variety of students who show up in K–12 classrooms. Precollegiate teachers must have a wide repertoire of teaching strategies and techniques to ensure that all students can access the curriculum. Unlike postsecondary teachers, K–12 teachers teach students who may or may not wish to be students. That means that their teaching must engage, cajole, convict, and perhaps even fool students into participation. Culturally relevant teachers understand that some of the pedagogical strategies that make teaching easier or more convenient for them may be exactly the kind of instruction they should avoid. For example, placing students in ability groups or tracks may serve to alienate struggling students further. Lecturing, no matter how efficient, may do nothing more than create greater gaps between successful students and those who are not. Even those strategies that progressive educators see as more democratic may fail to create the equal access teachers desire. In this instance, I refer to the almost unanimous belief that cooperative learning is a preferred teaching strategy. Many teacher preparation programs emphasize cooperative and other group strategies as preferable to more traditional classroom arrangements. However, when poorly managed, cooperative learning creates unequal workloads and instances in which students exclude other students from the process. High achievers sometimes resent being placed with struggling students and struggling students can be embarrassed by their inability to be full participants in the group setting.

Thus, if teachers must consider the ways that the social contexts of schooling impact their work and that their context may not be supportive, what, if anything, can they do? I argue that teachers must engage in a culturally relevant pedagogy that is designed to attend to the context while simultaneously preparing students for the traditional societal demands (i.e., high school completion, postsecondary education, workplace requirements, active and participatory citizenship). I next address the elements of culturally relevant pedagogy that teachers must attend to in order to achieve success with students who have been underserved by our schools.

Academic Achievement

When I wrote the words *academic achievement* almost ten years ago, I never dreamed that I would regret using this term. What I had in mind has nothing to do with the oppressive atmosphere of standardized tests; the wholesale retention of groups of students; scripted curricula; and the intimidation of students, teachers, and parents. Rather, what I envisioned is more accurately described as "student learning"—what it is that students actually know and are able to do as a result of pedagogical interactions with skilled teachers. However, because I started with the term *academic achievement*, I will stay with it for consistency's sake.

The teachers who focus on academic achievement (i.e., student learning) understand that this is their primary function. They are not attempting to get students to "feel good about themselves" or learn how to exercise self-control. Rather, they are most interested in the cultivation of students' minds and supporting their intellectual lives. They understand that through engaged learning students will develop self-esteem and self-control. They recognize that the outbursts and off-task behaviors are symptoms, not causes, and as teachers the one thing they have at their disposal are pedagogical tools to draw students into the learning in meaningful ways.

Culturally relevant teachers think deeply about what they teach and ask themselves why students should learn particular aspects of the curriculum. In these classrooms, teachers are vetting everything in the curriculum and often supplement the curriculum. For example, in a culturally relevant high school English class the teacher may understand that he or she has to teach *Romeo and Juliet* but would couch that book in the context of students' own struggles with parents over dating. There may even be a detailed discussion of suicide and the level of desperation that adolescents may experience when they cannot communicate with adults. Finally, the teacher may include some films, popular music, or other stories that take up the theme of young, forbidden love. The point here is that a culturally relevant teacher does not take the book as a given. Rather, the teacher asks himself or herself specific questions about what reading this book is supposed to accomplish. This same teacher might be quite explicit about the place of the text in the literary canon and the cachet and clout students acquire when they can speak intelligently about such texts. One of the major academic activities in the classroom of culturally relevant teachers is engaging in critique of texts and activities. Over and over students ask and are asked, "Why are we doing this?" "Why is this important?" and "How does this enrich my life and/or the life of others?"

For tasks that seem mundane, teachers may use a very pragmatic skill (e.g., changing a tire) to help students understand how simple component parts of a task (e.g., blocking and braking the car), are necessary prerequisites to the larger task. The chemistry teacher may spend time helping students learn the precise way to light and use a Bunsen burner, not because lighting a Bunsen burner is a marketable skill, but because having a lit Bunsen burner will be important for many of the subsequent labs.

Repeatedly, culturally relevant teachers speak in terms of long-term academic goals for students. They rarely focus on "What should I do on Monday?" and spend a considerable amount of their planning trying to figure out what the semester or yearlong goals are. They share those goals with students and provide them with insights into their teaching so that students know why they are doing what they are doing. These teachers use many real-life and familiar examples that help the classroom come alive. They may use metaphors to paint word pictures. One teacher refers to the classroom experience as a trip and uses many travel metaphors. "We're still in San Jose and you know we've got to get to L.A." is what she might say when the class is falling behind where she thinks it should be. Or, she can be heard to say, "Hey, Lamar, why are you in Petaluma?" when referring to a student who is off task and doing the exact opposite of what she wishes to accomplish.

Interestingly, Foster (1989) describes a community college teacher who structured her classroom as an economy. Even with adult learners, this teacher understood that the metaphorical language helped her students visualize their objectives. The students who were "on welfare" wanted to get jobs in "the bank." The symbolism and imagery resonated with the students and the teacher used it as a way to get the very best out of her students.

Cultural Competence

Of the three terms (*academic achievement, cultural competence, sociopolitical consciousness*) that I use to describe the components of culturally relevant pedagogy, I find the notion of cultural competence the most difficult to convey to teachers who wish to develop their own practice in this way. One of the problems is that like academic achievement, the term *cultural competence* has another set of meanings. Currently, many of the helping professions—such as medicine, nursing, counseling, social work—refer to something called "cultural competence." However, in these professions the notion of cultural competence refers to helping dominant group members become more skillful in reading the cultural messages of their clients. As a consequence, novice practitioners in these fields practice aspects of their work in ways that represent culturally sensitive behaviors—not pointing; speaking in direct, declarative sentences; directing questions and statements to an elder. Unfortunately, these practices reflect a static and essentialized view of culture and tend to reinforce stereotypes, rather than dispel them.

My sense of cultural competence refers to helping students to recognize and honor their own cultural beliefs and practices while acquiring access to the wider culture, where they are likely to have a chance of improving their socioeconomic status and making informed decisions about the lives they wish to lead. The point of my work is to maintain teachers' focus on what improves the lives of the students, families, and communities they serve—not to make teachers feel better about themselves. I presume that teachers who do learn more about their students' backgrounds, cultures, and experiences feel more capable and efficacious in their work as teachers, but the teachers are not my primary objective. In the most instrumental way, I think of the teachers as a vehicle for improving students' lives.

Teachers who foster cultural competence understand that they must work back and forth between the lives of their students and the life of school. Teachers have an obligation to expose their students to the very culture that oppresses them. That may seem paradoxical, but without the skills and knowledge of the dominant culture, students are unlikely to be able to engage that culture to effect meaningful change.

I visited two middle school teachers who created an etiquette unit in which they introduced students to information about manners. However, it was not a unit merely focused on what to do; it included historical, cultural, and sociological information about why these practices are as they are. At the end of the unit, the teachers took the students in small groups out to dinner at a quality restaurant. For many of the students, this was the first time they had attended a restaurant with linen napkins and multicourse dinners. The idea of this activity was not to attempt to make the students middle class but, rather, to have the students experience and critique middle-class ways. A surprising response to the dining experience was that of one female student, who said, "Now that I know what this is like I'm not going to let a guy take me to McDonald's and call that taking me out to dinner."

In one of the most powerful and striking instances of cultural competence, MacArthur Award winner,[4] teacher, and forensics coach Tommie Lindsey of James Logan High School in Union City, California, uses culturally specific speeches and dialogues to help his largely Black and Brown forensics team win local, state, and national competitions. The students use pieces from African American and Latina/Latino writers in the midst of a venue that can only be described as upper middle class and mainstream. Lindsey has successfully merged the students' cultural strengths with the forensics form. The students have exposure to a wider world without compromising aspects of their own culture.

Sociopolitical Consciousness

I can typically convince teachers (both preservice and in-service) that it is important to focus on student learning as well as make use of students' culture. However, the idea that developing sociopolitical consciousness is important is a much harder sell. One of the reasons that this aspect of the theory is difficult is that most of the teachers I encounter have not developed a sociopolitical consciousness of their own. True, most hold strong opinions about the sociopolitical issues they know about, but many do not know much about sociopolitical issues. When I talk to teachers about economic disparities, they rarely link these disparities with issues of race, class, and gender. Thus, the first thing teachers must do is educate themselves about both the local sociopolitical issues of their school community (e.g., school board policy, community events) and the larger sociopolitical issues (e.g., unemployment, health care, housing) that impinge upon their students' lives.

The second thing teachers need to do is incorporate those issues into their ongoing teaching. I am not talking about teachers pushing their own agendas to the detriment of student learning. Rather, the task here is to help students use the various skills they learn to better understand and critique their social position and context. For example, in my original study of cultural competence and sociopolitical awareness, a student complained about the deterioration of the community and expressed strong emotions about how unhappy he was living in a place that had lots of crime, drugs, and little in the way of commerce and recreational facilities. The teacher used the student's emotion to develop a community study. Although it is typical for students to study their community, this study involved a detailed examination of the reality of the community, not a superficial look at "community helpers." The teacher retrieved information from the historical society's archives so that the students could compare the community's present condition with that of the past and raise questions about how the decline had occurred. Ultimately, the students developed a land-use plan that they presented to the city council.

The Culpability of Teacher Education

Most discussions of what teachers fail to do give teacher education a pass. We presume that teachers are doing something separate and apart from their preparation. However, I argue that teacher preparation plays a large role in maintaining the status quo. Teacher educators are overwhelmingly White, middle-aged, and monolingual English speakers. Although more women are entering the academy as teacher educators, the cultural makeup of the teacher education profession is embarrassingly homogeneous. This cultural homogeneity of the teacher education profession makes it difficult to persuade preservice teachers convincingly that they should know and do anything different in their classrooms.

In addition to the overwhelming cultural homogeneity of the teacher education profession, we organize our profession in ways that suggest that issues of diversity and social justice are tangential to the enterprise. Most preservice teachers enter a program that ghettoizes issues of diversity. Somewhere in a separate course or workshop, students are given "multicultural information." It is here that students often are confused, angry, and frustrated because they do not know what to do with this information. Regularly preservice teachers report feelings of guilt and outrage because they receive information about inequity, racism, and social injustice in ways that destabilize their sense of themselves and make them feel responsible for the condition of poor children of color in our schools.

In some instances, preservice teachers participate in a teacher education program that requires them to have at least one field experience in a diverse classroom and/or community setting. When such field experiences are poorly done, this requirement becomes just another hoop through which students jump to earn a credential. Students in these circumstances regularly speak of "getting over" their diversity requirement. Rarely do such students want to do their most significant field experience—student teaching—in diverse classrooms. When these field experiences are well conceived, they allow preservice teachers to be placed in classrooms with skillful teachers and be supervised by careful teacher educators who can help them make sense of what they are experiencing and create useful applications for the multicultural knowledge they are learning.

Although the National Council for the Accreditation of Teacher Education includes a diversity standard in its accreditation process, most programs struggle to equip novice teachers fully to work with children who are poor, linguistically diverse, and/or from racial or ethnic minority groups. Teacher candidates may resist the lessons of diversity and social justice, but that resistance may be intimately tied to the lack of credibility their professors and teacher education instructors possess. Why should preservice students believe that teacher educators who spend much of their lives in the comforts of the academy can understand the challenges today's classrooms present? Why should tenuous 1960s civil rights credentials be made proxies for twenty-first century problems? I am not suggesting that participation in the civil rights struggle is an unimportant part of one's biography—it is a part of my own biography. Rather, I am suggesting that in this new time and space, that aspect of one's biography may not prove adequate for helping students navigate the multiple ways that race, class, gender, and language identities complicate the pedagogical project. Teacher education has much to answer for concerning its role in preparing teachers who fail to serve classrooms of poor children of color well.

What Is a Teacher To Do?

As I noted earlier, many well-meaning teachers lament the fact that they do not know what to do when it comes to meeting the educational needs of all students. Indeed, a group of soon-to-be teachers recently said to me, "Everybody keeps telling us about multicultural education, but nobody is telling us how to do it!" I responded, "Even if we could tell you how to do it, I would not want us to tell you how to do it." They looked at me with very confused expressions on their faces. I went on to say, "The reason I would not tell you what to do is that you would probably do it!" Now, the confused expressions became more pronounced. "In other words," I continued, "you would probably do exactly what I told you to do without any deep thought or critical analysis. You would do what I said regardless of the students in the classroom, their ages, their abilities, and their need for whatever it is I proposed." I concluded by asking the students who had taught them to "do democracy." They acknowledged that no one had taught them to do democracy, and I rejoined that doing democracy is one of their responsibilities. Slowly, the conversation moved to a discussion of how democracy is a goal for which we are all striving and although there are a few cases such as voting and public debate during which we participate in democracy, for the most part democracy is unevenly and episodically attended to. As teachers they have the responsibility to work toward educating citizens so that they are capable of participating in a democracy and nobody (and no teacher education program) is going to tell them how to do it. They are going to have to commit to democracy as a central principle of their pedagogy.

Eventually, the preservice teachers began to see multicultural education and teaching for social justice as less a thing and more an ethical position they need to take in order to ensure that students are getting the education to which they are entitled. As a teacher educator, I have worked hard to motivate preservice teachers to become reflective practitioners who care about the educational futures of their students. Often we are naïve enough to think that all teachers care about the educational futures of their students. The truth is that most teachers care about what happens to their students only while they have responsibility for them. To that end, they take on a tutorial role for some students, making sure they learn and advance. They take on a custodial role for some students, taking care of them in whatever state they are in but not advancing them educationally. They take on a referral agent role for others, shipping them off to someone else (e.g., a special educator, a parent volunteer, a student teacher) and expecting others to take responsibility for them educationally. But, how many teachers look at the students in their classrooms and envision them three, five, ten years down the road? Our responsibility to students is not merely for the nine months from September to June. It is a long-term commitment, not just to the students but also to society. Although we may have only a yearlong interaction with students, we ultimately have a lifelong impact on who they become and the kind of society in which we all will ultimately live.

An analogy I will use to illustrate this point is my experience with health-care professionals. I do this with full knowledge that many people have not benefited from our current health-care arrangements. Thus, this analogy uses an N of 1. Currently, I see four different physicians—an internist, an allergist, a gynecologist, and an oncologist. My internist is like my "homeroom" teacher. He tracks my schedule and makes sure I get to my other classes (i.e., the other physicians) on a regular basis. All of my physicians take responsibility not just for the aspect of my health in which he or she is expert but also for my total health. They all want my weight to be within a certain range. They all monitor my blood pressure. They all look at the various medications I am taking so that they can make intelligent decisions about what they should or should not prescribe. I am not so naïve to believe that the physicians are merely invested in me. I am arguing that my physicians are invested in the health of the community as well as my personal health. It does not benefit the community to have me be unhealthy within it. Similarly, it does not benefit our democracy to have uneducated and undereducated people within it. Our responsibility to the students who sit before us extends well into the future, both theirs and ours.

Conclusion

This chapter asks the question, Yes, but how do we do it? I have laid out an argument for why "doing" is less important than "being." I have argued that practicing culturally relevant pedagogy is one of the ways of "being" that will inform ways of "doing." I have suggested that our responsibility extends beyond the classroom and beyond the time students are assigned to us. It extends throughout their education because we contribute to (or detract from) that education. In a very real sense, the question is not how we do it but, rather, How can we not do it?

References

Apple, M. W. (2000). *Official knowledge: Democratic education in a conservative age.* New York: Routledge.

Collins, M., & Tamarkin, C. (1990). *Marva Collins' way.* New York: Penguin.

Dewey, J. (1997). *Experience and education.* New York: Simon & Schuster.

Foster, M. (1989). "It's cookin' now": A performance analysis of the speech events of a Black teacher in an urban community college. *Language in Society, 18*(1), 1–29.

Foster, M. (1997). *Black teachers on teaching.* New York: New Press.

Haberman, M. (1991). The pedagogy of poverty versus good teaching. *Phi Delta Kappan, 73,* 290–294.

Johnson, L. (1992). *My posse don't do homework.* New York: St. Martin's Press.

Ladson-Billings, G. (1994). *The Dreamkeepers: Successful teachers of African American children.* San Francisco: Jossey Bass.

Ladson-Billings, G. (1995). Toward a theory of culturally relevant pedagogy. *American Educational Research Journal, 31,* 465–69.

Ladson-Billings, G. (2005). No teacher left behind: Issues of equity and teacher quality. In C. A. Dwyer (Ed.), *Measurement and research in accountability era,* 141–162. Mahwah, NJ: Lawrence Erlbaum.

Mathews, J. (1988). *Escalante: The best teacher in America.* New York: Henry Holt.

Paley, V. (2000). *White teacher.* Cambridge, MA: Harvard University Press.

Rist, R. (1970). Student social class and teacher expectations: The self-fulfilling prophecy in ghetto education. *Harvard Educational Review, 40*(3), 411–451.

Shujaa, M. W. (Ed.). (1994). *Too much schooling, too little education: A paradox of Black life in White societies.* Trenton, NJ: Africa World Press.

Endnotes

1. I purposely chose examples that represent people who came from working-class and poor backgrounds.

2. I borrowed this term from Professor Pat Campbell, University of Maryland.

3. I first used this term in a school-funding equity case against the State of South Carolina.

4. The MacArthur Award is also referred to as a "genius" award.

QUESTIONS

1. Based on this chapter, how would you define *Culturally Relevant Pedagogy*?

2. The author notes that Culturally Relevant Pedagogy is a state of "being" and the focus should be less on "doing." What does this mean for teachers who work with students of color?

THE EMPTY DESK IN
THE THIRD ROW

Experiences of an African American Male Teacher

Robert Simmons

"It's not what you take but what you leave behind
that defines greatness."

—Edward Gardner

M any vivid moments are collected in my mind. Some of the moments allow me to reflect on positive experiences, whereas others conjure up memories of past failures. Despite the result of these experiences, vivid moments of the past have all influenced my life and have provided some interesting "educational" experiences that I would like to explore in this chapter.

Throughout my teaching career, I have developed my own, unique teaching style. It has been nurtured by my experiences in the Detroit public school system, the students whom I have taught, and the students who have taught me. This experience is a collection of vivid moments not only in the school system but, more specifically, in my interactions with one specific student, whom I will call Jason. The details about Jason are found a little later in this chapter.

As I take a look back at my teaching career in Detroit, I realize that the students whom I have encountered have made me a stronger teacher, a more

---

I dedicate the writing of this chapter to all of my students, past and present; my mother, Alma Simmons; my grandmother Henrietta Wyden; my uncles John and Leon; and my lovely and supportive wife, Dia.

committed community member, and a more dedicated educator. As I taught, I influenced and was influenced by many different people. The diversity of the students and their home lives both astounded and baffled me. How could such a large economic disparity exist in a country of such wealth? As a bright-eyed twenty-two-year-old, I began my adventure in the Detroit public schools.

Brown like me. Hip-hop like me. Experiences like me. From the hood like me. Entrusted to me, the minds of fourteen-year-olds, and the souls of African American children. Having a class of students who looked like me, and coming from a community that was familiar to me, provided me with great incentive every day. I often looked around at my students and saw my mission written on their faces, my passion in their music, and inspiration in their day-to-day struggles and victories. With a strong commitment to providing my students with a quality educational experience, I set out every day to defy the odds, and defeat the many age-old stereotypes.

Teaching African American children—a mission, a cause, a priority, and a debt owed to the community that nurtured me in her bosom. A mission in the way that Dr. Martin Luther King, Jr., Malcolm X, and other great African American leaders saw their roles in the civil rights movement. A cause in the way that it took Malcolm's life. A priority, as to eat to survive. A debt to all those people whom I owed so much.

Bang! Pow! Gunshots at night. Sirens sound. Babies cry. Children die. Liquor store on the corner. Crack in existence. The hood that brought me forth. The hood where I will teach. At first glance I notice the tall structure at the entrance to the school. About nine feet high, with a place for people to walk through and under. A prison? An airport? Did I miss my stop? Am I in the right location? What is that? A beep. A clang. A slight thud. "Why me? Empty my bag? Come on, dog? Take off my shoes? Man you trippin'!!" The sounds of the "inmates" as they enter the prison—oops, the sounds have me confused. I'm sorry, what did you say, Mr. Principal? You are not the warden? Oh, yeah, I almost forgot; this is a place of learning where dreams are nurtured. The students wait in line. The noise rises. I wait. I look. I wonder, "Why this line of people?" No flight to catch, just the metal detector at the front of the school.

Learning begins. "Good morning, Mr. Simmons. What up? How you living?" Greetings exchanged. Pounds given, handshakes abound. Chairs move. Sounds increase. My voice rises. Sounds decrease. My voice rises. Hands in motion. My voice rises. Notebooks move. Dreams beginning or dreams deferred? Wait a minute—what is that smell? Sniff, search, and nothing found. But the persistence of the smell continued to follow me. For several days this odd and intoxicating smell would enter my classroom, at approximately 9:30 A.M. At 10:30 A.M., the smell would leave. As the days went on, I began to encounter a student named Jason. The look in his eyes was mine. The sound of his voice, hip-hoppy, rhyming, and smooth. His look, baggy pants, sagging, of course, Fubu sweatshirt, medium build, large brown eyes, smooth brown skin, the bling-bling in his ears, the gold shines from his chest, and cornrows to set it off just right. Jason would eventually be my source of the persistent smell. Foul smelling, no. Annoying, yes. What is that? Why is it? So young. So strong. So indifferent to the world around him. So attracted to the smell of marijuana and alcohol.

Jason entered the world screaming. From his mother's womb, he would be introduced to the life of the forgotten, and the mishaps of misfits. With his older brother selling drugs, Jason was introduced to his life with the harshness of an Alaska winter. Money rolling. Dope holding. Alcohol drinking. All the ingredients to propel a dream into an abyss. By age eight, juvenile for a week. By age ten, boosting cars at the mall. By age twelve, selling crack to his mother's friends. At age thirteen, a future convict had been made.

Who are you, Jason, I want to know. I know that you have a story. What is it? Conversations with the counselor told me much. School records told me a little. My experience with you would tell it all. A stellar hoops star, but ineligible because of poor attendance and grades. Standardized test scores, no problem. Jason routinely was in the 80th percentile or above. Behavior problem, seemed like the other African American boys whom I encountered. He was confident in his style, boisterous when need be, and fully equipped to challenge the status quo.

Money was spent. Girls were his hobby. School was his intruder. With emotional baggage in the right hand, marijuana in his back pocket, and a strong will clenched tight in his right fist, Jason and I would begin a journey fit for men. A journey prepared by tragedy. A journey from two strong women's wombs. A journey along a track with trains ready to collide.

As time went on, conversations about life were exchanged. Jason wanted to dream of a life that no one knew of, the life of an engineer. With time and trust the smell dissipated but the habits still persisted. The depth of his mind and the breadth of the problems were immense. Emotions ran wild. His mouth was quick. All attached to a quick left jab, and a dominating right hook. A day approached in his life when he came to me with a choice he had to make. Engineering program on Saturdays or sitting at home? An obvious choice to many. A difficult choice for him. "Why sit at home?" To chill out he would reply. Sitting at home relieved him of the hustle of the street. The hustle had lost some of its luster as more friends were indoctrinated into the 50 percent of all Black men incarcerated. Some friends pushed up daisies, while others fantasized about their next high. Jason thought of his life. Looked at his past. He began to shed a tear for all the things he had done. What happened to the woman with three jobs whose car he had stolen? That mother buying crack—what were her kids going to eat? Engineering on Saturdays, okay, let's give it a try.

"Holla at you on Monday," was our standard phrase on Fridays. This was our fourth Friday of using such a greeting. "I need a new car so work on designing something 'phat' this weekend," I told him.

"Aw right, Mr. Simmons. I'll hook it up," Jason would always say. Black jeans sagging, cornrows shining, and pockets empty, except for bus fare, the future chief engineer for General Motors started toward the bus stop.

Learning begins. "Good morning, Mr. Simmons. What up? How you living?" Greetings exchanged. Pounds given, handshakes abound. Chairs move. Sounds increase. My voice rises. Sounds decrease. My voice rises. Hands in motion. My voice rises. Notebooks move. The dreams were no longer deferred but seen as visions of Moses. Visions of things that are possible. Dreams of things that will be done. Success at last. The small group of students soared in class. 90 percent. 85 percent. 100 percent. Test scores zoomed. Jason questioned. Another student answered. Dialogue was beginning. "Jason, I've seen you at school every day this month." "The hustle's getting old, Mr. Simmons." Old friends are moving on. Old habits die slowly. But big brother continues to thrive. Cash flows. Dope rolls. BMWs shine. Oh, wait; I forgot I got that engineering class. Be careful, Jason; you are at a crossroad. Boom, boom, the bass kicks. Lyrics blare. Profanity is used as water is drunk. BMW 325 pulls into the circle drive. Don't do it, Jason. Keep on walking. I know blood is thicker than water, but your life, your dreams. Run. Run faster. You're walking. You're getting in the car. You wave. The sound trails off. Don't forget that class on Saturday.

Learning begins. "Good morning, Mr. Simmons. What up? How you living?" Greetings exchanged. Pounds given, handshakes abound. Chairs move. Sounds increase. My voice rises. Sounds decrease. My voice rises. Hands in motion. My voice rises. Notebooks move. Discussion continues. A seat is empty. Jason, are you coming? We've done so well. A bond. A relationship. Some progress. Tick-tick. The clock seems to move slow, as if caught in a nuclear wind. A bump startles me as the door opens. Jason, is that you? No, it's the school secretary. Okay, maybe I'm paranoid. She hasn't seen Jason in school. Am I the only one concerned? Maybe my intuition is incorrect. Maybe I should call. My mind races. Students work. Ring, ring, ring. The bell tolls at 10:30. No Jason. This is only Monday. Oh, wait. I'm sorry. It is Wednesday, Mr. Simmons.

After school on Wednesday, I leave and head toward Jason's house. The sun is bright. "Oops, sorry, Mr. Simmons," as one student races to the bus stop. "Anyone seen Jason?" I inquire. No response. An agonizing ten minutes passes. I walk. I walk some more. 1256. 1258. 1260. Watch the bottle. 1262. This is the house. Holding the railing on the old rickety wooden steps is challenging. Thump, thump, thump. No answer from inside. Thump, thump, thump. I hear someone coming. A small woman in her midforties opens the door. Her eyes are red, and the smell of alcohol dominates the tiny, red brick home. "You must be Mr. Simmons," the woman says. "I am Jason's mother. I have heard a lot about you. You must be here to find out about Jason's absence." I shake my head in agreement. Her eyes seem blank. Her stare resembles that of my mother. Where have I seen this look before? My mother. My grandmother. Her voice shakes. Her hands sweat. My eyes water. We share memories. The desk in the third row will forever remain empty. Jason's dream was no longer alive. A shooter, looking for his brother, stole his dream. I rise up from the couch, hug the mother, and slowly exit the house. I walk. I walk some more.

The desk in the third row will forever remain empty. The body that was there is gone. The spirit is in me. The will to change is left in the community. Jason's courage to dream a dream foreign to his "colleagues," a dream absent from his home, and a dream left unfulfilled is why chairs move and my voice rises. Learning begins. "Good morning, Mr. Simmons. What up? How you living?" Greetings exchanged. Pounds given, handshakes abound. Chairs move. Sounds increase. My voice rises. Sounds decrease. My voice rises. Hands in motion. My voice rises. Notebooks move. The desk in the third row will forever remain empty.

That empty desk has taught me the power of faith in students. That empty desk displayed the violent impact of drugs on the community. That empty desk challenged me. That empty desk changed me. The innocent are stolen, dreams are denied, and tears will flow. That empty desk provided me perspective on the hardships of the world and validated my mission, my cause, my priorities, and my debt. Jason's mother looked like mine, felt pain like mine, but was unable to nurture like mine. My debt is now increased because I must now nurture another Jason, so that the desk in the third row can be occupied again.

What Can We Learn From the Empty Desk?

My experience with Jason during my first year teaching, 1997–1998, taught me a tremendous amount about students in urban schools. Having grown up in the city in which I taught, Detroit, I witnessed firsthand how the streets could devour young African American men. It is my experiences as a youth that helped me appreciate Jason's triumphs, respect his decisions, and cry when he fell. The following sections explore what teachers in the many urban schools around the country can do to prevent the "empty desk" experience.

Develop Relationships With Students

Too many times I have heard teachers discuss where they went to college, where they got their master's degrees or doctorates, or whom they know. The fact of the matter is that urban students do not care about that stuff. They want to know if you are "keeping it real." They want to know that when the chips are down you will "have their back." Certainly the quality of your education can impact your knowledge of subject matter, but it has no bearing on your ability to develop meaningful, positive relationships. The positive relationship with that tough-to-reach kid could mean the difference between life and death. It could mean the difference between success and failure. How can you establish that relationship? Do not read the student's entire school record file. Reading the file will taint your view. A tainted view of a student does not allow for an honest relationship, but a relationship built on conditions. Eat lunch with students in the cafeteria. There is no more authentic social experience than the school cafeteria. You will begin to see student interests, understand their perspectives on the world, and see their lives at home. Provide students with clear expectations. Too many students in urban schools have teachers who were not raised in that environment. With this lack of experience, many urban teachers assume that students will know all the "rules." Despite teachers' best efforts to provide students with a list of rules, it is the unspoken rules that often bring about the demise of the teacher/student relationship. Perhaps the most important tool in building authentic relationships with urban students is the need to know their "hood"/community. Get out into their communities, in the physical sense and the intellectual. Go to the local public library with your students to model research. Visit their places of worship. Attend sporting events. Go to their homes for dinner. Appreciate their culture and heritage by reading about their history (as written by their own authors).

Know the Urban Learner's World

The world of the urban learner is diverse. Students in urban schools are connected to a variety of fashions, have an eclectic appreciation for music, and possess a deep sense of social consciousness. Urban learners come from many different socioeconomic backgrounds. Answering the following questions will help you to know your students:

- Do you know what the latest fashions are in your school?
- Do you know who the most popular clothing designers are?
- Can you repeat the latest verse from the most recent hip-hop or R & B album?
- Do you understand the lyrics of the most popular songs?
- Do you know if your students live in an apartment or a house?
- Do you know who lives with your students or whether they live alone?
- Do you know who came to school this morning after working late last night?
- Do you know if any of your students' parents work third shift? Do you know what third shift is?
- Do you know where "sagging the pants" originated?
- Do you know why boys wear those extra long T-shirts?
- Do you know what the deal is with guys wearing pink clothes?
- Do you know the history of the "feminist" movement?
- Do you know the difference between being Hispanic and Latino/Latina?
- Do you know why African American students wear cornrows?

These are just a few questions that you should be asking yourself or your colleagues. Knowing the answers to these questions will better equip you to know the world that your students attempt to navigate on a daily basis.

Respect Who the Students Are

It is important to remember that there are many ways of doing things. There are many ways to speak. There are many ways to dance. There are many ways to think. Respect permeates the tone that teachers use when responding to criticism from students. Respect penetrates the ears of students when they are ridiculed. Respect is given by acknowledging your humanity, as well as theirs. Respect comes by seeing all of your students' cultures, races, and ethnic characteristics not as "minority," but as parts of the norm/mainstream. Respecting who they are means respecting their differences in gender, race, socioeconomic status, religion, ability, sexual preference, country of origin, native language, and age. Respecting who they are means they will respect you.

Revamp the Curriculum

One of the most needed changes in education is the revamping of all curricula. Do not think that you need the entire department or school on board. Start small. This can be done by looking at what is being taught in your classroom. When you question the truthfulness of the curriculum, some may be offended. Many may disrespect you. Several people may avoid you. This is a small price to pay when the curriculum avoids the truth, eliminates all sides to the story, or cultivates ideas that represent one point of view. Answers to the following questions will help you to discover what curricular changes need to be made:

- Does my classroom library have books that tell the stories of all members of our school community?
- Is the literature in my classroom library authentic or stereotypical?
- Is our social studies/history curriculum telling the "true" story?
- Are we still telling our students that Columbus discovered America?
- Do we engage students in discussions about the contributions of women and people of color to math and science?
- Do we dust off our heritage month curriculum every day or are we saving it for that one month?
- Do we play games in physical education that represent various cultures?

The questions that I have just posed represent a beginning to the dialogue on curriculum reform. If we want our urban learners to be successful, we must ensure that they see themselves in what is being taught. We must ensure that our students feel connected to what is being learned.

Conclusion

Urban learners face many challenges. It is our job as educators to inspire them passionately. I learned of the value of that inspiration through an experience with an empty desk. That empty desk changed my life. That empty desk tore me down, only to help build me up again. Use that empty desk to build yourself up. Use that empty to desk to inspire all urban learners. Use that empty desk to create your own vivid moments.

Reference

National Urban League. (2000). *State of Black America.* New York: Author.

QUESTIONS

1. What can educators learn from the "empty desk" in this chapter?
2. What can we learn about African American students by answering the questions in the section "Know the Urban Learner's World"?

5

BUT GOOD INTENTIONS ARE NOT ENOUGH

Doing What's Necessary to Teach for Diversity

H. Richard Milner

I n this chapter, I argue that it is not enough for teachers to have good intentions to meet the needs of their students. Having good intentions is important, but teachers must transform and enact those good intentions into thinking (that is, mindsets) and practices that allow all their students, including their culturally diverse students, to (1) find meaning in the classroom, (2) feel a sense of belonging in the space, and (3) build knowledge and skills for academic success. With special attention to issues of race, in the subsequent sections of this chapter, building from established research, theory, and practice in the field of education, I share what I call instructional principles that can assist teachers in transforming and moving their good intentions into actions that make a real difference for students in P–12 classrooms. Before discussing the four principles, I consider, in more depth, the importance of teachers moving their good intentions into effective practices. In short, I elucidate why it is critical for teachers to move beyond just having good intentions as they work to teach all students effectively. Teachers must do what is necessary to teach for diversity.[1]

Beyond Just Good Intentions

In my nearly 14 years of experience in education, I have rarely, if ever, met a teacher without good intentions: they purchase supplies for students from their own finances; they hold tutorial/after-school sessions to assist their students with complicated subject matter; they even volunteer to serve as coaches and club supervisors for their students. However, while teachers' good intentions are necessarily appropriate, they are inadequate—and frankly not enough—for the complex work of teaching in various social contexts across the United States. It is essential that teachers develop the competencies necessary to meet the instructional needs of *all* students in public school classrooms. Unfortunately, teachers, in particular, sometimes do not have the repertoire of knowledge and skills necessary to construct meaningful instructional practices for their culturally diverse students.[2]

Clearly, I am not attempting to criticize the many teachers across the United States who deliberately work to provide optimal learning opportunities for all students. I understand teaching as difficultly complex and multifaceted work. However, too many teachers are in denial about the reality of their classroom practices and students. They are in denial about why they are struggling to meet the needs of their students, and they are in denial about how their practices are sometimes inadequate to meet the needs of their students, especially their culturally diverse students. Teachers' locus of control—that is, the blame for lack of student academic success is often placed solely external to them. For instance, teachers may blame their students' lack of motivation or even lack of parental involvement for challenges they face in the classroom. While student motivation and the nature of parental involvement likely play important roles in what happens in classrooms, I argue that teachers must concurrently examine themselves and their practices as potential contributory factors in the successes and failures of the classroom culture and learning that takes place there.

Given the demography of the teaching force, it has become blatantly apparent that race needs to be a critical element of consideration in the teaching and learning exchange. Yet, many White teachers, in particular, struggle with even having conversations about the influences and relationships between race and pedagogy in the P–12 classroom. White teachers, who make up the vast majority of the U.S. teaching force in P–12 classrooms, can shut down during conversations about race and racism because they are uncomfortable confronting such issues. Based on research I have conducted over the years with White preservice teachers, several assertions can shape their positions to avoid the "taboo" topic of race:

- Assertion #1: If I acknowledge the racial or ethnic background of my students or myself, then I may be considered racist.

- Assertion #2: If I admit that people experience the world differently and that race is an important dimension of people's experiences, I may be seen as "politically incorrect." I may offend others in the teacher education classroom discourse if I express my beliefs and reservations about race.
- Assertion #3: I should treat all my students the same regardless of who they are, what their home situations are, or what their racial experiences happen to be. Race does not matter, and racism has ended and certainly has no place or relevance in the classroom.

Such assertions make it difficult for teachers to engage in the types of introspection necessary to address their instructional practices with students and especially with culturally diverse students.

Below, to further illuminate the racial demographics, I provide a snapshot of the U.S. public school teaching force and student population in Tables 5.1 and 5.2.

When teachers refuse to discuss race and how race can manifest in their instructional practices, they can disrupt possible opportunities for them to develop the kinds of mindsets and practices necessary for student academic success. Silence regarding race can be used as a weapon (Ladson-Billings, 1996) in classrooms, faculty meetings, or even private conversations because teachers are actually communicating when they are silent. The silent communication or dialogue (Delpit, 1995) relays to others that race is insignifi-

TABLE 5.1

Teaching Demographics in Public Elementary and Secondary School: Percentages of Teachers Represented in Types (Elementary or Secondary) of Schools

2007–2008	*Elementary Public School Teachers (%)*	*Secondary Public School Teachers (%)*
White	82.7	83.5
Black	7.1	6.9
Hispanic	7.5	6.8
Asian	1.2	1.3
Pacific Island	0.2	0.2
American Indian/Alaska Native	0.4	0.5
More than one race	0.9	0.9

Source: NCES (2008)

TABLE 5.2
Student Demographics: Percentage of Students, by Ethnicity Represented Over Four Years

Ethnicity	2003 (%)	2004 (%)	2005 (%)	2008 (%)
White	60.5	59.9	59.4	57.8
Black	14.9	14.9	14.8	16.0
Hispanic	17.7	18.2	18.7	20.4
Asian	3.6	3.7	3.7	4.4
Pacific Islander	0.2	0.2	0.2	n/a
American Indian/ Alaska Native	0.9	0.9	0.9	1.4
More than one race	2.2	2.3	2.3	n/a

Source: 2003-2005 Digest of Education Statistics (2008); NCES (2008)

cant and consequently inconsequential to teachers' work. It can be quite difficult for many White teachers to engage in real conversations about race and racism in teaching and learning, mainly because White teachers enjoy privileges (McIntosh, 1990) that allow them to avoid such taboo topics of conversations. White teachers' privileges allow them to not be necessarily concerned about the role of race in society and their work.

Such an avoidance is baffling because teachers realize there are racial tensions and realities prevalent in education and their classrooms when (1) they examine disparities among and between different racial groups on standardized test score data, (2) they examine disciplinary patterns among various racial groups of students, (3) when they investigate gifted and talented program referrals, (4) when they examine special education patterns in their school, or (5) when they look closely at student representation in prestigious clubs and organizations such as honor societies, the homecoming court, or student government.

Moreover, White teachers often recognize the tensions they encounter with culturally diverse students through classroom practices such as when they have difficulty with classroom management, and they see that their culturally diverse students are those whom they struggle with the most. Still, teachers too often refuse to confront these racialized issues head on in order to redress them. As Gordon (1990) maintained, "critiquing your own assumptions about the world—especially if you believe the world works for you" (p. 88) is indeed an arduously complex task. Thus, because the world works for these teachers and their own biological children, addressing race may seem trivial and irrelevant. At the same time, teachers may believe they are giving their students all that they have; again, teachers may have good intentions but fail to move outside of their comfort zones in order to construct more innovative learning opportunities for students.

In subsequent sections of this chapter, I share principles that I have found to be necessary in helping teachers transform, extend, and enact their good intentions into "good" practices. At the end of each of the four principles I outline, I provide a list of reflective questions to assist teachers in thinking deeply about themselves, their positions, as well as their practices regarding meeting the needs of their students, and especially their culturally diverse students. At the heart of the reflection questions for teachers is the following recurrent question: What do I, as teacher, need to change in order to better meet the needs of all my students? Critical self-reflection is an important process for teachers because careful and deliberate reflection (also see the work of McCutcheon, 2002; Milner, 2003) can assist teachers in uncovering issues, perspectives, practices, and ideas that have been hidden and covert otherwise. Freire (1998) explained, "as women and men, simultaneously reflecting on themselves and the world, increase the scope of their perceptions, they begin to *direct their observations towards previously inconspicuous phenomena*" (emphasis added, p. 63). Through reflection, teachers can begin to deal with some authentically real racialized issues that could bring them into new levels of consciousness. Put simply, what teachers think and believe show up in what they actually do (Gay, 2010; Milner, 2010). Throughout this chapter, I ask teachers to ask themselves several broad questions regarding themselves, their students, and their work such as:

- What has happened to me throughout my life experiences that may have influence on my thinking and positions inside the classrooms with my students?
- How might my pre- and misconceptions, thoughts, beliefs, reflections, and mindsets shape who I am and how I construct learning opportunities with my students?
- How do I, as teacher, situate myself in the education of others?

I turn next to an explanation of the principles that I believe can assist teachers in expanding and acting on their good intentions.

Principle One: Teachers transform their deficit thinking about students and build on the assets that students bring into the learning social context.

Even when teachers have good intentions, they sometimes do not really believe in the abilities and capacities of particular students. Teachers' thinking about their students, about their students' abilities, and about their students' established knowledge and possibilities can serve as a precursor to what is possible instructionally. For example, teacher thinking bears on how they develop the curriculum (McCutcheon, 2002), how they formulate questions to expand the curriculum, whose voice they allow to speak in the classroom, what they are willing to try differently in the classroom with different students, and how they enact and teach the curriculum.

One contributor to deficit thinking is that many teachers have never attended schools with individuals of a different race or ethnicity, or lived in cross-cultural/cross-racial neighborhoods, which adds to their already vague and inadequate understanding of students. Because many White teachers have a lack of exposure to and experience with people of color, they may adopt deficit orientations about their culturally diverse students. In light of this lack of exposure and understanding, teachers often rely on stereotypes of their students based on misconceptions they have acquired about the students' racial or ethnic group. Teachers' conceptions and perceptions of students may be constructed and extracted from television programming they have watched, the media (especially newspapers), misinformed colleagues in their school, or even family biases that have been communicated to them yet not critically examined. Unfortunately, stereotypical beliefs and thinking may force teachers to think about their culturally diverse students through deficit lenses—whether consciously, subconsciously, or unconsciously—and these counterproductive thoughts can contaminate teaching and learning, even when teachers have good intentions.

For some teachers, it is difficult for them to build on what students actually bring into the learning environment because they do not necessarily believe that students actually possess *useful* knowledge and skills that can be used as a foundation from which to draw and build. Deficit-minded/thinking-teachers' perceptions that culturally diverse students do not already possess skills, knowledge, and attitudes to succeed and learn can result in the development of curriculum and instruction that falls short of optimal teaching and related educational opportunities. *My argument here is that teachers need to build on what students already know; my argument is not that students already possess everything they necessarily need to know in order to function effectively in an oppressive and repressive society.* Thus, deficit thinking can result in inaccurate perceptions of marginalized students that hinder students' progress. Where cultural deficit theories are concerned, Ford (1996) wrote:

> These theories carry a "blame the victim" orientation, and supporters look upon Blacks and other minority groups as not only culturally but also intellectually inferior. According to deficit theories or perspectives, "different" is equated with deficient, inferior, and substandard. (p. 84)

Thus, deficit thinking can prevent teachers from realizing that all students are knowledgeable and bring a wealth of knowledge into the classroom that must be tapped into in order to capture students' interests and their engagement. It is essential that teachers acknowledge that there are varied ways of knowing and that culturally diverse students often enter the classroom with a set of knowledges and experiences that may be different, often outside of or inconsistent with their teachers', yet knowledges and experiences that should be valued and built upon in teaching and learning.

In short, deficit thinking can cause teachers to look upon culturally diverse students as liabilities rather than assets. Further, research suggests that teachers need to confront and change their deficit thinking in order to be more productive in their classrooms with culturally diverse learners (Ford & Grantham, 2003; Howard, 2001; Milner, 2010). Indeed, having good intentions is not enough. Teachers must become proactive in changing their negative mindsets and deficit thinking about culturally diverse students in order to deconstruct and transform their instructional practices to benefit all those in the learning milieu. In a quest to address deficit thinking for effective instructional practices, I invite educators to consider the following reflection questions:

- Do I believe that students have assets that can be used to build on and from in the classroom? Why or why not?
- What assets do students bring into the classroom that can be powerful curricular and instructional resources? (Examples of assets might include students' knowledge, skills, and interests.)
- How do I (or might I) build on student assets to better connect with students?
- What assets do I, as teacher, bring into the classroom, and how do I bridge my assets with those of my students?

- How might I negotiate the knowledge and skills that students bring into the classroom in order to build instructional practices?

Clearly, in an era of accountability, standardized testing, competition, and mindsets of meritocracy, it is easy for teachers to focus most of their attention on what they perceive as student deficits. I have come to understand that such thinking can prevent teachers from developing challenging and rigorous learning opportunities for students because teachers believe that watering down the curriculum and creating simple, mundane lessons will in fact help students catch up with peers whom society and those in education considers the norm or exceptional. Of course in many cases White students are considered the norm by which culturally diverse students are measured and compared. Taken together, the aforementioned examples and explanations of deficit thinking can result in less than meaningful learning opportunities for students.

Principle Two: Teachers understand the complex interplay between equity and equality for the benefit of students.

While it is critical that teachers transform their mindsets and, in particular, their deficit thinking regarding culturally diverse students and their capacity to succeed, it is also important that teachers understand the complex nature and interplay of equity and equality in their work to meet the needs of all students. Teachers sometimes confound equity with that of equality. When we define and practice equality in education, we are often attempting to provide the same educational opportunities, experiences, curriculum, and instruction for all students in different learning environments, regardless of the needs of those in the contexts (Ladson-Billings, 2000; Milner & Williams, 2008). Equity, however, means that teachers prepare a set of educational experiences that are tailored to meet the particular needs of their students. This means that what is necessary for success among one group of students may be very different from what is vital for others. The idea is that some students may need extra supports and opportunities for academic success, for example, while others may not. Such an ideal is grounded in notions of social justice (Secada, 1989).

Understanding equity and equality as sameness can mean that teachers aspire to and work toward the same educational opportunities for all students. This approach can be disadvantageously ineffective because in reality students do not enter schools with/in the exact same circumstances; consequently, we under-serve students and fail to meet their needs when we attempt to adopt and implement a one-size-fits-all approach to our work with students. From an educational historical perspective, Secada (1989) unpacked important differences between equality and equity:

> There is a history of using terms like equity and equality of education interchangeably. Though these constructs are related, equality is group-based and quantitative. Equity can be applied to groups or to individuals; it is qualitative in that equity is tied to notions of justice. (p. 23)

Equity, according to Secada (1989), is defined as judgments about whether or not a given state of affairs is just. For example, equity in education may mean that we are attempting to provide students, regardless of their racial, ethnic, cultural, or gender background with what they need to succeed—not some predetermined practices that may or may not be appropriate.

Ladson-Billings's (2000) discussion about notions of "equivalent" and "analogous" can help us think through the equity, equality, and sameness issue. She outlined some of her experiences related to equity in discussions with teachers:

> Discussants [teachers] want to talk in terms of who has suffered most. However, when we understand the ways in which oppression has worked against many groups of people based on their race, culture, class, gender, disability, and sexual orientation, we must recognize that there may be analogous experiences that are not necessarily equivalent ones. (p. 207)

In this way, it may be necessary to extend opportunities to certain groups of students based on the historical context that has shaped their experiences. Ladson-Billings (2000) goes on to explain that "our understanding of the commonalities of oppression cannot wash out the particularities and specifics of each experience" (p. 207). Thus as we examine the impact that the many phobias and isms have had on the educational experiences of culturally diverse students, it becomes clear that, from an equity standpoint, heightened attention and resources may be necessary to counter some of the negative influences and realities that different groups have endured both contemporarily and historically

In analyzing policy-related matters focusing on desegregation, Ladson-Billings (2000) maintained that "rhetoric of equality means sameness tended to ignore the distinctive qualities of African American culture and suggested that if schools were to make schooling experiences identical for African Americans, we somehow could achieve identical results" (p. 208). Logically, employing identical schooling experiences across the board without attending to the idiosyncrasies inherent to the particular group of students in a school will not necessarily result in promising outcomes. Several interrelated questions can provide insightful guidance for teachers as they attempt to disentangle the equity-equality conflation.

- Do I recognize that students bring varied experiences into the classroom, experiences that are not identical to each other?
- How can I develop learning experiences for students that address their particular situations, needs, and circumstances?
- Do I develop the curriculum, enact it, and gauge (assess) learning among my students through equitable lenses—taking into account each student's reality?
- How do I determine, negotiate, and reconcile equitable learning opportunities in my classroom that may not necessarily be the same for all students?

Indeed, attempting to uncover what it means to teach students based on who they are and what their needs happen to be is complex work that requires teachers to deeply understand how to differentiate instruction. While teachers may intend to meet the individual needs of students, in practice, it may seem difficult because they find it inappropriate to develop instructional and related practices that differ for students, depending on student-specific needs. Again, although teachers can have good intentions, they are not enough.

Principle Three: Teachers understand that both they and their students operate through power structures that should be acknowledged and negotiated in order to successfully function and thrive, both inside and outside of school.

Thus far, I have outlined two important principles essential to teachers' moving beyond good intentions to conceptions and practices that are advantageous for all their students. In particular, teachers transform their deficit thinking about students and build on the assets that students bring into the learning environment. Moreover, teachers understand the complex interplay between equity and equality for the benefit of students. A third principle has to do with the importance of teachers' ability to understand and articulate what power is and how it works in the lives of people (teachers and students in particular) both inside and outside of the classroom.

Even with the influx of high-stakes testing, teachers still have an enormous range of power and control over what actually happens (or not) in the classroom. As McCutcheon (2002) explained, teachers are more than mere curriculum implementers; they are curriculum developers as well. Even with scripted curriculum that is constructed by some outside source, teachers are not robots who are mindlessly disconnected to students' opportunities to learn. However, teachers often do not recognize or acknowledge the huge range of power they have in their teaching. For examples, some teachers do not embrace the agency they actually have that can make a meaningful difference with students. It is critical for teachers to understand their power in the classroom because it is part of their responsibility to help their students: (1) understand the power structure in the classroom and beyond, (2) survive and thrive in and through power structures, and (3) work to change inequitable, racist, and unjust power structures they encounter in their school and other environments.

Where the role of power among teachers in instruction is concerned, Freire (1998) asserted that good teaching and learning does not evolve from a banking theory, in which teachers see education as "an act of depositing, in which the students are the depositories and the teacher is the depositor" (p. 53). Rejecting the banking theory of education, Freire supported an educational process that is problem-centered and problem-posing. The banking approach to teaching has a top-down nature to it where teachers are considered the "knower" and students are considered the "learner" and too often the non-knower. Indeed, as discussed previously regarding asset-thinking, students have knowledge and teachers can learn from their students and with them. Through the banking approach of knowledge acquisition, teachers make deposits "which the students patiently receive, memorize, and repeat" (p. 53). This concept is important because individuals, whether teachers or students, are the experts on/about their experiences. A teacher, then, works in collaboration with their students to construct knowledge, relevance, and meaning in the classroom.

In order to negotiate some of the power in the classroom, teachers might pose questions which help students locate answers to questions and areas of interest, resulting in a teacher/student interaction that is dynamic and evolutionary. Such a partnership, where teachers are open to learning from their students, has the potential to minimize the power of the teacher because knowledge and expertise are negotiated and valued among all those in the social context. Teachers help students understand that learning is an ongoing process and that they can garner power through knowledge construction and acquisition because as students they are "not . . . a static reality but . . . in transformation" (Freire, 1998, p. 64).

In essence, power in the classroom can be understood as teachers answer the following questions: Is my role of teaching superior to the experiences and expertise of my students? Is there knowledge to be learned from my students? How do I situate and negotiate students' knowledge, experiences, and expertise in knowledge construction in the classroom?

In addition to Freire (1998), Delpit (1995) explained that there is a "culture of power" that must be addressed and understood as we work to problematize "normal" and "appropriate" behavior and ways of being and experiencing the world. In her explanation of how power works, Delpit described five aspects of power:

> (a) issues of power are enacted in classrooms; (b) there are codes or rules for participating in power; that is, there is a culture of power; (c) the rules of the culture of power are a reflection of the rules of the culture of those who have power; (d) if you are not already a participant in the culture of power, being told explicitly the rules of that culture makes acquiring power easier; and (e) those with power are frequently least aware of—or least willing to acknowledge—its existence. Those with less power are often most aware of its existence. (p. 24)

Delpit suggested that students deserve to be told explicitly the "rules" and the consequences of those in power. For students to have a chance at success in the classroom and society writ large, Delpit seemed to argue that students must understand that they live and operate in a system that is oppressive because those in power decide how one is supposed to behave, learn, and even exist. White teachers, in particular, possess a range of power that is complicated by other layers of power they possess beyond their role as teachers. Fundamentally, White teachers enjoy privileges associated with and as a consequence of their Whiteness. Thus, White teachers have to examine how their powered positions enable them to function in the classroom in particular. Success, rewards, and sustainability can be couched in a student's ability to understand, negotiate, and navigate through the culture of power, and it is teachers' responsibility to assist students in these processes while simultaneously building their own knowledge about what it means to have power in the space.

In essence, Freire, Delpit, and I argue that the onus of articulating the power structure of the classroom is on teachers—that is, those in power—to help students make the transition into navigating through the dominant culture in ways that allow them to succeed and, simultaneously, change unfair and unjust systems. Students must learn to adapt their behaviors and the ways in which they operate in their homes to the expectations of their mostly White teachers whose home experiences with their own children and whose expectations for what is appropriate, normal and consequently acceptable may be incongruent with their culturally diverse students. For students to make smooth shifts between what is expected at home and what is expected of them at school, Delpit declared that those in power must make the rules and expectations clear and overt to their students. The assumption that students would be taught a culture of power outside of the classroom is an irresponsible assumption. This point can be substantiated particularly if parents do not fully understand how to negotiate and live in a teacher's culture that she or he has cultivated in a classroom. Knowing *what* the culture of power actually is, *how* it works, and how power can be *achieved* are important competencies for students' success in the classroom, and again, teachers should help students in their development and knowledge of the culture.

The notion that there is more than one appropriate way to act, learn, and perceive the world means that teachers understand their own power and privileges and that they understand how and why certain individuals with and without power are able to navigate the system whereas others are not. Several reflective questions seem appropriate for teachers as they work to uncover and address the nature of power in their work:

- Do I understand that there are implicit and covert power structures that exist in the classroom?
- Am I prepared to explain and teach students these implicit and covert power structures?
- What are the power structures that exist in the classroom, and how do they enable or stifle learning opportunities among my students?
- In what ways am I willing to negotiate the power structure of the classroom in order to empower students to have voice, gain perspective, and garner power in the space?
- How can I empower and prepare students to transfer their enhanced understandings of power to other settings outside of school?

In essence, this principle encourages teachers to remember that there are multiple ways to live and act in the world; however, a teacher has the power to determine what is acceptable in his or her classroom and thus must be willing to explain and consecutively negotiate the culture of power so that students are able to function effectively.

Principle Four: Teachers understand that while incongruence between themselves and their students is inevitable, they can work to circumvent it through deliberate practices that focus on what they are doing and why.

A fourth and final principle that I discuss in this chapter has to do with the idea that cultural and racial incongruence, discontinuity, and inconsistency occur in classrooms where teachers and students do not possess the same or similar cultural and racial backgrounds, knowledge, and experiences. Such inconsistencies make it difficult for connections to occur in terms of pedagogy and related learning opportunities in the classroom. Incongruence can ensue due to a range of matters such as differences between teacher and student ages (generational discontinuity), differences that exist regarding teacher and student interests (interest discontinuity), and differences that exist between how teacher and student handle and resolve conflicts (conflict resolution discontinuity).

In short, research, theory, and practice suggest that the incongruence that can occur between teachers and students is often culturally and racially grounded and shaped. Because White teachers and culturally diverse students, in many ways, possess different racialized and cultural experiences and repertoires of knowledge and knowing both inside and outside the classroom, racial and cultural incongruence may serve as a roadblock for academic and social success (Irvine, 2003). A pivotal finding regarding cultural incongruence is that when teachers develop and employ examples to illuminate their subject matter in a classroom, when they interpret misbehavior among students in a classroom, or when they attempt to connect with their students' parents, they may be ineffective because they do not understand the role that race and culture play in these interactions (Howard, 2010; Irvine, 2003; Milner, 2010).

While the cultural and racial incongruence principle has merit and teachers should be mindful of such incongruence, research is also clear that teachers from any racial and/or ethnic background can be successful pedagogues of culturally diverse students (see Ladson-Billings, 2009, for more on this). To explain, Gay (2010) asserted that "similar ethnicity between students and teachers may be potentially beneficial, but it is not a guarantee of pedagogical effectiveness" (p. 205). Teachers from any ethnic, cultural, or racial background can be successful with any group of students when the teachers possess (or have the skills and *desire* to acquire) the knowledge, attitudes, dispositions, and beliefs necessary to meet the needs of all their students.

Thus, while teachers must be aware that they will encounter conflicts in their classrooms that are racially and culturally constructed and grounded, they should also be aware that they can develop the competencies necessary for them to work through those conflicts for the benefit of all their students. Recognizing that differences actually can exist is an important first step for teachers as they attempt to address discontinuity. In addition, recognizing that conflicts are not always racially motivated but are sometimes more generally shaped is essential. Perhaps most importantly, it is imperative that teachers realize that differences that are inevitable between themselves and their students do not have to halt success in the classroom as long as teachers are willing to exert the necessary energy and work to build their knowledge and skill to address, challenge, and work through conflicts. Teachers might consider the following questions when attempting to address cultural incongruence:

- Do I recognize that cultural and racial incongruence can exist in my classroom?
- What are some examples and signs of disconnections between students and teachers that may actually exist in a learning environment?
- How can I deepen my knowledge about myself and my students to find points of convergence?
- How can I deepen my knowledge and understanding about students when their ways of knowing and acting are inconsistent with my own?
- From a sociological perspective, how can I build knowledge about my students to "get along" better with them?
- From a curriculum and instructional perspective, how can I build knowledge about my students and their needs in the development of the curriculum and the enactment of it?

Indeed, understanding and addressing teacher and student incongruence in the classroom can potentially decrease the many conflicts that can exist in a space. As Sheets (1996) explained, students in her study revealed that they often felt disrespected, devalued, and misunderstood in the classroom due to conflicts with their teachers.

TABLE 5.3
Principles Beyond Good Intentions Chart

Principle	Explanation
Understand and Reject Deficit Thinking	Teachers transform their deficit thinking about students and build on the assets that students bring into the learning social context
Understand and Practice Equity versus Equality	Teachers understand that equity does not necessarily mean that they will employ the same practices with all students. Rather, equity and equality require a deep understanding of the contextual nature of teachers' work.
Understand and Negotiate Power Structures	Teachers understand that both they and their students operate through power structures that should be acknowledged and negotiated in order to successfully function and thrive, both inside and outside of school.
Understand and Navigate through Racial and Cultural Conflicts	Teachers understand that while incongruence between themselves and their students is inevitable, they can work to circumvent it through deliberate practices that focus on what they are doing and why.

Summary and Conclusion

In summary, in Table 5.3 I summarize the major principles explored in this chapter in hopes that teachers will move their good intentions into practices necessary for student academic and social success. Clearly, teachers should understand that both they and their students operate through power structures that should be understood in order to succeed both inside and outside of school. Teachers should understand the fundamental differences between equity and equality for the benefit of students; they should realize that they may not be able to implement the exact same practices among all their students because students enter the classroom with different needs and expectations. As well, teachers should understand that they and their students operate through and must navigate through power structures that have a huge bearing on opportunities to learn in the classroom. Teachers need to be told explicitly about the rules and expectations of the classroom and also about how power works in those spaces. In addition, teachers understand that while incongruence between themselves and their students is inevitable, they can work to circumvent it through deliberate practices about what they are doing and why.

Finally, teachers are challenged to develop new levels of understanding, awareness, and competencies around these four principles. Teachers' claims of having good intentions are simply not enough in an era when many students are desperate for challenging and relevant learning opportunities and experiences in social contexts (see, for example, Carter, 2005). I am hopeful and optimistic that teachers will not sit back innocently and unconcerned about the too many culturally diverse students who are not meeting and reaching their full capacity in classrooms across the United States. Indeed, I am hoping that teachers will *do* what is necessary to teach for diversity.

References

Carter, P. L. (2005). *Keepin' it real: School success beyond black and white*. New York, NY: Oxford University Press.

Delpit, L. (1995). *Other people's children: Cultural conflict in the classroom*. New York, NY: New Press.

Ford, D. Y. (1996). *Reversing underachievement among gifted Black students: Promising practices and programs*. New York, NY: Teachers College Press.

Ford, D. Y., & Grantham, T. C. (2003). Providing access for culturally diverse gifted students: From deficit to dynamic thinking. *Theory Into Practice, 42*(3), 217–225.

Freire, P. (1998). *Pedagogy of the oppressed*. New York, NY: Continuum.

Gay, G. (2010). *Culturally responsive teaching: Theory, research, & practice*. New York, NY: Teachers College Press.

Gordon, B. M. (1990). The necessity of African-American epistemology for educational theory and practice. *Journal of Education, 172*(3), 88–106.

Howard, T. C. (2001). Telling their side of the story: African American students' perceptions of culturally relevant pedagogy. *Urban Review, 33*(2), 131–149.

Howard, T. C. (2010). *Why race and culture matter in schools: Closing the achievement gap in America's classrooms*. New York, NY: Teachers College Press.

Irvine, J. J. (2003). *Educating teachers for diversity: Seeing with a cultural eye*. New York, NY: Teachers College Press.

Ladson-Billings, G. (2009). *The dreamkeepers: Successful teachers of African American children* (2nd ed.). San Francisco, CA: Jossey-Bass.

Ladson-Billings, G. (2000). Fighting for our lives: Preparing teachers to teach African American students. *Journal of Teacher Education, 51*(3), 206–214.

Ladson-Billings, G. (1996). Silences as weapons: Challenges of a Black professor teaching White students. *Theory Into Practice, 35,* 79–85.

McCutcheon, G. (2002). *Developing the curriculum: Solo and group deliberation.* Troy, NY: Educators' Press International.

McIntosh, P. (1990). White privilege: Unpacking the invisible knapsack. *Independent School, 90*(49), 31–36.

Milner, H. R. (2010). What does teacher education have to do with teaching? Implications for diversity studies. *Journal of Teacher Education, 60*(1/2), 118–131.

Milner, H. R. (2003). Reflection, racial competence, and critical pedagogy: How do we prepare preservice teachers to pose tough questions? *Race, Ethnicity, and Education, 6*(2), 193–208.

Milner, H. R. & Williams, S. M. (2008). Analyzing education policy and reform with attention to race and socio-economic status. *Journal of Public Management and Social Policy, 14*(2), 33–50.

Secada, W. G. (1989). Agenda setting, enlightened self-interest, and equity in mathematics education. *Peabody Journal of Education, 66*(2), 22–56.

Sheets, R. H. (1996). Urban classroom conflict: Student-teacher perception: Ethnic integrity, solidarity, and resistance. *The Urban Review, 28*(2), 165–183.

U.S. Department of Education, Institute of Education Sciences, National Center for Education Statistics. (2009). *Percentage distribution of school teachers, by race/ethnicity, school type, and selected school characteristics: 2007–08.* Retrieved from http://nces.ed.gov/pubs2009/2009324/tables/sass0708_2009324_t12n_02.asp

U.S. Department of Education, Institute of Education Sciences, National Center for Education Statistics. (2009). *Percentage distribution of students, by sex, race/ethnicity, school type, and selected school characteristics: 2007–08.* Retrieved from http://nces.ed.gov/pubs2009/2009321/tables/sass0708_2009321_s12n_03.asp

Endnotes

1. By "teach for diversity," I mean that teachers need to be equipped to understand the diversity among the students with whom they are working, and they need to construct learning opportunities in the classroom with a diversity-oriented commitment. In short, teaching for diversity means that teachers are *for* diversity and centralize matters of diversity as they develop and enact the curriculum.

2. I understand that there is diversity among all groups of students, even White students. However, to clarify, I refer to culturally diverse students as those students who live in poverty, are students of color, and are students whose first language is not English.

QUESTIONS

1. Why aren't good intentions enough for meeting the needs of your students, particularly your students of color?
2. Why are the three "assertions" presented in this chapter a barrier for White teachers in reaching their students of color?

6

THE UNINTENTIONAL UNDERMINING OF MULTICULTURAL EDUCATION

Educators at the Equity Crossroads

Paul Gorski

Mary and I stepped wearily into the conference room—a small, dimly lit space, just large enough for the meeting table and eight middle-aged, straight-postured, White administrators waiting for us to arrive. As Donald, the principal, flanked by his two top assistants, waved us in, our other hosts, having forgotten to leave space for us at the table, shifted and scooted to squeeze us in. With a knowing, understanding, but exasperated smile, Mary patted me lightly on the back, a gentle nudge of encouragement in the late afternoon of a disheartening day.

After lowering ourselves into our seats and participating in the requisite introductory banter, we initiated this focus group with the same question with which we had initiated the other groups we had met during two full days of data gathering. Looking at Donald, turning my body squarely toward him so there could be no confusion from whom I hoped to draw an answer, I asked, "How do you conceptualize multicultural education here at Northern High School?"

Shortly before this focus group with the administrators, Mary and I sat in a bare, white-tiled room adjacent to the cafeteria. We shared sandwiches, fries, and cooked carrots with twelve students of color, many of whom were members of Prism, Northern's multicultural student organization. They were African American, Asian American, Latina/Latino, and Native American, and whether counted in their individual racial or ethnic groups or as a diverse collective of students of color, they comprised a small, largely invisible percentage of the student population. Donald requested the development of Prism three years earlier in response to several racial incidents within the school—a common move for a well-meaning administrator, cautious of examining the roots of racial inequities within her or his school, and opting, instead, to conceptualize the problem as one beginning, and ending, with the students themselves.

As we transitioned from intergenerational comparisons of the nature and quality of school lunches to an exploration of the students' experiences at Northern, it became quickly, painfully apparent that nobody of decision-making consequence had taken much interest in their stories, their lives, their livelihoods at the school. When asked to describe those experiences, the students used words such as *alienation, discrimination, racism.* They described individual racist episodes and an institutionally racist environment. And, like many students of color whose mostly White teachers and administrators believe themselves to be committed authentically to the principles of multiculturalism, these students were exhausted and frustrated by "baby steps," by human relations and community development programs that never named or addressed racism.

Wrapping up after an hour with the students, we asked them what they felt the teachers and administrators needed to do to address their concerns. "I want somebody here to acknowledge that racism is rife at Northern," one student exclaimed, pounding her fist on the table and eliciting nods from her classmates. "Without acknowledging that and dealing with it directly, they're just making it worse. And I'm tired."

With that, Mary and I had headed to our next focus group: the administrators.

Donald leaned forward and smiled. His tie, covered with renderings of a diversity of smiling children, spilled out of his unbuttoned sports coat. His air, like his tie, exuded optimism. He was genuine. He wanted his diversity of students to be as happy as the characters on his tie. He truly believed that diversity was an asset, an essential element of effective education. He approved our visit and an endless array of other programs and budget hits focused on diversity and community.

"How do I conceptualize multicultural education?" he repeated. "Well, I believe that, at Northern High School, we must celebrate the joys of diversity. We must find ways to share our cultures—our food, our dress, our art.

We pride ourselves on celebrating our diversity." With that, he sat back, confident, smiling, and dedicated to his conception of multicultural education.

After years of facilitating diversity, multicultural education, and education equity workshops for schools across the United States, Mary and I were accustomed to hearing White educators describe this conservatively reframed version of multiculturalism. And, worse, we were used to hearing them describe it with pride and confidence in what they seemed to actually believe to be an authentically progressive and transformative approach to teaching and learning. But, perhaps because we had just come from a meeting with devastatingly disenfranchised students describing the painful realities of racism at the school, we felt the racist undertones of Donald's response in a particularly deep way.

As the meeting progressed, we continued hearing evidence of the disconnect between the reality of the students and the reframing of that reality by their administrators. One administrator mentioned the possibility of reinstituting the Korean culture festival. Another worried that the identity-specific student groups (such as the Black Student Union) modeled segregation and pushed for disbanding them. The principal, listening carefully to his colleagues' suggestions and nodding his approval, insisted that Northern should focus less on race and other "contentious issues" and more on "intellectual diversity."

So in place of a real examination of race and a plan to eliminate racism, the students of color at Northern were on a path to experience *less* attention to race and a celebration of "intellectual diversity." Leaving the meeting in quiet contemplation of how to push these administrators beyond their reframed conception of multicultural education, I turned to Mary with a suggestion of my own: "With all of this celebrating, perhaps they'll institute a 'Celebrate Your Oppression' day." That, after all, seemed to be what the administrators wanted the students of color to do.

This story illustrates a growing crisis that threatens the processes and movements toward equity and social justice that comprise multicultural education. The crisis is not about battling overt bigotry (though that is still a substantial part of the battle). It is not about struggling to push the concept of multicultural education into the mainstream consciousness or challenging P-12 educational leaders who openly endorse segregation and White supremacy. Instead, it is an internal crisis, a reframing of multicultural education that focuses not on eliminating the inequities and injustices that continue to pervade schools, but on human relations and celebrating diversity (Hidalgo,

Chávez-Chávez, & Ramage, 1996; Jackson, 2003). And what is most devastating about the crisis is that, while it is fueled in part by conservative voices, it is often cycled by the champions of multicultural education who believe, at least ostensibly, that all students, regardless of race, home language, gender, sexual orientation, (dis)ability, or socioeconomic status, are entitled to an effective, affirming, equitable education.

My intention, by focusing on how those of us who believe we are committed to multicultural education contribute to this crisis, is to help us understand how the current trend toward conservatism within multicultural education undermines the possibility of educational equity. Secondarily, I hope to document the conservatization of multicultural education in the United States, in order to help educators, scholars, and school activists in other countries identify and strategize against similar phenomena in their contexts.

I do not mean to suggest that this is a new crisis or that we can eliminate the temptation of the path of least resistance. Nor do I intend to assign blame. Instead, my goal is to uncover trends in the field so that we can reestablish a movement toward educational equity.

And I carry a sense of urgency into this discussion. We are in a time of larger education equity crises (Apple, 1999; Ladson-Billings, 2003): No Child Left Behind, vouchers, the looming threat of privatization, high-stakes testing, inequitable school funding, prescribed curricula, and the growing application of other policies and procedures that disempower students as well as teachers (and particularly those at high-poverty schools with high percentages of students of color). In light of this context, we must rededicate ourselves to ensuring that the work of multicultural education—the work for equity and social justice in education—continues to fight against, instead of bow to, the conservative tide. To do this, we cannot allow the field to be knocked from its social justice foundations, whether from within or without.

I present my challenge in three steps. First, I draw on the theory and philosophy of major scholars to establish a set of principles for multicultural education against which I can measure the current state of the field. Second, I expand on my description of the crisis, placing it in a larger social context. Third, I offer a set of strategies for reestablishing a fieldwide vision of multicultural education that insists upon equity and social justice in schools and schooling.

Defining Principles of Multicultural Education

In an attempt to identify a set of defining principles of multicultural education, I review definitions set forth by several of the field's pioneer and leading voices, including Sonia Nieto (2000), Christine Sleeter (1996), Carl Grant (with Sleeter, 1998), and James Banks (2004). I choose to focus on the field's leading scholars because, as Sleeter has argued, "One must distinguish between an approach as formulated by [multicultural education's] main theorists, and superficial applications of it that one often finds in schools as well as the literature" (1996, p. 8). I draw from the work of these theorists in order to uncover the well-intentioned but "superficial applications" that comprise many practices, policies, and programs that people routinely describe as multicultural education.

Although each of these scholars frames multicultural education in unique ways, they agree on several key principles:

1. Multicultural education is a political movement and process that attempts to secure social justice for individuals and communities, regardless of race, ethnicity, gender, home language, sexual orientation, (dis)ability, religion, socioeconomic status, or any other individual or group identity.
2. Multicultural education recognizes that, although some individual classroom practices are consistent with multicultural education philosophies, social justice is an institutional matter and, as such, can be secured only through comprehensive school reform.
3. Multicultural education insists that comprehensive school reform can only be achieved through a critical analysis of systems of power and privilege.
4. Multicultural education's underlying goal—the purpose of this critical analysis—is the elimination of educational inequities.
5. Multicultural education is good education for all students.

A brief exploration of each of these principles will provide useful connection points for my discussion of the crisis later in the chapter.

Securing Social Justice

According to Banks (2004), a key element of multicultural education is the notion that all students, whether of color or White, girls or boys, wealthy or poor, must have an "equal opportunity to learn in school" (p. 3). Nieto (2000) agrees, explaining, "It challenges and rejects racism and other forms of discrimination in schools and society and accepts and affirms the pluralism (ethnic, racial, linguistic, religious, economic, and gender, among others) that students, their communities, and teachers represent" (p. 305). She continues, arguing that multicultural education must be *explicitly* anti-oppression, consciously taking a social justice stand against discrimination. Sleeter, writing with Peter McLaren (1995), affirms Banks's and Nieto's social justice perspective, pointing out the need for an ongoing critique of the sociopolitical and socioeconomic contexts of schooling and whom these contexts serve. Sleeter (1996) describes this critical framework as "a form of resistance to dominant modes of schooling, and particularly to white supremacy" (p. 2). She then challenges all educators to grapple with our responsibility to secure social justice through multicultural education by recognizing

> the ethical dimensions of teaching other people's children, and work[ing] to provide them with the highest quality of education one would wish one's own children to have. This means that such a teacher recognizes the aspirations oppressed groups have for their children and the barriers, both interpersonal and institutional, that persistently thwart their efforts. (p. 239)

This point is crucial in that it emphasizes the notion that in order to secure social justice in our classrooms, schools, or districts, we must understand schools and schooling in a larger context. It is not enough to learn about the cultures of our students if that process does not include the significance of their place in the sociopolitical landscape. The mere process of learning about behavioral differences between girls and boys does not necessarily prepare us to provide gender equity. Instead, we must be committed to ensuring that we empower girls as much as we empower boys, that we call on girls as often as boys, that we do not make assumptions about abilities or interests based on gender and our own socialization.

Reforming Schools Comprehensively

Making small changes within a traditional classroom, school, or school system does not constitute multicultural education. Instead, multicultural education is broad based (Nieto, 2000), calling "for the reform of the entire classroom and the school itself" (Grant & Sleeter, 1998, p. 163). Nieto (2000) states that multicultural education must permeate school climate, culture, and practice—that it must be visible everywhere, including in decision-making processes such as textbook adoption, behavior policies, and program assessment.

Grant and Sleeter (1998) are even more specific, providing a detailed list of the aspects of schools and schooling that must be analyzed critically in the multicultural school reform process. Their list includes curriculum materials, curriculum content, the existence or absence of multiple perspectives, instructional strategies, language diversity, student evaluation, grouping practices, visuals, role models, home and community relationships, and extracurricular activities. Thus, whereas some people use the term to describe individual curricular practices or programs (such as food fairs or student clubs) within a traditional educational framework (Banks, 2004), multicultural education recognizes the institutional nature of educational inequities and serves as a framework for comprehensive reform. In fact, according to Sleeter (1996), educators who are truly committed to multicultural education even go beyond school walls, advocating for children from historically and presently oppressed groups "in broader civic life" (Sleeter, 1996).

So, although we might think multicultural simply means having diversity-themed bulletin boards or adding a diversity unit to our established curriculum, we must broaden our view. We must think not only about the content of our classes, but how we deliver that content. We must think not only of posters and bulletin boards, but also of the values and culture of the entire school. We must think not only about celebrating diversity, like the principal of Northern, but also about ensuring that all students, regardless of race, gender, sexual orientation, socioeconomic status, or any other identity, feel affirmed and welcomed in our classroom and school.

Critically Analyzing Systems of Power and Privilege

Because comprehensive school reform calls for institutional transformation that secures social justice, it must be based on a continual and critical analysis of institutional dynamics of power and privilege. According to Banks (2004), "To implement multicultural education in a school, we must reform its power relationships. . . . The institutional norms, social structures, cause-belief statements, values, and goals of the school must be transformed" (p. 23). For example, we must challenge the assumption that because a student does not speak English fluently she or he is less intelligent than students who do. We must question the normalcy of the gender imbalance as long as women comprise a large majority of classroom teachers and a minority of district- and state-level administrators. Sleeter (1996) recognizes that in order to reform power relationships in schools we must first understand those relationships in a larger societal and global context. She argues that "multicultural education should also direct our attention to concentrations of power and wealth in the hands of a small elite" (1996, p. 137).

Correspondingly, in their list of four goals of multicultural education, Grant and Sleeter (1998) include promotion "of awareness of the social issues involving unequal distribution of power and privilege that limits the opportunity of those not in the dominant group" (p. 164). By nurturing this awareness, multicultural education uncovers "policies and practices that are advantageous for some students at the expense of others" (Nieto, 2000, p. 315). At the institutional level, this may mean uncovering "power . . . configurations [that] serve to reproduce social relations and domination" (Sleeter & McLaren, 1995, p. 7), such as tracking and inequitable school funding.

At the individual classroom level, this may mean sharing power with students (Sleeter, 1996) by providing opportunities for them to make connections between what they learn and their own experiences or by allowing them to choose how their learning will be assessed (traditional multiple-choice test, essay, project, etc.). In either case, the sort of transformation described by the leading multicultural education scholars cannot happen through prejudice reduction workshops, the study of "other" cultures, international food fairs, and many of the other practices often referred to as multicultural education.

Eliminating Educational Inequities

One of the foundational ideals of multicultural education is equal opportunity (Grant & Sleeter, 1998)—a movement to "increase educational equity for a range of cultural, ethnic, and economic groups" (Banks, 2004, p. 7). Thus, once we uncover and acknowledge systems of power and privilege, multicultural education becomes a framework for exposing and eliminating the resulting educational inequities. For example, it calls for teacher education programs to "be reconceptualized to include awareness of the influence of culture and language on learning, the persistence of racism and discrimination in schools and society, and instructional and curricular strategies that encourage learning among a wide variety of students" (Nieto, 2000, p. 315). Increased awareness among pre- and in-service teachers, administrators, activists, and scholars prepares us for more informed, reflective, and equitable analysis of tracking, assessment, disciplinary policies, curricula, and other school practices and policies that may serve the interests of some students at the expense of others (Nieto, 2000).

And like other principles of multicultural education, the elimination of educational inequities relies on a deep understanding of the relationship between these inequities and larger sociopolitical systems. According to Sleeter and McLaren (1995), "Critical pedagogy and multicultural education are complementary approaches that enable a sustained criticism of the effects of global capitalism and its implication in the production of race and gender injustices in schools and other institutional settings" (p. 8). However, this sustained criticism and determination to dismantle injustices cannot be achieved through much of the work people refer to as multicultural education—work that never deals honestly with real equity concerns and stratification (Nieto, 2000).

Improving Education for All *Students*

When multicultural education exposes racism, heterosexism, classism, and other real equity concerns, opponents, such as Arthur Schlesinger (1998), denounce it as separatist or divisive. Grant and Sleeter (1998) challenge this denunciation, explaining that multicultural education does not value separatism, but cultural pluralism, a sharing and blending of cultures and identities for the benefit of the entire school community. In other words, while multicultural education advocates for students of color, socioeconomically disadvantaged students, and other students who continue to be left behind by the current education system, it recognizes that the elimination of this repression and the broadening of inclusivity in schools benefits *all* students.

A consensus panel of interdisciplinary scholars, gathered by the Center for Multicultural Education (at the University of Washington—Seattle) and including both Banks and Nieto, makes a particularly strong statement on this point:

> An important goal of [U.S.] schools should be to forge a common nation and destiny from the tremendous ethnic, cultural, and language diversity. To forge a common destiny, educators must respect and build upon the cultural strengths and characteristics that students from diverse groups bring to school. . . . Cultural, ethnic, and language diversity provide the nation and the schools with rich opportunities to incorporate diverse perspectives, issues, and characteristics into the nation and the schools in order to strengthen both. (Banks et al., 2001, p. 5)

Although more recent work in the field might critique the nationalistic (as opposed to global) spin of the panel's statement (Ladson-Billings, 2003; Sleeter, 2003), what is clear is that, at its core, multicultural education attempts to institutionalize inclusivity, to engage a broader set of worldviews that, woven together, provide all of us with a deeper understanding of the world and ourselves.

For example, a diversified curriculum drawing for varied perspectives and challenging the notion of a single historical narrative helps all students develop a deeper and more complete understanding of history as well as the present. And this awareness is transferable. Students who grasp the complexity of a multiperspective history will also begin to apply similar reflection to news programs and publications, Web sites, and any other single source of information.

Summary

Banks (2004), Nieto (2000), Sleeter (1996), and others describe a comprehensive movement and process grounded in equity and social justice and benefiting all students. Still, many teachers, teacher educators, and administrators understand and practice multicultural education in a significantly less transformational way. In fact, the very conception of multicultural education critiqued by the field's leading voices—human relations work, cultural celebrations, and periodic decontextualized references to "heroes" from disenfranchised groups—seems to be institutionalized in today's schools.

I want to be careful here. As I have stated, I do not mean to assign blame for this phenomenon. I believe that most attempts at multicultural education practice, though perhaps inconsistent with multicultural education theory, come from well-intentioned, authentically anti-inequity, committed educators. The problem is not a set of maliciously unaware and inequitable teachers. Instead, the challenge facing all of us is that we, as current and future educators, have been socialized by the same messages and social structures that shape our schools. It is in the process of digging through this socialization that we can ensure that we are not unintentionally contributing to the alienation and exclusion of our students, colleagues, and community members.

One way to start this process is by recognizing that, despite good intentions, much of what U.S. educators, activists, scholars, and others refer to as multicultural education is not multicultural education at all, but small changes and programs within an inequitable educational system (Ladson-Billings, 2003). And, worse, many of these superficial applications, despite the sincerest of intentions, contribute to the inequities and injustices that necessitate multicultural transformation (Nieto, 2000). This is the crisis we are facing today.

The Crisis

When I ask multicultural education professionals in the United States—public school coordinators of equity and diversity, multicultural resource teachers, members of districtwide diversity committees, school administrators, and others—to define multicultural education, their responses typically reflect a depoliticized notion of it. My prompt rarely elicits answers about eliminating achievement gaps or the inequities that facilitate them. Their definitions almost never speak to the need to expose and eradicate racism, sexism, classism, homophobia, and other forms of discrimination from classrooms and schools. Instead, a majority of well-intentioned diversity advocates, who would never support or endorse practices or policies they knew to be inequitable, most often tell me that multicultural education is about "learning about other cultures" (which brings to mind the question, Other than *what?*) or, as Donald, the sincere and well-intentioned principal of Northern High School, suggested, "celebrating diversity."

For example, multicultural curriculum reform has been institutionalized largely as Black History Month and other additive celebratory occasions that do not challenge the euro, male, Christian, heterosexual, English-speaking, upper-middle-classcentrism that raises the ire of pioneers of the field. Diversity-related professional development workshops often focus on the supposed cultural traits of various groups of color, poverty-stricken children, or students with other "deficits." In place of equity and social justice, we offer festivals, sensitivity training, and cultural tourism, often resulting in little more than a deeper entrenchment of stereotypes and assumptions (Ladson-Billings, 2003; Nieto, 2000; Sleeter & McLaren, 1995). Although I do not disregard the value of some of these programs—they may, indeed, be a *step toward* multicultural education—they too often are defined *as* multicultural education, as *the step*.

And, again, this is not a new phenomenon. It has been ten years since Sleeter and McLaren (1995) pointed out that "the new conservative agenda has been officializing a concept of democracy that conflates it with nationhood, making it inhospitable to the struggle of social justice" (p. 9). Nor is this phenomenon unique to multicultural education. The reframing of multicultural education is a manifestation of a process in the United States that recasts virtually all equity and social justice movements in two basic ways: (1) by reframing the movements as evil or anti-American concepts from the fringes of radical leftist thought, and (2) by reframing the movements as fluffy human relations work posing little threat to inequitable institutions. What may be unique, though, is the extent to which those of us who support multicultural education philosophically contribute to this reframing, often unintentionally, in practice (McLaren, 1994).

Multicultural Educators as Evildoers

Try this experiment: Next time you are teaching a class or conducting a workshop, ask participants how many identify as feminists. Then ask how many believe that women deserve the same rights and protections that men have, free from discrimination. Notice the drastic increase in raised hands. Why do so many people—including liberals—identify with the ideology of feminism, yet adamantly avoid the "feminist" label? (After all, being a feminist means that one is dedicated to the principle of gender equity, of the elimination of sexism.) They are caught in a reframing process that has cast feminists as radical, fringe, men-hating, lesbian, antifamily brutes. Such recasting is doubly powerful for men who wish to maintain their positions of privilege.

First, it distracts people from the collective critical reflection necessary for social change. Consider, for example, the way U.S. history books tend to equate capitalism with freedom and democracy. Then consider the way people in the United States are socialized to understand socialism and communism, not as alternative structures or points of entry into a critical dialogue about capitalism, but as the virtual opposites of freedom and democracy. In fact, a graduate student at the university where I teach who was in the process of attaining U.S. citizenship told me that during her interview the interviewer asked whether she had ever been a member of a communist group. The very act of asking such a question during a citizenship hearing demonstrates neither freedom nor democracy. As a result of these sorts of messages, of the collective socialized fear of these concepts (like that of feminism), one cannot discuss socialism, or even the scholarship of Karl Marx, without being cast to the "un-American" fringes.

Second, the recasting of progressive movements as evil, fringe concepts results in the demonization of the individuals who identify with the movements or to whom the public connects the movements. For example, the demonization of feminism becomes the public invalidation of feminists (or, as the reframing goes, "femi-Nazis"), lesbians (whether or not they are feminist activists), and any woman who chooses to exert her power by critiquing the status quo.

The same process used to discredit feminism and other progressive movements and frameworks has been applied to multicultural education. Conservative scholars complain that multicultural education is anti-White and antimale. Others respond to its critical curricular lenses by arguing that it is un-American or separatist (Berliner & Hull, 1995; Center for Educational Opportunity [CEO], 2005; Schlesinger, 1998). For example, the front page of the CEO (2005) Web site contains this statement under the heading "Bilingual Education": "Multiculturalists have a firm grip on both elementary and secondary schools and universities. Their ideology of racial and ethnic difference risks balkanizing our multicultural society." I frequently am challenged by this "separatism" notion when I conduct educational equity workshops. The argument usually goes something like this: "We do not have any problems with race [or gender or sexual orientation or whatever the issue under discussion happens to be] here. Multicultural education is the real problem, the way it lumps people into separate groups and labels everybody."

The implication of this argument, echoed by the CEO (2005), the Ayn Rand Institute (Berliner & Hull, 1995), Diane Ravitch (2002), and others, is that by acknowledging and attempting to eliminate inequities multicultural education is actually the *cause* of racial (or gender or class, etc.) conflict. Unfortunately, many educators who buy into these reframings are advocates for multicultural education, at least philosophically. We buy in when we conduct workshops or teach classes that portray multicultural education as cultural sensitivity or intercultural communications training. We buy in when we spend more time thinking about how to avoid alienating the most resistant of our students or participants than about how to develop the leadership capabilities of the most progressive.

The Softening of Multicultural Education

We also bow to the pressures of the "evildoer" label when we follow Donald's—the benevolent Northern High School principal's—lead, failing to ask the difficult questions, softening multicultural education, turning a transformative process and movement into cultural celebrations and student clubs. Again, this is not a new phenomenon, nor is it unique to multicultural education.

Consider, for example, the softening process we apply to our civil rights heroes such as Martin Luther King, Jr. Most White people remember King as a peace-loving civil rights activist who believed that the oppressed should love their oppressors. We, with the truest of intentions and respect, immortalize his eloquence and recite portions of his speeches. But with this image we ignore an enormous portion of what Dr. King and the civil rights movement were all about—and, alas, it is the most progressive, political portion that we ignore. Many of us forget that Dr. King spoke passionately against the Vietnam War. Toward the end of his life he spent as much energy critiquing the U.S. government's allegiance to corporate-friendly capitalism and disregard for poverty as he spent on racism. And he drew important connections between the two. Yet, just as many people have recast multicultural education from a movement for equitable and just policy and practice to one for changing individual attitudes, we have reshaped Dr. King's image to be more digestible, less transformational, less a threat to our own power and privilege. And he is not alone. Many of us remember Rosa Parks as a tired, helpless, old woman, disregarding her history of civil rights engagement before the day she refused to give up her bus seat. We remember the Black Panthers as extremist, militant separatists. Meanwhile, we fail to acknowledge how they fought poverty by organizing programs to feed and educate the neediest in their communities and by empowering the disempowered.

I believe that the attitudes underlying the reframing of these social justice activists also underlie what Sleeter and McLaren (1995) refer to as the domestication of multiculturalism. One such attitude values peace over justice (or equates the two). So we frame Dr. King's work as peace activism instead of social justice activism and we demonize the activists, such as the Black Panthers, whose work, though similar in purpose to Dr. King's, cannot be reframed so easily. Likewise, we remove the transformational, the overtly political, the institutionally critical principles of multicultural education and replace them with notions of peace and harmony—just enough of a shift to help us "be" together without disrupting the status quo (Vavrus, 2002). Another related attitude values comfort over change. If we acknowledge Dr. King's politically charged and transformational speeches and writings, we must grapple with our own power and privilege in ways that call for fundamental self and social change. And if we present a genuinely transformative image of multicultural education instead of a softened one, we may have to sacrifice our own comfort, our own privilege, our own institutional likeability. But in doing so, we may also show the most disenfranchised of our students that they have an advocate—somebody willing to stand up with them against that which alienates them.

So far, although some of us have taken that plunge, we, institutionally speaking, tend to fluff the multicultural education pillow until it is soft enough for the education mainstream, despite the continued discomfort and alienation this causes the already disenfranchised. We fluff the pillow when we soften multicultural education classes and workshops to make them less intimidating to dominant groups. We fluff it by encouraging multicultural student clubs to host dances and "ethnic" food nights instead of tackling inequities in their schools and communities. We fluff it any time we endorse any practice and policy under the guise of "multicultural education" that does not have the central aim of establishing and maintaining educational equity.

Repoliticizing Multicultural Education

So how do we turn the multicultural education tide back toward the political, toward the real, toward equity and social justice? I have developed a list of starting points and questions I must continually ask myself:

1. I must refrain from referring to simple changes in curricula, decorations, or programs as multicultural education and challenge others' notions that these additive steps are multicultural education. *Am I contributing to a "heroes and holidays" or human relations notion of multicultural education? Do I understand multicultural education as a framework for my work, or as a series of individual programs and additives?*

2. I must continually ask myself how, if at all, my work moves education (in a classroom, school, district, or larger context) closer to equity and social justice. If I cannot explain this to myself, I need to rethink how I am framing multicultural education. *Am I using resources earmarked for equity work or multicultural education for programs that, although fun and interesting, fail to challenge the status quo? Am I, like the principal of Northern High School, merely celebrating diversity, or am I working to eliminate inequities from my classroom, school, or district?*

3. I must ensure that I do not replicate inequitable dynamics in courses and professional development workshops I design and facilitate for teachers and administrators. *Am I putting the onus of responsibility on people from historically and presently oppressed groups to teach people of privilege about prejudice and discrimination? Am I designing my courses and workshops at the pace of the most resistant participants, thereby failing to provide leadership development in other participants? Am I challenging my students to study and understand the dynamics of power and privilege, or only to examine experiences of oppressed groups? Am I concerned primarily with the comfort of privileged participants or pushing the dialogue toward equity and social justice?*

4. I must examine critically the literature, speakers, and other resources

that I incorporate into classes and professional development workshops, especially those that have become standard multicultural education fare. I must ascertain whether their popularity is owing to depth and relevance or comfort and the avoidance of responsibility. *Am I choosing speakers and resources that encourage complex and critical thinking about diversity, multiculturalism, equity, and education? Am I providing a grounded sociopolitical framework that delves into issues at an institutional level and in a historical context or do they deal with surface-level culture in a way that contributes to stereotypes and assumptions?*

5. I must remain committed to the political, transformational nature of multicultural education and I must *not* turn multicultural education into a human relations, relativistic concept that values every perspective. Multicultural education is not about validating every perspective, but about eliminating racist, sexist, homophobic, classist, and other oppressive perspectives and policies from schools and society. *Am I validating oppressive statements as a matter of "opinion"? Am I failing to confront antigay sentiment in order to be "inclusive" of people with inequitable beliefs?*

6. I must frame multicultural education as an active process, remembering that "being there" philosophically is not the same as "being there" in practice. *Am I connecting multicultural education to progressive policies and practices or focusing only on changing attitudes?*

7. I must facilitate experiences through which educators learn to examine equity concerns such as high-stakes testing in a larger context of inequity. When they are removed from this larger context, it is easier to believe they can be eradicated through Band-Aid approaches (such as single-sex classrooms in response to sexism in math and science education) that never move us closer to educational equity. *Am I contextualizing educational equity in a larger societal or global framework?*

Conclusion

Although we must continue to battle the tendency to recast multicultural education as evil, un-American, or a "watering down" of traditional schooling, we can do so effectively only after we reflect on the ways in which we, the teachers, teacher educators, staff developers, activists, and scholars, contribute to the softened reframing of the field. Remembering the concept of multicultural education provided by leading voices in the field, we must reassess our own work and whether it strengthens or softens the push toward equity and social justice in our classrooms and schools. Only when we recommit ourselves to repoliticizing multicultural education will we be able to fill the gap in perception and experience that exists between Donald, the principal of Northern High School, and his students, and between the well intentioned and the despite-the-good-intentions disenfranchised.

I have suggested ways in which we can observe the reframing of multicultural education, such as the softening of the field, and several ways I have decided to ensure that I remain committed to authentic multicultural education. My hope is that this will open a dialogue about what I have described as a crisis—one for which we must hold ourselves accountable.

References

Apple, M. W. (1999). Between neo and post: Critique and transformation in critical educational studies. In C. Grant (Ed.), *Multicultural research: A reflective engagement with race, class, gender and sexual orientation* (pp. 54–67). Philadelphia: Falmer Press.

Banks, J. (2004). Multicultural education: Characteristics and goals. In J. Banks & C. Banks (Eds.), *Multicultural education: Issues and perspectives* (pp. 3–30). San Francisco: Jossey-Bass.

Banks, J., Cookson, P., Gay, G., Hawley, W., Irvine, J., Nieto, S., Schofield, J., & Stephan, W. (2001). *Diversity within unity: Essential principles for teaching and learning in a multicultural society.* Seattle: Center for Multicultural Education.

Berliner, M., & Hull, G. (1995). Diversity and multiculturalism: The new racism. *Ayn Rand Institute* [On-line]. Available: www.aynrand.org/site/PageServer? pagename = objectivism_diversity.

Center for Educational Opportunity (CEO). (2005, February). *Center for equal opportunity web site* [On-line]. Available: www.ceousa.org.

Grant, C., & Sleeter, C. (1998). *Turning on learning: Five approaches to multicultural teaching plans for race, class, gender, and disability.* Upper Saddle River, NJ: Prentice-Hall.

Hidalgo, F., Chávez-Chávez, R., & Ramage, J. (1996). Multicultural education: Landscape for reform in the twenty-first century. In J. Sikula, T. Buttery, & E. Guyton (Eds.), *Handbook of research on teacher education* (2nd ed.) (pp. 761–778). New York: MacMillan.

Jackson, C. W. (2003). Crystallizing my multicultural education core. In G. Gay (Ed.), *Becoming multicultural educators: Personal journey toward professional agency* (pp. 42–66). San Francisco: Jossey-Bass.

Ladson-Billings, G. (2003). New directions in multicultural education: Complexities, boundaries, and critical race theory. In J. Banks & C. Banks (Eds.), *Hand-*

book of research on multicultural education (2nd ed.) (pp. 50–65). San Francisco: Jossey-Bass.

McLaren, P. (1994). White terror and oppositional agency: Towards a critical multi-culturalism. In D. Goldberg (Ed.), *Multiculturalism: A critical reader* (pp. 45–74). Cambridge, MA: Blackwell.

Nieto, S. (2000). *Affirming diversity: The sociopolitical context of multicultural education* (3rd ed.). New York: Longman.

Ravitch, D. (2002). Diversity, tragedy, and the schools: A considered opinion. *The Brookings Review, 20*(1), 2–3.

Schlesinger, A. (1998). *The disuniting of America: Reflections on a multicultural society.* New York: W.W. Norton & Company.

Sleeter, C. (1996). *Multicultural education as social activism.* Albany, NY: State University of New York Press.

Sleeter, C. (2003). Teaching globalization. *Multicultural Education, 5*(2), 3–9.

Sleeter, C., & McLaren, P. (1995). Exploring connections to build a critical multi-culturalism. In C. Sleeter & P. McLaren (Eds.), *Multicultural education, critical pedagogy, and the politics of difference* (pp. 5–32). Albany, NY: State University of New York Press.

Vavrus, M. (2002). *Transforming the multicultural education of teachers: Theory, research, and practice.* New York: Teachers College Press.

QUESTIONS

1. How does "multicultural education," as we practice it in schools, with a focus on heroes, contribute to the inequities and injustices that necessitate multicultural transformation?
2. How do we assess our schools/school districts based on the section entitled "Repoliticizing Multicultural Education?" Where are we with the implementation of multicultural education?

7

WHITE WOMEN'S WORK

On the Front Lines in Urban Education

Stephen D. Hancock

I n an effort to close the sociocultural, socioeconomic, and sociopolitical gaps between White female teachers and urban elementary students, I enlisted the experiences of four seasoned White women teachers to bring a personal and professional voice to their plight as soldiers on the front lines of urban education. This chapter reveals the voices of these four teachers in an urban elementary school setting. Via a formal questionnaire, I compiled a small data pool to conduct a pilot study concerning issues that White women teachers feel are important to teachers who teach in urban schools. The qualitative data compiled in this pilot study are used to explore (1) what White women teachers believe is important for success in inner-city schools; (2) avenues that will encourage, enlighten, and empower White women to become more effective teachers in urban schools; and (3) ways in which White women teachers can smoothly navigate their sociocultural realities and the sociocultural realities of their students, and to give a voice to teachers working in the inner city.

Some subliminal second thoughts:
He's in my classroom, but he didn't choose to be there . . .
He didn't choose this school, and he didn't choose me as his
    teacher.
He didn't select his father's income, his mother's absence, or
    his crowded house.
He didn't choose to confound my pet curriculum and my pet
    teaching prescriptions.

He didn't choose to value different things than I, or to speak a
    different, albeit more colorful, idiom;
He just didn't choose . . .
He can't smile nicely when his world tells him to feel anger, nor
    can he frown away warmth and fair play . . . his mask is not
    like mine.
He could never comprehend the gap that separates his mercu-
    rial moods from my pale, practiced rightness.
He didn't decide one day to shape his nose, his brow, or his
    mouth into forms that trigger my discomfort and disdain.
He doesn't know that he won't learn if I don't think he can, or
    that my eyes and voice limit his circle of friends.
He doesn't know how much his future depends on ME.
He just doesn't know . . .

—White woman teacher, 1969
(Larson & Olson, 1969, p. 17)

Historical Background of Our Current Crisis

"He's in my classroom, but he didn't choose to
be there. . . ."

The confession (and particularly the first line) in the opening of this chapter
was born in a time of national turmoil and volatile change. It speaks of a
time when White teachers (particularly White women) found themselves in
the center of a political and racial blizzard where they would have to face
racially different students and either consciously or unconsciously acknowledge their innermost thoughts about and prejudices and fears toward those
students. This confession also speaks of the importance of understanding the
needs of diverse students as well as the power and influence of a teacher on
the life and future of a child.

It was a time when Black students left the familiar and affirming environments, albeit poor and dilapidated schools, to embark on an uncertain
and fearful journey into a world of alienation, confusion, and perceived
hope. These students carried the hopes of integration and educational equality for a people, a community, and a nation. They were met, however, with
the evil of racism powered by ignorance, beliefs in prejudice, and a passionate
longing for the status quo. This confession emerged in a time when *Brown
v. Board of Education* was forcefully implemented throughout the United
States. This implementation was met with massive resistance (Wolters, 1984).

The delayed and misdirected implementation of the *Brown v. Board of Education* decision had altered the face of education. Instead of providing students, schools, and communities with better learning environments, *Brown* created (and continues to create) environments where African American and other minority students and White women teachers share dysfunctional relationships built on fear, ignorance, mistrust, and resentment. It was not the original intent of *Brown* to create educational environments where cultural illiteracy and racial contempt would prevail and dominate school policy and classroom practices.

The delayed and forceful implementation of the *Brown* decision had many challenging and detrimental outcomes. One of the most problematic and paradoxical results of *Brown* is noted in the drastic reduction of African American teachers in public schools (Ladson-Billings, 2004).

Desegregation policies were forged in many cities by closing predominately African American schools, busing Black students to segregated White schools, and demoting or firing African American teachers and administrators (Anderson & Byrne, 2004). Epps (1999) contends that in the eleven years between 1954 and 1965, thirty-eight thousand African American teachers lost their jobs. Anderson & Byrne (1972) reported that 41,600 African American teachers were displaced or fired and more than 50 percent of the African American administrators were demoted or dismissed. Haney (1978) asserts that school districts systematically and institutionally imposed salary sanctions and intimidation tactics to dissuade African American teachers from teaching. In essence, many school systems overtly infused Jim Crow tactics and educational policy to lower successfully the number of African American teachers in southern states and throughout the nation. In North Carolina, for example, 128 of the 131 White superintendents successfully restricted African American teachers from applying to their school districts. (Haney, 1978). As a direct result of discriminating hiring practices, African American students saw fewer Black teachers and thus surmised that teaching was not an available profession (Robinson, 2000). Therefore, African American college students who might have aspired to teach saw teaching, especially elementary education, as White women's work, and these students entered fields of business, medicine, law, and other areas, leaving a minority void in elementary teaching.

The legacy of the misdirected implementation of *Brown* and the racist backlash is still evident today. Anderson and Byrne (2004) report that of the 3,022,258 teachers in the United States only 470,680, or 15.6 percent, are minority, and of the minority teachers 7.5 percent, or 227,505, are African

American. Despite the intent of *Brown,* today our urban schools are more segregated than ever before (Epps, 1999), and the crisis of urban schools (especially elementary) pivots on a delicate point where African American students and White women teachers must find mutual respect and relationship in an effort to gain academic, personal, and social growth.

The Present Context of Our Current Dilemma

"He didn't choose this school, and he didn't choose me as his teacher, . . . He didn't choose to confound my pet curriculum and my pet teaching prescriptions, He didn't choose to value different things than I, or to speak a different, albeit more colorful, idiom."

These words speak to the current dilemma of urban elementary schools in the United States and point to the sociocultural, sociopolitical, socio-economic, and racial differences among inner-city students and White women teachers. Urban school districts, university education programs, and community leaders must invest in resources, courses, and in-service opportunities designed to enhance positive and supportive relationships between teachers and students in urban schools. For the foreseeable future, the elementary teaching force will overwhelmingly comprise White women (Howard, 1999; U.S. Census Bureau, 2003), whereas the student population will be overwhelmingly populated by African American and Latino American students. If urban schools are to close the achievement gaps, maximally educate urban students, and create healthy rapport among students, teachers, and community, then addressing concepts of teacher preparation, cultural literacy, and relationship as essential learning and teaching methods must be a top priority.

The salience of preparing teachers to better understand, accept, and respect urban students is heralded by the current demographics in the urban school teacher and student population. The U.S. Census Bureau (2003) reports that 65.1 percent of all elementary and middle school teachers (grades 1–8) and 72.5 percent of all preschool and kindergarten teachers are White women. In urban school districts such as Cleveland-Lorain-Elyria, Ohio; Colorado Springs, Colorado; Tampa-St. Petersburg-Clearwater, Florida; Richmond-Petersburg, Virginia; Columbus, Ohio; and Charlotte-Mecklenburg, North Carolina, White women represent 75.1 percent of preschool and kindergarten teachers and 65.8 percent of elementary and middle school teachers (U.S. Census Bureau, 2003). Of the 7 million students in the Council of the Great City Schools, however, the African American, Asian, Alaskan/Native American, and Latino student population comprised 76.9 percent in 2003 and is likely to increase (Council of the Great City Schools, 2003). Current urban school districts report minority student enrollment that far surpasses the number of minority teachers. These statistics reveal the need to educate, support, and enlighten White women teachers about the different realities of minority students.

The figures given in Table 7.1 reinforce the primary dilemma and challenge of urban schools. Whereas the current teaching forces in urban schools are predominately White women, the current student population is predominately African American or Latino American. The reality that White women are on the front lines of urban education is clearly evident. While we continue to recruit and retain minority teachers, it is critical that we also focus our attention on helping to educate White women teachers about the realities of teaching students who may hold a different sociopolitical, sociocultural, and socioeconomic perspective.

TABLE 7.1
Student Enrollment of the Twelve Largest Urban School Districts by Race and Ethnicity

City	Enrollment	Asian (%)	Black (%)	Latino (%)	White (%)
New York	1,091,717	10.0	36.1	37.3	16.1
Los Angeles	735,000	6.0	12.9	71.4	9.6
Chicago	438,589	3.3	50.6	36.4	9.2
Miami	374,806	>2.0	30.1	57.2	10.6
Houston	212,099	3.0	30.5	57.1	9.3
Philadelphia	204,851	4.9	65.3	13.1	16.4
Detroit	187,590	1.0	90.1	2.8	5.2
Dallas	163,327	1.2	32.9	58.9	6.7
San Diego	141,171	17.2	15.6	39.7	26.6
Memphis	118,000	1.4	87.0	0.7	9.0
Charlotte-Mecklenburg	116,853	4.0	43.0	9.0	42.0
Milwaukee	105,000	3.6	58.96	12.5	22.2

Note: These figures come from Ladson-Billings (2004) and current district Web sites (Charlotte–Mecklenburg Schools).

Voices from the Front Lines

"He can't smile nicely when his world tells him to
feel anger, nor can he frown away warmth and
fair play . . . his mask is not like mine."

In casual conversation with White women teachers, I have found that many of their initial motives for teaching in urban schools were based on the "savior" or "missionary" mentality. With good intentions and zeal, many White women teachers head for inner-city schools to "save" urban students only to find out that they themselves were the ones who needed to change; to grow; to understand; to accept and remove the mask of superiority, self-righteousness, and judgment. Sandy, one of the teachers in the pilot study, confessed her challenge in trying to save students: "One challenge that I have faced is feeling too much empathy (if you can feel too much empathy). I must realize that I cannot save the world and that everyone may not have had the same situations I had, but that they can still survive and be all right."

The four teachers who responded to the pilot study were Julie, Mary, Jodie, and Sandy. Each teacher is a White woman from a middle-class socioeconomic background. Their teaching experience ranged from four to twenty years. I knew these teachers as a fellow faculty member of two years. We worked in an urban district where our school was ranked at the bottom of the ninety-two elementary schools. I arrived the same year as the new administrator, an African American man known for turning troubled schools onto the path to success. In those two years, our elementary school moved out of academic emergency while student and teacher morale as well as academic progress made great gains.

Each teacher was given a questionnaire. The questionnaire was divided into a ranking section and a response section. Summative results of the data revealed that each teacher expressed the importance of the development of relationships, genuine and realistic preparedness, and cultural awareness as benchmarks for academic success. The present context of our current dilemma is multifaceted, and, thus, there is no single formula for success. However, the development of relationships, cultural literacy, and teacher preparedness are essential elements for academic progress in urban schools (Hancock, 2003; Howard, 2001).

Relationships: An Essential for Academic Success

We have come to a place in our educational development where we can no longer rely solely on curriculum to guide learning opportunities or legislation to create a community of diverse learners. In a multiracial, multilingual, and multiethnic society, it is necessary that our schools develop multiple perspectives, methods, and practices in educating and understanding students. Along with curriculum as a teaching and learning guide, teachers should develop positive and informed relationships with students and their community in an effort to maximize success. When the teacher contends in the opening confession, *"He could never comprehend the gap that separates his mercurial moods from my pale, practiced rightness,"* she speaks of the learning gap as also a teaching gap that is formed as a result of a negative relationship. Research on student perspective in school contends that curriculum supported by a positive and informed relationship based on high expectations is one key to educating diverse students (Hollins & Spencer, 1990; Howard, 2001). Studies conducted on student perspectives found that African American students believed that positive and supportive relationships with teachers enhanced academic success, that teachers' awareness and interest in the personal lives of students promoted high achievement and made school a meaningful experience, and that teachers who empowered students' voices in classroom practices and discussions were preferred (Hancock, 2003; Hollins & Spencer, 1990; Howard, 2001).

Jody's Story: Education Supports Racial Cooperation and Relationship

My first year at this school was difficult because I had twenty-nine kids and one of them was a major terror to everyone. I've learned that in order to be successful all teachers (especially White women) are better off knowing something about the students' daily lives, their music, and what they like to do. I have learned that urban kids are very similar to suburban children when you get to the heart of a matter. If you talk about basic needs and values, they are not that far apart. They are very different in how they try to attain what they want. I have been fortunate to have similar interests in music and food with the (African American) staff at my school and the kids see that in various ways. They know who is uptight about talking to a person of a different race and who isn't. Without regular contact and relationship with people "different" in some way, there is no real understanding beyond stereotypes. College may help with racial understanding but not until there are more substantial numbers of "minority" kids going to predominately White colleges. I guess education does more for racial cooperation and understanding than anything else.

Summary

Experience and knowledge are two essential qualities in order to have racial cooperation and relationship. Experience and knowledge afford urban teachers the opportunity to understand the culture of urban students; be aware of the different and divergent perspectives of both self and students; and, finally, accept students' culture with respect and validation (Hancock, 2003). Jody believes that in order to develop genuine relationship, teachers must consistently interact with a diverse group of people. In addition, teachers should understand that urban student issues are not exclusive to urban settings. However, the way in which any student approaches an issue may have cultural influences. For example, both suburban and urban students deal with issues of teacher/student trust. Their attempts to deal with the issue, however, may be very different.

Julie's Story: Success Is Making Positive Connections with Urban Students

I think White women, as well as all people, regardless of race or gender, who did not grow up in or thoroughly experience an urban culture before teaching need to be told exactly what to expect and taught "a bag of tricks" to deal with the issues that arise in urban schools. Urban teachers need to know that unlike most children in a suburban setting (due to the fact that most suburban students are used to White women), urban children do not automatically respect you because you are an adult. You have to earn their respect, while getting them to learn to respect you. This happens when relationships are made between student and teacher. It's not an easy task to do, especially if you are a race other than the student's.

I remember during my first week of teaching in an urban setting a third-grade boy looked right at me and yelled, "You just hate me because I'm Black!" I had simply asked the child to put my book down and sit down. I had no good response to this, and my lack of control over the moment lost me some control over the class. White teachers, especially new teachers, need to know that comments like this one are not rare. And they need to be prepared with how to deal with them. Even better, teachers need to understand where these comments come from, which goes into a deeper understanding of the culture in which the students live.

Teachers, especially White teachers, need to know that their own race does play a part in how the students react to them. If I had been a Black teacher, I might not have gotten a comment like that one from a third-grade boy. The most important thing to know, though, is that, regardless of race, urban students can make a positive connection to you as their teacher. It may not be easy, but showing consistency, kindness, and love at all times, even when a child is not cooperative, is important. Children notice everything we do, and when we get frustrated and sigh, roll our eyes, or say something destructive, the students may think we do not like them, and a wall goes up. Urban children are like all children—they want love and acceptance—but their environment has taught them to be wary of people, and breaking down some of those walls is the hardest thing to do as an urban teacher.

Summary

Making positive connections with urban students should begin with teachers being prepared to navigate issues of racism and cultural illiteracy. In an effort to do this, teachers must understand the historical elements that may fuel student resistance and teacher prejudices. Julie asserts that White women teachers must be aware that they have a culture and that their culture directly affects their teaching. Another concept that White women teachers should understand is that in the African American community respect is a coveted principle that is not freely rendered; rather, it is earned. Julie contends that when positive connections and genuine relationships are formed, urban students are more likely to respect White teachers. It is relationship that helps break down walls in order to develop positive connections.

Both Jody's and Julie's stories have touched on a myriad of issues, concepts, and topics that cannot be covered in this chapter. They both, however, convey a strong message that White women not only must be aware of student culture but also must understand the implications and influence that their personal culture and race have on their teaching and learning. Julie and Jody feel that consistency and tenacity are two traits all teachers need to survive effectively the difficult and challenging reality that can be evident in urban schools. Goodard, Hoy, and Hoy (2004) state, "The higher teachers' sense of efficacy, the more likely they are to tenaciously overcome obstacles and persist in the face of failure. Such resiliency, in turn, tends to foster innovative teaching and student learning" (p. 4). Similarly, Stremmel (1997) contends that in order for teachers to be effective in diverse settings, first, they must develop an awareness of the cultural, racial, and historical experiences that shape their own White culture; second, they must understand that children construct their world within a sociocultural context; and, third, they must understand that diversity awareness is a process that moves individuals from a monolithic perspective to more critical and divergent thinking.

Cultural Literacy: A Prerequisite for Relationship Building and Academic Success

Before teachers can build positive connections with urban students, there must be an awareness, an acceptance, and a respect for their own as well as their students' culture. I describe the notion of awareness, acceptance, and respect for self and others as cultural literacy. I contend that teachers who are literate in others' cultures possess a critical conscience, are able to self-reflect, and are willing to challenge and examine personal perspectives as they relate to new and divergent ways of thinking. I also surmise that cultural literacy is a prerequisite for developing connections and relationships between and among urban students and White women teachers.

Stremmel (1997) states, "Systematically exploring one's attitudes and practices is essential to moving toward cultural self-awareness and multiculturalism" (p. 369). In short, critically navigating the deep-rooted beliefs and values that one possesses promotes self-knowledge and a capacity to know and respect others (Palmer, 1993). Howard (1999) suggests that if White women teachers are to develop as effective teachers of diverse students, there must be an awareness of how socioeconomic, sociocultural, and sociopolitical realities as well as how White privilege and social dominance influence urban students and educational outcomes. Cultural literacy is refreshing for urban students, because they can perceive that White teachers are able to focus critically on the realities of their Whiteness, rather than highlight perceived deficiencies in their students' culture (Howard, 1999).

Mary's Story: Cultural Literacy Yields Compassion

I believe that all children can learn. Teachers just have to do more culturally based teaching and help the young parents learn. We must realize that most caregivers do want to and try hard to work out of the poverty cycle. This is not easy to do when you come from generational poverty. Therefore, teachers should try to learn African American customs, language, family relationships (understand that everyone is a cousin) and that urban children need more encouragement and culturally supportive teaching since the caregiver is struggling to survive with little time or money to help with schoolwork and encouraging rewards or activities.

Summary

Cultural literacy fosters an awareness of the urban student and also the urban parent. In an effort to be an effective teacher, Mary asserts that White women must move beyond the notion of meritocracy and examine how White privilege blinds them to the reality of generational poverty. Many urban families in her school live in poverty, and she believes that an understanding of parental situations from a place of compassion and genuine care promotes cultural literacy and is essential to building relationships and academic success.

Sandy's Story: Becoming Culturally Literate

One thing I have learned about the African American culture is that when a student says, "He is my cousin," that may not always be the case. When I first started teaching at an urban school, I was amazed that everyone seemed to be related! I've come to learn that the African American culture views close family friends as cousins, so everyone is not "truly" a cousin. I've also learned that in our school, many children are being raised by grandparents, aunts, foster parents, or single mothers. In the community I teach in, everyone seems to know everyone else. It seems to be a close-knit neighborhood (with exceptions here and there). I have learned that urban parents want the best for their kids, whether the teacher is White, Black, red, or purple! If you're a good teacher and you treat their child fairly, then they respect you and appreciate what you're doing, regardless of color. I guess I was nervous my first year thinking that some parents may be biased against me because I'm White, but that was never the case.

I would have to say that my sociopolitical and socioeconomic views have changed a lot! I must honestly say that I had not ever been around people who lived in poverty, or people who were on food stamps, welfare, etc. Growing up in an upper-middle-class family, I just didn't see that lifestyle, except for what was portrayed on television. Honestly, I guess I must say that I had a somewhat negative attitude toward people in this situation; when you don't have an understanding of someone's situation, it's easy to "judge" them or view them in the wrong light. Now, I would say that I am in a totally opposite state of mind. I feel empathy and compassion for people who have no money, cannot buy groceries, have no beds for their children, sleep in shelters, etc. I now want to help people in these situations. I want the children to know that they have a choice and that they do not have to grow up and depend on welfare.

Teaching in urban schools has also changed my sociopolitical views as related to education. As far as the No Child Left Behind Act I believe it has ridiculous guidelines. I think the premise of it may have been on the right track, but it has turned out to be a disaster. Again, before I was teaching and living the middle-class lifestyle, I probably would have thought, "Great, my kids will have a better education because of all these standards!" But now that I am in the field and especially since I am teaching in an urban setting, the whole thing just frustrates me to no end.

Summary

From a position of cultural literacy, teachers are better able to connect with students. Sandy submitted three important components as benchmarks for cultural literacy: (1) White women should know that many African American communities in poverty have close community relationships; (2) parents will support White women if they trust and sense genuine care; and (3) teachers should reflect on personal biases, prejudices, and ignorance toward non-White cultures. Sandy also revealed how through experience with diversity cultural literacy possesses the capacity to change sociopolitical perspectives.

Julie's Story: Let's Communicate across Cultures and Socioeconomic Borders

After working in an urban school, I have a better understanding of what goes on in a different socioeconomic group than the one in which I was raised. I have definitely learned a lot about the problems that face people in a low-socioeconomic area. I see that to change things in an urban setting, it is going to take a lot of people and programs, which means money (which is hard to get, especially from the government). Even with the money people have to be willing to change, which is another battle that can be difficult to win. Since working in an urban environment, my views have changed, my world has become a little wider, and the social problems in our country have come a little closer to home for me.

When I first started working in an urban school, I learned that the students were very aware of their culture. They talk with their own lingo, dress in their own styles, and interact with each other in a different way than most middle-class people. Even though the students often conform to the culture around them, they do seem aware that people, like teachers, act and speak differently. The students often refer to this as "acting White." However, I've learned that just because someone does not share the exact same values as me doesn't mean we can't communicate. I have learned how to communicate without pushing my views on someone else or undermining their beliefs. I have also learned that I can accept and embrace my students' culture and show students that there is diversity among all people, different ways to act in different situations, and how having respect for others may help them in their own lives. For me, understanding their culture is an ongoing process that I hope to get better at and I hope to also improve my interactions with the students and parents with which I work. One thing I also have to keep in mind is not to typecast the children and their parents. Just because they fit into a certain socioeconomic status doesn't mean that children and adults reflect the stereotypical roles that society puts on them.

Summary

Communicating across cultures and socioeconomic boundaries requires teachers to have multiple perspectives in an effort to open their eyes to social challenges outside of their world. Urban students, especially African American and Latino American students, are aware of their culture, and teachers must accept and understand these cultures in order to communicate successfully. Julie contends that experience is one of the best teachers when it comes to understanding urban students. She confesses, however, that becoming culturally literate is a lifelong process of learning, growing, and challenging self-perceptions.

Teacher Preparedness: A Personal and Academic Journey for Teaching

"How is it possible, with so much research and information available about multicultural issues today, that prospective educators can complete their entire teacher education and certification program without gaining a deeper grasp of social reality?"

(Howard, 1999, p. 26)

Can teacher education programs alleviate the cultural illiteracy of White women teachers? This question has relevance and begs to be answered as we continue to see a cultural clash between urban students and White women teachers. The importance of preparing White women to teach in diverse settings is obvious, particularly because most White women teachers hail from middle-class neighborhoods and lifestyles where there is little to no genuine interaction with minorities (Howard, 1999). We can no longer graduate White teachers from colleges or schools of education who are not culturally literate. Too often White teachers are put in diverse settings and expected to competently navigate cultural realities that are not congruent with their own socialization patterns, perspectives, and racial experiences. Thus, it is incumbent upon teacher education programs to provide opportunities for student teachers to have prolonged experiences in urban scholars or schools where these White teachers are the minority.

Colleges must educate teachers to build and extend on the cultural knowledge that urban students bring to school, rather than try to force students to fit into the middle-class, eurocentric ideology of school curricular practices. Schools of education should also provide students with opportunities to engage in reflective practice as a means to understand and recognize culturally relevant teaching (Gay, 2000; Hancock, 2003; Hollins, 1993). I contend that teacher education programs can do much to alleviate cultural illiteracy among its teachers.

Sandy's Suggestions

I think there are several factors to consider when preparing new White women teachers to teach in an urban setting. One is to make sure they have knowledge and understandings of other cultures. It's one thing to know about another culture and it's another to accept it and appreciate it. On a personal level, White women teachers need to feel confident and secure with themselves (as they should anyway) and know that they are doing just as important work as if they were teaching in the most affluent of schools. I think that sometimes people look at urban schools and think, "Oh, that poor teacher got stuck there," or "That school must have bad teachers because it's in such a poverty-stricken area." Those issues are just not true, and I think teachers must have a sense of pride in their work.

As far as academically, I think teachers need to know that all children learn differently, and that techniques and strategies that worked in the "sterile" environment of the university and the affluent suburban schools may not work with children in an urban setting. You need to know their background and needs to figure out how to teach them. A teacher must know that there is more than one way to teach and she may need to try every strategy for some students. Working with children in an urban setting can be both challenging and rewarding. A teacher must be prepared for these challenges and be prepared for the unexpected. As far as professional factors, I think new teachers and current teachers must display the same professionalism in urban schools as would be expected in any school setting. We need to be mindful that we are examples to students. If the teacher is late to work every day, wears old jeans and T-shirts, then the students will sense that you may not have a strong work ethic.

Summary

Sandy suggests several factors for preparing White women teachers to teach in urban settings. One factor implies that more academic classes on issues concerning diversity and multiculturalism be available and required. Another factor is to provide experiences with other cultures, in order to gain genuine connections and acceptance. Finally, new teachers should understand, implement, and promote multiple intelligence theory, culturally responsive teaching, and cultural learning styles.

Jody's Words

White women should know that urban students want to be loved by their teacher, just like all other children. White women should know that urban elementary schoolchildren show affection in various ways. In some instances (especially in kindergarten), there will be a lot of body contact immediately. Urban teachers should learn that some children can do work when they are pushed. Teachers of urban students should also know that urban parents expect them to do well in school. Urban parents test teachers, just like the kids do. If the parent perceives that you want to help their child, they will usually go with you on issues. Be prepared to be challenged by students and parents. Most importantly, White women must know themselves and understand that their culture affects how they teach and see their students.

Mary's Words

In order to prepare White women to teach in urban schools, I believe that they must have more and longer opportunities to learn about cultural differences. Teachers today should be immersed in another culture to better understand and appreciate differences. Teachers of all races and genders need to respect students' culture and home talk, but also teach urban students business talk. These are two fundamental elements that White women teachers should know when being prepared to teach in urban schools.

Summary

A fundamental notion that teachers should understand is that all children seek love and acceptance from their teacher. At no time are teachers to pass judgment on students' culture. Mary contends that language is important and teachers should know how to teach students to code switch from their home talk to business talk. She is also a proponent of prolonged experiences in urban schools so that prospective teachers will have a better understanding of teaching in a diverse setting. White women should also promote self-reflection and self-knowledge to enable them to self-assess and reveal how their personal culture influences student and parent response. Jody suggests that White women must have genuine motives for educating urban students in an effort to gain parents' trust.

Conclusion

"He doesn't know that he won't learn if I don't think he can, or that my eyes and voice limit his circle of friends. He doesn't know how much his future depends on ME. He just doesn't know . . ."

The last lines of the poem summarize this chapter perfectly. They speak truth to the power that teachers possess in a student's life. These lines also reveal that urban elementary students are at the mercy of the knowledge, experience, and perspective of White women teachers. That is why it is imperative that we provide White women with opportunities to better enhance their understanding of teaching in urban schools.

As White women teachers seek cultural literacy, positive relationship, and proper preparation for urban teaching, it is important that these same teachers revisit self-reflection. I contend that in order to navigate racism, fears, prejudice, and ignorance teachers must critically assess personal motives and beliefs (Hancock, 2003).

Finally, as we move toward a society where people of color are rapidly becoming the majority of the population, we must move with all deliberate speed to support and educate White women to be more effective teachers of diverse students. Presently, White women make up 65 to 76 percent of the teaching force in elementary schools, while students of color represent 76 percent of the urban student population (U.S. Census Bureau, 2003). These numbers for both teachers and students are likely to increase; thus, there must be a clarion call to better prepare and support the White women who stand on the front lines every day.

References

Anderson, J., & Byrne, D. (2004). *The unfinished agenda of Brown v. Board of Education.* New Jersey: John Wiley & Sons.

Brandon, L. T. (2004). *W/righting history: A pedagogical approach with urban African Council of the Great City Schools.* (2003). Annual report [On-line]. Available: www.cgcs.org.

Epps, E. (1999). *Race and school desegregation: Contemporary legal and educational issues.* Available: www.urbanedjournal.org/articles/article0003.pdf.

Gay, G. (2000). *Culturally responsive teaching: Theory, research & practice.* New York: Teachers College Press.

Goodard, R., Hoy, W., & Hoy, A. (2004). Collective efficacy beliefs: Theoretical developments, empirical evidence, and future directions. *Educational Researcher, 33*(3), 3–13.

Hancock, S. (2003). *Creating positive spaces: A narrative account of the development of a multicultural learning community.* Unpublished doctoral dissertation, The Ohio State University, Columbus.

Haney, J. (1978). The effects of the Brown decision on Black educators. *The Journal of Negro Education, 47,* 88–95.

Hollins, E. (1993). Assessing teacher competence for diverse populations. *Theory into Practice, 32*(2), 93–99.

Hollins, E., & Spencer, K. (1990). African American and Latino children in high-poverty urban schools: How they perceive school climate. *Journal of Negro Education, 65*(1), 60–70.

Howard, G. (1999). *We can't teach what we don't know: White teachers, multiracial schools.* New York: Teachers College Press.

Howard, T. (2001). Telling their side of the story: African-American students' perceptions of culturally relevant teaching. *The Urban Review, 33*(2), 131–149.

Ladson-Billings, G. (2004). Landing on the wrong note: The price we paid for Brown. *Educational Researcher, 33*(7), 3–13.

Larson, R., & Olson, J. (1969). *I have a kind of fear: Confessions from the writings of white teachers and black students in city schools.* Chicago: Quadrangle Books.

Palmer, P. (1993). *To know as we are known: Education as a spiritual journey.* San Francisco: HarperCollins.

Robinson, R. (2000). *The debt: What America owes to Blacks.* New York: Dutton.

Stremmel, A. (1997). Diversity and the multicultural perspective. In C. Hart, D. Burts, & R. Charlesworth (Eds.), *Integral curriculum and developmentally appropriate practice: Birth to eight* (pp. 363–388). New York, NY: State University of New York Press.

Wolters, R. (1984). *The burden of Brown: Thirty years of school desegregation.* Knoxville: University of Tennessee Press.

QUESTIONS

1. The author notes that many White female teachers head into inner-city schools with a "savior" or "missionary" mentality. Why is this a barrier for these teachers?

2. According to this chapter, why should teachers not pass judgment on a student's culture?

8

WHEN TRUTH AND JOY ARE AT STAKE

Challenging the Status Quo in the High School English Class

Julie G. Landsman

More than ever, I believe that if teaching is to be effective, it must contain an element of the subversive. We close the door to our classroom; we turn toward the students; and we begin to teach, in our own way, often with our own materials. There is nothing more exhilarating, or more isolating, than the feeling just before the last bell. When it rings, you are the one to bring order out of the chaos: of girls applying makeup, of boys passing notes across the table, of chatter about a weekend party rising up from the inaudible hum to comprehensibility:

"Over on Park Avenue, at eight, you know, Denisha, the one with the pink beads? She havin' a party then. Don't matter you live on the North Side, you invited. Word!"

For a moment you want to listen to them speaking, some in hesitant English, some in dialect as imaginative as you will ever hear, using new words almost daily. For a moment you do not want to take over, call them to attention, because you are weary and you would rather read the novel tucked in your lunch bag, or listen to music on the CD player at the front of the room.

But you are there to provide safety, ritual, warmth, boundaries, and the world of words. So you step up to the music stand you have put in a corner of the room. It is November and they become quiet as you wait. This is part of the safety. They know that when you stand there, in that spot, it is time for work. As much as they may argue, or defy, or continue their exchange about the party on Park Avenue, you know that they are aware, out of the corner of their eye, or looking straight at you, that the ritual of class has begun.

Teaching is as much about these things—the structures we devise, the routines we create for the hour or ninety minutes we have with our students—as it is about content. The two are so interwoven that it seems artificial to separate them, but for the purposes of this paper I will. In reality, as they walk in the door before the official start of the hour, the poem on the board is just as important as the move behind the desk or even the sound of the bell. The comment you made about the new hat worn by your most troublesome student and his answering smile are just as important as the first chapter of the novel you have assigned for that day. This art of teaching is about our voices, our perceptions, along with those of the students we teach. It is also about the way we were raised and how we were taught, about intersecting with the homes the students come from, the music they hear, the mosque or church or synagogue they attend. It is hard to tease the strands apart. I will try to do this and then interweave these strands back together again.

How We Teach

Often, White teachers are much less demanding of students of color, especially African American students, than they are of White students:

"That's okay. You can turn it in in a week."

"Excuse me, Michael. Would you mind talking about that after class? I really need to get going. Sorry to interrupt your plans, though."

"If you want to go for a C, instead of the A contract, that is fine, Mary."

I said these same kinds of words until I understood from others who were better and more experienced teachers than I that I was making a lot of allowances for Black children that I did not make for the White children in my classes. This leniency was a form of subtle racism. It was a way of saying: "I assume you can't get it in on time, pay attention, do the A work, and so I will let you off. You are probably not going to need academics anyway."

There are teachers who rarely call home when young Black students are in trouble because they assume Black families are dysfunctional, illiterate, or unconcerned. I have talked with Black students in high schools who are aware that the teacher turns toward them when he or she has an easy question on a text and toward the White kids when he or she wants the answer to a more complex and difficult question. I have watched teachers allow Black students to saunter into class late with barely a recognizing nod of the head, whereas a White child who is late gets a frown and the mention of a phone call home. For years, I have spent much time talking with teachers about this problem; I have heard, time and time again, from teachers who say that until it was called to their attention, until it came to them from something they were reading, or until the light just dawned, they automatically expected less of their Black as well as their Indian, Hmong, and Latino students.

The subtle ways we make these allowances for minorities testify to their ingrained nature. A principal of a city school in St. Paul, Minnesota, tells this story:

A Black student was acting up constantly in the eleventh-grade class of a White English teacher. Finally, he threatened the teacher, and the teacher asked him to leave the room—they would talk in the principal's office. Later, after a brief discussion of the event that led up to the student's dismissal from class, the principal turned to the teacher and asked him what he wanted to happen as a result of this behavior.

"I want Jamal in my advanced placement class. I want his schedule changed so he can be in that more advanced class. He is a bright young man who has been misplaced."

Years later this teacher and his former student talk as a team about the difference that moment made in the student's life. By expecting great things, by assuming the ability of this young man to read literature and respond to it, the teacher was able to turn the young man's mind toward very real possibilities for his future. It did not happen overnight. There were bad days and discouraging times, parent conferences, and after-school sessions. Yet, this young man, Jamal, will tell you he can pinpoint the day his view of himself changed. He can describe the road afterward—starting with the different turn it took when it was *assumed* he would do well, *expected* that he would make it.

I am not naïve enough to think this is the answer to the problem of tough kids in the classroom or kids who act out. I do think, however, that it demonstrates what we can do as teachers when we assume that our students are capable of high achievement even though it runs counter to all our training, all those initial responses honed in a racist system. I believe it is an example of what it takes to teach all kids with equal expectations for greatness.

A teacher in a primarily Black high school simply asked that his advanced placement (AP) English classes be scheduled with students who did not necessarily have a particular grade point average (GPA) but who had the ability to read, and who expressed an interest in learning to understand literature. After he eliminated the GPA requirement, his classes became representative of the school population. Instead of classes of 84 percent White students, he had classes of 75 percent students of color. And he taught those students with exactly the same high expectations and requirements he had used in the previous years. His students of color took his class just as seriously and worked just as hard as his other classes filled with White students.

It took this teacher, as it took the teacher with Jamal, to disrupt a pattern, to abandon assumptions, and to reinvent requirements that had formerly limited students of color at every turn. This change is subversive: challenging the strictures that keep certain students from certain classes, requesting things that run counter to the way a school runs. The way we approach students can make all the difference.

Along with high expectations, as evidenced by whom we call on, what we demand, what we assume, we need consistency in structure. Black students have told me that if I let a homophobic slur go during a class hour, if I turn my back or pretend to ignore it, then this could happen when the word *nigger* is used, and, thus, the room is not safe for anybody. Part of the routine, the ritual, the expectations of our classes has to be a demand for civility and respect: from students to ourselves, from us to students, and from students to each other. By weaving these expectations into our everyday language and by spelling them out in signs along the walls of our rooms, we are making an inclusive and safe place for students of all kinds, even before we consider the materials we will use.

Part of the everyday routine of our class must be respect. I have never allowed use of the word *nigger* in my room, not from anyone. One evening in my urban education class at a nearby St. Paul college, a Black principal in a city high school told me he considered the word verbal abuse and did not let any student utter it in front of him. What never ceases to impress me is that students who appear tough, who are streetwise and even living on their own at seventeen or eighteen, accept this restriction without much complaint. They have an understanding of the history of this word, the pain it can cause, no matter how often they hear it in songs or use it with each other. They understand that when an adult in charge asks that this word stay out of the classroom it means that he or she is simply trying to make the room a safer place, the guidelines clear.

Student Voices: Part of How and What We Teach

As I turn the discussion toward content, I include the importance of student voices. The more we build in time for students to read aloud their own words, their own responses, the more our curriculum becomes inclusive and multicultural. For example, if we are reading a description of a "compare and contrast" essay, we can have students write quickly for ten minutes comparing a morning to an evening, a color to a sound, or any other two concepts. Next, we can let them read aloud what they have just written, going around the room without comment. Students can make lists: "I'd rather be a _____ than a _____," or "I used to be _____ but now I am _____." Once students have gotten used to this quick writing and reading aloud, they will ask on their own for free writing exercises. By asking for immediate responses to a topic or concept, we are helping students to make the concepts organic, part of their bodies and minds.

By having students write automatically, we refuse to let them become blocked. By listening to them read, we refuse to silence them. Once this reading and writing has happened a few times, you will feel a sense of community in the classroom. The students will write in the silence that follows an assigned topic, the traffic outside humming along as you, too, write with them. You will add your voice to the voices in your room as you read aloud what you have written. You do not lose your place as the conductor, the coach, the authority. Yet, even in that role, you are also part of the community of every class and, thus, your voice deserves its place. As a visiting writer, I am continually amazed at how carefully students listen to each other—and to me—as we read aloud. It is my chance to give them the generational viewpoint I hold, and I sense that they are hungry for this.

Allowing the Use of Dialect

I have often been asked about dialect, about what we allow, what we restrict in our classes. I have some thoughts on the topic, but for a fuller discussion I suggest reading the book *The Skin We Speak* (Delpit, 2002). It is important for all of us to keep in mind that Ebonics is a legitimate language with its own regularities and grammar, its own rules and logic. It is the language many of our students hear at home, use in conversation, and read in African American literature. If we negate or dismiss this language, then we will be disrespecting our students' home culture and family. We will be judging what they have been raised and nurtured on. And in this way we will create an obstacle between students and ourselves. In our lack of acceptance and appreciation for Ebonics as a rich, ever-changing, and creative language dialect, we can lose the trust and motivation of those students we most want to reach.

There are ways to allow dialect into the English class while exposing students to the language they will need to compete in a world of "standard English," where much of the economic power in the United States resides. I let kids use dialect in informal freewriting; in creative writing; and at other times of expressive work, such as poetry and short-story writing. When I want a paper done according to specifications or when I want an essay written for a final project or a college application form or a job requirement, I ask students to take what they may have written in freewriting sessions and *translate* it into standard English, the kind of language they read and hear every day. When put in this way, students find it more acceptable and it makes sense to them. They *translate* all the time when they take a second language. Put this way, we give respect to the language of their home, their culture while acknowledging the presence of another language they are adept at and into which much of their official work will be translated. In addition, they begin to see themselves as bidialectical, as students having an extra talent in their ability to switch from one dialect to another with great dexterity. We make it clear to them that they do this "code switching" all the time, emphasizing this as a talent, rather than a drawback. This translation can provide them entrée into the cultures in which they wish to participate.

We so give students little credit for what they already know: it is a primarily White world in places of power right now—in college admissions offices, in banks, in high schools, in corporate and professional America. To be able to be a doctor, a teacher, a lawyer, or a restaurateur, it is essential to talk the talk of the culture with which you wish to work.

Kids are very aware of this. They do this kind of bidialectical work all the time. They flip from Ebonics to street slang to standard English within a five-minute period in most high schools. By asking students to translate their work you are putting a name on what they do, without detracting from their home, how their grandmother or grandfather speaks, what their mother says when she is talking with their friends. By talking about *registers* of language, from intimate to formal, students begin to see their own linguistic variety and the way this fits into an organized pattern of understanding. By teaching these concepts, I believe we are lessening the chaos in these adolescents' lives. We are also including *all* the ways they speak. At the same time, we are adding to the diversity in our classrooms without denying them entry into any world.

There are so many ways to include both languages in our classrooms. These include translating Shakespeare, for example, into Ebonics, or translating Ebonics from music lyrics into standard English. In each case we play on students' strengths. We can have students create whole dictionaries of words in English and their Ebonics meanings, or vice versa. We can point out that many works of literature, such as the novel *Their Eyes Were Watching God*, by Zora Neale Hurston, include Ebonics and standard English side by side. Speakers can come into the classroom who have learned to code switch in order to maintain their jobs and their place in the world of power but who have kept their cultural identity. They can talk with students about what this means and how it can be done in a practical way, and what strengths it involves to be able to do this.

We can also ask our students' parents what they want from us as teachers. Often White teachers are surprised when parents ask that teachers make sure their sons and daughters know how to navigate the world of power. We often assume they simply want their children to be "happy" in school. To achieve this goal, we can enlist parents' support in urging students to become fluent in writing in both dialects. We can also invite parents to visit the classroom to talk with students about their jobs, lives, and thoughts on language. We can become familiar with and draw upon the community from which our students come for help in encouraging them to celebrate their own language and inventiveness while becoming comfortable using the language of a certain world where they may wish to work. All of this must come from a place of comfort within ourselves, a real and true belief in the beauty and structure and legitimacy of the home languages and dialects of all our students.

What We Teach

We can have "Black poets' month" in our English classrooms just the way we can have Black History Month in February, or "Harriet Tubman month" as some Black kids at a local St. Paul, Minnesota, high school call it. This limited recognition is better than not recognizing Black achievements at all. However, the natural way to include writers of all cultures in our English classrooms is to weave them in all year. If we teach genres, Langston Hughes can be there along with Walt Whitman in a unit on American poetry. Or John Edgar Wideman can be included with Amit Chaudri and Jane Eyre in a study of novels of place. This way Black writers are not marginalized, but simply part of the lineup.

My favorite way of teaching literature is to teach according to themes. When studying the family as a theme, include August Wilson's play *Fences* with Shakespeare's *King Lear*. Include Toni Morrison's *Beloved* with Gabriel Garcia Marquez's *Love in a Time of Cholera* when discussing the supernatural in novels. Everything is open when we look at assigning literature this way. Genres combine in amazing ways around themes. In a unit on war we can read from the poems of Seamus Heaney, Rita Dove, Walt Whitman, and Rupert Brooke; and the fiction of Leslie Marmon Silko's *Ceremony*, Li Pao's *Monkey Bridge*, Bobby Ann Mason's *In Country*, and Hemingway's *For Whom the Bell Tolls*.

We need to find literature that is compelling, excellent, and multicultural. This task is not difficult. Once you begin to read (probably in the summer if you are an overworked secondary teacher), you will find so many titles you want to read that you will not be able to fit them all in. One of the most effective ways of learning about other cultures is to read fiction. So besides finding literature to prepare for your subject area, be sure to read fiction. This will allow you to find a way into the cultures of the kids you teach, in an intimate way that research and descriptive nonfiction cannot always give you.

Include poetry in your class every day. You can write a new poem on the board when you open each class, or a poem on each worksheet or lesson you give out. In response to these poems, students should have the silence and the time to absorb them. Choose a line or the topic of the poem and let students write in their daily journal. On Fridays, they can read a selected entry from these journals. The silent writing time, combined with the poem itself, selected from different cultures all during the year, is one example of the way *what* and *how* you teach come together. There are a myriad of anthologies. One of the best is entitled *Unsettling America*, which has poems for every theme you can imagine teaching and from all sorts of poets from all kinds of ethnic backgrounds.

Another possibility is to make up your own anthologies, by cutting out new poems from magazines and looking back in old anthologies for poems that would fit your chosen theme. The combination of new and old works is important for students. So many of them see no connection between the past and the present. They want to see this, but we have not been showing it to them. Thus, a poem by Auden combined with one by Reggie Gaines or Sekou Sundiata on identity, on war, on cities can bring worlds together and make even their history classes more relevant to young people. Poetry has the advantage of being short. To a young man or woman with no time on his or her hands, this looks manageable. In our MTV world, our world of poetry slams and spoken word, urban word poetry, we have an entrée here.

Bringing Together the *What* and the *How*

Before I go on to a final moment of reflection on our system as a whole, I wish to bring together the *what* and the *how*. George Roberts, a man who is now retired and who taught most of his life at North Community High, an inner-city Minneapolis high school, had a method that combined insightful pedagogy and the curriculum in one brilliant beginning to each class hour. He had each student pick a day to be in charge of typing up lyrics to a song that was meaningful to him or her. The student also had to type up a paragraph about why he or she thought the song was important. After the song was played at the beginning of the hour, he let the class discuss it, structuring that discussion by throwing a soft Koosh® ball toward the person who brought in the song and letting him or her begin the exchange, passing the Koosh to the next person who wished to talk. In this way the conversation found its way around the room for ten minutes. In the meantime, George had put up a rubric on the board with which he wanted students to structure their discussion. What is the tone of the song? What is the theme? What about the word choice? What happens in the song? Students became excellent "readers" of the lyrics, noticing how word choice reinforced theme, how the "story" was created over the time of the song, how the tone seemed angry or lonely, and how both music and vocabulary contributed to the mood.

Later in class, when the students began to talk about a story, a novel, a poem, or a memoir they were reading, George put the same rubric on the board he had put up when they were talking about their own music. What is the theme of this story? What is the tone of this poem, this novel? How does word choice contribute to these things? They could be talking about a sonnet by Shakespeare, an essay by James Baldwin, a novel by Toni Morrison, or a short story by Sherman Alexie. From the ease of discussing their own music of the moment using this rubric, they were able to transfer a similar ease to a discussion of the literature they were assigned in class. In this way George had included student voices, made a connection to their own lives, and provided a challenging and provocative way of thinking and speaking about all kinds of literature.

One day when I participated in George's class, we listened to a song that involved a young man who felt bereft because he never knew his father. This is a common theme among many groups of students, be they in the suburbs or the inner city. On impulse, George asked that we stop for a while and write about fathers. We all wrote in silence, which seemed unusually powerful to me. Instead of the ten minutes for quick writes, it became clear to George that we needed more time. So he decided to toss out his plan for the day, and we kept going. Students looked up after about twenty minutes, became restless after twenty-five. We stopped and began to read around the room, George and I included. As people read often wistful or angry or lonely accounts of their relationship with their fathers, I felt a kind of heightened intensity, just as I had felt a charged kind of silence in this classroom, on this morning, in the heart of Minneapolis's North Side.

After everyone had read, we were silent again. A few tears, some statements like "ain't nobody gonna tell nobody what we said in here, right?" and then we turned toward George. He did what I felt like doing: he thanked all the students for their fine work, their willingness to share such immediate and personal writing and hoped they would consider using this work in their future essays or poems. There was a half hour left to the class. We spent that time talking about fathers, about why such a topic would be so powerful. George had on hand some poems written over the years about fatherhood. He mentioned a short story he liked about a boy and his father. We then talked about loss and how primal these father-child relationships are in our lives even when the father is absent, and where we can go to fill that lost place in ourselves.

If we are truly subversive, we can create this kind of class. Creation takes knowing all kinds of literature so well that it is at our fingertips; it takes being confident in letting students write and read work that is close to their hearts; it takes making connections between the world students come from and what goes on in class. It also involves expecting a lot from them: that they will read the literature we are talking about, that they will rework their writing with patience and perseverance, and that they will respect the teacher and fellow students throughout all these activities.

Beyond the How and the What to the System

Teaching equitably is even more than making our isolated classrooms dynamic, challenging, and welcoming places. It is being willing to take a chance, to redefine standards, to change definitions. The class on fathers was the one called AP English for which students were chosen not for their high GPA, as is usual, but for their desire to read literature. And, most important, it was a class students signed up for because George, a popular teacher at

North High, was the person offering the class. By redefining the standards for admittance to AP, he found students of color who would have been passed over, who, in many schools, have been passed over for years.

Just as it defines qualifications for AP English, our system often defines who gets admitted to gifted programs, who takes international baccalaureate classes, who is in the academic track, who is in vocational. All of these placements depend on expectations. Students know this is how the system treats them. They sit and do word puzzles in "basic English" and are very aware that this is not demanding enough for them. They see the surprised look on the face of their eighth-grade teacher when they recognize Chopin, can say the first words of a sonnet that is recited in their home, or see the symbolism in a poem. This look tells them that they were not expected to know these things.

By changing requirements, by expanding "the canon" in programs for advanced kids, by making kids of a multitude of cultures feel welcome in our classes by making the literature from those cultures visible, we can challenge the systems of education all across the country that expect less of students of color. Last year, students at Carleton College, a demanding liberal arts college in Minnesota, told me that they knew from about the third grade on who were going to be the college-bound students and who were on the "lower tracks." And when I asked them if there were students of color in those advanced tracks, in the gifted groups who took a special trip to the theater in the fourth grade and went to the museums in the fifth grade, they said there were very few. It split quite evenly along racial and cultural lines.

Until this changes, until we expect to see the mixture of students in our schools at all levels of instruction or, even better, until we get rid of the rigid separation of these levels altogether, we will not have anywhere near democratic and inclusive education in our schools. To change this is subversive work. In these days of standardized testing of prescribed literature selections authored by primarily White males, it is risky to close the door and chuck the lesson plan and write about fathers. It is bucking the system to assign Rohan Mistry instead of Dickens in some districts, even though the former is a genius at creating and maintaining characters in his long novels. Yet we cannot afford to be safe. We cannot afford to lose students of color. In most of our schools, the percentage of these students will reach 40 to 50 percent by 2020. Until we look at the statistics as a cause for celebration and innovation in our system, we are failing large numbers of young people all across the United States.

In addition to closing the door and turning to the Latino visiting poet who is not on the uniform lesson plan for the day but is an expert on North and Central American literature, we must act in larger ways to challenge our inherently racist system of education. We may do this by challenging the test used to determine which students get the "gifted label" and, thus, the special privileges. We can question entrance requirements for such programs. When programs for gifted students are organized around an academic definition of "giftedness" instead of around a definition that includes original thinking and problem solving, often second-language learners and those without books and an academic environment in their home are excluded from such programs. This leads to a tracking system very early on in our schools. Those who are in the "lower" tracks are often Black, second-language learners or poor of all cultures and colors. In this way, our education system is perpetuating the unfair system. In our own school, our own district we can step in to change the direction of this system. We can encourage parents and community members to look at where the money and programs are going, and who is selected for them. We can also advocate for resources for schools where students are failing standardized tests.

Thus, we must ask how students are selected and what ways they are measured to be included in programs and tracks for giftedness. We must also look carefully at special education to discover whether students of color make up an inordinate number of students in those classes. We may advocate getting rid of gifted programs altogether or, instead, providing the curriculum used in such closed programs for all students. We may insist that our schools look at assigning individual novels and self-designed packets instead of the textbook that is usually chosen every four years even though it rarely makes the perspectives of people of color a part of the history or literature it presents.

These are ways we must go beyond our classrooms to change the way the system works. Making change is tough going right now at this point in our country's history, yet this change has to do with the survival of our students, the advancement of culture and beauty in the United States. Therefore, it is perhaps the most important work we can do. There is no question in my mind that it is essential to the health of all our students, whether they are in predominantly White schools or in those with a broad mix of cultures. It is essential for White students to get an innovative, rich curriculum, just as it is for students of color. Our work world, our university world, is already peopled with many ethnic groups. It is a real disservice to any single group of students to provide them with a public education that contains a single

version of the world, a single-sided perspective of history and literature, celebrations, and definitions.

By being subversive, by changing the way things are done, we are helping to shape our country, making our own lives meaningful and giving *all*
children the gift of expectation, dreams, and a vision for themselves in a
multicultural world.

References

Delpit, L. (2002). *The skin we speak.* New York: New Press.

QUESTIONS

1. Why are White teachers less demanding of students of color?
2. Based on this chapter, how can teachers bring the *what* and *how* together in the classroom?

9

COLOR BLINDNESS, UNCONSCIOUS BIAS, AND STUDENT ACHIEVEMENT IN SUBURBAN SCHOOLS

Justin Grinage

It was my first day as a high school teacher. I woke up in the morning with my mind racing. I was excited and hopeful, yet in the back of my mind I had a nervous feeling of uncertainty. What if I am not good at this? What if I chose the wrong career path? What if I cannot live up to the high expectations I set for myself? I knew I wanted to actively help my community, but it wasn't until after I graduated from college with an English degree that I thought about becoming a teacher.

Being Black and male I saw a huge absence of teachers that looked like me and had experiences that related to my own. I personally did not have a teacher of color until my junior year of college and many of my friends growing up never had a teacher of color, ever. I saw myself as someone who could fill this much-needed void in my community and be a positive influence in students' lives. I envisioned myself working in an inner-city school with a large student of color population. So it was a little odd that I would be starting my first day of teaching at a large suburban high school.

That day was the first time I met my new colleagues and toured the school. As I got into my car a feeling of relief came over me as I realized I would have a whole week of orientation to get ready before the kids showed up; it felt good to go to school and not have to teach, yet. I left my tiny apartment early so I could arrive at school on time. I did not want to be late on the first day. This would be the second time I drove to the school, the first being for my interview. Considering my sense of direction is horrible, I wanted to leave as early as possible because the school was in an unfamiliar area to me. As I turned off the highway onto the road I thought I was supposed to turn on, a feeling of dread came over me when I realized: this is the wrong road.

To get back on my original route I proceeded to turn around, but for some reason I felt more lost than before. At this point I began to panic. I did not know where to go. I took a deep breath and tried to calm my nerves, but all I kept thinking was, "My coworkers are going to think that I am late all the time because I am Black." As I thought more and more about my coworkers judging me on my lateness, my nervousness increased. I was not able to think as clearly or concentrate on what I was doing. Speeding down the road, my mind racing, I lost focus and suddenly slammed on my breaks. I had almost rear-ended the car in front of me.

I finally reached the school, almost an hour late. All the staff was gathered in the gymnasium, sitting and listening to the principal speak about the upcoming school year. Trying to look composed and confident, I entered the gym and found a spot to sit on the bleachers. It felt like time moved in slow motion as I made my way to find a seat. It felt like every staff members' eyes were on me. I began to feel flustered and I blushed with embarrassment and shame. I felt like they were thinking, "He is Black and he is late, that is not surprising."

As the principal continued to talk I scanned the faces in the crowd. I was not shocked to notice that the majority of the crowd was made up of white faces. I saw a few black and brown faces peppered among the staff, which surprised me. I feared that I might be the only Black staff member at the school (other than our bi-racial principal). At the conclusion of the presentation all the new staff were asked to stand up and everyone clapped for us. In addition, we had four new security staff (essentially hall monitors), two of whom were Black (one female and one male). The other two were White and male. They were asked to come to the front and the principal personally introduced them to the staff.

We were then instructed to walk around the significantly large school for what the principal called a "diversity gallery walk." It was an opportunity to give the returning staff a chance to reconnect with each other and give the new staff a chance to meet other staff and get acquainted with the school—all while observing different displays that some of our school's vastly diverse student groups had created.

As the staff strolled out of the gymnasium a couple of my Language Arts colleagues rushed up to me to introduce themselves. I felt a little relieved seeing their smiling, friendly faces. I proceeded to walk around the school and look at the displays students had created. Many staff members greeted me very warmly as we walked, talked, and took in all the beautiful student work. Most of our conversations consisted of: Hi, how are you doing? I am so and so. I teach this subject. I have worked here this long. Are you new? What do you teach? I was very pleased at how friendly and welcoming the staff was.

I had several conversations with teachers and other staff members and I began to notice a pattern in some of the conversations. I and another staff member would be engaged in discussion and inevitably the question of what I teach or what my job is here would come up. I would answer accordingly: "I am a new English teacher here." However, several staff members, instead of asking me what my job was, simply stated, "You must be one of the new security guards here. Nice to meet you." The first time this happened I simply corrected them and chalked it up to being an honest mistake. But the next three times it happened, it really started to bother me. These staff members perceived me to be a security guard instead of a teacher. Once again, I felt like people were judging me because I was Black. At the end of the day, I thought to myself, "Oh boy, this is going to be a long year."

I tell this story about my first day as a teacher for two distinct reasons: (1) Teachers have biases based on race, whether conscious or unconscious, and (2) Negative stereotypes of people of color affect them in adverse ways. In this essay I explore these two issues and apply them to what it means to be a White educator in a suburban school and what it means to be a student of color in a suburban school. I will conclude with suggestions to help teachers recognize the impact that race has on teaching and learning.

Noticing Racism in the Age of Color Blindness

My discussion of White teachers and students of color will largely reflect an individual point of view, but it is necessary to place these individual interactions between teacher and student in a larger context. Teachers need to recognize that their classrooms exist as a microcosm of society and that their students enter with various experiences within this society. Racism still exists in America. It has changed and evolved over the years, but is present within all institutions and social structures, including schools and classrooms. Confronting this reality is the first step toward equity and toward noticing and observing instances of racism in your school and classroom. For many years—during slavery and through Jim Crow—it was socially acceptable to be overtly racist. It was common to hear derogatory slurs directed toward people of color and blatant acts of racism were frequent and permissible. Racism changed after the Civil Rights Movement; it was no longer socially acceptable to be overtly racist. However, that does not mean racism vanished. It simply transformed into a more hidden, acceptable form, embedded into our nation's laws and policies.

On the surface, racism seemed to disappear according to many White people because to them it had only been overtly visible. Whites began to perceive society as being equal for all individuals: everyone can succeed as long as they work hard. People began to argue that race was no longer a significant factor for people of color. Many White people recognized that racism existed, but felt that it typically was not a major impediment for upward mobility. Hence, the age of color blindness began.

Color blindness affects many White teachers in suburban schools. Suburban teachers tend to see students as individuals and do not acknowledge racial and cultural differences, which may be crucial to their students' identities. It is fine to see students as individuals, but being blind to students' racial and cultural identities can be extremely harmful. White teachers go so far as to avoid talking about race in any context, out of fear of being labeled racist. Mica Pollock calls this phenomenon colormute. During Pollock's (2004) ethnographic study in a large, racially diverse high school she found that the staff members deliberately avoided talking about race, and often noticeably steered away from conversations about race when it involved their relationship with students. In suburban schools it is often easier for teachers to be colormute because there are fewer students of color in their classes than there are in most inner city, urban schools. In this context if a student of color does not fit into the system, it is not attributed to their race or racism within the classroom or school—since color blindness dictates that race is not a significant factor in teaching and learning—but to their inability to succeed in school. Therefore, students become the victims and no blame attaches to the teachers who fail to realize the impact that race and racism have on teaching and learning.

White educators in suburban schools who do not adhere to the colorblind ideology often fail to see racism beyond an individual level. It is not enough to notice race and its impact on students' lives. One has to go a step further and identify how racism exists within a school's structure. Institutional racism goes hand-in-hand with color blindness. Teachers do not need to be racists to perpetuate racist systems. Racist systems function regardless of who is working within them because the inequities are built into the values, customs, policies, and procedures that make up the system.

The concept of institutional racism or structural racism can be elucidated using theorist Iris Marion Young's (2000) metaphor of the birdcage. The bird, representing a person of color, is locked in a cage, representing structural racism. Michele Alexander (2010), in her book *The New Jim Crow*, extends this metaphor:

> If one thinks about racism by examining only one wire of the cage, or one form of disadvantage, it is difficult to understand how and why the bird is trapped. Only a large number of wires arranged in a specific way serve to enclose the bird and ensure that it cannot escape. (p. 179)

Applying the birdcage metaphor to a school one may describe the individual wire bars on the cage as specific structural inequities within the institution. Let's say that a particular student of color is not succeeding in your classroom and you do not know why. It is important to examine the birdcage as it may provide a key to understanding why this student is not achieving. For example, one bar may represent unequal discipline policies, while another bar may symbolize the lack of relevant curriculum being taught in classes, and yet another bar the consequence of teachers' color blindness when working with students of color. We know that a student's experiences do not take place exclusively within school, so outside societal forces must be considered part of the wire cage. Therefore, another wire bar may be the inequitable way in which the police department patrols and harasses students of color in their neighborhoods. The more wires a teacher can see the easier it is to work with that particular student and understand why she or he is trapped in the cage. It is essential for teachers to understand the complicated ways in which the wire cage is constructed in order to disassemble the cage and let the bird go free. It is important to keep in mind, as the discussion narrows to discussing individual students of color or individual White teachers' interactions with them, that we consider the larger societal factors that impact the relationship between teachers and these students.

Suburban vs. Inner City Schools

As I mentioned previously, I was very reluctant to teach at a suburban school because I thought, in a way, I was "selling out." For kids of color growing up in the city, suburban schools denoted rich, privileged White kids. True or not, that is how I thought about those schools growing up. Why would I teach at a school full of privileged White kids when I wanted to be a positive role model for Black students and other kids of color? Conversely, I think many educators who grew up in the suburbs have similar misconceptions about inner city or urban schools. Many aspiring educators have a clear vision of the kind of student they want to teach, whether they are conscious of it or not. Some White teachers who grew up in isolated, predominantly White suburbs, tend to see themselves teaching students that have a similar background to their own. Others who want to teach in the inner city often have aspirations similar to Michelle Pfeiffer's character in *Dangerous Minds* or Hilary Swank's character in *Freedom Writers*. They want to be the heroes who swoop in and save those kids. So, for the most part, teachers seem to end up where they want to end up.

The words "suburban" and "inner city" (or urban) have essentially become racial code words for White and Black. In our color-blind society where White people rarely mention race, a teacher can say he wants to teach White children or not teach Black children just by saying he wants to teach in a suburban school or not teach in an inner city school. Educators working in suburban schools have difficulty confronting the possibility that they may not be as equipped to teach the increasing number of students of color that are entering their suburban classrooms. They may not have ever envisioned that they would be teaching "those" children.

The reason that White educators may not have seen themselves teaching students of color cuts deeper than just wanting to teach in a suburban school. Many White teachers who grew up in suburban areas have experienced segregation their whole lives. I have White colleagues and friends who grew up in the suburbs or small Midwest rural towns, both of which were often primarily White communities. They grew up with a handful of people of color, but their peers, classmates, and close friends were mostly White people. They attended schools with White teachers and White student bodies. How can these teachers begin to understand the complex cultural and racial histories of their students of color if, for a large portion of their lives, they have only been around other White people? I find that a lot of my close White friends and colleagues consider me their only friend of color. White educators need to seek out authentic relationships with people from different ethnic and cultural backgrounds. White teachers can learn a lot about what their students of color experience just by being around and talking with other people of color.

After working at the suburban school that hired me I realized that I was not "selling out" after all. I began to understand that there were plenty of students of color in that school that considered me a role model, and I feel extremely lucky to have worked with them. Also, something happened that I did not anticipate; I began to make a major difference in the lives of my White students. Many of my students had never had a teacher of color until stepping foot into my classroom. Opening up about my experiences with racism and having conversations about injustice allowed my White students to learn from my experiences and empowered my students of color because they felt like I could relate to what they were going through. Ultimately, I began to understand that every student, regardless of color, needed to confront and understand issues of racism and oppression within our society. This teaching and learning can occur just as easily in a suburban school as it can in an inner city, urban school.

Unconscious Bias

To explore the concept of unconscious bias it is necessary to return to the narrative at the beginning of this chapter. During the gallery walk meet-and-greet, a few staff members assumed that I was one of the new security staff instead of a new Language Arts teacher. Analyzing these interactions reveals the very subtle ways in which individuals carry assumptions based on race. Why would these staff members automatically assume that I was a security guard after meeting me for only a brief moment? Well, one could say that half of the new security staff was Black and since there were few Black staff members it was only logical to assume that since I was Black, I was a security guard, if you played the percentages. But there were also more White male security guards than Black male security guards—two to one. Is it likely that some of the new White male teachers were mistaken as new security staff? And as the other Black male security guard was walking around and meeting other staff members, was he mistaken for the new Black male teacher (many staff members did see me stand up when the new teachers were asked to, even though I was not introduced in front of everyone)? I suspect this did not occur in either case.

These particular staff members, I assume, were not consciously and purposely judging me by the color of my skin. In fact, they were extremely friendly and seemed to genuinely want to get to know me. However, they still made some pretty large assumptions about me based on my race, even though on the surface these assumptions seemed very subtle. This is an example of unconscious bias. Educators who claim to not see race or deny it as a factor in teaching and learning still, unconsciously, categorize, judge, and discriminate based on race. Even educators who are not color blind and understand racism's impact on education make unconscious decisions based on race everyday—we all make these judgments, no matter what race we are.

Often, historically embedded stereotypes are the driving force behind the race-based judgments that we make. For example, why would the staff members who mistook me for a security guard not assume that I was a teacher in the first place? Or, why would they not mistake the Black security guard for the new Black teacher? The answer lies behind the stereotypical images of who are typically teachers and who are typically security guards. If you ask the average person to describe what a teacher typically looks like, you would probably receive the answer, White and female, fairly frequently. If you asked that same person about security guards the answer might vary a little more, but you would probably receive the answer, young Black male, much more frequently than the answer to the teacher question. How often did those staff members see teachers depicted in the media as White and female, while security guards were depicted as Black and male? How many of those same staff members have ever had teachers of color growing up (remember I did not even have a teacher of color until well into college)? When I introduce myself to new people and they ask me what I do for a living, they often think I am lying when I say I am an English teacher. People find it easy to believe that as a Black male I love basketball, but find it harder to believe that I am a voracious reader and love classic works of literature. It is no coincidence that these staff members initially perceived me as a security guard instead of a teacher.

These few comments by staff members had a large impact on my first year of teaching. I was more conscious of how others perceived me as a professional because I am young, Black, and male. I thought that other staff members who did not verbally express that they thought I was a security guard were thinking it all the same. It made me feel like I had to prove myself and that somehow I had to gain additional credibility for other staff members to respect me as a professional. I worked extremely hard my first year of teaching to prove that I deserved to be there and to gain the respect of my fellow colleagues.

Another example of unconscious bias that I have witnessed at my school involves patterns in the way teachers and administrators discipline students. I often see students walking in the hallways for various reasons. Frequently, I have seen staff members stop students of color and ask for a hall pass, while White students are ignored. Similarly, before and after school, the areas where the majority of students of color hang out usually have more staff members monitoring those spaces. Are these staff members consciously targeting students of color while ignoring White students? I think in some cases this may be true, but most of the time these are unconscious decisions, meaning that staff members are not aware of the biases that they are showing toward students.

In schools where a disproportionate amount of students of color get into trouble for disciplinary reasons the blame is often placed on their behaviors, while overlooking other factors that may be contributing to the situation. If students of color are targeted and monitored more frequently than White students, inevitably they will get away with less, and get caught more often for misbehaving, thus creating the disproportional statistics. Conversely, if White students are ignored and not monitored as frequently, they get away with more and get in trouble less frequently than students of color, therefore making the statistical gap seem even larger. Administrators can then look at this data and justify targeting students of color, while still being unaware of the racism that these students face within the school and in their neighborhoods, which may be contributing to their behaviors (remember the birdcage metaphor).

Effects of Unconscious Bias and Stereotyping

A few assumptions made about who I was professionally deeply affected the way I approached the rest of the school year, and definitely made me more aware of how my fellow colleagues judged me. If just a few comments based on my race influenced me, imagine how much daily assumptions and perceived biases can influence students of color in suburban schools. Students who feel they are being negatively stereotyped and judged because of their race can have a variety of feelings and reactions that can adversely affect their school performance. Students may lose trust in teachers who they think are making judgments about who they are because of the color of their skin. Continued stereotyping may result in those students automatically not trusting any teacher. In extreme circumstances students may begin to feel like school is an unsafe place and reject the education system completely. Students may lose faith in themselves and lash out against the system that they feel does not support them.

Enduring repeated stereotyping and judgment from staff members and fellow students is emotionally damaging to students of color. Students who are continuously judged and stereotyped may internalize some of these presumptions and believe they are true. This phenomenon is often called internalized racism (also known as internalized oppression). Donna Bivens (2005) describes internalized racism: "As people of color are victimized by racism we internalize it. That is, we develop ideas, beliefs, actions, and behaviors that support or collude with racism" (p. 50). Internalized racism can cause adverse affects on achievement and a decreased investment in school for students of color. Based on how some staff members did not perceive me as an educator, I started to doubt my teaching abilities. I started to think that maybe I was not fit to be a teacher. I internalized some of these negative perceptions of the way people thought of me professionally. Luckily, I had enough confidence in my abilities that I was able to overcome the negative stereotypes I was internalizing. Also, it helped that I did not experience ongoing stereotyping from my colleagues over the course of that first school year, although it was often in the back of my mind. The student who is repeatedly singled out, monitored, or targeted because of their race may not be so lucky. The student that is constantly in trouble or failing may attribute this to the fact that they are Latino (for example) and internalize the stereotype that Latino's are supposed to get into trouble and drop out of school. It becomes a self-fulfilling prophecy that some students cannot overcome.

Another potential effect of unconscious bias and stereotyping is a concept first used by Claude Steele and Joshua Aronson (1995) called stereotype threat. Steele and Aronson define stereotype threat on the website reducing stereotypethreat.org as "being at risk of confirming, as self-characteristic, a negative stereotype about one's group." The results of their initial study found that Black college students performed more poorly on standardized tests than White students when they were made conscious of their race. However, when their race was not emphasized they performed on equivalent levels with White students. Additional studies on the concept of stereotype threat show that when students feel they are at risk of fulfilling a negative racial stereotype their school performance suffers.

As I mentioned in the narrative at the beginning of this chapter, on my way to school on my first day as a teacher, I drove down the wrong road and got lost. As I tried to get back on course I was terrified of being late out of fear of confirming the negative stereotype that Black people are always late. My mind was fixed on this outcome and, as a result, I could not concentrate on driving and almost caused an accident. My awareness of confirming a negative stereotype hindered my ability to perform a task, in this case driving. Stereotype threat was definitely a factor in my driving abilities that day.

Similarly, students of color in suburban schools are susceptible to stereotype threat, especially if they feel like they have or are being judged based on their race. In a classroom where students feel as if the teacher has racial biases, they may be more aware of how their race factors into their interactions with the teacher and the curriculum, thus becoming more vulnerable to stereotype threat.

Let's say there is a teacher who consistently favors her White students over her Black students. The teacher may often call on her White students, while ignoring her students of color. She may be more than willing to help her White students, but is more reluctant to help and less patient with her Black students. Overall, this teacher expects a lot more from her White students, but is unconcerned if the Black students do not meet expectations. Remember that the patterns of behavior a teacher displays do not have to be conscious. It is very possible that a teacher is not aware of the biases he or she may have. All it takes is for some of the Black students in the class to pick up on some of these behaviors, and they start to think the teacher expects the White students to do well and the Black students not to succeed in the class. As a result, they become more aware of the stereotype that Blacks are not as intelligent and do more poorly in school than Whites. Out of fear of confirming this stereotype many Black students in the class feel anxiety and nervousness during the big unit test, and do poorly as a result. Those students experienced a stereotype threat heightened by their teacher's unconscious racial biases.

Suggestions for Educators

In this last section my intention is to give educators suggestions on how to identify and reduce prejudice and stereotyping. Teachers should not consider these suggestions strategies that will ensure that all racism and biases are eliminated from their instruction. Recognizing and eliminating racism is not something that can be solved with a few simple strategies or steps. Centuries of racism cannot be undone by a set of strategies; if that were the case, racism would have been eliminated long ago. Instead, these suggestions are meant to be a start, or a continuation of, what will be a lifelong personal and collective struggle to fight oppression and racism in education and in society.

Acknowledge and confront the fact that you have prejudices based on race. The first step to noticing and eliminating racism is to admit that as a White teacher you hold stereotypes and prejudices about your students of color. If you ignore that you have biases based on race you will never be able to make unconscious assumptions visible within your teaching.

Seek to understand the complex ways in which racism exists in society. Once you admit that racism has an impact on your life and your students' lives, it is essential to learn how racism has influenced society. If you can better understand the historical, socio-economic, and political ways in which racism exists, you will begin to realize why you have prejudices based on race. By not only understanding individual racism, but also how institutional racism functions, you will start to identify instances where you are being biased and also start to recognize systemic inequalities occurring in society and in your school.

See past the historically ingrained stereotypical depictions of your students. Making positive, meaningful connections with your students will help to reduce the unconscious presumptions you make based on race. The more you understand each student as an individual—while acknowledging that their cultural background influences who they are, but does not totally define who they are—the more you will reduce biases that you may have toward that student because of their race.

Seek to create authentic relationships with people of color. Understanding how people of color experience racism is important to understanding how racism functions in society. White teachers should seek to establish relationships with people of color, both personally and professionally. Teachers of all nationalities and backgrounds need to unite and share each other's experiences. As educators we can all learn a lot about racism from learning about each other.

Create support systems within your own school and community.

Acknowledge that working to understand and eliminate racism is difficult work. You will need colleagues and friends who are working toward the same goals to encourage you and support you when times get tough. As educators you can begin to support each other by having meaningful conversations about racial issues within your school and your classrooms.

References

Alexander, M. (2010). *The new Jim Crow: Mass incarceration in the age of colorblindness.* New York, NY: The New Press.

Bivens, D. (2005). What is internalized racism? In M. Potapchuk & S. Leiderman (Eds.), *Flipping the script: White privilege and community building* (pp. 49–58). Conshohocken, PA: Center for Assessment and Policy Development.

Pollock, M. (2004). *Colormute: Race talk dilemmas in an American school.* Princeton, NJ: Princeton University Press.

Steele, C. M., & Aronson, J. (1995). Stereotype threat and the intellectual test performance of African Americans. *Journal of Personality and Social Psychology, 69,* 797–811. Retrieved from http://www.reducingsterreotypethreat.org/definition .html

Young, I. M. (2000). *Inclusion and democracy.* New York, NY: Oxford University Press.

QUESTIONS

1. The author notes that all teachers have biases based on race, whether conscious or unconscious. What are your conscious and unconscious biases based on race?

2. The author provides several recommendations for educators for how to identify and reduce prejudice and stereotyping. How can we get all educators on board to genuinely go through this exercise?

TIPS FOR SCHOOL PRINCIPALS AND TEACHERS

Helping Black Students Achieve

Dorothy Garrison-Wade and Chance W. Lewis

"For these are all our children. . . . We will profit by, or pay for, whatever they become."

—James Baldwin

No Child Left Behind legislation challenges school principals to improve the achievement gap between Black and White students. Still, Black students lag far behind their White peers on standardized tests used to measure academic achievement. Ladson-Billings (1994) states, "No challenge has been more daunting than that of improving achievement of African American students" (p. ix).

There are many reasons for Black students' achievement gap, but we contend that one of the reasons may be a shortage of teachers with an understanding of their cultural needs. This chapter explores this shortage of such teachers and provides the characteristics that Black students look for in their teachers. At the end of the chapter, we present tips to aid school principals and teachers in promoting the academic achievement of Black students.

Shortage of Black Teachers

More and more, Black students are being educated by people who are not of their race or cultural background. Wilder (2000) states that because many students of color will not have teachers of color, Black teachers in particular, they will never have opportunities to have teachers with an understanding of their culture, communities, or learning needs. Five decades after *Brown vs. Board of Education* (1954), the majority of U.S. public school students can go through their entire K–12 educational career without having an African American teacher (Hawkins, 1994; Orfield & Lee, 2004). According to Irvine (2003), 44 percent of our schools have no teacher of color on staff. Additionally, the American Association of Colleges for Teacher Education (1999) cites that White teachers comprise 70 percent of the public school population. Whereas, in the new millennium, Black students will consist of 20 percent of the total student enrollment, Black teachers will make up only 8 percent of the teaching force nationwide, with male Black teachers making up only 1 percent (Kunjufu, 2002; Lewis, 2006; National Education Association, 2001). This number is projected to decline to less than 6 percent in the next decade (Wilder, 2000). Furthermore, there are slightly more Black school administrators. The National Center for Education Statistics (2004) reports that only 9.8 percent of U.S. school principals are Black. Consequently, many Black students could go through their entire school experience without having a principal or teacher who understands their diverse needs. This is not to say that Black teachers or teachers of color are the only teachers equipped to understand the diverse needs of their students. Nor do we intend to say that all Black teachers can address students' diverse needs. Nevertheless, the shortage of Black teachers decreases the opportunity of Black students to have teachers who are familiar with their culture and communities (Wilder, 2000).

Given that a significant number of Black students in the K–12 educational setting will be largely educated by White teachers, there is a pressing need for all teachers to learn culturally responsive strategies. Ladson-Billings (1994) states that the educational community has come to a consensus in recommending that more African Americans are needed to deliver "culturally relevant pedagogy" to a more ethnically diverse student population. All teachers, not just White teachers, must learn culturally responsive teaching strategies to address students' diverse needs.

Listening to students' perceptions and interpretations of educational practices is crucial in identifying viable solutions for educators. Rarely do we hear from the students' perspective what they need to be successful. Unfortunately, limited studies examine the effectiveness of culturally responsive pedagogical practices from students' perspectives (Howard, 2001). Therefore, the next section gives students a voice. It explores students' impressions of what is needed for their academic success.

Students Speak Out

In an effort to include students' voices in this chapter, we invited Black students enrolled in a suburban and an urban school district in Northern Colorado and students from the Denver metropolitan area to participate in focus group discussions. Eight students responded to the invitation to participate in this research. We divided the students into two groups of four (Northern Colorado suburban/urban schools and Denver metropolitan urban schools). Their ages ranged from thirteen to eighteen. Questions focused on the role that White teachers play in facilitating Black students' academic success or failure, Black students' perceptions on whether White teachers' views of them interfere with addressing their educational needs, and Black students' perceptions on academic achievement. The focus groups' data were part of an ongoing, in-depth research study of the impact of White teachers on the academic achievement of Black students. The proceeding points were generated from the focus groups' conversations with the students.

Respect

One word, *respect*, continually cropped up throughout both focus group discussions, demonstrating that it was a major issue for Black students. Yet, when we talked with the students, we found that the word *respect* had many meanings. These meanings were the teacher being nice and not rude, helping out with assignments, and being sensitive. One student stated that respect was a good quality:

> "I think it's important that . . . it's one good quality that everyone respect each other because if you don't then you can't really have a relationship with the students whether you're Black, white, Hispanic, or whatever. So it's always good to have in the classroom and I've always felt I was respected and for instance, if we were to have a discussion on slavery or something, I would always be pulled to the side and told this is what we're gonna talk about are you okay, blah, blah, blah. Would you like to read something or I would be alerted ahead of time so I wouldn't be uncomfortable, so I think I was always respected and shown respect in school."

Students were also in total agreement that embarrassment was synonymous with disrespect. Any time students felt the teachers were embarrassing them, they interpreted the behavior as disrespectful. Students who felt respected by their teachers exhibited the same respect to the teachers:

"See I would like a teacher that's respectful and I'll respect them back so everything would go a little bit easier with this, with each other. . . . He'd do things for me, I'd do things for him."

Students who perceived their teachers as respectful expressed affection toward their teachers. Students who "liked" their teachers tended to work harder, listen more to their teachers, and show more interest in academic success:

"Say like your boss, if you hated your boss, you ain't gonna be cool with him or nothing. You won't really do as good a job, I don't think you'll do as good a job as when you like your teacher and they're working for you, just as well as you working for them, then it's easier for you to work and understand. I can do all the work in our school, but when you get bored in class like your teacher is boring or something, I could just go to sleep or something, just quit that. Teacher gotta be interesting, you gotta respect. When teachers are rude and mean you lose respect for 'em. And when I don't have no respect for somebody I don't listen to 'em anyway and I'm not gonna do what they say anyway."

Some students who perceived that their teachers weren't respectful might give up or demonstrate negative behavior, whereas other students who did not receive respect from their teachers might demand it through their actions:

"I think I get respect in the classroom because I command respect from my teachers because I give respect to my teachers pretty much. Like honestly, pretty much if a teacher disrespects me or I feel like I'm disrespected, I'm gonna say something. I'm gonna tell them I'm not gonna listen to you because that's just me, I got a mouth."

One male student described lack of respect as "threatening" him to perform better:

"I felt really disrespected from a teacher when she threatened me like five times in a day and she said it's your grade, so you have to do it, it's your grade. They always talking about if you don't do it, it's your grade. They won't actually help you out."

Another student provided an example of disrespect, mentioning the times her teachers had trouble remembering and pronouncing her name:

"Or when my teachers call me _____, _____, _____, all these names. When they first say it, if I'm new or they're a new teacher, it's cool then I'll tell them my name and then they'll mess it up again and I'll tell them again and they're like whatever, it's close enough. Your mama shouldn't have said it with a A. They say it's pronounced _____, and I say but it's _____."

Respect is not important just to African American students; it's important to all students. Even adults seek the same in their personal interactions. Unfortunately, too often teachers forget that respect is important. They sometimes unintentionally belittle students. Once respect is lost, it is nearly impossible to regain.

☞ **Tip 1: Show students respect and it will be reciprocated.**

Stereotype

Students voiced that another issue, stereotype, was a major deterrent to their achievement. They indicated that many teachers had established set stereotypes of Black students—false stereotypes, such as, "They aren't interested in learning"; "They're not as intelligent as other students"; "They're loud and trouble makers"; "Their parents aren't interested in their education." Landsman (2001) stated that from the time they enter school Blacks and other students of color are often not expected to do well. One student seemed to agree with her:

"I know the stereotype is that Black people don't learn as well or aren't as intelligent as other people are."

Several students stated that teachers automatically thought that Black students were bad:

"A lot of White teachers or some Black people too automatically think (we're all trouble makers because we're Black), 'Oh, he or she's bad, they got a referral and this and that.' Yea, they do, they do think that. They be thinking that about me and I make good grades."

"Some teachers at my school, when you first get in their class they assume that you're bad and stuff. Like they think, 'I can tell this person is going to be bad.' And they don't even know you that much."

Additionally, many students perceived that these stereotypes resulted in teachers falsely judging them. According to the students, many false assumptions were made based on their race and/or the way they dressed:

"And the way I dress, it's the stereotypes pretty much. You know, Black people are thugs and they smoke weed and they drink Kool-Aid. You know all that. That's what they be trying to do. They be trying to put that on you and some people do that but that's just not my thing. I'm trying to do something with my life, like my whole demeanor is that I'm gonna be the best at whatever I do pretty much."

"You won't be able to understand until you walk out into the world and be Black and go through discrimination and racism and people being racist with you and stuff."

"And I think it's [stereotype] a lot about appearance because of the way I dress, the way I am. If you didn't know me, you wouldn't know I'm just funny, happy, loud. A lot of people think I'm just mad, just think I'm mad and stuff but once you get to know somebody that's when all the barriers go down."

Surprisingly, many of the students understood the origin of stereotyping. They acknowledged that they were also guilty of false stereotyping, caused by negative television images of African Americans and other races and from influences of parents, family members, and/or friends:

"I think that's a universal thing, that's everywhere. Like us as Black people, we look at White people like, I know I do. Like if I see a White person that's not looking right, don't got their hair up, they're not dressed right, I'm gonna judge them quick because like, oh, they must be poor White trash or something. That's how it is everywhere, you just have that perception just because of TV and my parents, my mom, everybody, my whole family, people I hang around."

The solution, according to one student, was to judge people based on their character, not their skin color:

"Just like Martin Luther King said, judge us just by the character not the color of our skin. So just see us all as equal, don't think less of a person because of the color of their skin."

We have all judged others based on stereotype. But until we acknowledge it's wrong, students will suffer from our biases. In *Awakening Brilliance* (Sims, 1997), a teacher named Sarah states, "Our judgments about our students' abilities aren't always right. We can't see into their souls. We're only privileged to see a small part of their potential. Yet we judge them and act toward them as if we're all-knowing. We are often wrong" (p. 67).

The end result of stereotyping may be a "self-fulfilling prophesy" for some students, in which students act out others' negative perceptions of them. After being judged by teachers who have preconceived notions and after seeing stereotypes of the Black community through the media, students may judge themselves with these stereotypes. Instead of considering their own individuality and breaking past stereotypes, students may accept them as true. This would be detrimental to their personal growth.

☞ **Tip 2: Consider your first impression of a student. Avoid judging the student based on stereotypes.**

Connection

When students were asked to share a quality of a "good teacher" the word *connection* appeared over and over again. One may ask, "What is connection?" *Merriam Webster's Collegiate Dictionary,* 10th edition (1993) defines *connection* as "the act of connecting . . . , the state of being connected . . . , causal or logical relation or sequence . . . , a means of communication or transport . . . , a person connected with another esp. by marriage, kinship, or common interest . . ."(p. 245). Students had plenty to say about connection and provided advice on how to develop one. They indicated that connections were made when their teachers shared information about themselves with students, observed students' interests, and learned more about students' backgrounds. Several students offered advice on how to develop connections with students:

> "Just being yourself, telling them who you really are and showing them that you can do your work and stuff and they'll eventually know and they'll treat you differently and you'll get a connection."
> "You don't know all their backgrounds. You don't know everything about them and what they're hiding so you have to find out on your own."
> "We can't talk to them. I think when you have teachers [you] should have a relationship, [you] should discuss [your] work and when you have problems you should be able to come to them and ask them to help you."

Humor was always effective in connecting with students:

> "I actually connected to one teacher because I always used to be nice to my teachers but one day I was trying to do my work and he was trying to be hip hop and he was like "yeah what's up" and he's Jewish. He

made me laugh and I asked if I could have help with this problem and he'll help me. He'll try to make it fun."

Spending additional time with students helped develop connections:

"I was on the basketball team, he was also a coach. Fort Hamilton Middle School and just talking out there and playing basketball, spending more time other than just school, we connected."

Race did not have to be a deterrent in building connections:

"I never thought race mattered in anything I've done my whole entire life. Personally, I think everybody is created equal no matter what, it's all about you as a person and that's why you can click with that person. Because you click with people, you don't click with their race, that's basically it."

One student had advice for administrators for building relationships with students:

"Administrators need to just chill and not try to be like the authority figure and try to build relationships with students as well. They don't just have to . . . do their job but most of them don't really know students because students see them as authority figure and they not gonna go to that person, so they need to try to build some relationships with students as well."

Although some might not view establishing connections with students as a factor in enhancing their achievement, students revealed to us that they work harder for teachers who care for and listen to them, as well as help them. They also responded more when teachers made the lesson fun and interesting. For the students, establishing connections with their teacher created a comfort zone that opened the door to learning.

☞ **Tip 3: Take the time to learn about your students' backgrounds and interests. This will help you develop a connection with them that may create an environment conducive to learning.**

Cultural Understandings

The majority of students whom we talked to in the focus groups implied that they had limited exposure to teachers of color. Only a few students indicated that they had a Black teacher for a core academic subject; students might have had a Black teacher as a coach or elective teachers. Consequently, students felt that many of their teachers did not seem to have an understanding of their culture. Additionally, their curriculum was devoid of cultural representatives. Landsman (2001) stated that it may be alienating to students who never see representatives of their culture within the curriculum, such as in literature or in history. If this is true, then feelings of alienation and isolation might interfere with students' achievement. From the focus group discussions, we found that teachers who appeared to reach out to students in an attempt to learn more about their cultural backgrounds were more popular with the students. Of course, all teachers, regardless of their cultural background, should be cognizant of their students' cultural needs. Effective teachers' classrooms reflect a multiculturally responsive curriculum. Following are some of the students' views on cultural differences:

> "I would say your teacher has to understand what you're doing and he has to understand you so he can know what you're going through. Say if you have a problem or question and he has to understand."
> "She (teacher) knows about a lot of different cultures and stuff. She is real interested in African Americans and every time we have a discussion in class about that she always comes to me and tells me what we're going to talk about and let me know ahead of time so I don't feel uncomfortable in the classroom or anything. She's just cool like that."

Students noticed when teachers did not take time to learn about their cultural background or incorporate multicultural curriculum. For some students, these oversights seemed to indicate that some teachers might be afraid to present cultural topics. Two students voiced their opinion on their teachers avoiding cultural topics:

> "We skip Black history. He [teacher] don't even like messing with that stuff. He'll go straight to the Greeks, the Indians, forget about Black history and what the Ku Klux Klan and all that did because I only heard about the Ku Klux Klan once and I heard that in elementary school."
> "I think they don't think it's important about slavery and stuff. They think that's the past and whatever and they don't want to talk about it. Because Black people might get mad and look at White people differently or something, maybe they're afraid of that."

In our focus group discussions, students said that they really appreciated teachers who exposed them to Black authors and Black history, and discussed culturally sensitive issues. In addition, students seemed to appreciate teachers who shared their views on these issues. One student said:

> "I remember Mr. H., he talked about it. He's White because he found some of his ancestors had some slaves and he talked about it. It was embarrassing for him because he said a long time ago his name was in the article he was talking about and one of the kids was like that's your name and he looked it up to see if that his ancestors and it was. He felt embarrassed because he was talking about the situation and he didn't know that was his grandpa or great-great grandpa or whatever."

By avoiding cultural topics, teachers might be widening the achievement gap for students of color by alienating them.

It is almost as if some teachers think that culturally sensitive topics are better hidden under the rug. For students of color this only creates a void, a curiosity to learn more. Gordon (2000) states that students "desire a more honest representation in the curriculum of the diversity of ideas and skills that contributed to the development of America" (p. 1). We need to honor students' culture and create a culturally responsive environment to promote their achievement.

☞ Tip 4: Recognize cultural differences and develop a multicultural curriculum.

High Standards

Teachers' attitudes and expectations greatly affect all students. The students whom we talked with implied that their teachers' perception of their ability greatly impacted their academic performance. They responded favorably to teachers who held them to higher standards. Some students provided reasons that their teachers pushed them to excel:

> "Well, my teachers hold me to a higher standard because they expect it and it's just because when I meet my teachers I show 'em that I'm willing to learn. My mom lets them know too that they don't have a choice. They expect me to do good, when I do bad my teachers are shocked like 'what are you doing' is everything okay." They're shocked.
> "I think they hold me to a higher standard because my dad has always been involved in school. He'll go and make sure that I'm going to school, that we're doing good in classes and stuff, so by him doing that, they kinda know that I'm supposed to do what I can and be the best I can be, so I think they hold me to a higher standard, just by that not necessarily because of my race or anything."
> "Basically, I think they hold us to higher standards because we hold our-

selves to higher standards. We're not gonna settle for just the average, we want the best."

"Another reason why I think they hold me to a higher standard is because I express to them my goals and what I wanna be in life and so then they wanna help me with that and the only way they're gonna help me with that is by enforcing what I need to do and they know what I need to do because they've been there."

Unfortunately, some students reported that teachers seemed to lower their standards for Black students. Beady and Hansell (1981) implied that Black teachers held Black students to higher expectations than White teachers. Given that many Black students will not have Black teachers, all their teachers must rise to the challenge and establish high expectations and standards for all students. Landsman (2001) eloquently stated it best:

Somehow educators must find a way to make it safe for all students to believe and espouse the belief that they can succeed. But for this to happen, educators themselves must believe that every child, and every young adult, can learn. Unfortunately, the deep and abiding racism that affects everyone in this country, in ways both subtle and obvious, prevents students of color from having teachers who believe in their ability to learn. (p. 21)

☞ **Tip 5: Establish high expectations and standards for all students and they will meet the challenge.**

Conclusion

While there are many worthy ideas for promoting achievement for Black students, we addressed five major areas: (1) respect, (2) stereotype, (3) connection, (4) cultural understandings, and (5) high standards. In addition, we provided five tips to assist educators in working with Black students:

1. Show students respect and it will be reciprocated.
2. Consider your first impression of a student. Avoid judging the student based on stereotypes.
3. Take the time to learn about your students' backgrounds and interests. This will help you develop a connection with them that may create an environment conducive to learning.
4. Recognize cultural differences and develop a multicultural curriculum.

5. Establish high expectations and standards for all students and they will meet the challenge.

Although these recommendations are aimed at improving achievement for Black students, they are applicable to all students, regardless of race. We hope that the voices of the students in this chapter will help teachers and administrators improve the academic achievement of Black students.

References

American Association of Colleges for Teacher Education. (1999). *Teacher education pipeline IV: Schools, colleges and departments of education enrollments by race and ethnicity.* Washington, DC: Author.

Beady, C., & Hansell, S. (1981). Teacher race and expectations for student achievement. *American Educational Research Journal, 18*(2), 191–206.

Brown v. Board of Educ., 347 U.S. 483 (1954).

Gordon, J. (2000). *The color of teaching.* New York: Routledge-Farmer.

Hawkins, B. (1994). Casualties: Losses among black educators were high after *Brown. Black Issues in Higher Education, 10*(23), 26–31.

Howard, T. C. (2001). Telling their side of the story: African-American students' perceptions of culturally relevant teaching. *The Urban Review, 33*(2), 131–149.

Irvine, J. J. (2003). *Educating teachers for diversity: Seeing with a cultural eye.* New York: Teachers College Press.

Kunjufu, J. (2002). *Black students: Middle class teachers.* Chicago: Black Images.

Ladson-Billings, G. (1994). *The Dreamkeepers: Successful teachers of Black children.* San Francisco: Jossey-Bass.

Landsman, J. (2001). *A white teacher's perspective on race in the classroom.* Minneapolis: University of Minnesota Law School, The Institute on Race & Poverty.

Lewis, C. (2006). African American male teachers in public schools: An examination of three urban school districts. *Teachers College Record, 108*(2), 224–245.

Merriam-Webster's collegiate dictionary (10th ed.). (1993). Springfield, MA: Merriam-Webster.

National Center for Education Statistics. (January 11, 2004). *Characteristics of school principals* [On-line]. Available: http://nces.ed.gov/programs/coe/2004/section4/table.asp?tableID=77

National Education Association. (2001). *The disappearing minority teacher.* Washington, DC: Authors.

Orfield, G., & Lee, C. (2004). *Brown at 50: King's dream or Plessy's nightmare?* Cambridge, MA: Harvard University, The Civil Rights Project.

Sims, P. (1997). *Awakening brilliance.* Atlanta: Bayhampton Publications.

Wilder, M. (2000). Increasing African-American teachers' presence in American schools: Voices of students who care. *Urban Education, 35*(2), 205–220.

QUESTIONS

1. This chapter provides several tips for principals and teachers. How can these "tips" be implemented throughout a school or school district?
2. What can educators learn from the voices of students in this chapter?

II

HOW CAN SERVICE-LEARNING INCREASE THE ACADEMIC ACHIEVEMENT OF URBAN AFRICAN AMERICAN STUDENTS?

Verna Cornelia Price

U rban schools all over the United States are asking for help in reaching and teaching African American students, particularly male students. For many African American students, school is not a place to learn or a pathway that can lead to a better quality of life. On the contrary, school has become a place where failure is a norm; where disengagement and dysfunctional behavior are expected; where being suspended is more common than getting homework; where you go to hang with your "homies"; where you have your own personal stage to display the latest rap/pop culture "gear" and attitudes, be it clothes, shoes, jewelry, technology, your vocabulary, or your sexuality. School for many urban youths has deteriorated into a combination of nonengaging academic activities interconnected with a series of negative interactions with teachers and administrators, whom they see as absolutely irrelevant to their "reality." African American students, particularly males, have high rates of suspensions and behavior referrals and low rates of high school graduation and college attendance (Smith, 2004). Large percentages of African American students drop out, and many of those who stay have developed a prison mentality of "doing my time" about school.

A study by the National Academy of Sciences found that in many urban high schools with large concentrations of students living in poverty and students of color, it is common for fewer than half of the ninth-graders who enter to leave with a high school diploma. Dropping out of school is the most visible indication of pervasive disengagement from the academic purpose and programs of these schools. Many of the students who do not drop out altogether attend irregularly, exert modest effort on schoolwork, and learn little (National Academy of Sciences, 2004). The increasing rate of dropout and low academic achievement is further complicated by the fact that many urban public schools lack the funding and resources needed to provide students with the information, skills, and guidance that will prepare them to pursue their dreams. This inequity, noted in a National Black Caucus of State Legislators's (2001) education report, has been harmful to the future of too many African American students, jeopardizing their chances of becoming productive and successful citizens and increasing their chances of ending up underemployed or incarcerated. It is therefore unacceptable and must end.

The academic condition of African American students, however, involves many other factors, such as the impact of teacher perceptions about, interactions with, and expectations of African American students (Simmons, 1996); the role of the media in its "glamorization of thug life" (Price, S., 2005) on student motivation to stay in school and achieve academically; the impact of politics on education; the undercurrent of institutional racism; the role or lack thereof of parental involvement; the role of African American communities; and the role of socioeconomics, specifically poverty, lack of adequate housing, unemployment, and lack of adequate health care. In other words, the whole picture that the low academic achievement of African American students paints is both complex and complicated.

So how can service-learning impact the academic achievement of African American students? Before answering this question, it is important to understand the definition of service-learning—how it relates to other educational reforms and initiatives; what the research says about its impact on student behavior, achievement, and motivation; and why you should integrate service-learning into your teaching approach and educational paradigm. In other words, what benefits does service-learning offer to all students and particularly African American students? This information is imperative because it builds the case for why service-learning, when effectively integrated, can provide educators with strategies and techniques that will not only academically engage African American students but also their parents and the local

African American community. This chapter offers a specific service-learning integration paradigm that combines the ideals of community development and social change as a unique approach to teaching African American students, particularly in urban schools. It concludes with a structured format for where to and how to start integrating a community development and social change service-learning model into your curriculum and pedagogy.

What Is Service-Learning?

In the last twenty years, service-learning has become one of the leading practices in educational reform and the restructuring of how we teach students to learn, lead, and serve. As an educational pedagogy, service-learning is defined as follows:[1]

1. Service-learning is a form of experiential learning in which students learn through hands-on service projects.

   Example: *Students study how different communities function and what it takes to have a healthy and productive community. They decide to interview local community members and small-business owners as a hands-on way to gather authentic research data that they will then use to write a report about the local community.*

2. Service-learning is integrated into the core curriculum so that students learn the "real-life" application of the academic curriculum.

   Example: *To study the local community, students study social studies, reading, English, technology, history, literature, geography, political science, and math.*

3. Service-learning utilizes higher-order, critical thinking skills where students use reflection to pose critical questions and to solve "real" problems.

   Example: *To study the local community, the teacher asks students to raise critical questions about why the community has a certain population, what the history of the community is, what the relationship between the local community and their school is, what the role of the local community in supporting state funding for their school is, and*

---

[1] Adapted from *The Service-Learning Integration Guide* (2004) by Dr. Verna Cornelia Price for the USA Network "Give Where You Live Project," a partnership between Topics in Education, HandsOnNetwork, and USA Network (www.usanetwork.com/givewhereyoulive).

how the community can help students feel accepted even though many are bused to the school.

4. Service-learning is about addressing authentic community needs. Students work with the community to identify its authentic needs and assets so that the service project is relevant and meaningful for all involved.

    Example: *Students develop a community survey that they use to interview local community members about the needs and assets of the community and how the community and school can become partners in helping the community, school, and students be more successful.*

5. Service-learning is designed to help students, teachers, and community members create partnerships through which their service can help solve the authentic community need.

    Example: *Students work with the local community to create a community garden located at the school as a way to create and build relationships with the community at large and specific community members and small-business owners.*

6. Service-learning is a proven paradigm and educational reform known for building character, leadership skills, and developmental assets in students.

    Example: *Students work with community members who are ethnically and culturally different from themselves to learn about the importance of respect, team building, and civility.*

In many ways, service-learning is unique because of how it interconnects and interfaces with the multidimensional aspects of school, youth, community, and society. Service-learning occurs within three broad paradigms:

1. As a "best practices" teaching pedagogy, service-learning
    * integrates a multiple intelligence approach to teaching and learning that helps students tap into their unique style of learning (Gardner, 1989)
    * utilizes cooperative teaching and learning techniques to help students create teams and learning partnerships in which they can be the teacher and the learner
    * integrates project-based learning to help students exercise voice, ownership, and leadership in choosing and completing specific projects
    * exercises experiential learning to help students not only read about

a specific topic or issue but immerse them in a hands-on experience with that topic

2. As a community development model, service-learning
   - creates a process for the community to look critically at the "real" issues and how to help solve them using youths as a resource
   - develops critical partnerships between the school and community to build productive relationships that are good for youths and adults
   - becomes a "change-agent" structure for community to begin asking the hard questions necessary to begin addressing the needs
   - provides opportunities for communities to identify their assets and get the resources necessary to address the identified needs

3. As a philosophy of social change, service-learning
   - is a philosophy of hope for creating positive social change so that the community becomes a place for youths and adults to live, lead, and learn
   - provides a new paradigm of youths as civic resources and productive citizens
   - offers an authentic partnership between the educational system and the community that can lead to the civic engagement of both youths and adults
   - demonstrates authentic reciprocity for all involved in the service-learning project and process
   - offers the community a vehicle for not only raising the hard questions but learning how to work together to create strategies for addressing and solving the authentic community needs

How Does Service-Learning Connect to Other Educational Reforms and Initiatives?

Service-learning is compatible with many school and educational reforms. A study by the American Youth Policy found that the principles and practices of service-learning were compatible to highly compatible with twenty-eight different educational reforms. The study concluded that "service-learning is a powerful tool for reaching both the academic and social objectives of education. It has the potential to reinvigorate the education reform movement by encouraging the creation of a caring community of students to improve the school's culture and positively impact our world" (Pearson, 2002, p. 11). However, there are four specific bodies of educational research of importance to the academic achievement of African American students involved in service-learning:[2]

1. *Developmental Assets Research*[3]: The Search Institute identified building blocks of development that help young people grow up healthy, caring, and responsible. This research found a correlation between number of assets and success in school and life. Service-learning is a proven assets builder for youths because it helps them develop a positive attitude about themselves and others; teaches them social competencies such as planning and decision making, interpersonal communication, cultural awareness, and conflict resolution; empowers and helps them build a positive identity; and strengthens their commitment to academic learning and creating change in their community. Service-learning creates a learning process in which African American students discover and build their assets through authentic connections with the local and broader community. It positively increases the teacher's and local community's perceptions about the role of student leadership in helping solve real community issues.

2. *Resiliency research:* This research is interesting because it measures a student's ability to bounce back from difficult circumstances and life situations—in other words, how a student succeeds against the odds. More than ever, youths have challenging experiences that threaten to keep them from succeeding in school and life. Service-learning supports resilience in students in the personal and social domain by giving youths opportunities to feel empowered, to demonstrate respect for self and others, to develop self-confidence, and to avoid risk behaviors (Billig, 2000; Laird & Black, 2002). Many African American students in urban settings are faced with complex situations that can decrease their self-confidence and motivation to succeed. African American students who participate in service-learning discover opportunities to demonstrate to themselves, their teachers, and their community that they are capable, talented, and intelligent people who can and will make a positive difference despite life's challenges.

---

[2] Adapted from *The Service-Learning Integration Guide* (2004) by Dr. Verna Cornelia Price for the USA Network "Give Where You Live Project," a partnership between Topics in Education, HandsOnNetwork, and USA Network (www.usanetwork.com/givewhereyoulive).

[3] Synopsis of a study by the Search Institute, Minneapolis, Minnesota. www.search-institute.org

3. *Multiple intelligence:* Service-learning is set apart from volunteering and community service because of the intentional learning embedded into the practice through connections to the curriculum and reflection. According to the multiple intelligence research, students can learn using eight types of intelligence (verbal, visual, logical, musical, interpersonal, intrapersonal, bodily, and naturalist) (Gardner, 1993). Service-learning, through its practice of reflection, affirms a student's intelligence but also promotes the practice of all intelligences. Students learn how to use their intelligence as they prepare for, complete, and learn from their service-learning experience. A multiple intelligence approach is critical because it provides opportunities for African American students to explore and utilize their unique learning and teaching styles. When students are given the opportunity to demonstrate learning using their unique intelligence, they begin to believe in themselves as learners while gaining a greater respect and trust for their teachers and the overall educational process. The end result is increased levels of academic engagement and greater internal motivation to achieve.

4. *Dropout prevention:* According to this body of research, success in school is directly related to dropout rates. In other words, a student who is successful in school both academically and socially is more likely to complete his or her formal K–12 education and vice versa. This is important, because, according to the research,[4] youths who are engaged in service-learning
   - Attend school more often.
   - Report that school is relevant and meaningful.
   - Are more likely to have a positive attitude toward school.
   - Are more likely to have a positive attitude toward teachers.
   - Are more engaged in academic learning.
   - Are more engaged in community activities.
   - Are less engaged in discipline problems.
   - Are more likely to increase academic achievement.
   - Are more likely to increase their grade point average (GPA).

The bottom line is that many African American students see school as irrelevant and meaningless to their present and future. Students must see the

---

[4] RMC Research Corporation, Brandeis University study and the UC Berkeley study in California (Billig, 2000).

importance and relevance of education from a whole new perspective. Service-learning motivates an authentic "need to know" in students in which they are given opportunities to apply the curriculum to "real-life" situations as a way to help solve authentic community needs. As more African American students experience the importance of having and applying knowledge, more students will begin to value the educational process and achieve academically.

Why Teachers Should Integrate Service-Learning Into Their Practice: The Benefits of Service-Learning to Students, Teachers, Schools, and the Community[5]

The following benefits of service-learning are based on research findings[6] and more than a decade of experience in the service-learning field:

Benefits to Students
- Students see learning as meaningful and relevant.
- School attendance increases.
- Confidence in academic abilities increases.
- Higher GPAs are achieved.
- Students become empowered to create change in their communities.
- New friendships that are cross-cultural are built.
- Students learn how to work with teams.
- Students become empowered to set goals.
- Students become resources and leaders in their community.
- Students become active citizens.

Benefits to Teachers
- Students are more motivated to learn.
- Students become self-directed learners.
- The level of completion of academic work increases.
- More students complete homework on time.
- Students exhibit less negative behavior.

---

[5] Adapted from *The Service-Learning Integration Guide* (2004) by Dr. Verna Cornelia Price for the USA Network "Give Where You Live Project," a partnership between Topics in Education, HandsOnNetwork, and USA Network (www.usanetwork.com/givewhereyoulive).

[6] Search Institute, Minneapolis, Minnesota; Brandeis University Study and the UC Berkeley Study in California, RMC Research Corporation; National Youth Leadership Council Diversity/Equity Project.

- Students exhibit more positive behavior.
- More students become academically engaged.
- Student attendance increases.
- The sense of community within the classroom increases.
- Students see learning as relevant.
- Parents and community members become more involved.
- More resources from the community become available.
- Collegiality with other teachers increases.

Benefits to Schools
- The local community is more involved.
- Teachers are more motivated to teach.
- Students are more motivated to learn.
- School pride and sense of community increase.
- Students exhibit less negative behavior.
- Students exhibit more positive behavior.
- Student academic achievement increases overall.
- Taxpayer support from the local community increases.

Benefits to the Community
- Students become active and positive citizens.
- Positive relationships are built with the school.
- Students become resources to the community.
- Student civic engagement increases.
- Students exhibit less negative behavior in the community.
- Students exhibit more positive behavior in the community.
- Student achievement increases.
- Public relations for the community increases.
- Community members become meaningfully involved in the school.
- Students address authentic needs.
- Authentic partnerships are created with the school.
- The community becomes a resource to the school.

How Can Integrating an Approach to Service-learning of Community Development for a Positive Social Change into Urban Public Education Improve the Academic Success of African American Students?

Traditionally, K–12 education has mostly utilized service-learning as a pedagogy to enhance the curriculum. However, in urban public schools where large percentages of students are African American, service-learning must transcend pedagogy to become a catalyst for urban community development that results in positive social change. The integration of an approach to community development and positive social change must take into consideration a number of factors related to African American culture and the impact of race and racism on urban communities.

First, African American students typically come from communities where family is very important. Therefore, when positive community development occurs, it provides an additional support base for the family structure. Families now have greater access to jobs, health care, child care, positive community role models, economic networks, and educational resources. The "community school" movement in education has created a process whereby many urban public schools are attended by students from the immediate community. The reality of this structural change in urban schools is what appears to be segregated schools: in some schools up to 95 percent of the student population consists of African Americans and/or a combination of African Americans and Latinos. A community development service-learning model redefines how school takes place and who is responsible for student achievement. This model puts both the community and the school in a significant position to impact student achievement. In addition, this model creates an academic structure that allows African American students to begin to see themselves as positive change agents in their community (Dittman, 2004).

Second, most African American students are leadership motivated. What does that mean? African American students are naturally attracted to people whom they see as dynamic leaders. They also gravitate toward learning processes that place them in leadership positions and/or allow them to be recognized for their leadership skills and talents. This leadership factor combined with a need for a sense of community is a core factor that contributes to the increased involvement of African American students in gang organizations and activities (Burnett & Walz, 2000). Service-learning provides students with other examples of community members and other students who are role models and leaders, thereby giving students positive leadership role models to admire and follow, rather than negative leaders such as street gangs.

Third, most, if not all, African American students have experienced some form of subtle discrimination or blatant racism that made them feel unworthy and powerless. Unfortunately, racial discrimination is built into the very fiber of our social and political structures and schools. Service-learning from a community development social change paradigm provides African American students with a safe and supportive process for addressing difficult and often very political issues around race, class, power, and privilege (West, 2001).

Fourth, schools cannot increase the academic achievement of African American students without the significant involvement of all aspects of the African American community, whether it is parents or faith-based, grassroots, government, corporate, or civic organizations. The reality is that many schools and teachers are "burnt out" trying to "eliminate" the achievement gap, and they cannot do this work alone. As the academic achievement gap between African American and White students continues to widen, African American communities must become more determined and committed to working with the existing educational structures to improve the academic achievement of their youths. The research of Kretzmann and McKnight (1993) demonstrated that authentic partnerships is a key strategy. These researchers concluded that effective and productive community building is asset based, internally focused, and relationship driven. They state,

> Many community planning efforts achieve limited results because only the recognized, visible leaders of the community are invited to participate. One result is that since the full range of local problem-solving potential is not at the table, the planning leaders constantly pulled toward a dependence upon only external resources. An alternative approach attempts not only to make the planning process as open and participatory as possible, but also to pay particular attention to including people as representatives of community assets. Thus an expanded community planning table would include many participants not normally thought of as community leaders. These participants would each, in a sense, be bringing the assets of his/her own group to the table as part of the larger community problem solving capacity. (p. 352)

Therefore, when school administrators, teachers, and especially the African American students join the community development "table" and form authentic and reciprocal partnerships with local community members and organizations, the entire community can help create and implement a strategic plan for increasing the academic success of its African American students.

How to Begin Integrating an Approach to Service-learning for Community Development and Positive Social Change

The following are specific steps with examples from actual projects and strategies for beginning the process of creating a community development for positive social change service-learning project.

Step 1: Learn More about Service-Learning

As indicated earlier, service-learning is a sound and proven pedagogy that when integrated into the curriculum leads to increased academic outcomes for students. The first step in the process, then, is to begin by learning about the essential elements of service-learning: research and best practices. (See Appendix A for a list of service-learning resources.) (Price, V. C., 2004).

> **Example:** A high school planning to integrate service-learning into its curriculum hosts a daylong service-learning training session in which the teachers participate in a simulated service-learning exercise that immerses them in both the research and the actual "doing" of a service-learning project.

Step 2: Begin with the Students

Service-learning must begin with the student. Typically, students know their community much better than teachers. Ask your students about their community. What do they see as the assets or the things they like? What do they see as the needs or the things they do not like or wish to change? Whom do they know in the community who is making positive things happen? Assign your students to do further research on their community, such as analyzing stories in the local newspaper, or interviewing community members and conducting a survey asking family and friends about the community's assets, needs, and resources. Work with students to analyze their results and identify these assets, needs, and community resources.

> **Example:** A sixth- to eighth-grade English language learners (ELL) class whose school is experiencing a rapid increase in immigrant Spanish-speaking students decides to work with local community organizations to design a "Welcome Kit" for the new families. The students' goal is to decrease some of the discriminatory and racist attitudes existing in the community about the families and to help the families have a sense of belonging and community in their new neighborhoods.

Step 3: Work with the Local Community

Ask students to invite at least one community organization or member to be partners with them in helping them discuss their research, inform their research, and decide on a particular need. This will begin the community development model component of your service-learning project. Challenge yourself, students, and community members to ask the difficult questions about why certain needs exist in the community and how students becoming a resource to the community can help address those difficult issues. Also invite other members of the community to join you in that conversation. As a partnership (teacher, student, community members), create an authentic assessment strategy to "test" student achievement and project outcomes. Also as a partnership, follow the entire service-learning process of planning, performing, assessing, and celebrating the project outcomes and completion. (See Appendix B for additional strategies on how to form authentic community partnerships.)

> **Example:** In the process of researching, designing, and creating the "Welcome Kit" (see the previous example), the ELL students build relationships and partnerships with the local community, including the media. This project creates greater community pride and spirit between the school and the community. In the process, the ELL students become authentic community developers who learn how to address the issue of racism in a meaningful and productive way.

Step 4: Develop the Curriculum

Focus on one subject or curriculum area that you are required to teach students. Discuss with your students and the community partner the core academic outcomes for that particular subject matter. For example, if you teach math, a curriculum objective might be understanding fractions. Ask your students how they could learn about the subject matter and achieve the academic goal by working with the community to address and help solve the identified community need. Incorporate your subject matter into every possible aspect of the plan to help solve the need. Work with your community partner to provide ideas on how to incorporate "real-life" experiences into every level of the project. As a partnership (teacher, student, community members), create the goals, objectives, and community and student learning outcomes for the project (Figure 11.1).

> **Example:** ELL students and their teacher work with community partners to decide on learning outcomes for the students who are also first-generation Spanish speakers learning English as a second language. Community partners help design the learning outcomes and become guest speakers in the ELL class. Students have to learn how to communicate with community partners in English and in the process teach the community partners Spanish. The project helps the ELL students become proficient English speakers while community partners gain insight

FIGURE 11.1
Key Audiences Impacted by Community Development
for Positive Social Change Service

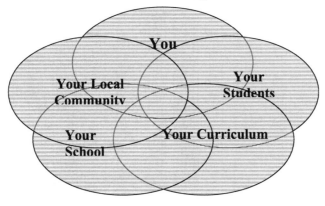

into what it means to be in an educational system in which only English is spoken.

Now What? Integrating an Approach to Service-Learning for Community Development and Positive Social Change as a Strategy for Increasing Academic Achievement

Community development and social change is an innovative service-learning approach that can increase the academic achievement of African American students. The following is an example of a service-learning project in an urban public school with a large percentage of African American students that is based in a pedagogy model but has incorporated some aspects of community development and social change (National Youth Leadership Council, 2004). To help you better understand how service-learning can help increase the academic achievement of African American students, an additional component to the approach to service-learning for community development and positive social change has been added.

Philadelphia Public Schools—Got Work? Philadelphia Middle School Students Help Homeless Meet Challenge

When Grover Washington Jr. Middle School's "learning support" class of eighth-graders began working with Need In Deed, a Philadelphia-based nonprofit committed to preparing youths for civic responsibility and service to others, to identify a service-learning project, the students chose the issue of homelessness because many of them saw it as a "real" need in their community. The project gained momentum after the students read an article about a local organization, Ready, Willing and Able (RWA), that helps men achieve stability and sufficiency as they overcome homelessness, welfare, dependency, incarceration, and substance abuse. Graduates of RWA visited the students' classroom and shared their personal stories about being homeless. Students also visited the RWA facility to learn more about the plight of homelessness and find out more about how they could help. As the students learned more about homelessness, they began to understand that unemployment is one of the greatest challenges for homeless people. Thus, for their service-learning project, the students decided to support the homeless men in their quest for jobs by talking with local businesses about potential job opportunities for which RWA men could apply. With the guidance of their teacher and their Need In Deed facilitator, the students prepared a "pitch" for the local businesses. The Need In Deed facilitator said that at first "the students were nervous and shy. This really took them out of their comfort zone. But soon the students felt so empowered and encouraged that they convinced their teacher to allow them to approach more employers." The project helped the teacher achieve many academic goals such as using formal communication skills; reading critically in content areas; implementing math standards around inferences, probability, and predictions; and meeting social studies objectives that centered on citizenship and community building. Though those involved cannot say for sure that the students' project led to specific jobs, the impact at RWA was evident by this comment from one of the RWA graduates: "To have these kids campaigning for men who are trying to turn their lives around, that really touches my heart. They are giving us all hope." (p. 13)

How to Integrate the Community Development and Social Change Model into the Example Service-Learning Project

The questions in this section offer a structure to begin integrating an approach to service-learning for community development and positive social change into your curriculum and your interactions with African American students. You must realize, however, that this is an approach that will take time, planning, and an element of courage. Why? Because as educators we cannot do this work alone, and the notion of community development takes us beyond the school and classroom walls into communities where we may not feel comfortable or wanted. Nevertheless, this approach promises to rapidly engage African American students while motivating them to greater levels of academic achievement. The bottom line, however, is that when an approach to service-learning for community development and positive social change is integrated, African Americans—all students for that matter—will begin to see themselves as true learners, change agents, and responsible citizens who understand "how" to create positive change in their communities.

1. Is there a process for community and students to look critically at the "real" issues?
   - The class and local community organizations could create a formal partnership to address the issue. This partnership could become a vehicle for inviting local community members, lawmakers, and community organizations to the table to discuss the root cause associated with homelessness while creating "doable" solutions for preparing and placing the homeless in stable positions of employment.
2. Is there an agreed-upon process of how youths can become a resource for helping the community create "real" change around the issue?
   - The eighth-graders along with the teacher could clearly present their learning objectives and curriculum goals to their community partners and ask them for ideas on how they could accomplish those goals. This would provide the community with an avenue to become "real-life teachers" to the students. It would also give the community a better idea of what it takes to educate today's youth. The youths would also begin to see themselves as productive, contributing citizens and members of the community.
3. How can the partnerships between the school and community build productive relationships that are good for youths and adults?
   - Infuse reciprocity throughout the process by providing opportunities for both the youths and community members to learn from each other and learn about each other.
   - Involve everyone in the process of teaching and learning, including the homeless individuals. Remember that regardless of a person's current situation, he or she can still teach lessons learned from his or her life's experiences.
   - Create clear boundaries and expectations for interactions between the community members and youths. This can be as simple as making sure that students work in pairs to conduct interviews with

community members and are well prepared with questions, and reviewing interviewing skills prior to the interviews.

4. How can students become change agents for their community?
   - Provide students with opportunities to research the "state of their community" using a variety of resources including community interviews, newspapers, local legislations, and releases from press conferences with local law officials.
   - Empower students to ask the difficult questions about themselves, the educational process, and the community, which is necessary to begin addressing needs.

5. Have the community and youths sufficiently identified the community assets and discussed the necessary actions to address the identified needs productively and successfully?
   - Ask students to arrange and facilitate a community meeting so that members from the businesses, grassroots community organizations, organizations specifically dedicated to assisting the homeless, lawmakers, parents, teachers, and schools can discuss the community assets available to address the issue of homelessness in the community.
   - Ask the community members to brainstorm possible strategies for helping the homeless that youths can implement.

6. Is a philosophy of hope for creating positive social change in which the community becomes a place for youths and adults to live, lead, and learn built into the service-learning process?
   - Ensure that community members feel they are being heard.
   - Ensure that the students feel they are being heard.
   - Treat the population being served with honor, dignity, and respect by inviting them to be an integral part of the solution to the identified need.
   - Ensure that the service-learning project and process are based on reciprocity for all involved. In other words, be sure that everyone feels they are important teachers and learners in the process.

7. Has the authentic partnership among the school, students, teachers, and the community produced measurable results and outcomes for the students and the community?
   - Provide "real" solutions to the identified need.
     Implement "real" solutions provided by the students and the community.

- Give students an opportunity to be civic resources and productive citizens in their community.

Appendix A: Service-Learning Resources[7]

Publications

- Billig, Shelley H. "Research on K–12 School-Based Service-Learning: The Evidence Builds." *Phi Delta Kappan*, May 2000.
- Born, Patricia. *Ethics and Service: A Values Based Approach to Community Service-learning.* Camden, ME: Institute for Global Ethics, 1999.
- Education Commission of the States. *Learning That Lasts: How Service-Learning Can Become an Integral Part of Schools, States, and Communities.* Denver: Education Commission of the States, 2002. www.ecs.org/clearinghouse/40/54/4054.pdf.
- Kaye, Cathryn Berger. *The Complete Guide to Service-Learning: Proven, Practical Ways to Engage Students in Civic Responsibility, Academic Curriculum, and Social Action.* Minneapolis: Free Spirit, 2004.
- Kielsmeier, James C. "To Be of Service: The Grassroots Initiative of Service-Learning in the United States." *ZipLine* (Fall 1998).
- Kielsmeier, James C., and Carole Klopp. "Service-Learning: Positive Youth Development in the Classroom and Community." *Community Youth Development Journal* (2002).
- Master Teacher. *Lesson Plans for Service-learning.* Manhattan, KS: Master Teacher, 1999.
- National Commission on Service-Learning. *Learning In Deed: The Power of Service-Learning for American Schools.* Newton, MA: National Commission on Service-Learning, 2002. www.learningindeed .org.
- National Service-Learning Clearinghouse. *Impacts and Outcomes of Service-Learning: K–12 Selected Resources.* Scotts Valley, CA: Author, 2004
- Service-learning 2000 Center (1994). *Learning through Service: Ideas*

---

[7] Adapted from *The Service-Learning Integration Guide* (2004) by Dr. Verna Cornelia Price for the USA Network "Give Where You Live Project," a partnership between Topics in Education, HandsOnNetwork, and USA Network (www.usanetwork.com/givewhereyou live).

from the Field. Palo Alto, CA: Youth Service California. (www.yscal.org).

- *The Service-Learning Integration Guide* by Dr. Verna Cornelia Price for the USA Network "Give Where You Live Project," a partnership among Topics in Education, HandsOnNetwork, and USA Network, 2004. Download free from www.usanetwork.com/givewhereyoulive
- Toole, Pamela, Ed. *Essential Elements of Service-Learning.* St. Paul, MN: National Youth Leadership Council Publication, 1999.
- Wade, Rahima C. *Community Service-learning: A Guide to Including Service in the Public School Curriculum.* Ithaca: State University of New York Press, 1997.
- Winings, Kathy. *Building Character through Service-learning.* Chapel Hill, NC: Character Development Group, 2002.
- Witmer, Judith T., and Carolyn S. Anderson. *How to Establish a High School Service-learning Program.* Alexandria, VA: Association for Supervision and Curriculum Development, 1994.

National Service-Learning Organizations and Other Educational Networks

Academy for Educational Development: www.aed.org
American Youth Policy Forum: www.aypf.org
America's Promise—The Alliance for Youth: www.americaspromise.org
Corporation for National & Community Service: www.cns.gov
Hands On Network: www.handsonnetwork.org
Innovation Center for Community and Youth Development: www.the innovationcenter.org
The Institute for Community Research—Youth Action Research Institute: www.incommunityresearch.org/research/yari.htm

National Council of Nonprofit Associations: www.ncna.org
National Service-Learning Clearinghouse: www.servicelearning.org
National Service-Learning Partnership: www.service-learningpartnership.org
National Youth Development Information Center—A Project of the National Collaboration for Youth: www.nydic.org
National Youth Leadership Council: www.nylc.org
YouthActionNet: www.youthactionnet.org
Youth Leadership Institute: www.yli.org
Youth Service America: www.ysa.org

Appendix B: Tips for Forming Authentic and Reciprocal Partnerships with the Local Community

1. Ask the community what it needs. According to a well-known community developer, John Perkins (1995), "A fundamental premise in community development is affirming the dignity of people by motivating them to take responsibility for their own lives. Beginning with community's felt needs establishes relationship and trust, which then enables us to move to deeper issues of development" (pp. 17–18). The community must be honored first by being asked about its needs and assets versus having assumptions made about it.
2. Ask the community how you and your students can help.
3. Invite community members into your classroom(s) and visit them out in the community. Ask them to teach you and your students about their culture, norms, values, assets, traditions, and history. Ask students who live in the local community to voice their perspectives.
4. Discuss with the community members who you are, what your learning objectives are for your students, and what your students wish to learn, and ask how you and your students can work with them to help solve a given community need or help strengthen a community asset.
5. Respect and value what community members have to say and the work they have already done to better their community.
6. Express your thanks for the opportunity to work alongside the community through conversations, written notes, and strategic recognition of your partnership, such as in newsletters, at local board meetings, and at school assemblies.
7. Encourage your students and community members to see the mutuality and reciprocity of giving and learning, which is a critical component in creating successful and productive community partnership.

References

Billig, S. H. (2000). Research on K–12 school-based service-learning: The evidence builds. *Phi Delta Kappa, 81*(9), 658–664.

Burnett, G., & Walz, G. (2000). *Gangs in the schools*. ERIC Digest 99. ERIC Clearinghouse on Urban Education, New York/ERIC Clearinghouse on Counseling and Student Services, Greensboro, NC (www.ericdigests.org/1995-1/gangs.htm).

Dittman, M. (2004, September). Fifty years later: Desegregating urban schools. *APA Online, 35*(8).

Gardner, H. (1993). *Multiple intelligences: The theory in practice*. New York: Basic Books.

Gardner, H., & Hatch, T. (1989), Multiple intelligences go to school: Educational implications of the theory of multiple intelligences. *Educational Researcher, 18*(8), 4–9

Kretzmann, J., & McKnight, J. L. (1993). *Building communities from the inside out: A path toward finding and mobilizing a community's assets.* Chicago: ACTA Publications.

Laird, M., & Black, S. (2002). *Service-learning evaluation project: Program effects for at-risk students.* Presentation, Second International Service-Learning Research Conference: Nashville, TN.

National Academy Press (2004). *Engaging schools: Fostering high school students' motivation to learn.* Washington, DC: Author.

National Black Caucus of State Legislators. (2001). *Closing the achievement gap: Improving educational outcomes for African American children.* Washington, DC: Author.

Pearson, S. S. (2002). *Finding common ground: Service-learning and education reform.* Paper presented at the American Youth Policy Forum Sponsored by W. K. Kellogg Foundation, Washington, DC.

Perkins, J. M. (Ed.). (1995). *Restoring at-risk communities: Doing it together and doing it right.* Grand Rapids, MI: Baker Books.

Price, S., & Price, V. (in press). *The glamorization of thug life.* Minneapolis, MN: JCAMA Publishers.

Price, V. C. (2004). *The service-learning integration guide.* Commissioned for the USA Network "Give Where You Live Project," a partnership among Topics in Education, HandsOnNetwork, and USA Network (www.usanetwork.com/givewhereyoulive).

Rosen, E. (2005). Got work? Philadelphia middle school: Students help homeless meet challenge. *The Generator, 22*(4), 13.

Simmons, V. C. (1996). *The impact of classroom social systems on the academic achievement of African American students.* Unpublished doctoral dissertation, Minneapolis: University of Minnesota.

Smith, R. A. (2004, February 1). Saving Black boys. *The American Prospect Online, 15*(2), 20 paragraphs.

West, C. (2001). *Race matters.* Boston: Beacon.

QUESTIONS

1. Based on the four steps for integration of service-learning in a school, what necessary steps will be needed at your school to utilize this concept on a large-scale basis?

2. In what ways can service-learning as presented in this chapter improve school/community relations?

PART THREE

KNOWING WHO IS IN THE CLASSROOM: HOW WHITE TEACHERS CAN ENSURE ALL CHILDREN ACHIEVE

12

WHAT ARE YOU? ARE YOU INDIAN? ARE YOU CHINESE?

The Lifelong Journey of an Adopted Latina

Stephanie A. Flores-Koulish

As a little girl I frequently heard those questions. So much so that they have become burned into my memory. I am a Latina adoptee, raised by a White mother and Mexican American father. I was nurtured in the days of Charo, before Dora the Explorer, J-Lo, and Shakira made being Latina cool, or even distinctive. My skin color was different from my Black and White classmates; I had no "accent," and I did not speak Spanish. Such exotic characteristics made my fellow students wonder why my skin was neither pale like a Caucasian nor deep chocolate like my African American classmates. My hair too was blacker than my White classmates' hair and straighter than my Black classmates' hair.

During the early 1970s in working-class Prince George's County, Maryland, I was a walking and talking paradox, and my mere existence begged the implicit and explicit questioning of both classmates and teachers. This feeling of not fitting in at school compounded my internal identity struggles, having been removed from my family of origin as a baby and placed in a "foreign" space I had to accept as my own.

Now, I am a Ph.D. Latina, Colombian-American who has very little command of the Spanish language, and most of my social circle consists of academics, many who are White. Though I have attained a level of success that is far from my humble beginnings (I have crossed the class hurdle), I continue to struggle with my identity. And so I share my story here in an attempt to sensitize teachers to the complex identity plight of adopted people, especially those in transcultural[1] families. And more specifically, I hope to show how my own example illustrates a part of the rich tapestry of Latino/a culture in the United States.

From what I have uncovered, my Colombian birth mother was among the first in the new wave of immigrants to the United States following the 1965 Immigration Act, which was also the year I was conceived. I've been told that she came alone to work for the diplomatic corps as a domestic in Washington D.C. according to the adoption agency's non-identifying records. My father was also a Colombian living in Washington D.C. That is about the extent of my knowledge of the two people who created me. Colombian, however, is what I am. But growing up I did not have many opportunities to know what that meant.

During my years in public and Catholic schools in Prince George's County, I began a lifelong quest to understand and accept my own identity. I could not answer the questions: "What am I?" "Who am I?" I knew I was Colombian by birth, but I didn't "feel" it. I didn't know what it meant to be Colombian. I did not know any other Colombians until a mysterious neighbor moved down the street when I was 14. I kept the leather change purse that she gave me, embossed with "Colombia" in cursive, the one time she and I spoke. I cherished this token of my bloodline, but continued to accept my ethnicity as a mix of Mexican, like my adopted dad, and Irish/ English, like my adopted mom.

Ever the alien, all I could do at the time was yearn to connect with something I was not, and so I was attracted to new cultures through books, television, and the rare student who would come to my school from a "different" land. I was a pop culture addict who embraced the other on television.

In fact, I gravitated toward differences like a magnet to metal. For example, I have clear memories of drinking tea with milk for the first time with my school friend Marilyn. Her family was from India, but had most recently lived in Guyana. Consuelo moved in to the house behind ours and we became friends, my first Latina friend. I found out later that she was from the first wave of refugees from El Salvador around 1980. And the girls' church group I belonged to provided me with the opportunity to explore world cultures through our studies of missionaries who were spreading imperial messages of Christianity throughout the developing world. I also became enamored with Australia after a few popular culture icons from there influenced me. I wrote to the Australian Embassy in Washington D.C. to ask for any literature they could send me on their country, and I studied my television heroes so that I could pick up and replicate their particular accent. I knew I was different. I knew I was strange. And I craved connections with others, like myself, who were on the outside of mainstream society. Harnessing my school-aged curiosity and channeling it toward self-discovery could have helped me develop a healthy Latina identity.

The second part of this chapter aims to offer some suggestions for teachers. First, when teachers consider the complexities of adopted children, in this case specifically transculturally adopted Latino/as, they gain new tools for appreciating the distinctiveness of the Latino community's rich ethnic tapestry and complex struggles. They also gain the facility to deal with children from diverse family backgrounds. As this book attests, peoples of color share great diversity and a common struggle against racist forces in the United States. A population that is frequently overlooked in "multicultural" literature is adoptees. As a member of this tribe, I intend to provide a voice that reminds teachers that our story might help them understand the larger collective quest for dignity and equity in a new way.

First, it is important to acknowledge the broad differences within the Latino/a community. Because of my fragmented life, my own story helps provide a case study in such diversity to counter the mythic monolith. Further, racism has impacted the Latino community, whether an adoptee or a native Spanish speaker visiting our country. Currently, in fact, the state of Arizona has passed a new law[2] that can stop anyone resembling me to question his or her legal status in the United States. I realize that I am far from what the authorities want, yet I share a visage with those labeled "alien" or "criminal." It is important for teachers to realize the impact that negative media has on their own views of their Latino students, and their students' sense of themselves. Often, this awareness is subconscious, drilled into our thinking by repeated broadcasts of racist claims. Therefore, it is imperative for all of us to interrogate the messages presented to us by the media so that we might be able to avoid the pitfalls associated with the many negative stereotypes presented. These stereotypes affect all Latinos, whether immigrant, adopted, or naturalized.

Beyond the impact of the media and popular culture on my identity, being adopted into a White/Mexican American working-class family had its own set of identity complications. Before entering into the specifics of transcultural adoption, it is important for teachers to understand what it means to be adopted. As a result of litigious secrecy, the origins of my own existence remain out of my permissible grasp. I am not allowed to obtain my original birth certificate. I am not allowed to know the names of my Colombian birth parents. I have been denied a basic human right afforded to all other non-adopted individuals in our country. That shroud of secrecy can easily create internal angst.

What could have been remains at the level of the imaginary, forever. As an adopted person with vague genealogical awareness, I have had to carve out my identity from the environment at my disposal. I have always known that I was adopted. My parents told me that "I was special" because they chose me, while other families "got stuck" with their children. But what lay dormant beneath this fairytale was that they were able to choose me because someone else, my biological mother, rejected me. In order never to be rejected again, I often fell into an obedient role, especially at school.

Being an adoptee in a transcultural family compounded my confusion.

> I feel I am a captive
> Aboard the refugee ship.
> The ship that will never dock.
> El barco que nunca atraca.
> —Cervantes (1981)

The stanza from Lorna Dee Cervantes' poem, "Refugee Ship," describes the sense of alienation one feels after looking at their reflection in the mirror. Later in the poem, Cervantes uses the word "orphaned" from her Spanish name. I am the protagonist in this poem. The visage in the mirror, my presentation to others, is Latina. With that image comes expectations and assumptions about who I am. I belie those assumptions. As a transcultural adoptee, the emptiness I have felt inside is distanced from my facade, like the drifting ship Cervantes describes.

As I explained earlier, I grew up in a mixed race, White and Black, working class and poor, community. This environment made it difficult for me to begin the journey of self-discovery. As Middleton, Coleman, and Lewis (2006) found in this volume:

> [W]e see African American youth raised in predominately White settings as "at risk" as they experience isolation, identity issues, categorization, and a lack of community and family connectedness. We see these experiences occurring in African American families and in White families with adopted children of color. (p. 168)

In many ways, I too was at risk. Yet, I was also such a "good girl" no school authorities ever raised suspicions about me being at risk. I was well-behaved and an above average student until I reached adolescence. I continued to be well-behaved in school, but my grades slipped to an average level that I felt internally met my potential. At the same time, around age 12, I started drinking alcohol after school, and pushed those limits for the remainder of my adolescence and through my 20s. In hindsight, I was probably experiencing immense grief and turmoil associated with my challenging identity quest. I no longer wanted to handle being asked what I was when I had no idea myself.

In their study *Beyond Culture Camp: Promoting Healthy Identity Formation in Adoption*, (2009) the Donaldson Institute documents their research of insensitivities that occur to transracially/transculturally adopted children across ethnic and racial lines. For example, they found that 39 percent of Korean adult adoptees[3] reported experiencing racial discrimination as children from their teachers. Regrettably, it is still relevant to infer that similar discrimination can occur to Latino/a adoptees. What is it then that teachers can do to ensure that they are combating exclusion and promoting inclusion?

For Latino/as, regardless of their generational or adoptive status, or language abilities, educational success should be imperative. For teachers to promote educational achievement for Latino/as, they need to become aware of the vast realities facing this population and teach in complex, culturally responsive ways, avoiding a monolithic "Hispanic" culture. Hence, they must become socially engaged teachers. To become such an educator, notions of educational success and learning must be broadened beyond contemporary understandings (e.g., test scores). Books like this one should be frequent reads, so that educators internalize White privilege alongside Brown potential. Therefore, it must be thought of as pragmatic for teachers to "go off script," to question why the script says what it does, for what purpose, to what ends. This practice of inquiry ties together the joint realities of Latino/as and adoptees. That is, critical inquiry contributes to self-understanding, or the integration of emotional and intellectual knowing. We feel empowered by acknowledging how our systems, whether of curriculum or adoption policies, can be corrupt, can be wrong, and/or can be disconnected from the realities of the human existence. I think that if teachers had taught me in this way during my adolescence, I would have felt empowered given my own internal struggles for justice, and thus achieved a better sense of peace overall.

Like Gorski (2006, p. 75), I endeavor to politicize multicultural education, starting with a list of questions and suggestions related to teaching students who are adopted.

1. To what extent do you ask who a student looks most like in his/her family? Even if the question is asked of a non-adoptee, adoptees hear this question and it leads them to an uncomfortable place. Furthermore, be sensitive in high school genetics lessons and try to balance nature with nurture.

2. Why ask students where they are from, especially when it is removed from context? Asking where a student is from can be problematic because s/he may not know precisely.

3. Do you ask your students to complete family trees? As an alternative, assign a "family story" after describing "family" broadly. This way, adoptees can choose to include elements of their biological heritage, to the extent that they know about it, and their adopted family's heritage. Additionally, a family story provides spaces for students to include their school family, their family of friends, etc.

4. Do you discuss genealogy? For older students, acknowledging rights in terms of one's identity, or lack thereof, can be empowering. Links can be made with African Americans who are often unable to trace their genealogy due to slavery, and as well with some children conceived through Assisted Reproductive Technologies. The parallels of how one's history has been erased by human-made structures can create solidarity.

5. To what extent does your classroom library include relevant literature for adoptees and/or alternative families? Read picture books featuring adoption or simply have them available as classroom resources (see Supplemental Readings list below).

Supplemental Readings and Websites

Selected Children's Literature on Adoption

Three Names of Me by Mary Cummings and Lin Wang
The Day We Met You by Phoebe Koehler
Brown Like Me by Noelle Lamperti
Did My First Mother Love Me by Kathryn M. Miller
We Belong Together: A Book about Adoption by Todd Parr
A Day, A Dog by Gabrielle Vincent
Why Can't You Look Like Me? by Ola Zuri and Jenn Simpson

Websites/Blogs About Adoption and Transracial Adoption

http://www.pactadopt.org/ (includes an excellent expanded list to previous)

http://johnraible.wordpress.com/

http://www.adoptioninitiative.org/

http://www.americanadoptioncongress.org/

http://www.adoptioninstitute.org/index.php

http://www.nancyverrier.com/

References

Evan B. Donaldson Adoption Institute. (2009). *Beyond culture camp: Promoting healthy identity formation in adoption.* New York, NY: Author.

Gorski, P. (2006). The unintentional undermining of multicultural education: Educators at the equity crossroads. In J. Landsman & C. Lewis (Eds.), *White teachers/diverse classrooms: A guide to building inclusive schools, promoting high expectations, and eliminating racism* (1st ed., 61–78). Sterling, VA: Stylus.

Middletown, V., Coleman, K., & Lewis, C. (2006). Black/African American families: Coming of age in predominately White communities. In J. Landsman & C. Lewis (Eds.), *White teachers/diverse classrooms: A guide to building inclusive schools, promoting high expectations, and eliminating racism* (1st ed., 162–181). Sterling, VA: Stylus.

Endnotes

1. The Evan B. Donaldson Adoption Institute (2009) defines transracial adoption "as the adoption of a child of one race by one or two parents of a different race (domestic or international)." Transcultural "may be racially similar but ethnically different from the parents" (p. 3).

2. Governor Jan Brewer signed SB 1070 into law on April 23, 2010.

3. Their study focused on Korean adult adoptees given the availability and size of this population in the United States. They write, "1-in-10 of all Korean American citizens came to the United States through adoption" (p. 4).

QUESTIONS

1. In what ways do you engage with students as unique individuals? Do you assume anything about a student based on his or her appearance, be he or she White, Brown or Black? To what extent do your students teach you?

2. To do this work takes an effort to rethink what we have been taught from our earliest days. What are some experiences, moments, or anecdotes that have caused you to rethink, to go outside the script, as Flores-Koulish says we must do?

13

DARING TO TEACH

Challenging the Western Narrative of American Indians in the Classroom

Beverly J. Klug

Teaching for social justice includes creating equitable opportunities for learning and correcting Western narratives about underrepresented populations. It also means sharing educational power with those who know their students the best. The stereotypes created about American Indians throughout history have diminished our abilities to recognize Native cultures and American Indian students in terms of their uniqueness and strengths, especially when considering educational practices for Native children. We must learn to re-evaluate what we have learned about American Indians in order to offer education appropriate for all of our students. This chapter offers a brief history of education for American Indians, examples of stereotypes held by teachers and teacher candidates that can impede teaching and learning processes for Native students, covers key legislation focusing on American Indian education, and presents recommendations for culturally relevant pedagogy for Native students.

Teaching for social justice means that we must create opportunities for all children to learn in school, share power in education with diverse populations, and correct the predominant Western narratives that concern underrepresented populations. In terms of teaching American Indian[1] students, we

---

[1] The terms *American Indian, Native American, indigenous,* and *Native peoples/students* are used interchangeably of their future students.

are faced with a history of cultural misrepresentations by the dominant culture as well as a pedagogical system that refuses to recognize the strengths of indigenous students unless they have been assimilated to the dominant culture.

For those students who are raised traditionally or biculturally, negotiating the educational school system can be particularly challenging. Indeed, the current dropout rate for American Indian students who begin 9th grade is 49.3 percent (National Indian Education Association, n.d.). This figure does not include the many Native students who choose to leave school between 7th and 9th grades.

As a result of the injustices that have been perpetrated against indigenous peoples in the past, many American Indians are instinctively reluctant to trust teachers with their children. It is difficult for people with good intentions to face the suspicion of others. Because non-Native teachers are not familiar with what has happened in the past with Native peoples, they are put into positions where there may be cultural misunderstandings because they have only been exposed to the narrative of American Indians through the filter of the dominant culture. In addition, the majority of teacher education programs don't prepare candidates to work with the diversity of backgrounds. This unpreparedness sets in motion a process where not understanding differences can mean lowering expectations for Native students and treating them in ways that will lessen their abilities to be successful in schools.

An example of this comes from one of my early experiences of having my teacher candidates present stories to children in a public school located on a reservation. After their experience, many of the candidates felt defeated because the students did not "act enthusiastic" about listening to the stories and participating in the follow-up activities provided. What I realized is that my teacher candidates were relying on the type of feedback that they received when they presented their stories to other audiences; namely, they were looking for facial and body language that would tell them the children enjoyed being a part of these presentations. Because these children were primarily being raised in a traditional Native American culture, they knew that the most important thing for them to do was to listen so that they could remember the story and be able to tell it to others. The children were not smiling and laughing during the presentations, but listening very hard, so their facial expressions did not give the teacher candidates clues that they were attending to the stories. The end result was that the teacher candidates were frustrated and felt they had failed, while the children did not understand why the people telling the stories would be "mad" at them. Clearly, it was time to look at what was really happening and draw the teacher candidates into the circle of cultural understandings.

Even though most of the candidates had grown up in the region where the reservation was located, they had absorbed the stereotypes—all of them negative—about American Indians that abound in border communities. As students going through their own K–12 educations, most had never had an American Indian peer. They had not attended events held on the reservation, such as the yearly summer powwow and festival, and if athletes, had only played Native students on their own school turfs. Therefore, the candidates had no real knowledge of their neighbors. They did not understand that the children's aboriginal language was an oral language that had not been written down until recently. People who grow up in oral communities are taught to rely on their memories for retaining important information, and this was exactly what the children were doing during the story presentations. Proof that the children found the stories worthwhile was that they were retelling the stories to each other with a high degree of detail and accuracy. Once the candidates recognized this, their perceptions of the Native students changed dramatically.

Understanding That We All Have Cultures

One of the misperceptions that many Euro-American people carry is that they have no culture, they are "American," and therefore everyone should be the same. We need to discuss the importance of culture in shaping us as human beings and explore our own "cultural remnants." In other words, what celebrations do we have and why do we have them; in what ways do children interact with adults; what types of foods do we eat that are different from others; what non-English languages or words were spoken in our homes reflecting the heritage of our ancestors? Because of the two World Wars, there was an active campaign to make everyone "American" since in many cases war was being waged against our own relatives. Those of European and other ancestries were supposed to forget their heritages and become part of the American "melting pot." In addition, people of Japanese ancestry, as well as some of German and Italian ancestry, were interned in camps in the United States during World War II. This resulted in denial that "Americans" were the product of different cultures. Once Americans realize that we are products of different cultures, it becomes easier for people to understand why it is important to acknowledge the cultures of others and that it is alright for us to think differently and do things in different ways.

That said, it is also important for non-Native teachers to learn about indigenous peoples' past, especially in terms of education, so that we can understand why there may be reticence on the part of American Indians to fully embrace "White man's education." As teachers, we need to open our hearts and minds to learn about the best practices for teaching Native students, expecting them to work to their highest potentials through ensuring that what and how we teach are meaningful for them.

The Influence of Language in Shaping Views of "The Other"

Josephy (1991) estimated that there were approximately 7 million people speaking over 2,200 different languages inhabiting Alaska, Canada, and the 48 contiguous United States; others put the numbers between 9 and 100 million (Stiffarm & Lane, 1992; Wax, 1971). Since the time of Christopher Columbus' "discovery" of the New World in 1492, Europeans and Euro-Americans have had both a fascination and a disdain for Native peoples who were so different from themselves. From the time of Columbus' second visit to the New World when obtaining gold for the Spanish crown became the main reason for making contact with indigenous peoples in the Caribbean (Shenkman, 1989), peoples native to the Americas have been vilified in terms of their cultures, languages, and mores as conquerors rationalized their enslavement of Natives as well as the pillaging and plundering of Native communities and lands (Usner, 2009). The language used to describe Native peoples deliberately polarized these differences and the supposed superiority of their European conquerors in efforts to justify genocide, colonization, and Christianization of Native peoples (Miller, 2006; Usner, 2009).

Stereotypes portrayed American Indians as blood-thirsty heathen savages who were lazy, superstitious, and stupid people who did not know how to use the land that was in their territory, and therefore needed others (Europeans) to take over for them (Usner, 2009). On the opposite end was the "noble savage" stereotype, which was just as harmful in illustrating American Indians as primitive peoples who were facing extinction in the near, industrialized, future (Berkhofer, 1978). These stereotypes do a severe injustice to Native peoples that make up the 564 federally recognized sovereign American Indian Nations (White House, 2010), other state-recognized American Indian Nations, and those who had their tribal status stripped from them after World War II in an effort to terminate Indian Nations and the government's responsibilities to them that had been established through treaties (Sheffield, 1997).

We are all shaped by our environments and the social influences around us. The history books used in classrooms in schools throughout the United States do not include information about the enslavement of Native peoples by Europeans; about the genocide of American Indians that occurred; about the massive numbers of Native peoples who lost their lives due to exposure to European diseases such as smallpox; nor about the loss of Native lands due to continual shrinkage of reservation boundaries by the government, even though these lands were promised to American Indians "in perpetuity" (Adams, 1999; Berkhofer, 1978; Josephy, 1991; Mihesuah, 1996).

Popular media have continued to shape negative perceptions of American Indians through such outlets as books, radio, television, and film. There have been relatively few resources produced by the dominant culture to counteract this narrative. The long-lasting effect of these stereotypes does not encourage teachers to examine the reality of American Indian histories and the contributions of Native peoples to the way we live, the foods we eat, many of the pharmaceuticals we use, or the history of how our own government system is based on the Iroquois Confederacy (Weatherford, 1978). These stereotypes have been entrenched and promulgated by all types of media to contribute to misrepresentations of American Indians and the intergenerational trauma that exists on many reservations and within urban Indian communities today.

In schools, the prejudicial reactions to Native students, lack of understanding of Native cultures, and the way Native students are treated and spoken to may be the product of these stereotypes. The result of these actions may be ineffective teaching of Native students who are very capable of learning. Unless we can open our hearts and minds to learning about the students with whom we work, we will not be able to figure out the best ways to teach them.

Education for American Indian Students

It is impossible to understand the reluctance of Native Americans to involve their children in the American educational system unless we understand some of the historical efforts to assimilate American Indians to Western culture through education. With colonization and Christianization came the demand for American Indian assimilation into the dominant culture through stripping Native peoples of their heritages and languages. As public schools became more established in the United States throughout the 1800s, schools were also established by the Cherokee and Choctaw Nations in order to teach children their traditional languages and cultures as well as to expose them to English and the dominant culture (Spring, 2006). However, as education became one of the promises established in treaties in exchange for tribal land holdings, the establishment of government and missionary boarding schools for American Indian children in the later half of the 1800's took precedence. At first the schools were located close to the children's Native communities. However, they were moved further and further away from them as the schools became seen as the way to completely assimilate Native students. In these schools, the children could speak only English and were punished severely if they spoke their own languages or attempted to continue any of their cultural or spiritual practices. Their Indian clothing was removed and Western clothing substituted. Their hair was cut short, a practice usually reserved in tribal communities for mourning a family member's death. Their jewelry was removed, and children were given English names in these schools. Children were mixed in with other Native children from different tribes in order to discourage them from continuing to think of themselves in terms of their native identities. Following the example set by Col. Richard Henry Pratt, director of the first government boarding school at Carlisle, Pennsylvania, many boarding schools adopted the practice of treating the students as if they were in the military by having them wear uniforms, participate in drills, and by dispensing harsh punishments (Spring, 2006).

In 1924, American Indians were given citizenship in the United States as a result of their willingness to defend the country when at war. Now American Indians had dual citizenship in the United States and their own sovereign nations. However, there was something wrong with the educational system that was leaving many Native Americans devastated in its wake.

An investigation into the boarding schools commissioned by the government resulted in the 1928 *Meriam Report* in which monumental problems and abuses of students were exposed publicly for the first time (Meriam, 1930/1977). Near-starvation conditions existed in many schools where children provided much of the labor to keep the schools running. Physical, mental, and sexual abuses of Native students were revealed (Johanson, 2000; McGillivray & Comaskey, 2000). While there were examples of American Indians who left the boarding schools and went on to become professionals, laborers, or domestic workers, the vast majority of former students were living in poverty at the turn of the 19th century. Since the majority of these children were forced to leave their tribes when they were young and could not return home until graduation, they no longer fit in with their natal communities because they did not speak their native languages well or at all. They had not developed the traditional skills or arts relied upon by tribal members to supply labor needed in their communities. Having been taught only Western ways, and that these were superior, it was impossible for them as young adults to jump the chasm between the two cultures in terms of beliefs, values, and ways of living. After these disclosures were made through the Meriam Report, the government decided to reverse its policies by establishing day schools on or near reservations that were intended to integrate native cultural life and languages with educational endeavors to try to undo the harm that boarding schools had inflicted on Native societies and resurrect their cultural identities (Lomawaima, 1995; Mankiller, 1991).

Unsurprisingly, the boarding school era had a profoundly negative effect on the American Indian peoples' view of formal education. Some boarding schools continued after the Meriam Report was released, and changes were made to reflect the concerns voiced in the report. However, for some Native people, the boarding school debacle represents reasons for continued opposition to formal education today. Conversely, many Native people support education's role in preparing their children to survive and thrive in the dominant culture while retaining their native identities.

The goal of having Native languages and cultures represented in school curricula has yet to be actualized in public schools despite numerous pieces of legislation enacted to ensure this would occur, including the 1934 Indian Reorganization Act; the 1968 Bilingual Education Act; the 1972 Indian Education Act; the 1975 Indian Self-Determination and Education Assistance Act; the 1990 Native American Languages Act (Public Law 101–477, Title I); the 1998 Executive Order 13096 to research best practices in education for teaching American Indians; and the 2004 Executive Order 13336 to reinforce the need to incorporate native languages and cultures in school curricula as part of the efforts of the 2001 No Child Left Behind Act (NCLB).

Considerations for Teaching American Indian Students

There is no one answer to the question, "What is the best way to teach American Indian students?" just as there is no one answer for the best way to teach children from any other racial/ethnic group. Rather, the answer lies in considering a constellation of factors that we know influence indigenous students' willingness to learn and to become part of the educational system. While there are many issues that are more fully enumerated in several books (Author & Whitfield, 2003; Cleary & Peacock, 1998; Gilliland, 1995; Reyhner, 1988), various areas are briefly addressed below to increase understanding of educating American Indian students.

Suspension of Beliefs One Holds About American Indians

One of the most critical keys for success when teaching American Indian students is to be open to learning about who the students are and about their cultures since each tribal Nation is unique. Native students may come to school having different understandings of the world and mores, or ways of doing things, than their teachers and non-Native classmates. This is particularly true for indigenous students who are growing up on reservations as many of them—though not all—are being raised in traditional cultural ways. Therefore, we must ask about the expectations Native communities hold for their children to understand where conflicts may arise between non-Native teachers and their Native students. When I work with American Indian children in schools, I start with the assumption that they are being raised traditionally because it is imperative to build their trust and for students to know that I respect them. For many students, the recognition that you understand their traditions provides the pathway to be able to forge relationships with them, whether or not they are being raised as strictly traditional American Indians.

Consider that it is generally a traditional practice that children do not make eye contact with adults because this is a sign of disrespect. When teachers force children who are being raised traditionally to make eye contact, the students are being made to violate the teachings of their families. Children who are being raised biculturally (or as acculturated), to act one way in the dominant culture and another way within their own culture, may not experience this conflict. Children who are being raised as assimilated to the dominant culture will act as other children who are being raised with dominant cultural values. Therefore, they will give eye contact readily when expected to do so by their teachers. The children who do not give eye contact may be judged negatively by teachers who are not familiar with this teaching, even to the point of receiving punishment for disobeying their teachers.

Another area that causes difficulties concerns the amount of oral discourse that takes place in typical classrooms taught by non-Native teachers. Those of us who have grown up in the dominant culture are used to listening to others speak on a continual basis. This becomes reinforced through radio, television, cell phone usage, and other forms of technology used for communication. We are uncomfortable with silence, and feel "cut off" when we do not experience the continual barrage of conversation. This carries over into our classrooms where we ask many questions of students and expect them to respond to us quickly; teach using the lecture mode to present a lot of information that we expect students to learn; have students engage through reading aloud; and involve students in classroom discussions. While these are time-honored pedagogical techniques, the amount of oral discourse can be overwhelming for more traditional American Indian students. A sixth grade teacher who had American Indian students in her classroom for the first time recently gave an example of this. About halfway through the second semester, one of her students with whom she had built a relationship stated, "I just wish the teachers would stop talking and let us do our work" (E. Hall, personal communication, March 10, 2010). This young lady was attending a school off the reservation for the first time, and clearly she wished for more silence in the classroom. The teacher did not understand why her student would make this comment until she learned more about the student's traditional culture.

Non-Native teachers tend to think that Native students who do not speak much in their classrooms, or who do not give long oral or written reports, do not really understand the concepts being presented in class. In truth, the students usually do understand—unless they have learning difficulties—but they are responding in culturally appropriate ways to what they are being asked to do in school. In many Native communities, language is considered a sacred gift from the Creator that should not be overused. White teachers need to be sensitive to this issue and not mistake culturally learned behaviors for lack of intelligence. Another example of cultural misunderstandings concerns giving answers to teachers' questioning in class. Teachers complain that they teach the same material over and over again, and the children still don't "get it." Usually, teachers make this judgment when they call on individual students in class to give the right answers. Since it is inappropriate to embarrass others in many American Indian cultures, as this would disrupt harmony, traditional students may give the wrong answer even though they understand what the teacher is asking. This is to save the students who do not understand the question from embarrassment. Instead of asking individual students to respond, a better way is to have the students work together in small groups. This way, students can give the answers that represent their group's responses.

One common complaint from Native parents/grandparents is that teachers do not attend events held on reservations or in cities that focus on American Indian cultures whereas these same teachers attend events in the areas where they are living. This contributes to the perceptions that teachers do not respect Native students and are not interested in building relationships with them and their families. Consequently, teachers do not take advantage of these occasions to become acquainted with parents, grandparents, and students' extended families; or to expand their knowledge and appreciation of students' cultures. When Native people see teachers attending various Native American events that are open to the public, they know that the teachers working with their children care for them.

Successful Pathways for Teaching American Indian Students

Vygotsky (1978) and Piaget (Flavell, 1977) are known for their work in the area of constructivist pedagogy, wherein students learn from working with objects and ideas as opposed to just memorizing information. While Piaget focuses on individual student growth through his work with stages of cognitive development, Vygotsky emphasizes the need to learn in concert with teachers and peers. Vygotsky views teachers as sociocultural mediators, which has implications for teachers of American Indian children, as many traditional and bicultural Native children do not have the background knowledge teachers expect of them. This is true especially if they are from low socioeconomic circumstances and have not had the same opportunities as middle-class students. There are also circumstances related to students' physical surroundings that play a role in the development of their knowledge. Children who live in desert areas are not always familiar with shells, in contrast to those who have traveled to the ocean shores, have seen pictures of shells, or perhaps have a collection of shells in their homes. Therefore, when reading a story that takes place on a beach and features children collecting shells, teachers need to prepare students for the story by letting them see and hold real shells, as well as talk about the ocean creatures that produce the shells. Comparisons can be made to the types of animals with which the students are familiar—how they live, what they eat, where they make their homes, how they protect themselves—to help students better understand the life of animals in the ocean. Multimedia and computer technology can provide additional ways of presenting information to build students' knowledge of unfamiliar environments. As a result, students will be prepared to engage with a story that would otherwise make no sense to them, and allow children to focus on comprehending the story rather than simply reading the words.

American Indian children are taught to learn through observation from the time they are babies. Using observation, hands-on, and experiential learning activities in classrooms are pedagogical techniques that are very valuable and more compatible with traditional and bicultural American Indian students (Author & Whitfield, 2003; Pewewardy, 1998). In addition, it is important to connect school curriculum to what the students already know, approaching learning in an holistic fashion instead of presenting information piecemeal, as is frequently the case in mainstream curricula. Using thematic approaches to learning, where literature becomes central to both reading and writing activities is one way to provide this type of learning. In addition, mathematics can be tied in to literature selections. A book about a journey can be used as a springboard to ask questions such as the length of the journey in miles and time, using this information to learn measurement and actually walking a distance to understand what a mile feels like. Social studies can be tied in with discussions about the communities represented in the book. Scientific concepts can be explored, especially biological and geographical, through discussions related to the types of animals and plants encountered on the journey.

Mathematics is an area that many teachers of Native students feel is a challenge. Yet, explaining concepts in a way that is familiar to students can make a huge difference. In almost every indigenous community, there is intricate beadwork production of some type. Using beadwork, teachers can explain mathematical concepts of addition, subtraction, multiplication, division, and many geometrical concepts.

Another way to explain mathematical concepts is to use communal experiences. One teacher used his experience of seeing teepees taken down after the annual festival to teach his second grade students about subtraction. He asked if any of his students had ever watched or been part of the taking down process, and after they talked about this, he drew several teepees on the board, and they proceeded to "take down" different numbers of teepees. The next step was to present the information in mathematical terms. The children understood the concept of "subtraction" from then on (F. Anderson, personal communication, November 9, 2009).

"We liked you because you always taught both sides [of history]" (S. Rainey, personal communication, June 12, 2010). This statement was made by a former student to her 4th grade teacher. Teaching social studies and American History in a way that is holistic and acknowledges all sides of the complicated history of many peoples is paramount to involving American Indian students in this often painful content area. There are also many books that feature different American Indian stories and topics about different tribal Nations that can be used in classrooms as a way to provide authentic reading experiences to students in conjunction with textbooks. While some Native students are very eclectic in their reading tastes, we have found that having books that focus on Native peoples can spark interest in reading for many children considered to be reticent about reading literature. Having discussions in class about historical events allows students to develop critical thinking skills and gives them opportunities to express their ideas concerning events that took place in our nation's history.

Learning and Demonstrating What Was Learned

In general, cooperation is valued over competition in Native communities. Therefore, cooperative learning activities and service learning in students' communities make a difference in not only how much students learn, but in their comfort levels as they work toward achieving common goals (Little Soldier, 1989; López, 1999).

American Indian children possess strengths in all of the Multiple Intelligences as identified by Gardner (1999) which include visual-spatial, bodily kinesthetic, musical, interpersonal, intrapersonal, linguistic, and logical mathematical intelligence. Incorporation of the arts as part of teaching and learning capitalizes on the strong visual intelligence that many American Indian children possess (Author & Whitfield, in press). We have used movement activities as a way to help children follow story sequence and understand a story's plot. Through visual arts, American Indian children can express their responses toward stories in a non-verbal sign system as well as giving their own unique endings to stories to increase comprehension skills.

Many Native children are very interested in and knowledgeable about nature. Connecting activities with growing plants, having animals as part of the classroom, and going on field trips to explore the world around them, are all activities that can be used to enhance students' understandings of scientific concepts. Many American Indian students are kinesthetic learners who enjoy athletics and being involved in learning through physically active games where they work together on teams. Many educational concepts can be explored through the use of games and physical activities. Board games can be created by teachers around vocabulary terms; treasure hunts for information and objects can be used for library work. The way games can be used is only limited by the creativity of the teacher.

There Is No "Pan Indian" Culture

Though the boarding school era provided opportunities for many native students to learn about other tribal Nations and some Nations adopted different styles of dancing at powwows and festivals held throughout North America, it is important to recognize that someone who is Cherokee can be as different from someone who is Mohawk as European Americans may be from people who are from Asia. While there may be some cultural overlaps, as we have all been exposed to different ways of living, especially through the advent of world-wide media, this still doesn't mean that we are all alike and do not need to know about other peoples and their values and traditions. The same is true about generalizing from one tribal Nation to another. This is especially true in terms of stereotypes, in thinking that all Indian people lived in teepees and ate the same foods, dressed in deerskins, and spoke the same way. Each tribal Nation is unique and, as teachers, we need to know the histories and cultures of the students we teach. Many tribal Nations have developed teaching materials that are available for use in classrooms, and these materials can be accessed by teachers who want to use them to help their students learn about people in other parts of the country. By using these materials, teachers help dispel the stereotypes about Native peoples that have such a strong hold on this country, to the benefit of all students in the class.

Changing Views, Changing Lives

The current implementation of NCLB leaves a false view of American Indian students' capabilities. Even though calls for attention to issues surrounding American Indian education were required by Executive Order 13336 (2004), the issue was ignored by those involved in carrying out NCLB. Because of the way the accountability system is presently designed, students who have made great strides are not rewarded for their progress if they have not met the lowest level of "basic" on the standardized assessment instruments. In the recently released document, *A Blueprint for Reform* (U.S. Department of Education, 2010), several considerations for the reauthorization of NCLB are called for, including looking at the amount of progress students are making (what we call a "growth model") and considerations for American Indian education. If we can change the accountability model from one-size-fits-all, we may finally return to what matters the most: teaching all children in ways that will promote their optimum growth and allow teachers to use techniques that they know are best for their students. In doing so, we hope to see a change in how American Indian children are viewed within the educational system, focusing on their strengths and using those strengths to ensure that they learn the content that is important for them to master so that they can become successful citizens in both worlds. We know that culture and heritage contribute to the resilience of our American Indian youth. By incorporating culturally relevant pedagogy for American Indian students into our teaching, we create counter-narratives that focus on their abilities and success in contrast to the dominant cultural views of Native students. In doing so, we create stronger educational communities and a stronger America for all of its citizens.

Selected Resources

Alaska Native Knowledge Network. (1998). *Alaska standards for culturally responsive schools.* Anchorage, AL: Author. Retrieved from http://www.ankn.uaf.edu/standards/standards.html

Anthropology Outreach Office. *A critical bibliography on North American Indians, K-12.* Washington, DC: Smithsonian. Retrieved from http://www.nmnh.si.edu/anthro/outreach/Indbibl/

Baylor, B. (1978). *The other way to listen.* New York, NY: Simon & Schuster.

Bigelow, B., & Peterson, B. (1998). *Rethinking Columbus: The next 500 years.* Milwaukee, WI: Rethinking Schools.

Caduto, M. J., & Bruchac, J. (1988). *Keepers of the Earth: Native American stories and environmental activities for children.* Golden, CO: Fulcrum.

Giese, P. (1996). *Native American Indian resources.* Retrieved from http://www.kstrom.net/isk/

Goble, P. (1986). *Buffalo woman.* New York, NY: Macmillan.

Hirschfelder, A. B., & Beamer, Y. (2000). *The American Indian: Yesterday, today, & tomorrow. A handbook for educators.* Sacramento, CA: California Department of Education.

Katz, J. B. (1975). *Let me be a free man: A documentary history of Indian resistance.* Minneapolis, MN: Lerner.

Kubinski, E. (2008). *Resources for working with American Indian/Alaska Native students.* Madison, WI: Department of Public Instruction. Retrieved from http://dpi.wi.gov/sped/doc/disp-res-amind.doc

Montana Office of Public Instruction. (2010). *Indian education for all: Essential understandings regarding Montana Indians.* Helena, MT: Author. Retrieved from http//www.Opi.mt.gov/pdf/indianed/resources/essential/understandings

O'Dell, S. (1960). *Island of the blue dolphins.* Boston, MA: Houghton Mifflin.

Ross, G. (1995). *How Turtle's back was cracked.* New York, NY: Dial.

Weatherford, J. (1989). *Indian givers: How the Indians of the Americas transformed the world.* New York, NY: Ballentine Books.

References

Adams, H. (1999). *Tortured people: The politics of colonization* (Rev. ed.). Penticton, British Columbia: Theytus Books Ltd.

Berkhofer, R. F. (1978). *The White man's Indian. Images of the American Indian from Columbus to the present.* New York, NY: Random House.

Bilingual Act of 1965, 20 U.S.C. § 7401 *et seq.* (U.S.C. 2000)

Cleary, L. M., & Peacock, T. D. (1998). *Collected wisdom: American Indian education.* Boston, MA: Allyn & Bacon.

Exec. Order No. 13336, 3 C.F.R. 25295. (2004)

Flavell, J. H. (1977). *Cognitive development.* Englewood Cliffs, NJ: Prentice-Hall.

Gardner, H. (1999). *Intelligence reframed: Multiple intelligences for the 21st century.* New York, NY: Basic Books.

Gilliland, H. (1995). *Teaching the Native American* (3rd ed.). Dubuque, IA: Kendall-Hunt.

Indian Education Act of 1972, 20 U.S.C. § 3385 *et seq.* (U.S.C. 2000)

Indian Reorganization Act of 1934, 25 U.S.C. § 461 (U.S.C. 2000)

Indian Self-Determination and Education Assistance Act of 1975, 25 U.S.C. § 450f. (U.S.C. 2000)

Johanson, B. E. (2000). Education: The nightmare and the dream. *Native Peoples Magazine, 13*(1), 10–20.

Josephy, A. (1991). *The Indian heritage of America.* Boston, MA: Houghton Mifflin.

Klug, B. & Whitfield, P. T. (2003). *Widening the circle: Culturally relevant pedagogy for American Indian children.* New York: RoutledgeFalmer.

Klug, B. & Whitfield, P. T. (in press). A mind with a view: Education through the kaleidoscopic lenses of the arts. In C. J. Craig & L. F. Deretchin (Eds.), *The role of teachers and teacher educators: Part II. ATE Annual Yearbook XVIII.* Lanham, MD: Rowman & Littlefield Education.

Little Soldier, L. (1989). Cooperative learning and the Native American student. *Phi Delta Kappan, 71*(2), 161–163.

Lomawaima, K. T. (1995). Educating Native Americans. In J. A. Banks (Ed.), *Handbook of research on multicultural education* (pp. 331–347). New York, NY: Simon & Schuster MacMillan.

López, A. (1999). Return to the heartbeat of Turtle Island. *The heartbeat of Turtle Island: A journal of Native Service-Learning* (pp. 37–47).

Mankiller, W. (1991). Education and Native Americans: Entering the twenty-first century on our own terms. *National Forum, LXXI*(2), 5–9.

McGillivray, A., & Comaskey, B. (2000). *Black eyes all of the time: Intimate violence, aboriginal women, and the justice system.* Toronto, Canada: University of Toronto Press.

Mihesuah, D. A. (1996). *American Indians: Stereotypes & realities.* Atlanta, GA: Clarity Press, Inc.

Miller, R. J. (2006). *Native America discovered and conquered: Thomas Jefferson, Lewis & Clark, and Manifest Destiny*. Westport, CT: Praeger.

National Indian Education Association. (n.d.). *Native education 101: Basic facts about American Indian, Alaska Native, and Native Hawaiian education*. Washington, DC: Author.

Native American Languages Act of 1990 Pub. L. No. 101–477, Title I, 25 *U.S.C.* 450b (U.S.C. 2000)

No Child Left Behind Act of 2001: Reauthorization of the Elementary and Secondary Education Act of 1965, 20 U.S.C. § 6301 et seq. (U.S.C. 2001)

Pewewardy, C. (1998). Our children can't wait: Recapturing the essence of indigenous schools in the United States. *Cultural Survival Quarterly, 22*(1), 29–34.

Reyhner, J. A. (1988). *Teaching the Indian child: A bilingual/multicultural approach* (2nd ed.). Billings, MT: Eastern Montana College.

Sheffield, G. K. (1997). *The arbitrary Indian: The Indian arts and crafts act of 1990*. Norman, OK: University of Oklahoma Press.

Shenkman, R. (1989). *Legends, lies, and cherished myths of American history*. New York, NY: Harper & Row.

Spring, J. H. (2006). *Deculturalization and the struggle for equality: A brief history of the education of dominated cultures in the United States* (5th ed.). New York, NY: McGraw-Hill.

Stiffarm, L. A., & Lane, P. (1992). The demography of Native North America: A question of American Indian survival. In M. A. Jaimes (Ed.), *State of Native America: Genocide, colonization, and resistance*. Boston, MA: South End Press.

U.S. Department of Education. (2010). *A blueprint for reform: The reauthorization of the Elementary and Secondary Education Act*. Washington, DC: Author. Retrieved from www2.ed.gov/policy/elsec/blueprint/blueprint.pdf

Usner, D. H., Jr. (2009). *Indian work; Language and livelihood in Native American history*. Cambridge, MA: Harvard University Press.

Vygotsky, L. (1978). *Mind in society: The development of higher psychological processes*. Cambridge, MA: Harvard University Press.

Wax, M. (1971). *Indian Americans: Unity and diversity*. Englewood Cliffs, NJ: Prentice-Hall.

Weatherford, J. (1978). *Indian givers: How the Indians of the Americas transformed the world*. New York, NY: Fawcett Columbine.

White House. (2010). *Forging a new and better future together: 2010 White House Tribal Nations Conference* [Progress Report, Executive Summary]. Washington, DC: Author. Retrieved from www.whitehouse.gov/sites/default/files/rss.../nc_progress_report.pdf

QUESTIONS

1. How do you express or demonstrate the culture in which you were brought up? Many Whites do not even think they have a culture.

Examine your own life, celebrations, values, ways of interacting. Do your students have ways of speaking, moving, and responding that are identical to yours? What do you do about it if they do not, but are rather more silent, oral, and communal than you were raised to be?

2. How much history of different tribes and cultures of Native Americans have you learned? Why do you think this subject is rarely explored in depth in American education? What does it mean for Native students? How does it affect the way you teach? How does learning history from the perspective of American Indians influence your understanding of history as a whole?

14

EDUCATING BLACK MALES
Interview With Professor Emeritus Joseph White,
Ph.D., Author of *Black Man Emerging*

Julie G. Landsman

JL: Before we focus on specific areas of education—curriculum, pedagogy, links with community peer group, home and school—I have one or
two general questions I would like to ask.

JW: Go right ahead.

JL: We hear these days that the testing mandated by No Child Left Behind [NCLB] is making it impossible to make changes in our schools in
terms of pedagogy and curriculum. What is your response to the teacher who
says, "I can't add anything else. My principal says I have to teach to the
test"? What is your opinion of the NCLB program? Are these tests another
example of biased instruments used to test African American students?

JW: We always have to make sure we go from problem definition to
problem solution. In this case, the problem is how do we work around or
within guidelines, especially if we do not agree with such guidelines. Yet if
we believe that nothing can be done, we are stopped cold.

We have to use such high-stakes testing in one way—a prescriptive
way—not an evaluative way. Any test used on [a] minority child should
come out with prescriptive ideas for helping the child do better, never as a
statement of ability.

JL: I have often heard that the best way to help African American students do well in school is to have a structured, authoritative classroom. There
is a school here that has a strictly structured program, is 99 percent African
American students and mostly Black teachers, and is increasing students' test

scores and school attendance in great numbers. I have also read that we must adapt to the open, interactive style of our students, that African Americans are verbal, demonstrative, and talkative in their cultural style. How do we do both—provide structure and quiet, obedience and orderliness—and still adapt to the style of our African American students? Can we do both? How?

JW: There is no one solution for pedagogy and no one learning style that will work for African American children all the time. Either/or is a way of getting out of designing a unique way of teaching. It is important to look at the best mix, to create a way to mix authoritative and cultural styles. First find out what turns a child on; once he is turned on by something he will respond to anything if the connections are made. When a student is turned on by football, he will follow discipline of practice in that sport. Can do this in academics as well.

To capture the high energy of African American males, it works often to build in drama, role plays, active participation to really draw upon their energy. We know when any students actively participate, their alertness goes up, attention span increases, and retention of information is higher: all this by making active participation a part of teaching.

JL: Many writers and experts in education have emphasized that they want their children or students to be able to make it in the White world. They say their kids are already fluent in rap, or singing, and that is not what they are in schools for. They should be learning "standard English" and all the material that will allow them to compete in a White, corporate world of power. How do we connect with students' culture and also make sure they get plenty of mainstream cultural capital when there is a limited amount of time? Can schools do it all?

JW: Schools can't do it all. Effective learning is additive. Build on what a child already has. If a child already knows hip-hop, draw energy and build on top of it. If he can comprehend a rap song and its vocabulary and create raps of his own, he is showing an ability to engage in complex behavior. Can we build additively on that so he can be bicultural? Of course. We can build on both cultures. We need to create opportunities for him to see bicultural role models bringing in speakers, high-achieving Black men and women who have kept their cultural identity but who have made it in the "mainstream" world. We need to show them individuals who can engage in either world. Thus, we can make them see they can do both: be down with hood and be in with mainstream economy.

We need to build on a child's experience. Bob Moses's algebra project starts out in Roxbury, Cambridge, Massachusetts. His teachers take children on rides, providing direct experience in their community to engage them in math problems. How much money was spent? How many stops? How much time spent? How much time at each of the stops? How far did they go in miles? The students get off and picnic together and then get on again, calculating what the teacher asks. In this way they have experienced concretely what they will be working with in a classroom. They can assign values to elements—time, distance, money—once they get the fundamental concepts at a rudimentary level. They can put symbol to concrete experience and can take this and build symbolic language.

Concrete hands-on experience is essential to African American students. They need to see connections to their lives and what they need and want. If they have this experience, they can learn. Excite them and build on concrete experiences.

JL: Now I would like to look at the categories you have presented in your outline "Enhancing Educational Achievement with Black Males." But, first, why have you spent so much of your time working on psychology and study of Black males? Aren't Black females in trouble too? And if they are not, can you explain the gender difference?

JW: Black females have role models all the way through their childhood and early adulthood. Sixty to 70 percent of Black children are without a stable male figure in home. The Black female has her mom, aunt, and grandmother. She enters school, then may have a female and even Black female teacher. On through middle school this will often be the case. There may be a few more Black males in high school, but there are still very few. There are more Black females. Black students will seldom see a Black male in a responsible educational role. Thus, he thinks education is a White male thing, or a female thing—but definitely not a male thing.

At home, Black mothers cut their males a little more slack and expect more of their female children. The saying is, "We raise our female children, love our male children."

And, finally, given this scenario, those Black males who do connect to education and see it as something males can connect to will have trouble with their peers. I picked my focus on the Black male because of this lack in their lives, and also because I experienced this myself. I have raised three girls, two are Ph.D.s.

JL: Let's start with curriculum and Black males in education. What is the curriculum that will make sense for students? What does it do about Ebonics, the cool pose Black males often use as a survival mechanism and the bilingualism students bring to the classroom? How do we use these strengths to help students achieve while at the same time maintaining a classroom that is effective for all students, including those who are quiet, are not African American? What can we do in the selection of materials, books, topics, subjects to appeal to Black students?

JW: We have to have teaching and learning strategies that capitalize on cultural and learning styles. There are seven underlying concepts I like to stress:

1. Curriculum that makes sense to the child
2. Involvement of active participation
3. Role models in the classroom that look like students
4. Use of a strategy that involves peer reinforcement
5. Learning plans that have excitement to them
6. Capitalizing on the intrinsic motivation of the child
7. Drawing upon the creative energy of the child.

Role models: There are not many Black educational models, and it is important to know that we are not going to get that many more males in the field. One way to help this situation is to use our colleges and universities. Have Black male undergraduate students in the building. Bring them in as hall monitors; have them present in the environment in multiple ways, as coaches, tutors, mentors; use them in meaningful roles. Find men who come from the same community as the students, so that they can be concrete examples of those trying to do bicultural peace. Give these students real training as Black male role models; don't dump them in.

Intrinsic motivation: In schools based on external motivation, the belief of all involved is that students are there because the law says they must go, and tells students what they have to do. Yet, without this legal mandate, why do kids learn more from birth to age five than they do in any period of their life? How is this? Most never went to formal school. They have intrinsic drive to learn, a real curiosity about the world. Bring some of that fascination into the school to tap into this intrinsic drive of kids to learn, into their excitement, their exploratory drive, their curiosity, their natural psychological drive to learn. The mechanisms of birth to age five can be used with older students. We can't use external motivators but need to tap into internal motivators present in all students.

Rappers must have a way to be creative, to use rhythm, and a facility with what is going on in the community. They must have knowledge of the latest street happenings. If they have the capacity to understand all of that, it is important to use their ability as a vehicle, as a mechanism to reach students, to move them along and to teach other things. [See a fuller exposition of this in *Black Man Emerging* (White & Cones, 1999, p. 96)].

The curriculum has to make sense in a real-world sense to students. The Black male student must see the world around him reflected in the curriculum. He must see the world in which he lives in the books he reads, on the walls, in the music, math examples, science problems, and real-world experiences.

JL: I would like to call the next topic pedagogy: how teachers teach. Body language, tone, attitude play such an important part in reaching young people. What are some ways you have found in your research that White teachers and Black teachers can use to create a relationship with students? What are the attitudes of Whites toward Black students as found in research and anecdotal information? How do we get at that? How can teachers let classrooms be used as to allow exploration of identity and culture? What will it take in training teachers to be able to do this?

JW: Somewhere in every community there are successful teachers, Black and White, who are reaching these kids. Find out who they are, debrief them, and put them on film and video. Beginning teachers can then see all of this. Let a beginning teacher sit in the classroom of an effective teacher. Use video to show teachers behavioral interactions: eye contact, pull back, lean forward, body language, and interpersonal interaction. This will show how nonverbal responses can be more important than verbal ones. If a teacher "gives off bad vibes" the kids will back off.

Cognitive: Teach about a student's culture's whole being. Saturate the curriculum with this rather than one course on the side in multicultural education. Don't put multicultural education over on the side, but saturate the whole curriculum.

My impression is that twenty- to twenty-two-year-old White girls who start out going into teaching are highly motivated and want to do the right thing. After a while they don't get support in their struggle to understand and they tune out, burn out. Yet they truly want to make a difference. We need to give them the tools and support or they will quit. The majority of K-6 teachers will be White female. It is important to get across to them not to write kids off. If they find themselves doing this they need to see if they can find some help.

It is important to continue to work with institutions that are working with the kids even if they don't want to change. There will be institutional conflict, and out of this can come change.

JL: How can teachers use the bilingualism of students in their instruction? What will this do for their classroom and community connection? Some parents will say, "I don't want my child to speak Black English or Ebonics. He can do that anytime in the neighborhood. I want him to learn mainstream English so he can get a job." How can teachers do it all?

JW: Communicate clearly what we are doing and why: learning is most meaningful when it is additive. Expand skill base by adding on to what they already know, to get to normative skill level in standard oral English based on what they bring to us. If we ignore what they have, we won't be building a solid house. You can teach Shakespeare by providing a transitional piece by having them translate a play into inner-city language, then come back to standard oral English and then to Shakespearean English. . . so they clearly see meaning in all three and have exposure to this language. They need to see the goal. Again, it is the additive learning thing like teaching math by riding the neighborhood subway.

JL: How can schools connect to the homes of their students?

JW: Through a paradigm shift. This is fundamental. We approach parents wanting them to do certain things that we define as effective parent behavior. We don't ask them, What do they want? We need to start out asking, What do the parents need from us? Presentable clothes? Help in filling out a job application? Literacy skills? Job referral? Schools are part of a larger community. They must partner with groups in the community. They need to find ways to make alliances to provide parents with what they think they need. Then they can also move to suggestions to turn TV off. Schools must also use other resources in the community and build stronger links between home, peer group, community, and school.

JL: How can schools become part of the community? Connect to the community? Where does this leave the topic of bussing? Many schools are becoming "racially isolated." Do we try and fix this by bussing, or work with it to establish home schools situated in their communities and not worry about integration, even though data suggest that African American students do better academically in integrated schools?

JW: Get churches, radio stations, brothers on the corner—get all of them behind the educational message. Know people out there like the Urban League, for example, and ask them to take some responsibility. Do this so that everywhere a child goes, everyone is saying the same thing.

Peer group: Involve peer group in educational process or you will lose kids. From fifth grade on, peers are an important support system. Listen to the peer group. They think education is for White folks: America will not honor us; why mix with oppressors? Make them understand you can have an integrated identity of skills to make it and still be down with hood keeping your Black identity. Hip has to mean you can read and count. Right now hip does not mean that. Many authentic people are gangsters in the neighborhood. America has done this with movies, TV, music, rap, clothes. An authentic Black man is often pictured or reported on as a gangster or athlete.

People are tired of the bussing fight. Don't want to abandon integrated education. Figure out how to get mixture of ethnics . . . magnet schools. Figure out ways to draw people together. White folks will go where quality education is. Rethink concept of where we put the good schools. Makes this complicated. Create a menu of these things, including strong ethnic schools. This is often looked at as either/or, and there are more creative solutions out there.

JL: How can schools compete with the peer group? What can they do to make learning and classroom achievement "cool"? How can we reach African American males who have "dropped out" emotionally by fourth or fifth grade?

JW: Acknowledge up front that peer group is more powerful than we are. Work with peer group as a group . . . have an ongoing dialogue with peer group. Why are they so turned off?

As individual teachers, tell students that we know you want to speak and be heard. We also know you need to learn how to read, count, etc. to make it. We are acknowledging something they do already know deep down. Be straight with them. Talk to them about the fact that if they are out on the street and if they participate in the underground economy they will go to jail. Tell them you don't want them to fail and that you know they don't want to fail. Work on masculinity: masculinity does not have to mean going to jail. Often students believe this jail time is a rite of passage. They are continually trying out their swagger, their challenge stance. Tell them they don't need to go through this step. First talk it out. Help them establish their identity: have them sit down, ask themselves questions. Who am I? What do I want to do? Lecture and talk in small groups of eight to ten. Be aware they feel they have to put on a façade of toughness even though they have a lot going on. Intensive interaction in small groups will get to their core questions and positive values and motivation.

JL: How do we foster motivation?

JW: Connection through curriculum that builds on strengths of each child. Find something that excites them and then you will have an entrée into discipline and precision.

In any major human endeavor, relationship is key. More than words, body language and true expressed feelings matter to all students. Teacher has to have style of relating that can connect with children growing up in neighborhoods they themselves may not have grown up in. These teachers may need to learn that the style of connecting may be very different in these communities, something they may not realize at first but can learn.

JL: How do we foster hope?

JW: Help children dream the impossible dream. Give them the tools that will move them toward that dream. If they dig deep enough, they will find the strengths that they need. We did not survive all these four hundred years—and some thrived—without having psychological strengths. Help children learn what those core strengths are and how they can use these core strengths to achieve the impossible dream. These core strengths come from the African American history and culture. They are improvisation, resilience, connectedness to others, the value of direct experience, spirituality, gallows humor, and a healthy suspicion of White folks. We must recognize those strengths and use them to reach young men in school.

Children have to learn that there is such a thing as plan A *and* plan B, that there is nothing wrong with wanting to be a basketball player but you also need a backup plan. Pro athletes will tell them that. Keep a course *parallel* to athlete course. Know what to do in life.

JL: How do we foster resilience?

JW: Foster resilience: teach seven strengths; expose kids to examples of resilience in biographies of African Americans. Help them find strength within themselves; teach them how to heal, and get stronger in the broken places. All this is part of the Black experience.

JL: How do we foster resourcefulness?

JW: It is one of the basic, core strengths and involves improvisation and creativity. It has to be taught and demonstrated in childhood and means often making something from nothing, or "make a way when there is no way." Teachers can do some of this. Kids can also figure out that in every neighborhood there are some options and opportunities available, and teachers have to be open to discussions about what these are. They also need to know that opportunity won't just come walking in your door. Also, students need to learn to overcome disappointment and will have to adapt to a certain extent, or "You have to kiss a few frogs before you find a prince" is another way of putting it.

JL: Finally, what would a school look like that included Roger's requirement that they address *feelings and ideas?*

JW: As far as ideas go, school would be a place that knows that education is a cognitive process, that involves music, plays, psychodrama, poems . . . places and activities where the feelings come out.

School would also send alternative messages out, about testing, about giftedness, about resilience.

I learned because of my own internal motivation. It worked twice for me and took me further.

One, learning how to read. Funny papers fascinated me. My older brother and sister would not read to me when they were supposed to. I tried to tell my mother but she could not protect me from my siblings. I wanted to be independent of them. I wanted to find out what was on the page without a big hassle. . . . I was four years old. I began to memorize words. I was trying to learn from memory yet could not put them into a meaningful sequence. My method was raggedy. My mother put me in preschool. I showed kids what I was trying to do with my shoe box full of words in show-and-tell one day. Got the attention of my young teacher, who decided to help me learn to read. I could read when I got into regular school. The motivation came from inside of me.

Two, when I was nineteen years old I was in college listening to lecture on psychology—all about the unconscious mind. Whole thing fascinated me. I knew there was more to things than what I had known before. Here was something that connected with me. My grades went from C + to A. All came from me. I figured out what to do once the internal motivation came.

If we can figure out what internal motivation is for each child the rest will happen.

Reference

White, J. L., & Cones, J. H. III (1999). *Black man emerging: Facing the past and seizing a future in America.* New York: W. H. Freeeman.

QUESTIONS

1. Joseph White says we need to find out what our students need and what their parents need and want before we dictate to them what they ought to want. How does this apply to your experience working with African American communities? How do you communicate with parents or family members of your Black students?

2. Dr. White suggests we need a mix of authoritative and cultural styles to reach African American students. What does he mean by this? When he says to build on the strengths of students and on what they already know and do, what does he mean? How does this lead to motivating students?

15

BLACK/AFRICAN AMERICAN FAMILIES

Coming of Age in Predominately White Communities

Val Middleton, Kieran Coleman, and Chance W. Lewis

T he wave of middle-class Black/African American youth being reared and educated in predominately White communities is on the rise, and in its wake is a force undermining their social, emotional, and educational well-being, as the following scenario illustrates:

> Jeremiah continually ended up in the principal's office of his pre-dominately White junior high school after having yelled at, tripped, or hit one of his peers. Jeremiah stands a head or two above his peers, dark chocolate skin, unkempt black curly hair, and a smile that should have been able to get him out of any amount of trouble he had gotten himself into. In conversation, Jeremiah would acknowledge that he felt like no one understood him, that his peers call him names, make racist remarks, tell racist jokes, and pull his hair because they want to know if it will "bounce back." He says, "Sometimes I can just ignore it, but other times it's just too much." He is the youngest of four and the only one adopted into his White family. He is struggling with what

---

The ethnic identity categories of *African American* and *Black* are used interchangeably to refer to individuals of African ancestry. Black may also be used to include individuals who are perceived to be Black or African American (e.g., African, Jamaican, multiracial) and who currently live in the United States.

it means to be coming of age as a Black man in this predominately White community.

Jeremiah is in the process of coming to terms with and bringing to the
forefront his concerns about difference, identity, and disconnectedness in
this predominately White setting. With few positive outlets for such crisis
situations, Jeremiah and other African American youth are "at risk" emotionally and academically. This chapter explores issues related to understanding and supporting African American youth coming of age in predominately
White school settings. Narrative experiences of Black families living in predominately White settings detailing expectations for nurturing student
growth and success are shared. It is our hope that these narratives will support current and future teachers in understanding and addressing the unique
needs of this diverse student population.

Black/African American Children and Families

For many, the media determines the perception of Black or African American. The stereotypical portrayals of Black men as rappers, athletes, gang-
bangers, pimps, thieves, drug dealers, and criminals; of Black females as
maids, pregnant teens, prostitutes, and single mothers on welfare; and of
Black families as living in poverty in urban ghettos, in dilapidated housing,
or in the projects are rampant. More recently, the stereotypes have expanded
to include those African Americans with newfound wealth or status based on
their ability to be stereotypical media icons (e.g., cast members of *The Real
World*, rappers, and athletes), further perpetuating the idea "you can take
them out of the ghetto, but you can't take the ghetto out of them."

Amid the backdrop of these stereotypical portrayals of African Americans, *The Cosby Show* aired and brought to the forefront the social world of
the Black/African American, suburban family. This TV show provided a
portrait much more complex and diverse than the previous stereotypes seen
in the media and, ultimately, became a portal through which society could
redefine African Americans as both economically and academically successful.

The number of African American families living and being educated in
predominately White communities is on the rise, as are issues of isolation,
identity, and connectedness for African American youth. Media portrayals
confound the issues for both White and Black youth, as the following narratives illustrate:

Heath is not only struggling with his identity, but also keeping up with his friends . . . who come and pick him up in Jaguars and Range Rovers. He is not able to keep up economically. We are also dealing with substance abuse of pot. . . . You don't have to buy it, because they [White boys] have it. They are walking around with money in their pocket and it is assumed because he is Black that he is supposed to act like the videos. If not, he is not being true to his own, because he has been told that by other Black kids. He's struggling. (Parent L)

Sue likes to be around other Blacks. She says, "I like being around my people." Although she does it jokingly, she tries to imitate what the media portrays as the Blacks being cool. (Parents F and G)

The complexity of racial self-concept can be seen in these narratives and in African American youth as they struggle to develop a dual identity as one who is part of the mainstream and one who is apart from the mainstream. Dual identity is an acculturation position in which students have positive beliefs both about their own ethnic group and about their membership in the larger society. In establishing a dual identity, they struggle with the dichotomy of demonstrating their true nature or identity through positive interactions in an effort to tear down the typical negative stereotypes when the expectation was for them to live up to the stereotypical image (Glenn, 2003).

Meet the Families

You have already been introduced to three members of twelve families who share stories throughout the chapter regarding their experiences and/or their children's experiences in predominately White school communities. The parents of color sharing stories in this chapter grew up in segregated or racially diverse communities and were all educated at four-year colleges/universities with the exception of one, who was educated at a technical school. The children who are represented range in age from four to seventeen years and are from four school districts. Pseudonyms are used to protect the identity and location of the parents and their children.

Parent A is a married female from a large metropolitan area in the West. She grew up in an ethnically diverse environment. After graduating from college and living on the West Coast, her husband was transferred to a predominately White community, where she has lived for approximately six years, serving as program director of an early education program. They have three children schooled predominately in this community. She describes her children as follows:

> *Janae is the oldest child and a junior in high school. She is active in the music program and runs track. She wants to attend a college outside of the state in which she currently resides. The majority of her friends are White, Mexican-American, and Asian. She enjoys school. Tina is in middle school and has a diverse core of friends . . . a more diversified group of friends. Jordan is in elementary school, has a mild disposition, and is active in sports. He is like his father, who is also mellow and relaxed. He earns good grades. He received several commendations from the principal because he is calm and he is a leader.*

Parent B is a divorced female from a midsize city in the southern part of the United States. After graduating from a historically Black college, she received a fellowship to pursue a graduate degree at a university in a predominately White community. She has one son, Micah, and his prior schooling occurred in a predominately Black elementary school setting. Micah is currently enrolled in an ethnically diverse elementary school. She states, "He is a sociable young person. He doesn't have problems making friends, and he is very outgoing and loves school."

Parent C is a single female from a large metropolitan city on the West Coast. She grew up in an ethnically diverse neighborhood because her family lived in Navy housing. After graduating from a university on the West Coast, she applied to a graduate program in a predominately White community. Her son originally attended a predominately Black Christian academy on the West Coast and is now in first grade at a predominately White elementary school. She states, "Antonio is playful and he will be himself. He loves school."

Parent D is a single female who grew up in a diverse community in the Midwest. Through a desegregation program, she attended a racially diverse suburban high school. After graduating from college, she worked in a community college setting before taking an administrative position at a predominately White university. Her first-grade daughter attends a predominately White school. She states, "Amaya is very outgoing, very creative, artistic, and friendly."

Parent E is a married male from a large metropolitan area on the East Coast. He moved to a predominately White area where he worked as a school paraprofessional and later in an administrative position at a university. Two of his children are enrolled in school, one in a prekindergarten program and the other in an elementary school. While describing his school-aged children, he states, "Jalen is excited and fascinated to be among his peers and he loves attending school and playing with his friends. Erica is happy-go-lucky and she is always happy to be around her friends."

Parents F and G come from a large metropolitan city in the Midwest. They grew up in a predominately Black school setting and later worked in diverse settings in their executive positions in a nationally recognized company. They have two children in high school and one child in middle school. They share the following descriptions about their children:

> Malcolm, the oldest, is quiet, and probably cerebral. He is athletic and popular. As a result, everybody knows him and likes him. Sue is the artistic type. She loves dancing and music. Cindi, the youngest, is a tomboy. She is probably more of the leadership/student council–type student. She loves art. She is involved in basketball and volleyball.

Parent H is a divorced male from North Africa. He grew up in a predominately Black African setting. American missionaries heavily influenced his educational experiences. After graduating from college, he relocated to the United States to attend graduate school and worked in an administrative position at that predominately White university. He has two children in a predominately White elementary school. When describing his daughter and son, he states, "Angelica is a well-organized girl for her age. She is very helpful at home and according to her teachers, she is well behaved in school. Keenan is a good child who likes to receive lots of direction."

Parent I is a married male from western Africa. He grew up in a predominately Black African setting strongly influenced by British traditions. After graduating from a boarding high school in western Africa, he came to the United States for better educational opportunities, graduated from college, and worked as a corporate senior administrator in several metropolitan areas across the United States. He has one daughter enrolled in a private Christian academy at the elementary level. When talking about his daughter, he states, "Iman loves school and enjoys playing with her friends."

Parent J is a married female from Central America. Missionaries influenced her educational experiences. While in the United States, she met her husband and eventually they relocated to a predominately White community. They have two children and the oldest child is in elementary school. Parent J has this to say about her:

> Monica is a very energetic, inquisitive child. She is highly perceptive about people and their feelings. She has a high sense of justice and equality. She notices when she is treated differently from others and that distinction bothers her.

Parent K is a single female from the southern part of the United States. She attended an experimental racially diverse high school and later graduated from a historically Black college. Afterward, she lived and worked professionally in several metropolitan cities across the United States. She relocated to a predominately White community for a corporate job. She has three children. The oldest child started school in the area but returned to the South. The other two children attend a public elementary and high school, respectively. In describing her children, she states the following:

> *Johnny is smart and athletic. He has the ability to retain trivial knowledge. He is kind and passive, but he is also passionate about many things. He likes to keep peace. Louis is very athletic, but he is totally opposite from the oldest child. He stands up for his rights and for the rights of others. He likes to take up for the underdog. He loves a challenge and a debate. Sharon is very loving, kind, quiet, and soft-spoken. She is artistic. She loves to read, and she doesn't mind being alone.*

Parent L is a married biracial female from a large metropolitan city on the West Coast. She grew up in a predominately White community, was a student leader in a small international academy, and after high school she married and relocated overseas because her husband was in the military. After a period of years, she returned to the States and eventually moved to a predominately White community. She has three children enrolled in public schools, two in high school and one in elementary school. When discussing her children, she shares the following information:

> *Heath is athletic and loves basketball and wrestling. He is self-motivated. He likes socializing with his friends. Tommy is athletic—basketball, football, and track. He likes math and he is very aggressive and competitive. Lisa prefers basketball and swimming. She is very active in school and church. She does well in school.*

The narrative descriptions shared by these families come from extensive interviews that were part of a research study (Coleman, 2003) and our daily work in schools with youth and their families. The family portraits and detailed accounts of their experiences frame a picture of expectations toward supporting the education of African American youth in predominately White schools. The narratives and the conclusions drawn from them support current research aimed at helping teachers understand and address the unique needs of this diverse student population.

Issues Affecting African American Youth in Predominately White Schools

Despite parental socioeconomic status and academic abilities, we see African American youth raised in predominately White settings as "at risk" as they experience isolation, identity issues, categorization, and a lack of community and family connectedness. We see these experiences occurring in African American families and in White families with adopted children of color. As parents, we wonder about the consequences of raising and educating our African American children in this particular type of community and our responsibility in meeting their cultural, social, and educational needs.

One of the major issues for schools in educating their diverse student population is the schools' *invitational* nature. Invitational Theory (Purkey & Schmidt, 1990) contends that inviting climates are predicated upon feelings of care, respect, and trust. The success of the climate is dependent on how intentional schools are about establishing inviting environments. *Intentionally disinviting* schools are obvious in their attempts to attract and retain a certain population of students; however, *unintentionally disinviting* schools are likely not aware of the factors that make them disinviting (Purkey & Schmidt, 1990).

The following narratives invite readers to delve into the experiences of African American children in predominately White schools as their parents highlight the invitational nature of schools. These stories are beneficial because they bring to the surface unintentionally disinviting behaviors occurring in schools while providing opportunities to deconstruct and reconstruct through dialogue intentionally inviting schools for educating African American youth.

It's the Intent

Many parents of children of color will utilize the "school choice policy" to search for schools in their predominately White communities that are intentional about creating and fostering a climate in which diversity is recognized, acknowledged, and affirmed. Generally, parents look for schools with excellent academics, meaningful lessons, and supportive personnel. Although some parents believe that it is important to have a diverse staff and student population, they are as likely to choose schools that are intentionally inviting and schools that have White teachers who are committed to sustaining a supportive and embracing environment for their children. The following statements from parents indicate what they believe is the essence of *intent:*

We were not impressed [with the neighborhood school], and we had a negative experience at our neighborhood school. We went there and when we met with the principal we wanted to know about the staff people of color and they couldn't tell us. Even with the students, it's a difference when you walk into the class and the students think, "Hey, that is a new person" versus a look of "Wow—I've never seen your type before." You could see it in their eyes. Me and my wife decided that there is no way we will put our son through that. If they do that to us, what about our son? So, we immediately erased that school off our list and went to our next school to interview. This would have been his first educational experience. Going into that environment? No way!

At the school of choice, the one thing I liked was that they weren't taken back with, "Why was he asking me? Why is he pursuing this? Why is this important?" It was more like, "This is great; could you give me more insight? If you need anything else or have any ideas, just come back." They have been great in this situation. An issue at the [choice] school is that staffwise it is not that diverse. What is important is there is an appreciation, awareness pictures, and multiculturalism—the intent is there. She [principal] made an impact in everything. So to answer your question, "Yes, we do feel comfortable with the school." In this school, someone is trying versus another school where it is not even a try. He would have been lost. (Parent E)

The school has an inviting atmosphere and the environment is colorful. They make you want to be there. They make you feel like this is the place where I am going to learn something. I have been to some schools, coming from where I come from, the environments are not conducive to learning. It is drab and the kids don't want to be there. It doesn't invigorate the mind. . . . But, this school has a wall picture of a globe or whatever that shows where students from different places come from. They boast about this map. That's a very proud thing to know that they have students from all different points of the country. I thought it was nice. A lot of these kids are away from home for the first time to see something that represents their country on the walls. They also have pictures of kids, like children from Turkey. I think that is nice and positive. (Parent B)

I checked the statistics on the Internet on the school district. I wanted to know . . . how many other African American or people of different cultures or backgrounds are enrolled in that school. . . . There was not a diverse faculty, but I got the impression that they do a lot of work even for teachers who were raised in this state. They have sought out extra training . . . to get a feel for what is going on outside of this state. This school is rated as excellent. I thought the school was old and cluttered—that was my first impression. It was cluttered with articles and garments from different countries. I thought that was pretty neat to bring in people's cultural background into the school setting so it can be discussed. So, I liked that part about the school. They are very open. They have posted around the school, in different languages, what the room is, so if it is the bathroom, it's written in Spanish on the door and it's written in English. I thought this was pretty good. I wanted Amaya to learn another language as well. You know, there are few schools in this area that are culturally reflective. This is also one of the schools that had the most diverse population as far as people from different cultures and I don't just mean African American, but they have students from fifteen different countries in that school. (Parent D)

I feel that they are genuine. They want to try to make a better transition. They understand that my children are minorities and they are going to have a harder time. It is just the way life is. I feel they are sincere and they try to be an advocate for my kids. They want to make my children comfortable. They set up a plan—if you have questions or problems, come to them so that they can address it immediately. (Parent E)

Sharon really likes her teachers. I think the teachers have a great impact on her. They are very encouraging with little notes, "excellent job," and "keep up the good work." All these things really build her self-esteem and make her want to continue to do better and take initiative. She likes that. (Parent K)

The positive experience in public school is none. I took Monica out of public school because I felt that the only thing they were teaching is that the White culture [uses his hands] is here and everybody else is down here. The new school, a Christian school, teaches all kids are equal. They go through lessons about "it's okay if someone has blue or brown skin, but we are all God's children." They have an interest in establishing cultural programs so after we are gone it continues—a sustaining program. That is the biggest attraction for me. I don't think it is appease and move on. I know what it looks like. Intent is there. (Parent J)

The unconscious acts of prejudice and discrimination of unintentionally disinviting school environments and the conscious acts involved in making schools intentionally inviting are evident in these narratives. Bringing the disinviting actions to the forefront for deconstruction and, ultimately, reconstruction into intentionally inviting actions is the focus of the remainder of this chapter.

In Case You Didn't Know: Deconstructing Stereotypes and Assumptions

In case you didn't know refers to parents' clear and adamant statements regarding their desire not only for their children to receive a quality education, but to make sure that school officials unfamiliar with the Black middle-class family make no assumptions about their ability and willingness to be involved in their children's educational process. The following narratives clarify misconceptions regarding parental involvement and high expectations from a racial group barely seen in the community:

> We are more involved than our parents. We are very involved with our children. . . . We have always been involved, because if you are not involved, the school system feels you don't care. Then, they don't care. If something is not going right, we want to know about it, and we expect you to tell us about it. Don't write us off and we find out down the road that it has been going on for a while. (Parents F and G)

> I think I did a good job of clarifying most things when I first arrived—like establishing rapport. Letting them know who we are, where we were from, where Antonio came from in regards to schooling, what he had been learning, and the environment he had grown up in so far. I made sure that I told the teachers and principal in such a way that there were not any misconceptions. I made sure that I had persistence at the school so there were no misconceptions. I think that my persistence is a better indicator because I was able to verbally discuss with them face-to-face instead of over the telephone. I feel like when you have a personal contact with somebody it is a better way to communicate. They can see visually and hear what you are saying so that they can get both sides of it. (Parent C)

> I think it is important to let them know that we care about our children's education. We are not just sending Amaya there and expecting that they will be her sole teacher and not the parents. We want to be involved and also in the process. (Parent I)

> I have always been involved because I wanted to make sure that I or my kids didn't fall into those stereotypes of single Black parents. Oh, they don't care about their kids. They just send them to school. They don't care about what is going on and they don't participate. So, I made an effort to make sure that I stopped by the school to check and see what is going on. I want them to do well and I want them to succeed. Your foundation, education, is the key. When we came here, it wasn't that I wanted to show my kids that I cared, but I wanted to show the teachers and the principal and all these other people that the stereotypes they may have in their head is not me. You need to erase that off because that's not me. I'm not that typical or whatever you have in your mind of a typical single Black mother. I wanted to show them the difference. (Parent K)

My oldest son, Heath, has dyslexia and he is in the special education program. He is mainstreamed, but he also takes a resource class. He maintains a 3.0 but struggles with comprehension so I have to get tutors for him. I know that people with dyslexia can be successful. Most people with dyslexia have high IQs. We went for an IEP [Individualized Education Plan] meeting, making sure he is eligible for next year's program. Well, she asked him, "What are his goals?" He was like, "I'm going to college." She looks at him. . . . She said to him, "Well, you know you don't have to go to college. Maybe you should think of other options. Maybe college is not for you. You can go to a junior college or maybe a trade school." We just looked at her. She later wanted to know why I was involved because she told me last year that he is in high school so I really don't have to set up these meetings or his classes. He can do his own classes. I said, "I'm here to help him achieve his goals." (Parent L)

These narratives demonstrate parents' purposeful efforts to combat stereotypes of "the uninvolved parent of color" by establishing lines of communication with school personnel and frequenting the school. This process erases the prevailing misconceptions or stereotypes school personnel may have about parents of color and assures them that parents of color are serious about being involved in and staying informed of their children's progress and behavior. Parents also want school personnel to know that they have no hesitation in confronting the system to ensure that their children are being treated fairly and receive a quality education.

At What Cost?

At what cost? refers to the mixed emotions of parents regarding their children's experiences in predominately White schools. Generally, parents felt good about their children's academic experiences and their diverse friendships, as illustrated in the following narratives:

Jordan has a diverse amount of friends. (Parent A)

Amaya enjoys her friends. They call her on the telephone, and, of course, she is still the only African American child in her class. (Parent D)

Jalen's positive experience is that he is gaining good friends and good social skills. He is a part of the parties—the social things. Lots of time, if you are from a different group, you get excluded. He has been a part of all of that. White students call our house and get together outside of the classroom to do things. (Parent E)

Angelica and Keenan like school. They like their friends. They love their teachers. They say that their teachers are cool. (Parent H)

The high school is new and they have done well . . . they have had the opportunity to become involved in a lot of extracurricular activities. (Parents F and G)

Micah loves school. He gets involved. He is excited about learning. It's opening up his mind to other places. He can understand that this person is from Turkey. . . . I think it helps him open his mind up to really see what it means to be from different parts of the world. Everything is just not the U.S.—right here centrally focused. There are other parts of the world. There are other people that come from different parts of the world, and he is a part of it. (Parent B)

The school draws in a lot of people that want to focus on diversity and have their children learn about diversity. It teaches them about characteristics, like compassion. They want students to come out with a well-rounded education, not just book smarts, but also understanding how to be compassionate and understanding of other people and differences. Students do art about different cultures, and they learn about cultures. (Parent C)

Although parents generally agreed that their children were in good academic schools and had excellent teachers, their concerns pertaining to cultural issues such as overcompensation and isolation forced them to continually evaluate the pros and cons and ask themselves, "At what cost?"

Overcompensation

Parents recognized that teachers tried to be culturally sensitive, but because of a lack of knowledge or experience in working with students of color they oftentimes fell short. For instance, teachers would allow students of color to have more chances than their White counterparts. Although these teachers were intentionally trying to be helpful, many of the parents felt that the teachers were too lenient and that their children were getting away with too much. These parents believed that the teachers were "overcompensating" to make sure they were not seen as racist or insensitive, as the following narratives illustrate:

When I went to a parent-teacher conference, I found out a lot of stuff that I didn't know was happening. She began explaining to me about Micah's overbearing nature. She expressed that she didn't want to send him to the office because she didn't want him to be labeled as a problem child. I think they overcompensated because they didn't know how to discipline him so they made allowances by letting him do more things than someone else.

Honestly, coming from Black schools, a lot of these things would not be handled this way. They would have gotten him in line. He is the type of person who is going to push as far as you let him push. When he sees he can push you and get around you, he will. When he was in school at home in an all-Black school with Black teachers, they would be like, "No way. We're not going to have that." He would have to check himself. . . . "Don't let him push you, okay? You deal with him and tell him, 'You stay your butt here for recess or you won't do this. This is taken away from you.'" She asked, "Can I do that?" I had to give her permission to control her student. (Parent B)

Another type of overcompensation involves going "above and beyond" in response to cultural situations, as illustrated in the following narrative about Tina:

When Tina was in third grade the class did an assignment: trace your ancestors back to their original country. Additionally, there are a huge number of children who are adopted in this community. Our African American relatives are harder to trace. So, I went to talk to the teacher. I told the teacher it wasn't fair. . . . So, we compromised—we came up with an alternate project. When we got to the school this woman made Tina the queen of the heritage search. Our point wasn't to point her out or have special attention. We wanted to help the teacher recognize that not everybody can trace their heritage back to the Mayflower or England or whatever. We had to go back and address her overcompensation. (Parent A)

The cost of overcompensation is that it gives students a false sense of the reality they will need to deal with as adults of color (i.e., racism) and feeds their feelings of difference among their peers. That sense of reality and the need to prepare students of color for future interactions is illustrated in the following scenario:

Parent L shares that Lisa told the teacher a kid on the school bus called her a "nigger." Parent L took this matter back to the school. After the counselor promised her that this would never happen again, she told the counselor, "You can't promise me this won't happen, maybe not tomorrow or at this school, but it will happen."

Isolation of Being: Different, Only, One of a Few

Feelings of isolation brought to the forefront by teachers' lack of knowledge, overcompensation, or by students of color being "different," "the only," or "one of a few" in a classroom must be addressed in order for students to gain a sense of identity and belonging. The following narratives speak to the importance of having teachers provide a classroom environment that actively and purposefully nurtures diversity:

> *When he reached first grade, Jalen came to me and said, "Daddy, I am the only one that is brown in my classroom. There are no brown faces in my classroom. I see brown faces during the break, lunch, and recess, but they are not in my classroom." He also has reflected this in his work assignments, whether it is art or anything: drawing brown on everything is his focus. (Parent E)*

> *In a teacher's conference, I asked the teacher, "What is Iman's interaction with children in her class? Who does she interact with?" The teacher was stunned. She couldn't give me an answer. She couldn't tell me who. She had no idea. This was important because she never came home talking about a friend. She would say nobody likes me because I'm different. So, I wanted to find out had the teacher noticed. It is not the responsibility of the school to force children to be social, but if a child is going to spend so many hours in school, if there is no relationship, that's a very empty place to be. (Parent I)*

> *There was an Indian girl who was about the same skin tone as Amaya. All the other kids were Caucasian with light skin complexions. Amaya and the Indian girl could not be in their club. . . . "They didn't want to play with us today." That made me think because they were the only dark-skin people in the class-room and the only two excluded from the little girl's club. I talked to the teacher about it, and she sort of blew me off. She knew the little girl's personality and she changed the seating. (Parent D)*

The parents clearly explain the cost of educating their children in these narratives. Overall, they describe their desire for their children to receive a quality education within these predominately White settings and adamantly declare their willingness to confront a disinviting system through parental involvement, purposeful communication, and high expectations for their children. Additionally, parents recognize that there are some things predominately White schools can provide for their children and some things they cannot. For further assistance in supporting African American youth in predominately White settings, schools and families often turn to local community agencies and the church.

Church and Community Support for African American Youth

In predominately White communities, a multiracial church can be critical for survival of African American youth, as in the following example.

> *There was one day that the church had just been remodeled. Lin was on a ladder changing a lightbulb and all the men were holding the ladder. They were supporting her. I thought this was all symbolic. (Parent A)*

Role Models Who "Look Like Me"

Role models who "look like me" identifies that additional supports are needed for educating African American youth coming of age in predominately White settings. We have had many preservice teachers in our teacher education courses become defensive at the statement, "White teachers need support in teaching students of color," and minimize it with the retort, "All teachers need support, not just White ones." While they are accurate in recognizing that all teachers need support, they are also unveiling a belief system of *privilege*. Getting White teachers to understand and acknowledge that children of color have different needs from those of their White counterparts is critical to creating inviting school environments. Additionally, the families of students of color want teachers to know that the identity development of African American children must be *purposefully* supported.

The narratives in this section use the context of the African American or multiracial church as a partner in schooling African American youth because it plays a unique role for many African American families and specifically for those families raising children in predominately White environments. Parent E illustrates this point by stating, "The church, particularly the Black church, fills that need as far as social need, spiritual need, social interaction, relationship, guidance, and programming that they are not receiving in the school."

The church described in this chapter provides a lens through which school personnel can understand and develop plans for meeting the educational and developmental needs of its African American students. It demonstrates the importance of involving other entities in the growth and development of African American youth, as the following narratives illustrate:

> *The school plays a different part. Jordan is getting educated as far as writing, math, reading, and listening skills, but that is it. We have to be intentional about other extracurricular events that the school is not providing. . . . It fills the needs that the school district cannot do or accomplish by providing people that look like him—cultural identity. He expressed that he loves his friends at school but he wants to see people who look like him. It serves a spiritual need as well as a network for support for people who look like him. (Parent A)*

> *My sons have a lot of male role models in the church that are successful Black men, highly educated. (Parent L)*

> *Identity—they see whole groups of people of color in the church who look similar to them. They are not walking in and they are the only ones standing out. . . . The kids look like them. (Parent H)*

> *I think culturally the church gives them an opportunity to be around their own. They don't have to deal with stereotypes. They can relax and be themselves. They can talk slang, minus subject and verb agreement, without marring their image, without being misunderstood. To be around other Blacks—it is their getaway. It has been their haven. . . . They don't have to explain the culture things . . . all the questions and attention of little things that comes naturally for us. (Parents F and G)*

> *Most of the kids look like her. The teacher, for the most part, looks like her. So, there is a different self-concept than at school, where she is sitting there and she's the only one sitting there and the teacher looks White. Everything looks White. She is the only dark spot. She has a sense of belonging. She can be at ease. (Parent I)*

> *Amaya has the opportunity to meet other Black families and kids her age. She also has the opportunity to see individuals who serve as role models. There are teenagers who are looking out for the younger children and that's the whole village thing. It takes a village to raise a child and the church is our village. (Parent D)*

Curriculum

African American youth must see themselves widely represented and successful not only in the community, but also in the curriculum. When diversity is not readily infused into the curriculum, these youth must be taught to think critically about what has been included as well as omitted. They must also be prepared to respond to a society that continually stereotypes them as criminals and rappers. Parents speak to the church as a community agency, providing opportunities for critical thinking and countering stereotypes.

> *They do debates, different types of subjects, hip-hop, women's issues, teen pregnancy, and things that are important. The teacher doesn't sugarcoat these things because you are setting them up for failure, and I think what he does is he hits the issues right on the head. He relates to them too. What do you think about this? What is this rap song saying? What do you think this means? He breaks it down for them. So the next time they hear another song, instead of them just hearing the beat and popping their fingers and tapping their toes, now they are analyzing the words and thinking. . . . It is like a school setting because they are learning in a different way and different things. (Parent K)*

> *I'm not expecting to go anywhere and be prejudice free; that's unrealistic. The children need to understand that is not going to happen. . . . They need to be aware that they are Black and be proud of who they are. (Parents F and G)*

Care and Support

Parents want a caring and supportive network that provides opportunities to establish meaningful relationships with peers, community leaders, adults, and others from a variety of cultures. In Gilligan's (1982) book, *In a Different Voice*, *care* is based on needs, response, and relationships. Care urges individuals to be carers and to demonstrate the principles of care with others.

Noddings (1992) bases care on four major components: (1) *modeling*, which enables individuals not only to care, but to show others how to care through the development of relationships; (2) *dialogue*, which allows individuals to exchange ideas through open-ended conversations; (3) *practice*, which gives individuals the opportunity to develop and apply skills needed in making significant contributions to society; and (4) *confirmation*, the act of affirming and encouraging the best in others. When encouragement occurs, individuals contribute to the development of others, and care and support are manifested within the community.

> *Eventually, you want to make sure the children have the right foundation so they can be successful and care about other people and help make society better. . . . That's the ultimate goal. (Parent K)*

Even in areas where African American students appear to "have it all," these children cannot survive without a supportive and caring culture. Parents viewed the church as a place where their children felt a sense of care and belonging while leadership, social skills, cognitive skills, and identity were cultivated. Parents also recognized that the church is only one partner in the education of their children and that schools were the other. These parents wanted partners that would help their children be well rounded and involved. Additionally, they wanted commitments toward caring and culturally responsive teaching methods and curriculum that is academically rigorous.

The institutions of church and school have a significant influence on the social as well as the academic success of students, and they play a significant role in introducing alternative thought that will assist them in the development of character and influence behavior. However, parents recognize that not every community will have one entity to partner with in meeting the needs of African American youth and offer the following messages to predominately White schools regarding efforts toward diversity:

> *It is a wonderful community to raise a family, but there are some shortcomings in the community when it comes to cultural awareness. . . . They need to do more cultural awareness trainings. The teachers in the community need to understand that when Black kids come into the school they are going to be different. . . . They need to do some type of piece about racism, its meanings and harms—just like you teach everything else. These kids need to know. These kids are coming to school and they are saying things that are not so nice, that maybe they heard their parents say. They can't understand that's damaging. That hurts. Talking about racism and bringing it into a part of the fabric of the school. (Parent B)*

> *Even though the school is an institution, each child is an individual. They should be treated individually. The schools should serve as mentors and guides to help mold the child, not just on a school level, but also on a personal level. (Parent K)*

> *I would say for an African American child raised in a predominately White area or a predominately White school district . . . get your child involved in something that is culturally based. Become involved. (Parent D)*

> *When you have children in the minority—it doesn't matter if it's color, physical ability, level, or language—they need to pay careful attention to these children, especially young children. . . . Teachers should look and see what is happening*

and talk to them, to the class, about acceptance and embracing differences. Do some of that bridging. Watch what is happening with that child and if that child is being isolated. I know, academically, Iman is doing well. Unfortunately, she is experiencing a poor social environment. It kills me and hurts me like a knife to my stomach to hear her talk about it. (Parent I)

My message would be for teachers to open your eyes and recognize the contributions of other cultures in America. Teach the truth and the whole truth to the students. (Parent J)

My message for schools would be that although we live in a community with very little diversity that as a teacher or as a leader they need to realize they have a large impact on every child's life. They need to be open-minded and understanding to different cultures. They have to be sensitive to diversity. I just hope, I can't even say, that they can even read a book that gives them that. They have to open up their minds and hearts and be willing to accept each child for who they are regardless of their race. (Parent L)

Further recommendations for educating children of color in predominately White communities are as follows:

- Establish relationships/form partnerships with entities committed to working with diverse populations.
- Be aware of issues faced by families with international backgrounds who may have a different understanding of their role regarding parent-family-school relationships.
- Participate in discussions aimed at providing meaningful experiences for students of color in predominately White communities.
- Develop programs that will meet the needs of specific groups of students of color.
- Support mentoring and volunteering programs in schools as a way to develop meaningful relationships and discredit stereotypes.
- Embrace differences and find ways to make a difference for the diversity that exists within the student population.

One of the greatest challenges faced by schools with a growing diverse student population is moving from an ideology of assimilation to one of acculturation, which recognizes and celebrates the uniqueness all students bring to the school community. The family narratives that we have presented highlight ways to enhance school environments so that diversity is recognized, appreciated, and used to build a foundation of respect, trust, and intentionality toward supporting the physical, psychological, and academic potential of their youth.

References

Coleman, K. (2003). *Parental perceptions regarding the experiences of African American children in multiple settings (church and school) located within predominately white communities.* Unpublished doctoral dissertation. Fort Collins: Colorado State University.

Gilligan, C. (1982). *In a different voice.* Cambridge, MA: Harvard University Press.

Glenn, D. (2003). *Minority students with complex beliefs about ethnic identity are found to do better in school* [On-line]. Available: http://chronicle.com/daily/2003/06/2003060201n.htm.

Noddings, N. (1992). *The challenge to care in schools: An alternative approach to education.* New York: Teachers College Press.

Purkey, W., & Schmidt, J. (1990). *Invitational learning for counseling and development.* Ann Arbor, MI: Eric Counseling and Personnel Services Clearinghouse.

QUESTIONS

1. What do the authors of this chapter mean when they talk about the "complexity of racial self concept" for young people? Why is this made even more complex by being Black in a predominantly White school? What can be done about it in your school?

2. What are some of the things that African American parents look for in choosing a school for their child in a predominantly White system? If you had to begin changing your school to one that welcomes Black students, where would you start? Name three beginning steps you might take.

16

UNDERSTANDING KOREAN AMERICAN STUDENTS

Facts, Not Myth

Ok-Hee Lee

A mong children of immigrants, Asian Americans represent one of the fastest-growing student populations in U.S. schools today. According to the U.S. Census Bureau, in 1999 it was estimated that approximately 2.6 million Asian American students were enrolled in the nation's P–12 schools, accounting for 5 percent of the total student enrollment, a dramatic increase from a meager 1 percent in 1972. The demographics of Asian Americans help explain the increase; 88 percent of Asian American students have a foreign-born parent, compared with 65 percent and 20 percent of Hispanic students and all U.S. students, respectively.

With this increase of Asian American students, their academic achievement and success in schools have received heightened attention from both the mainstream media and academia. Various statistics on student achievement in the United States show that Asian American students outperform White, Black, and Hispanic students in GPA, SAT, and high school graduation rate (CARE & College Board, 2008; Lee, 2009; Lew, 2006; Tuan, 1998). Praised as a "model minority," Asian American students have been portrayed as a smart, quiet, dependable, and industrious minority fulfilling the American dream.

Indeed, many Asian American students are exceptionally successful, and they become a source of pride and inspiration for many other Asian American students. However, seeing them as typical would simply be a mistake.

Often, aggregate data on Asian American students fail to capture important disparities within and among Asian American students, which may lead educators and policymakers to believe the stereotype of Asian American students as model students. While there are multiple reasons for including this group under one umbrella in certain cases, it is critical for educators and policymakers to recognize that students who comprise this group occupy positions along the full range of the socioeconomic spectrum—from the poor and marginalized to the affluent and highly successful. There is no single description that can capture the characteristics of Asian American students or communities as a whole (CARE & College Board, 2008; Lee, 2009; Lew, 2006).

Of the many ethnic groups lumped together as Asian Americans, this chapter specifically focuses on Korean American students and discusses their characteristics, both those shared by other Asian American groups and those that are unique to Korean Americans. This information will help White teachers understand who Korean American students are and how to better meet their needs in the classroom. More specifically, the purpose of this chapter is fourfold. First, it offers a brief history of Korean immigration and current demographics of Korean Americans in the United States, highlighting some of the prominent characteristics of Korean Americans as a group and the diversity that is found in this group. Second, it examines how the stereotype of Asian Americans as perceived foreigners or as a model minority plays into racial relations in America in general and Asian Americans' experience in particular. Third, it considers some of the challenges Korean American students and their families face. It concludes with suggestions about what teachers can do to meet the needs of Korean American students in their classrooms.

Immigration History and Demographics of Korean Americans

Korean Americans are one of the fastest growing Asian American ethnic groups in the United States. According to the 2000 U.S. Census, 1,076,872 people identified themselves as Korean only and 1,228,427 identified themselves as Koreans in combination with another Asian or other races. This constituted 0.38 percent of the 281,422,000 U.S. population (http://www .census.gov).

The history of Korean immigration to the United States spans over 100 years with the first Korean immigration dating back to 1883 (NAKA, 2003). During the first 80 years of Korean immigration history, however, there was little immigration. The immigrant population was mostly comprised of plantation laborers in Hawaii until 1924 when the U.S. government banned Asian immigration. Later immigration waves consisted mainly of the Korean brides of American soldiers who fought in the Korean War from 1950 to 1953, Korean War-orphans who were adopted by American families, and Korean students who were sponsored by the United States between 1945 and 1965 (Yu, Choe, & Han, 2002).

The influx of Korean immigrants came after the U.S. government passed the Immigration Act of 1965, which allowed employment and family immigration. Due to these changes in the immigration law, many Korean professionals seeking employment in the United States, including physicians and guest nurses, were not only able to apply for permanent residence visas, but could also enter the United States as families rather than as individuals as their predecessors had to do. In addition, these professionals could petition for permission for their parents or siblings to immigrate as well. Thus, Korean immigration to the United States accelerated dramatically from 6,231 during the 1950s to 34,526 during the 1960s, and to 267,638 during the 1970s. The biggest growth yet happened during the 1980s when 333,746 Koreans were admitted, ranking Korea fourth after Mexico, the Philippines, and China in number of immigrants to America.

The influx of highly-educated professionals during the 1970s and 1980s, however, significantly slowed down in the 1990s. Subsequent waves of immigrants have included poorer and less-educated immigrants from Korea and other Asian countries. This is critical to understanding the Korean American population along with other Asian Americans: the change in the immigration pattern has resulted in a polarized distribution of social class within the Asian American category (CARE & College Board, 2008; Lee, 2009).

In terms of demographics, due to the nature of their initial immigration history, Korean Americans have traditionally been concentrated in the Western states, Hawaii and California being home to a great majority until the 1950s. However, the pattern of geographic distribution of Korean Americans has changed significantly to include all the 50 states since the 1960s even though California and New York still remain home to 43 percent of all Korean Americans and metropolitan areas of 10 states are where heavy concentrations of Korean Americans are to be found (Noonan, 2004). Ninety-six percent of Korean Americans reside in large metropolitan areas, in comparison to 80 percent of the general population. Of Korean Americans living in metropolitan areas, 57 percent make their home in the suburbs and 40 percent in urban areas. Some scientists attribute this to Korean American parents' efforts to send their children to better schools (Lee, 2009; Lew, 2006).

According to the 2000 U.S. census, Korean Americans continue to hold one of the highest levels of educational achievement compared to the national average. Of Korean Americans 25 years of age and older, 49.2 percent had at least a bachelor's degree, which was more than double the national average of 20 percent. Also compared to the general population in the United States, Korean Americans show a lower divorce or separation rate as the figure of 6.1 percent divorces for Korean Americans compared to 11.8 percent divorces for any ethnicity from the 2000 U.S. Census attests. The figure reflects a relatively stable family structure in Korean American households.

In terms of work, about one-third of Korean American householders run self-owned small businesses, about one-fifth are in professional work including doctors, lawyers, and engineers, with the rest in other occupations. A typical pattern in the 1970s for a newly arriving family was to "start a small business with capital saved from a few years of labor on assembly lines, maintenance companies, and other blue-collar jobs" (Yu et al., 2002, p. 72). Today's immigrants start businesses shortly after arriving in part due to the strong economy and the liberalization of foreign exchange law in Korea. Even though Korean Americans constitute only 0.38 percent of the U.S. population, they own 1.49 percent of all retail businesses in the United States.

According to Yu and associates (2002), the tendency for Korean Americans to start small businesses is because of language and cultural barriers that hinder their ability to find jobs in mainstream society that fit their level of education and work experience. In order to stay competitive in the small business world, Korean Americans work long hours, mobilize ethnic resources, and utilize family labor. Typically in the small business world, some Korean American business owners do well, but others struggle as evidenced by the income data discussed below. Another reason for the high concentration of small businesses among Korean Americans is that they like controlling their work environment (Yu et al., 2002). Many Korean Americans face discrepancy in their status in the United States because they cannot find a job commensurate with their level of education and work experience. Thus, being one's own boss is an attractive option because it provides a certain degree of psychological satisfaction and compensation for the loss of self-esteem.

Related to income, Korean Americans make far less than what is commensurate with their educational achievement and work experience, mainly because many Korean Americans do not work in the occupations for which they are educated, and instead own small retail and personal businesses where profit margins are slim. Also, there is a significant disparity in income among Korean Americans themselves as evidenced by the fact that the mean income for Korean Americans is notably higher than their median income and that their respective standard deviations are the highest of all Asian and other racial groups. That means that economic status is severely polarized among Korean Americans in the United States. Thus teachers should not be misled by Korean Americans' mean or median income by assuming that most Korean Americans are prospering economically. There are many poor Korean Americans and therefore many Korean American students from poor families.

Moreover, the pattern of business ownership in the Korean community changes significantly as second-generation Korean Americans do not necessarily inherit or manage their first-generation immigrant parents' small businesses, significantly changing the characteristics of Korean Americans' occupations and residency. The following section addresses how the stereotypes of Asian Americans (including Korean Americans) as perceived foreigners or as a model minority play into American race relations. It also covers Asian Americans' experiences as immigrants.

Foreigner or Model Minority: Race Relations and Asian Americans

As a racial minority, what has been Korean Americans' experience living in the United States? Where do they stand in terms of racial relations? Are they always going to be perceived as foreigners or as a model minority? How do race relations play into Korean American students' experiences in schools? These are some of the important questions that need to be investigated to understand the challenges Korean American students and their families face, as well as to find ways to meet their needs in schools. However, discussions about Korean Americans' standing in race relations cannot be complete without contextualizing their experience more broadly within Asian Americans' experience because race, not ethnicity, has been the dominant category in the discourse about relations among different groups of people.

The dominant discourse of race including race relations and racial inequity in the United States has traditionally centered on Blacks and Whites (Ancheta, 2006; Hune, 1995; Okihiro, 1994; Tuan, 1998; Wu, 2002). Shaped primarily through historical inequities and conflicts between the two groups, the discourse on race relations leaves little room to discuss different groups' experiences separately from the Black and White framework.

In this paradigm of Black- and White-centered racial discourse, Asian Americans—being neither White nor Black—have been situated within the racial frame of both White and Black (Ancheta, 2006; Hune, 1995; Okihiro, 1994; Tuan, 1998; Wu, 2002). That means there have been times when Asian Americans were likened to Blacks or Whites depending on the historical, social, and political context of the time. According to Ancheta (2006), Asian Americans have been treated primarily as "constructive Blacks" throughout most of U.S. history. He states, for example, "the courts even classified Asian Americans as if they were [B]lack" and consequently Asian Americans "endured many of the same disabilities of racial subordination as African Americans—racial violence, segregation, unequal access to public institutions and discrimination in housing, employment, and education" until the early 20th century (p. 5).

However, it would be an overstatement that the Black and White racial paradigm completely accounts for the ways in which Asian Americans have been racialized in the United States (Park & Park, 1999; Tuan, 1998; Wu, 2002). According to Tuan (1998), the subordination of Asian Americans has happened largely by portraying Asian Americans as foreigners who are unwilling to assimilate into mainstream American culture and society, which often leaves many Asian Americans' loyalty and patriotism to the United States in question. During World War II, for example, Japanese Americans were subject to internment in harsh and inhumane conditions out of suspicion that they might have betrayed the United States.

The persistent stereotype of Asian Americans as foreigners affects the lives of all Asian Americans. The following statement, made by a Korean who was adopted by White parents, reveals how she struggles to identify herself in the midst of the foreigner stereotype:

> I didn't know what Korean culture was; it wasn't an option. So I did my best to be American. But I was constantly told I wasn't fulfilling it because I wasn't a perfect American because I was Asian. I didn't look American. I wasn't blonde. I wasn't tall. (quoted in Ancheta, 2006, p. 142)

Contrary to European immigrants who were accepted as authentic Americans soon after their arrival in the United States, third-, fourth-, and even fifth-generation Asian Americans are often perceived to be foreign (Ancheta,

2006; Tuan, 1998; Wu, 2002). It is typical for Asian Americans to be asked where they are from when in fact not only they but also their grandparents were born and raised in the United States.

Due to the perpetual foreigner stereotype of Asian Americans, they are excluded from the dominant discourse of race. When Asian Americans are brought in to the discourse on race, it is usually to identify Asian Americans as model minorities (Bascara, 2006; Lee, 2009; Lew, 2004; Tuan, 1998).

The construction of the term *model minority* illuminates how racial relations generally work in America and how Asian Americans are positioned in racial relations in particular. The term *model minority* first appeared in the 1966 *New York Times* article "Success Story Japanese American Style" by William Peterson. In his article, Peterson complemented Japanese Americans for not becoming a "problem minority." This article appeared coincidentally with the Civil Rights Movement during the 1960s. More specifically the article was published months after the Voting Rights Act of 1965 was passed and the 1965 Watts Riots occurred. Grounded in the social and political context of the birth of the term, critics of the model minority notion have argued that the emergence of the stereotype at that particular moment in history reflected the desire to maintain the status quo of White dominance, silencing the political actions taken by African Americans against racial injustice (Lee, 2009; Wu, 2002).

It was also during the mid-1960s that social scientists began to frame poverty as a cultural phenomenon. Devoid of any consideration given to the social, political, economic, and historical context of poverty, poor people were described as living in a culture of poverty that shaped their actions and behaviors in ways that trapped them in poverty. In the process, poverty was associated most closely with Blacks living in inner cities. Since then, Blacks have been equated with urban blight, cultural deficiency, and dysfunctional families. In contrast to the representation of Blacks during this period, Asian Americans were portrayed as model minorities with strong families and healthy cultures that did not need to depend on the government to achieve social mobility (Zhou & Kim, 2006). In this racial discourse, African Americans were implicitly told to model themselves after Asian Americans, which ultimately pitted Asian Americans against other minorities.

The model minority stereotype not only complicates Asian Americans' race relations with other minorities, but it also perpetuates the illusion of a color-blind society and meritocracy. Often coupled with the model minority stereotype, Asian Americans' success stories are used to prove that members of any racial group can achieve success if they work hard. The implicit message is that success in life depends solely on each individual's hard work and effort. In other words, if one fails, it is one's fault. The model minority success of Asian Americans is interpreted as evidence that markets are neutral and color-blind. In the process Asian Americans become "honorary Whites," a status that denies the fact that Asian Americans experience racism (Ancheta, 2006; Tuan, 1998; Wu, 2002). Thus in the ideology of meritocracy, the existence of unequal racial relations, institutional discriminations against certain groups of people, and unequal power relations between the majority and the Asian American population is conveniently obscured. The model minority stereotype maintains the dominance of Whites in the racial hierarchy not only by concealing racial inequity but also by setting the standards for how minorities should behave.

In the nexus of complex racial relations, some Asian Americans have embraced the model minority label, seeing it as their ultimate ticket toward gaining social acceptance. Simultaneously, others reject the designation altogether. For example, many high school students in Stacy Lee's study (2009) on Korean American youth were convinced that with hard work, patience, and a little help from the model minority stereotype, they would someday gain the full approval of White Americans. They viewed incidents involving racism or discrimination as the acts of ignorant individuals, isolated experiences that they did not take seriously. What must be pointed out, however, is that students who adopted this strategy were usually foreign-born. Native-born Asian American students, conversely, were more likely to be suspicious of the model minority stereotype, to view racism as systemic, and to feel a sense of camaraderie with other minority groups. As longtime Americans who struggled to be seen as such, they were skeptical that full social acceptance would ever be forthcoming.

What makes it difficult to break the model minority stereotype is that there is some evidence to support the idea that Asian Americans are successful; Asian American students are indeed overly represented among high achieving students. However, the success of those students masks the growing academic struggles of other Asian American youth. Jamie Lew's study (2006) on Korean American students' achievement gap reveals that there is a significant and ever growing achievement gap within Korean American students especially corresponding to socioeconomic status. After noting the growing dropout rates among Korean American high school students in New York city, she identified three larger social factors by which Korean American high school students' achievement and aspirations were primarily shaped: "the socioeconomic backgrounds of their families, access to social capital at home and in their community, and structural support and caring relationships with teachers and counselors at school" (Lew, 2004, p. 318). That means Korean American students buttressed by those factors tend to succeed in schools, but those without them struggle and are dropping out of high schools.

The study done by CARE and College Board (2008) also suggests that there is a significant number of Asian American students who struggle with poverty, who are English-language learners with a high likelihood of leaving school with rudimentary language skills, who are at risk of dropping out, joining gangs, and remaining on the margins of society, and who are subjected to violence and discrimination on account of race, class, gender, ethnicity, or language. By describing Asian Americans exclusively as model minorities, the diverse and complex experiences of Asian Americans remain hidden or neglected.

Challenges Faced by Korean American Students

As discussed in the previous section, most of the Korean immigrants to the United States during the 1970s and 1980s were young adults. Those immigrants are the parents of the majority of today's Korean American students. Many of these immigrants were educated in Korea and have a relatively shorter period of residence in America compared to immigrant adults who have been in this country since their youth. Educators need to consider the multiple implications of the challenges these parents face, and what kinds of support they can or cannot provide to their children who are in the U.S. school system

First, considering the short immigration history of Korean Americans, it is likely that many Korean American students' parents, and thus in many cases Korean American students, are still going through the acculturation process, negotiating cultural values of their origin with cultural values in the United States. For example, traditionally Confucian values are integrated into every aspect of social life in Korea. Thus group harmony, cooperation, blending with the group, modesty, obedience, and respectfulness are ingrained values of Korean culture. However, these values are inconsistent with the dominant cultural values in the United States which emphasize independence over interdependence, self-expression over group harmony, and individualism over collectivism (Wu, 2002). Consequently, living in the United States after growing up and being educated in Korean culture requires an extensive cultural adjustment, which often causes Korean Americans to endure stressful life experiences such as feeling a loss of control, feeling helplessness, losing self-confidence, dealing with role conflicts, and having verbal and nonverbal communication barriers (Yeh et al., 2005). Facing value conflicts within oneself is already challenging, but the challenge is exacerbated when it also introduces a source of conflict between parents and children. This happens when Korean parents expect their children to hold on to Korean culture but their children absorb American culture instead.

Another important implication for educators of Korean American students with foreign-born parents is that the parents are far less informed about the U.S. educational system compared to parents who were educated in the United States. Their unfamiliarity with the American education system limits their ability to help their children do their homework and make decisions about coursework or application to institutions of higher education. In other words, many Korean American students, especially those with parents who were educated in Korea, are less likely to get guidance or support from their parents while they attempt to succeed in school.

It is not only the Korean parents' lack of exposure to the American education system that restricts their ability to support their children, but their limited English language skills as well. The Korean language is very different than the English language in its form of writing, phonetics, and grammar rules. For example, in English, sentences usually follow the grammatical pattern of subject, verb, and object—John enjoys reading. However, in Korean grammar, the verb comes at the end of the sentence—John reading enjoys. Also in Korean, there are no *R, F, V,* or *Z* sounds. Therefore, it is difficult for Koreans to pronounce certain English words correctly. These are just a few of the major differences between the two languages; there are numerous other examples, which all add up to make the already challenging task of learning another language more difficult for Koreans. The lack of English skills of many Korean American parents not only hinders their ability to help their children with homework, but limits their ability to be involved in school activities as well. Also, parents who are not fluent in English sometimes depend on their children to translate for them, which occasionally reverses the parent-child relationship and makes parenting much more complicated.

As far as parental involvement in school activities is concerned, another factor comes in to play. In the context of Korean culture, and typical of many Asian countries influenced by Confucianism, teachers are highly respected by both parents and students. Once their children are enrolled in school, Korean parents try to leave their children's education up to the teacher believing he/she has the wisdom and expertise to educate their children to their fullest potential. Within such a cultural atmosphere, asking questions, let alone voicing opinions different from the teacher's, becomes difficult for Korean parents because they fear their act might be viewed as disrespectful. Such cultural norms remain within the Korean American community even after they have immigrated to the United States until they become fully acculturated into American society. Consequently, there may be Korean American parents who do not see themselves as equal partners with teachers in their child's education. Thus, American teachers might misinterpret the lack of parental involvement by Koreans as disinterest.

Finally, Korean culture places great importance on family relations. Coupled with a strong belief in the power of education for social mobility, many Korean parents make sacrifices for their children, especially for their children's education. In fact, one of the main reasons Korean American parents initially came to the United States was for better education opportunities and a better future for their children (Jo, 1999; Sohn & Wang, 2006). Children, in return, respect their parents and generally assume the responsibility to support them when they become elderly. However, this seemingly positive and strong family relation sometimes can be a burden to Korean American students who do not live up to their parents' expectations, especially when they are not successful in school. As suggested in different studies on Korean American students' achievement gap (e.g., Lee, 2004; Lee, 2009; Lew, 2006), working-class Korean American students in particular have far more disadvantage than their middle-class counterparts due to the lack of resources that are crucial for educational attainment and social mobility. The following response from a Korean American high school student explains the specific challenges working-class Korean American students encounter:

> My parents could not help me in school because school and education in high school today is too much for them. I mean a lot of the kids come into school with poor immigrant parents, and they don't even know what the hell their kids are doing. I think basically, like, parents say do your work, try your best, that kind of thing . . . but it's difficult for most parents to help because they are not even sure what or how they can help except by *pushing them* [emphasis added]. (as cited in Lew, 2006, p. 42)

When students are pushed to do well in the absence of parental support that consists of vital information and resources, they often become frustrated with their circumstances, and some give up school entirely if nobody reaches out to assist them.

What Teachers Need To Do

Solid multicultural education embedded into every aspect of schooling would benefit not only Korean American students and other Asian American students, but also students from other cultural backgrounds including students from the dominant culture. Transforming schools so that students from different cultural backgrounds have an equal opportunity to experience school success should be an ultimate goal. If school transformation seems to be a daunting task, however, individual teachers can make small changes and gradually branch out their efforts to create school-wide transformation.

One of the most important factors in making every student feel welcome in the classroom is the teacher. A teacher who shows a sincere interest in each and every individual student will make students feel comfortable and motivate them to learn. It would not be realistic to expect teachers to be equipped with multicultural knowledge and skills for every single culture represented in their classroom; however, the teacher's openness to different perspectives, accepting differences as valuable assets to our lives and to the classroom, being interested in learning about other cultures, and caring about every student will help students from different cultural backgrounds feel valued. In the process other students will learn to appreciate and celebrate diversity.

When it comes to meeting the needs of Korean American students, the most important thing for teachers to remember is that diversity exists among Korean American students. Notwithstanding that Koreans are relatively homogeneous in terms of ethnicity, language, and culture compared with other Asian Americans, the most salient differences within the group include length of residence in the United States, parents' educational level, ability to speak English, familiarity with the U.S. school system, and religion. Due to the many variables affecting each individual student, therefore, teachers should not assume Korean American students are homogeneous and expect all of them to respond identically to their school experiences. The model stereotype simply does not fit each Korean American student and, consequently, one strategy will not work for all. Thus, devising a tool to gather information on each student and family might be a good starting place so that teachers can better understand their students and meet their needs.

In spite of the diversity found among Korean Americans, there are some characteristics that most Korean American students and families share as discussed in the previous section. Based on some of the specific challenges that Korean American parents and students face, the following are some suggestions for teachers to consider when they strive to meet Korean American students' and their families' needs.

First, one of the biggest obstacles for Korean Americans in their endeavor to survive, to find a job, and to be successful in U.S. schools is their limited English speaking ability. Again, there are privileged Korean Americans who can speak English fluently even when they enter the United States for the first time as a result of their school and private education in Korea. Yet, the majority of the population experiences difficulties communicating in English. Stemming from the way in which they are taught English in Korea, focusing mainly on reading and writing, oral communication is a nerve wracking experience for many Korean American parents. In order to invite those Korean American parents into schools who shy away from face-to-face conversations, teachers and schools will need to provide such services as interpreters to assist at parent-teacher conferences and in translating school letters into Korean using community resources. Another strategy teachers and schools can use for better communication with Korean American parents, while taking into account their comfort level with reading and writing in English, is communicating via email or through written memos which allow them to read and respond asynchronously rather than synchronously as in face-to-face conversation.

For Korean American students with limited English speaking skills, more effective and extensive ESL or ELL programs would be beneficial. More importantly, teachers should create a classroom atmosphere in which Korean American ESL or ELL students' accents or inaccurate pronunciations are not ridiculed by non-ESL or ELL students so that they feel comfortable making mistakes when they speak in class. Another strategy is to involve ESL or ELL students in small group work whenever possible so that they have opportunities to express themselves in English in a small group setting without being intimidated by a larger group of peers. Also developing a program in which students from diverse backgrounds could share their own struggles and triumphs would provide them with a space to form friendships and to support one another.

In relation to Korean American parents' unfamiliarity with the U.S. school system, an information session or classes for parents held in Korean utilizing community resources would help them to better understand the school system and to become able to better support their children. Even if community resources are not available, written information in plain English, free of jargon or acronyms, would be a valuable resource to which parents could refer whenever needed. From the students' perspective, more extensive counseling on career options and subsequent pathways for coursework would help them make informed decisions about their future. As Lew (2006) pointed out in her book, a caring relationship with teachers and counselors is crucial in preventing at-risk students from dropping out of school, especially those without parental support, not because of indifferent parents, but because of the lack of information or resources parents could provide or afford.

In summary, teachers and schools need to recognize that diversity exists within and among Korean American students and families, to identify each individual student and family's needs, and to make the best efforts to meet those needs. In addition, teachers should adopt various strategies not only to communicate with Korean American parents but also to inform them about the U.S. school systems in general and the particular school system their children attend in particular.

References

Ancheta, A. (2006). *Race, rights, and the Asian American experience* (2nd ed.). New Brunswick, NJ: Rutgers University Press.

Bascara, V. (2006). *Model-minority imperialism.* Minneapolis, MN: University of Minnesota Press.

CARE (National Commission on Asian American and Pacific Islander Research in Education) & College Board. (2008). *Asian Americans and Pacific Islanders: Facts, not fiction: Setting the record straight.* Retrieved from http://www.nyu.edu/projects/care/CARE_Report-Revised.pdf

Hune, S. (1995). Rethinking race: Paradigms and policy formation. *Amerasia Journal, 21*(1&2), 29–40.

Jo, M. (1999). *Korean immigrants and the challenge of adjustment.* Westport, CT: Greenwood Press.

Kwon, K., Suh, Y., Bang, Y., Jung, J., & Moon, S. (2010). The note of discord: Examining educational perspectives between teachers and Korean parents in the U.S. *Teaching and Teacher Education, 26*(3), 497–506.

Lee, S. J. (2009). *Unraveling the "model minority" stereotype: Listening to Asian American youth* (2nd ed.). New York, NY: Teachers College Press.

Lee, S. S. (2004). Class matters: Racial and ethnic identities of working- and middle-class second-generation Korean Americans in New York City. In P. Kasinitz & M. Waters (Eds.), *Becoming New Yorkers: Ethnographies of the new second generation* (pp. 313–338). New York, NY: Russell Sage Foundation.

Lew, J. (2004). The "Other" story of model minorities: Korean American high school dropouts in an urban context. *Anthropology and Education Quarterly, 35*(3), 303–323.

Lew, J. (2006). *Asian Americans in class: Charting the achievement gap among Korean American youth*. New York, NY: Teachers College Press.

NAKA (National Association of Korean Americans). (2003). *In observance of centennial of Korean immigration to the U.S.* Retrieved from http://www.naka.org/resources/history.asp

Noonan, S. (2004). *Korean immigration*. Philadelphia, PA: Mason Crest Publishers.

Okihiro, G. (1994). *Margins and mainstreams: Asians in American history and culture*. Seattle, WA: University of Washington Press.

Park, E., & Park, S. (1999). A new American dilemma? Asian Americans and Latinos in race theorizing. *Journal of Asian American Studies, 2*(3), 289–309.

Sohn, S., & Wang, X. (2006). Immigrant parents' involvement in American schools: Perspectives from Korean mothers. *Early Childhood Education Journal, 34*(2), 125–132.

Tuan, M. (1998). *Forever foreigners or honorary whites?* New Brunswick, NJ: Rutgers University Press.

Wu, F. (2002). *Yellow: Race in America beyond Black and White*. New York, NY: Basic Books.

Yeh, C. J., Ma, P., Madan-Bahel, A., Hunter, C. D., Jung, S., Kim, A. B., . . . Sasaki, K. (2005). The cultural negotiations of Korean immigrant youth. *Journal of Counseling and Development, 83*(2), 172–182.

Yu, E., Choe, P., & Han, S. (Spring/Summer, 2002). Korean population in the United States, 2000: Demographic characteristics and socio-economic status. *International Journal of Korean Studies, VI*(1), 71–107.

Zhou, M., & Kim, S. (2006). Community forces, social capital, and educational achievement: The case of supplementary education in the Chinese and Korean immigrant communities. *Harvard Educational Review, 76*(1), 1–29.

QUESTIONS

1. "When it comes to meeting the needs of Korean American students, the most important thing for teachers to remember is the diversity that exists among Korean American students." What does the author mean by this? What are some of the differences among Korean students themselves that teachers may not be aware of?

2. What are three ways Ok-Hee Lee suggests teachers can help Korean students succeed? How does she feel about the concepts: "model minority" and "culture of poverty"? What are the drawbacks to these two terms and ways of looking at Korean Americans?

17

LOW EXPECTATIONS ARE THE WORST FORM OF RACISM

Carolyn L. Holbrook

"Low expectations are the worst form of racism."

—(The late) Sally Rudel, Assistant Principal,
South High School, Minneapolis

It's 7:30 on a chilly October morning. I'm writing in my journal and peering out the window, as I do every morning at this time. I love the early morning, especially in the fall, when I can take in the remainder of the nighttime view and witness the spectacular autumn sunrise.

I live two and a half miles from downtown Minneapolis, but the city skyline looks like it's right outside my window. On a clear night, the skyscrapers remind me of sentinels standing guard over the University of Minnesota's imposing West Bank Office Building, which sits rooted firmly in the ground across the freeway, almost within touching distance from my place.

As I pan slightly to the right, orange lights move in perfect synchronicity, like a chorus line, atop a silo high above the city. Each hoofer gets her moment on stage as the lights spell out "G-o-l-d M-e-d-a-l F-l-o-u-r," illuminating the old mill that was recently converted into a museum to educate the public about Minneapolis's legendary flour industry.

Straight ahead a series of bridges marks the communities on the east and west banks of the Mississippi River. On the first bridge, the Hennepin Avenue Bridge, an arc of green lights casts mysterious shadows over the next bridge, which crosses the river from 3rd Avenue. As my gaze moves in closer to my neighborhood, I see two rows of yellow lights slanting downward beneath the Stone Arch Bridge. They kiss the river and tip their hats, alerting night-floating barges of potential danger.

Just as the sun is about to make its appearance, caravans of yellow school buses cross the bridge directly in front of my window. One caravan crosses west to east, the other in the opposite direction. As I glance at the children bouncing around inside the buses, I wonder, How many of them began their day with a nourishing breakfast and how many are waiting to get to school for free or reduced-price meals? How many were encouraged to do their homework last night? How many witnessed violence in their neighborhood or experienced it in their homes? How many boarded the bus from a home-less shelter? How many homeless children will miss school today because their families couldn't find shelter last night? Where are the children who have run away from unbearable home environments? Have they found their way to safe places, alternative schools, perhaps? How many children on those buses are native English speakers? Which ones speak Ebonics as their mother tongue? Which children dreaded getting on the bus this morning, knowing they would have to face a bully? And who are the children who couldn't wait to get on the bus so they could harass a child whom they consider an easy mark? Which children will be greeted this morning by a smiling teacher, happy to see them, and which ones will be greeted by teachers who will take the glint out of their eyes?

An hour ago, rush-hour traffic began to whiz by on the freeway. I won-dered, How many of the commuters were teachers on their way to school? How many of those teachers were driving into an urban school from a subur-ban area? Which ones were driving from one city neighborhood to another? Who among those teachers slept well last night and left home this morning with a full heart? How many fought with their partners or their children before leaving home this morning? How many are lonely? Which teachers are excited to be going to school this morning and will greet their students with a smile? And I wondered, How many of those teachers want to know all they can about the children in their charge in order to more effectively help them learn? Which ones are discouraged? Which ones are frustrated because classroom size prevents them from giving students the attention they need and deserve? Which of the White teachers have allowed racism to color their perceptions of children of color? Which teachers with dark skin take the rage and powerlessness of internalized racism out on students who look like themselves or students from other communities of color? Which teachers are burned out on teaching?

First Impressions—Reflecting on How We Think and Act

Later today, when it's time to go to the office, I will drive my sleek red Honda out onto the street. If I turn right and drive up to the Seven Corners area, I will see students and professors walking to and from classes at the University of Minnesota, actors and dancers going to work at one of the theaters in the district, and travelers coming and going from the Holiday Inn. If I keep driving, I will see people from around the globe—Somali women, young and old, dressed in colorful veils; Indians garbed in saris and turbans; people with Arabic, Asian, and African features—many of them students, many others, refugees. I wonder, How many will be shunned today or denied something because of their accent or the way they look? How many of their children will be harassed at school, labeled as terrorists?

If, instead, I turn left onto the street that will take me to Mississippi River Parkway, the scenic drive that accompanies the river, I will see cars parked along the street, many with "U of M" stickers glued to the rear windshields. If I drive a half block in that direction, I will pass a row of low-income housing units that are neatly hidden from the view of the campus.

Last Saturday afternoon when I turned in that direction on my way to the supermarket, I saw three grungy-looking adolescents walk toward a man who was ambling toward his parked car; a thin White man dressed in jeans, a Lands' End vest covering a blue and grey plaid flannel shirt, and a long ponytail swinging down the middle of his back. When he saw the youths he picked up his pace, quickly unlocked his car, jumped in, and took off, leaving behind thick black exhaust trailing from his tailpipe, blurring his "Who Will Save the Children?" bumper sticker.

The youths moved back into the street, gesturing with their arms for me to stop. I rolled down my window and listened as the first young man, a hefty Latino, explained that the three friends were raising money for a field trip they wanted to attend with the neighborhood community center. The second youth, a tall, extremely handsome young man whose skin color and hair texture caused me to guess that one of his parents was Black and the other White, nodded in eager agreement. The third, a skinny blond girl, made the request for a five-dollar donation. "I don't have any cash right now," I responded and promised to stop back by when I was finished shopping. For the next few minutes, we enjoyed an animated conversation as they told me about their field trip and asked questions about my car and my long, silver dreadlocks.

I drove away feeling sad, because, at such a young age, those kids were already so accustomed to people turning their backs on them in fear that it didn't faze them, at least not outwardly. However, it's common knowledge that unless there are caring adults in their lives—at home, at school, at church, in their community—they are in danger of becoming the next generation's statistics. The two boys are in danger of becoming chemically dependent, spending much of their lives behind bars or meeting an early death, and the girl might join a class of children that America prefers not to acknowledge: inner-city White kids from low-income households who become teen parents, gang bangers, drug dealers, addicts, or worse.

Countering Stereotypes in Our Own and Others' Minds—Checking Myths vs. Reality

For a number of years, I worked as a writer-in-residence, visiting parenting classes for teen parents. Because most of the advertising I have seen about the prevention of teen pregnancy is directed at African American girls, my initial expectation was that I would use my personal experience as an African American teenage mother to encourage young Black moms. I was surprised that many White kids were in the classes I visited. In one classroom, I was also delighted to see young fathers participating side by side with their partners. It was refreshing to work with a teacher who acknowledged that the girls, White or Black, did not become pregnant by themselves.

The numbers of White youths involved in the teen-parenting programs that I visited aroused my curiosity about the demographics of teen pregnancies. A search of the National Campaign to Prevent Teen Pregnancy's Web site[1] revealed that, although the rate of pregnancy among African American teens surpasses that of other races, the actual number of teen pregnancies reported in the United States in the year 2000 was 787,610. Of that number, 346,980 were White teens and 235,650 were African American. The remaining teens were listed as Latino. In that same year, Minnesota reported 5,580 White teen pregnancies and 1,400 African American. My surprise turned to anger and frustration when I returned to the site's home page. In less than a minute, six photos of teen parents flashed. Two or three young parents were pictured in each photo but five of the six photos featured Black kids. Why is it that stereotypes are so ingrained, so pervasive that an organization can support the very misinformation that it disputes?

---

[1] www.teenpregnancy.org

Single-Parent Dreams

As I drove slowly up River Parkway last Saturday afternoon, I remembered when my children were teenagers. We didn't live in a beautiful condominium back then, nor did I own a sporty red car. Our living conditions were as grim as the conditions I imagined the kids I had just left were living in. I was a divorced single mother struggling to feed five children while trying to cope with what I now recognize as depression. I wanted to be a productive member of society yet I also wanted to be a stay-at-home mom, an option that I could ill afford. But it was important to me that my face be the last one my children saw when they left for school in the morning and that I be there with snacks ready when they returned home in the afternoon. At the same time, I wanted to instill in my children a deep knowing that the poverty they were growing up in was not a life sentence, that they could have better lives as adults. I resolved my dilemma by starting a home-based secretarial service, teaching my children the practical skills of typing and proofreading. In addition, I enlisted the services of Big Brothers/Big Sisters and Hospitality House, a faith-based youth-serving organization based in Minneapolis. I insisted that my children's Big Brothers and Big Sisters be African American so that they could see living examples of what they could become. My younger son, Julian, recently told me that having a Big Brother and being involved in the programs at Hospitality House were the major factors that helped him resist negative pressures from his peer group. Unfortunately, those resources were not helpful to my elder son. He had bipolar disorder, which was not diagnosed until he had spent many years medicating himself on crack cocaine. He is currently serving a lengthy prison sentence.

Blackboard Jungle

Fifty years ago, in 1955, the film *Blackboard Jungle*[2] was released. The story, based on a novel by the same title, revolves around Richard Dadier, an idealistic English teacher on his first job in an all-male high school in a big city. The school is plagued by gang violence, but the teacher finds himself surrounded by apathetic teachers and a principal who doesn't want to admit that the school has disciplinary problems. One of the film's stars is the magnificent actor Sidney Poitier, who plays the role of Gregory Miller, one of

---

[2] http://destgulch.com/movies/bjungle/

only five or six African American students in the school, and the only Black actor in the film with a speaking part.

At the beginning of the film, none of Mr. Dadier's students like their new teacher, including Gregory Miller and Artie West, a gloomy, morose, White gang leader who has uncanny control over the other class members, who look up to him and fear him. However, Dadier soon notices that Miller is the most intelligent student in the school, and the least bitter. Miller doesn't get perturbed when his classmates call him "Black boy" and make other derogatory remarks referring to the very dark tone of his skin. During the course of the film, Dadier gradually wins Miller over and, by the end, Miller becomes the teacher's sidekick, breaking up the gangs and bringing peace to the school. In many ways, the Gregory Miller character reminds me of Yoda, the all-wise, all-knowing, unflappable, and completely asexual Jedi master of *Star Wars*, except that he isn't green.

I was a student in the Minneapolis public schools in the 1950s and 1960s, and even though I was a girl, my experience was nothing like what Gregory Miller experienced in *Blackboard Jungle*. Nor were the experiences of my male peers. When we were growing up, our south side Minneapolis neighborhood was undergoing the classic American transition—Blacks were moving in and Whites were moving out. Like Gregory Miller, I was one of a handful of Black students in the schools I attended. But, unlike Miller, neither I nor my Black classmates were singled out as wise or brilliant leaders. In fact, we were hardly noticed unless our skin was light or a teacher wanted to humiliate us.

I recently talked with a male friend, Archie Givens, Jr., who related a story that is typical of what our generation experienced in the Minneapolis public schools. "I remember going to a college fair and feeling excited that I was going to have an opportunity to see what various colleges offered," he said. "But when we got there, a man from Goodyear Tire Company called all of the Black boys into a separate room and, instead of encouraging us to go to college, he told us about the great careers we should consider in auto repair. I remember vividly how humiliating it was, first of all, to see the White kids watching as the Black boys were called to the side as though we were criminals and then to be told that we weren't good enough to go to college."

It's a good thing Givens's family taught him to believe in the importance of books, education, and ideas. It's a good thing his parents instilled in him the kind of pride and confidence that encouraged him to believe in himself. He never doubted that he was qualified to do more with his life than repair cars. Today, he holds a master's degree in hospital administration and presides over the prestigious Givens Foundation for African American Literature, the largest, most distinguished collection of its kind in the world. Located at the University of Minnesota, the collection contains more than nine thousand books, manuscripts, correspondence, and other materials, including many rare and first editions, and is committed to celebrating and promoting African American literature through a variety of programs.[3]

Thoughts for Teachers

When I reached the supermarket last Saturday, I parked my car, went in, grabbed a shopping cart, and began my stroll through the aisles. Because it was a Saturday afternoon, there were many young parents with children of all ages in tow. Some of the families were clearly enjoying their shopping trip, but other families were struggling. The children were screaming and the parents were trying to quiet them or were threatening them.

As I watched the families, I tried to determine which of the children were successful in school. I remembered how confusing school was for me, and I hope teachers will learn two things from my experience. First, teachers need to realize that the assumptions they make about their students may not always be correct, that things aren't always the way they seem. Students who tend to "act out," no matter their race or ethnicity, are more than likely suffering in ways they don't know how to express in positive ways. Second, teachers need to know, and be okay with, the fact that even though they may never be the ones to see the results of any good work they do with difficult students, these students may be forever changed by their good work.

Language and Community

From elementary school until I dropped out in high school, my best grades were always in the language arts. Teachers seemed puzzled by my ability to switch back and forth between standard English in the classroom to what is now termed Ebonics when I was with my peers. But, rather than praise me for my bilingual skills, my teachers tried to make me use standard English in all situations, just as they tried to make me use my unfamiliar right hand to write with, giving me the message, in more ways than one, that I was not acceptable the way I was. To make matters worse, the same teachers who

---

[3] Givens Foundation Web site: http://givens.org

acknowledged my talent in the language arts led me to believe that I would be wasting my time if I considered becoming anything more than a low-level clerical worker.

In the 1950s and 1960s, African Americans' bilingualism was not honored by the people who held authority over their education. Unfortunately, that is still the case. As the African American linguist Lisa Delpit (2002) points out in her groundbreaking essay "No Kinda Sense," "Our language has always been a part of our very souls. When we are with our own, we revel in the rhythms and cadences of connection, in the 'sho nuf's' and 'what go roun' come roun's' and in the 'ain't nothin' like the real things'." (p. 37). I was the same as most of my peers: we all spoke two languages and our first language was not acknowledged or accepted by the people in authority.

By the time I reached my teens, the principal's office had become my second home. I fought with other students, talked back to teachers, and was often suspended from school. I believe that most people, both my peers and the adults in my life, saw me as selfish, lazy, and uncaring. In truth, I was a shy girl who had successfully constructed a believable image of female bravado in order to mask the considerable emotional pain I was suffering because of conditions at home.

There was one exception: my eighth-grade English teacher, Miss Johnson. She seemed to understand that my negative behaviors coupled with my propensity for daydreaming masked a fertile, imaginative mind. Instead of punishing me, she often gave me books to read and encouraged me to write poems and stories. Unfortunately, however, by the time she came into my life, a pattern had already been set.

At the age of sixteen, I became a mother and dropped out of school. For the next thirty years, I lived a chaotic life, which included a failed marriage, single parenthood, and untreated depression with all of its ramifications. Yet Miss Johnson's encouragement stayed with me and eventually led me to pursue a career in the literary arts. Today I am a writer and an arts administrator, and I teach college-level English and creative writing. I am proud that four of my five children are living successful lives with impressive careers and strong, loving families.

Because memory isn't always accurate, I am aware that the facts about my interactions with Miss Johnson may be different from what I remember. I may very well be romanticizing her. But there is no mistake about the emotional memory that has stayed under my skin since eighth grade.

There is no mistaking the lasting power that teachers have in shaping children's lives, for good or for ill. It is very likely that, if she is still living,

Miss Johnson forgot about me a long time ago. But even if she does remember me, she doesn't know that she saved my life. If I could find her today, I would tell her so. I would also tell her that I try to emulate her example with my own students.

Real Life, 24/7, Right Now

As I walked through the supermarket that Saturday, I hoped that twenty years from now the kids from the housing project would have a "Miss Johnson" stored in their memories. But my mind also floated back to the ponytailed man who had turned his back on them and I felt dismayed that after all of the work that has been done over the last three decades to try to erase racism and classism they are still pervasive in American society.

I recently joined a weight loss program. I was impressed with the leader, who was a fabulous presenter. She mentioned that she is a teacher and I thought her students were really blessed to have such a knowledgeable teacher who presents so clearly. At the end of each meeting, new members are invited to stay around for an orientation. I was the only new member the day I joined, and I listened intently and appreciatively as she briefly explained the program and answered my questions.

Two weeks later, a friend joined me. We had planned to go to the gym and work out afterward so I stayed for her orientation. I was taken aback when the leader explained the program in detail to my friend, who is White. She even gave her handouts and recipes, saying that she gives those things to all new members. Did I miss something? I looked through everything I had collected since I had started the program, but nowhere did I find the items that the leader claimed she gives to all new members. When I mentioned that I hadn't received the handouts and recipes during my orientation, the leader looked at me blankly—a look that, in retrospect, I realized she had given me during my orientation. Her response was an offhanded, "Oh, I didn't give them to you?" She then gave me the items while she continued having an animated conversation with my friend.

For the next few weeks I watched in horror as she subtly passed over the other two Black members of the group or paid them minimal attention. In my mind, those adults became the students of color who have to face this woman every day in her classroom, and my memory took me back to my own school years and to those of my children. This woman's racial bias also caused me to think of my grandchildren who are students in Twin Cities public schools now.

Every Day in Schools, Still

Memory took me back to my middle daughter Tania's junior year in a public high school. On conference night, we moved from teacher to teacher, all with high praises for her academic achievements. At one point, as we were waiting in line for a teacher who was having an especially long conference with another child's parents, one of the school counselors, Mr. McCoy, stopped to talk with us and complimented my daughter on her intelligence and her consistently high GPA.

"Where do you plan to go to college?" he asked. Mr. McCoy, a Black man, always showed great interest in the African American students.

"The 'U,' I guess," Tania responded, referring to the University of Minnesota.

"Why don't you consider Vassar or Wellesley?" he asked, a sincere smile spreading across his face.

We hadn't started looking at colleges yet, but Tania had already expressed discomfort about going to the University of Minnesota, a very large school. Mr. McCoy's comment was just what we needed to hear. Tania and I looked at each other and the decision was made in that instant. She would apply to smaller, more prestigious colleges as well as the "U."

The morning after she received her letter of acceptance to Vassar College, Tania left for school excited to tell Mr. McCoy. But, to my dismay, she came home that evening, shoulders slumped, as she tearfully recalled Mr. McCoy proudly announcing her acceptance to teachers and other counselors. One counselor, a White woman, started what seemed like a chain reaction of discouragement, assuring Tania that she was out of her league. "My daughter did just fine at the 'U,'" the teacher remarked, in a condescending tone. Tania heard similar remarks by teachers, causing her to doubt her abilities and causing me to have to spend a lot of time reassuring her.

Well, Tania did just fine at Vassar College, without the encouragement she should have received from her high school teachers. She is now enrolled in a graduate program at the "U."

The Great Force of Expectations and Assumptions

In *A White Teacher Talks about Race*, Julie Landsman (2001) quotes a principal who once told her, "Within two weeks of arriving at this school, students can tell which teachers like them and which teachers do not. They know exactly who will help them and exactly who will make them suffer, without assistance, through the credits necessary to graduate." Although Landsman was referring to the alternative school where she taught, that statement is true no matter the type of school in which a child is enrolled. Children know when they're being treated differently from other children and it takes a powerful toll on their motivation to learn.

It is vitally important that teachers, no matter what their racial or ethnic background, be honest with themselves about how they feel about certain young people. My granddaughter, who attends a suburban school for the arts, observed that her fifth-grade teacher consistently treated African American children differently than the White kids. She spoke to them harshly and punished them for things the White kids got away with. At the same time, my eldest son, who attended an alternative high school where the student body was primarily African American, had a discouraging experience with a Black teacher. The teacher was extremely rigid and it seems that internalized racism caused her to convey a message through her behavior that she was wasting her time and energy because "niggers like them" couldn't learn anyway.

A little honest self-reflection will inform a teacher about whether she or he feels differently about one group of kids than another. For most of us, myself included, taking a look at the parts of ourselves that we don't wish to face can be uncomfortable. However, when you are responsible for children's lives, this kind of honesty is vital.

Finally, along with my five children and my eight grandchildren, I urge teachers to have a sense of humor and to be flexible enough to understand that if a student's learning style is different from what you are comfortable with that student should not be rendered unteachable. I am continually surprised at the numbers of students in my college freshman composition class who are convinced that they do not have the ability to write well. On closer investigation, it becomes clear that their fear of writing is based on the discouragement given by a teacher in elementary, middle, or high school.

When I finished my shopping last Saturday, I pushed my cart through the cashier's line and I wrote my check for ten dollars over the amount. The cashier handed me my change and I walked out of the supermarket, climbed into my car, and headed back down River Parkway, hoping the three adolescents would still be there. And now, as I sit looking out my window, I remember the mixture of surprise and gratitude I saw in their eyes when I put the money in the girl's hand. Their field trip is this weekend. I send them a blessing and a hope that they will have a wonderful time.

References

Delpit, L. (2002). No kinda sense. In L. Delpit & J. K. Dowdy. *The skin that we speak: Thoughts on language and culture in the classroom* (pp. 31–48). New York: New Press.

Landsman, J. (2001). *A White teacher talks about race*. London: Scarecrow Press.

QUESTIONS

1. In this chapter, Holbrook is talking about assumptions made about African Americans based on their race. What are some of these assumptions you found yourself admitting to in the privacy of your own thoughts? Have you spoken up when those around you, in the teachers' lounges, at meetings, or at the lunch or dinner table make negative assumptions about students based on their skin color? How can we begin to change the very way we are brought up to think, react, and assume?

2. In each building there are allies, those we can work with to change how students are tracked, how they are counseled and what courses are offered to them. Do you have such a group in your school? Do you involve students or their families in such discussions and plans?

18

HOW EDUCATORS CAN SUPPORT THE HIGH EXPECTATIONS FOR EDUCATION THAT EXIST IN THE LATINO FAMILY AND STUDENT COMMUNITY

Jennifer Godinez

"Demography as Destiny": The Growth of the Country Will Depend on the Progress of Latino Youth in America

D emography is Destiny," these three words capture succinctly the challenge of predominantly White educators shaping the educational experiences of Latino students in the United States. It is no surprise that the United States is experiencing one of the largest demographic shifts in U.S. public schools. According to the Pew Hispanic Center,

> One-in-five schoolchildren is Hispanic. One-in-four newborns is Hispanic. Never before in this country's history has a minority ethnic group made up so large a share of the youngest Americans. By force of numbers alone, the kinds of adults these young Latinos become will help shape the kind of society America becomes in the 21st century. (Pew Hispanic Center, 2009)

As baby boomers retire, and the Latino population increases—the economic and social progress of the United States will rely heavily on what will occur with our Latino students population.

President Barack Obama has shown significant investment in education budgets, exemplifying the need to invest considerably in education for purposes of building the new economy. Coupled with the challenge of a shifting demographic, the President and education leaders agree that rigorous and equitable educational systems need to be developed within the next 10 years in order to train the human capital required to ensure the United States remains competitive in the global economy.

Not only do we need to prepare more children of Latino immigrants than ever before to become the *new knowledge workers* who will contribute to our tax base, we will need to develop *innovators* and *change agents* to keep our economy vibrant and competitive. Latino students in our schools today need to be tomorrow's social leaders, inventors, energy crisis solvers, and reform educators. All teachers need to have the skills to develop educational settings that train Latino youth to be the next generation's equivalent of Steve Jobs, Sonia Sotomayor, Bill Gates, and Jorge Ramos in order to stabilize and build and innovate our economy and our communities. Americans need to view our Latino student population as more than what the common narrative currently expects from them—"pregnant teens" or "gang members."

It is clear that we need to develop more Latino talent. Educators need to build upon Latinos' personal and communal resources—and essentially meet the community's own high expectations for educational success in this country.

My journey through education was shaped by my Mexican immigrant parents who emotionally (and whenever possible, financially) supported my academic and extracurricular activities as a child, through college, and upon completing graduate school. I can still recall my immigrant father showing up at parent-teacher conferences right after his daily grind as a welder. He and my mother proudly showed up in "ropa profesional" (professional clothes) to hear what my teachers had to say about my progress. My parents might not have known what the recent Iowa Tests of Basic Skills were, but they were eager to support my teachers as these teachers, in turn, supported my talent and my dream to go to college. My inspiration to write on the topic of "high expectations" also comes from the hundreds of young Latina and Latino students and other students of color that I have encountered as I work on college access program development and education policy development in Minnesota. The inspirational talks I have with Latino parents at their kitchen tables, over beans and rice, discussing school, college, and the dreams they came with to "Los Estados Unidos." With every serving of hot, steamy Mexican food, I get "helpings" of Latino parents who believe in the American dream. A confidence from Latino families that they deeply feel they are raising the next Bill Gates or Sonia Sotomayor as they ask urgently, "What is college? How do you pay for it? What can I do to support my niño or niña so that they can achieve success through education?"

To address this issue of reframing our conversation around the talents and assets of Latino families and their students, this section begins by highlighting promising practices for involving and engaging Latino parents. It also describes the dreams, aspirations, and leadership qualities of a growing sub-group of Latino youth, undocumented students from the Development, Relief, and Education for Alien Minors (DREAM) Act movement.

We must emphasize that not *all* Latino youth are undocumented. Researchers estimate that there are approximately 65,000 undocumented seniors who graduate from American high schools each year (though not all such graduates are Latino) (Gonzales, 2009). While not all Latino students are undocumented, the purpose of describing examples of DREAM Act student leaders' civic engagement toward college access is twofold. First teachers need to encourage students to exhibit the persistence and leadership qualities of this undocumented population in their quest to change public policy and access higher education. Likewise, educators need to recognize that this population sits within a growing population in schools and communities and will shape that community as well. Latino youth constitute 20 percent of the U.S. school population and by 2025 one-of-four public schools will be Latino (Gándara, 2010). The reality is that these students are probably in mixed-status families. Latino families have a mix of family members—residents, undocumented, and citizens. The very issue of undocumented youth will impact the larger question of accelerating educational excellence from a growing and influential population (Gándara, 2010; Gonzales, 2009). Put simply, how these students perform academically impacts their families and communities, and the growth of the Latino community in this country impacts us all.

The following chapter provides a more accurate representation of the aspiration and persistence of Latino families and an influential population of Latino, immigrant students. Ultimately, these case studies and educational strategies urge you as educators to reframe the conversation from basing strategies on misconceptions toward educational approaches based on Latino family and student strengths, civic engagement and their own high expectations and aspirations for educational success.

The Aspirations of Latino Parents—Minneapolis Education Advocates Provide Examples From the Field

The high aspirations for Latino children by their families and the information on education sought out specifically by Latino parents suggest strategies that can be used by teachers to build strong parent partnerships to cultivate more academic success from Latino youth.

According to leading researchers, studies find that Latino immigrant families have a deep belief in U.S. education. Studies by researchers Marcelo Suárez-Orozco and Carola Suárez-Orozco have long revealed how much Latino immigrant parents influence their children's early attitudes toward schooling:

> The children of immigrants arrive in our schools with very positive attitudes toward teachers and other school authorities. In a study of adolescents of various backgrounds (Mexican immigrants, second-generation Mexican Americans, and a control group of non-immigrant, non-Latino Whites), we asked our informants to respond "yes" or "no" to the statement: "In life, school is the most important thing." While only 40 percent of the non-Latino White students responded yes, 84 percent of the Mexican immigrant students did so. (Suárez-Orozco & Suárez-Orozco, 2001)

The research concludes, "Immigrant parents and their children are very aware of the importance of education to their future success. We asked immigrant parents: 'How do you get ahead in the United States?' and a reference to education was by far the most frequent response." (Suárez-Orozco & Suárez-Orozco, 2001). In this section, I describe three models of Latino family involvement, based on two interviews with educators working with Latino families and my own experience leading "La Escuelita," a youth development organization.

Rosita Balch, educator and parent advocate, has over 15 years of experience working with Latino families in Minneapolis and other parts of Minnesota. From her experience, the place to start building a relationship with Latino families is to understand their own past experience with education in Latin America. According to Rosita, "Teachers must reflect on the experiences of Latino families in Latin American education systems. These school systems had different structures, respect for teachers, standardized curriculum. These adults were students in Latin America and now have students in the system here. The parent advocacy model in the [United States] is very different from what families are used to in their country. No one in the U.S. system is the main person responsible for 'how to navigate U.S. systems'"

(Balch Interview, February 2010). Perhaps her most important observation is that when teachers understand they need to better guide and navigate Latino families through the U.S. education system, they begin to stop blaming parents for not caring enough about education—and, by doing so, remove a barrier to progress in working with Latino families. "White teachers blame the poor success of their students with the excuse that 'Latino parents do not value education,'" states Rosita. Rosita also emphasizes how much parents view the teacher (as in Latin American contexts) as a mentor and friend *as well as* educator. This, she states, requires educational systems that can reinforce such a bond and encourage more open involvement from Latino parents in schools—to build their trust with educators and involve them in reinforcing the teachers' lessons in the home. This will happen to the extent that schools reflect strong Latino pride and strength of their communities.

David Greenberg, a local Minneapolis educator who has led the charter school, El Colegio, has worked with several Latino families in the El Colegio school setting. David responds to the question of engaging more Latino families with the following insight,

> I think White teachers first and foremost need to understand that Latino parents do have dreams for their children—they want their children to succeed in school, go to college, and have a better life than they have. The reality is that many Latino parents may not have gone to college themselves, let alone graduate from high school, so they may not understand the system—what questions to ask, what classes their student should take, how to fill out the forms, etc. (Greenberg Interview, February 2010)

Reinforcing Rosita's observation, David reiterates the need to start with the vision families have for their children:

> As teachers, we need to ask parents what their dreams are for their students, while understanding what experience the family has had. Even if parents don't have the experience or understanding of the system, they can support their students by ensuring they have the time and a place at home to study and do homework for example. Sometimes parents may think that since they don't have the experience of going through the process they can't help their child. As educators, we can give ideas to parents about how they can support their students. (Greenberg Interview)

Through my own experience with after-school program development with the La Escuelita organization and college access initiatives, one constant was the extent to which families sought information about education. When programming was done in a culturally competent manner, such as utilizing Latino trainers and holding sessions in Spanish, the families were even more involved in our programs and asked more questions related to education success and college attainment. Reflecting on my experiences in providing families with information about college access, both in church settings (where the families gather) and in classrooms (invited by teachers for college nights), I have observed the drive families have for understanding the system. Schools, however, often fail to provide information in the parents' language, which places the burden on nonprofit efforts. It is important for schools and policymakers to develop new initiatives to meet Latino parent needs for more information on college success. The following three recommendations are for the classroom and school settings.

Further Recommendations for Engaging Parents in the Education of Their Sons and Daughters

1. *Begin by dispelling myths—Reframe the relationship of Latino families and educators.* As we reflect on the Latino student survey data, recognize barriers that exist in the system, recognize the movements Latino, immigrant youth lead for greater access and opportunity, and listen to families' requests for "understanding the system," there is strong evidence of the value and importance placed on education by Latino youth and families. As educator Rosita Balch and others have stated, teachers and education policymakers from the dominant culture often "blame" parents for "not caring enough about education." Educators must dispel such myths, point toward the systemic failures that prohibit greater success of Latino students (lack of staff, lack of policy reform changes) and look within themselves to make necessary attitude changes in their approach to Latino youth and families. Viewing families as core contributors to students' motivation is key to working with Latino parents.

2. *Develop college knowledge information centers or staff teams in your school.* While motivation for increased parental involvement in the their children's education exists, the information about the U.S. education system must be well articulated to families as they engage with the school system. As parent advocates have articulated for this chapter and I have experienced, Latino families seek a distinct "go-to" place in schools for information about such topics as what a GPA is

and how immigrant families can finance a college education. These information centers or teams of bilingual staff can be started through a community-based partnership or with a local church that most Latino families attend. College access experts are more than willing to make special visits to schools for parent sessions, but instituting this information within the school staff is more efficient. The key is that schools recognize the need for such information to guide parents toward greater support of their youth—with consistent, accurate, and timely information.

3. *Highlight the contribution of Latino families and local Latino businesses at your school.* To engage more Latino families, educators can highlight the contributions that local Latino families and businesses bring to the community. Latino students need to be reminded of these contributions so that they can feel pride and ownership of the school-community they are a part of. Honoring a parent for their hard work and sacrifices can remind educators and students that all families work hard to support their students in education. Often, Latino families are the least recognized or honored—not fitting a traditional "bill" of PTA parent or roles typically played by U.S.-born parents. Challenge your school to develop opportunities for Latino parent leadership—from teaching a course on the history of their family coming to the United States to providing time for a local Latino business leader to give a presentation about their role in the community. This kind of parent-community engagement will signify to the entire school that the Latino community is a strong part of the school-community partnership.

High Aspirations—Reframing the Conversation on Talent in the Latino Community and How Educators Can Build Upon These Aspirations

The high dropout rate of Latino youth and persistent achievement gap is the dominant narrative of Latino youth academic persistence in the United States (Lopez, 2009). This generalization is a misinformed and limited narrative of Latino youth ambition and must be reframed. The *untold* stories consist of the aspirations and goals that Latino youth express as they persist through our education system.

Data also supports these high aspirations of our emerging Latino youth population. According to a survey of young Latino adults conducted by the

Pew Hispanic Center, Latino youth understand that a college education is important for getting ahead in life. "Young Hispanics (89 percent) are more likely than all young people (84 percent) to agree that a college degree is important for getting ahead in life than all young people ages 16 to 25" (Lopez, 2009). In a study by the National Women's Law Center (NWLC) and the Mexican American Legal Defense and Educational Fund (MAL-DEF), the conclusion drawn from survey data is that Latina girls have high aspirations with regard to their future and education. The report concludes, "Many of the Latina girls surveyed and interviewed for this project had very high aspirations for the future. Substantial numbers of them want to have professional careers as doctors, lawyers, nurses, and scientists and understand that they cannot reach those goals without education. In fact, 80 percent of the students surveyed want to graduate from college and perhaps go further. And 98 percent reported that they wanted to graduate from high school" (NWLC & MALDEF, 2009).

> My name is Dulce, I recently heard about you from Isabel Morales from the girls scouts about the help that you offer young Latinos that wish to go to college but don't have the legal status, I myself am found in that situation. I really have high hopes for myself and I wish to attend college to be in the business industry someday but as we all know you need college to have more knowledge and to learn more things that I still have not had the chance to look at. I was brought to this country and I'm thankful for it I just wish this can happen for me to accomplish my American dream. I know this country gives out so many opportunities I just hope it can give me this one. I would love hear back from you! I hope you can take some time and help me with my situation. (email to chapter author, Fall 2009)

The email above is one of countless emails I receive in my work as a youth advocate and supporter of education equity. For the past 10 years, I have been involved in creating Latino youth development programs and college access initiatives that have revealed a lot about the perspective of Latino youth and their aspirations for a college education.

One particular movement that showcases the high aspiration of young Latino, immigrant leaders is the DREAM Act movement. Approximately 65,000 Latino immigrant youth nationwide identify a clear "roadblock" to continued education success in this country—lack of a pathway to citizenship that allows them to take full advantage of a college education in this country (Gonzales, 2009). It must be stated that the supreme court case, *Plyler v. Doe (1982)* ensures that all undocumented children have full access to a primary and secondary education (Gonzales, 2009). However, the law does not extend to access to federal aid for college or in-state residency at state colleges in most states. The DREAM Act is a public policy that would recognize U.S.-raised undocumented immigrant youth as residents for purposes of qualifying for in-state tuition rates at U.S. colleges. If passed by Congress, "The DREAM Act is designed to allow undocumented immigrant youth who *were brought to the country as children* to obtain legal permanent resident status if they remain in the school through high school graduation and go on to college or military service" (Gonzales, 2009). The DREAM Act movement in the United States is led by thousands of aspiring immigrant youths who have been advocating to change policy around higher education access for undocumented children who are raised in the United States.

According to author Roberto Gonzales and other advocates of immigrant youth, the critical issue is that the students most impacted by these policy shifts are *high achieving immigrant youth*:

> Their [undocumented immigrant children] mannerisms, interests, and aspirations are identical to those of their American-born peers. They are honor roll students, athletes, class presidents, valedictorians, and aspiring teachers, engineers, and doctors. They also tend to be bicultural, and almost all of them are fluent in English. . . . They have high aspirations, encouraged at home and in school, yet are at risk of being forced into the margins of society. (Gonzales, 2009)

These are the stories of potential for driving accelerated learning and greater civic leadership from Latino students, despite their legal status challenges or other challenges. In fact, it is these challenges that push them further into roles of community leadership. The high aspirations of these young people have led to their organizing of coalitions that advocate for the passage of the DREAM Act and education initiatives for their families and communities. "An important aspect of the student advocacy groups' effects has involved educating the public about the benefits of the DREAM Act. . . . The wide spectrum of these activities add to the vibrancy of the immigrant community as a whole" (Rincón, 2008).

In Minnesota, my experience has been with a self-organized youth group, Necessary And Valuable Insight to Gain Access Toward Education (NAVIGATE). The youth from this group have produced tools to educate other high aspiring youth on the steps to get into college in Minnesota (www.navigatemn.org). These youth leaders continue to educate others about the public policy issues of access to higher education in general as well as for immigrant youth, while becoming role models to younger students, siblings, and neighbors in the community. According to youth leader Juventino Meza,

> Through NAVIGATE, we build social change at the institutional level advocating for greater access at universities and through state policies, and we build social change through social interactions. We get younger siblings to follow our behavior of aspiring for college and we interact with other Latino students and, by doing this, we change the perception of those students so they know college is a possibility. (Meza Interview, February 2010)

Another young leader in the movement, Alejandra, articulates this advice to teachers and counselors:

> My advice to counselors (and teachers) is to help ensure that students are prepared to become the next generation of leaders, professionals, parents, workers, and citizens. Every student needs guidance, support, and expanding opportunities, so counselors [and teachers] must build stronger and closer relationships with students and their parents. (Alejandra Interview, September/October 2010)

The DREAM Act movement, led by Latino, immigrant youth, is clear evidence of the high aspirations that drive the growing Latino youth community. As exemplified by the youth leaders quoted previously, these youth are committed not only to their own success, but to the civic advancement of their peers and the progress of the overall community. These students are civic actors. To ignore this is to ignore the opportunity to shape a new narrative of Latino youth potential and talent—needed for greater impact in our education systems nationwide.

What Educators Can Do to Develop Academic Success From a High-Aspiring Latino Youth Generation

1. *Build communities of college access support.* As Latino youth aspire for college and advocate for policies that provide greater access to higher education in the United States, educators will need to build more "communities of college access support" at their schools. Additionally, more teachers and counselors will need to emphasize college course-taking (not remedial tracking) for all students. Emphasizing an overall college-going culture means instituting more activities of

college awareness (school visits and college admissions visits), advising more Latino students about college preparatory classes, and providing ongoing information about financing a college education. Bilingual and bicultural staff will be a *must* in communities of college access support. This staff will be able to communicate new concepts of college access to predominantly Spanish-speaking family members of Latino students who aspire to attend college. Most importantly, all staff and teachers must be trained to fully embrace a school culture that shifts to an *everyone-can-and-must-pursue-college* culture from an *only-some-can-get-there* school culture.

2. *Connect education to real-world career opportunities.* Reassuring students that their school achievements are tied directly to future job prospects is key to successfully empowering Latino students. One more step of support could be to provide college-career connections for youth while still in high school through internships, tours of local businesses, and sessions on growing job markets. Teachers must see themselves as mentors who guide students to see the direct correlation between school and work—especially when students may seek financial opportunities for themselves and their families and forgo education because of a lack of "connections" made between school and work. While aspirations to college are high, the reality of financial instability "pulls students" toward taking jobs during high school and could eventually lead them to drop out of school altogether.

3. *Develop a speaker series featuring Latino and Latina college graduates.* Educational institutions can provide ongoing mentorship and role models to aspiring students through a "speakers series" of past alumni who have gone on to college and successful careers. Latino or Latina alumni from your school can provide examples of Latinos who have already been through the high school to college to career transition. Most of these alumni are more than willing to "give something back" to their high schools, but are rarely asked to do so. The DREAM Act youth are great examples of how older students can mentor younger students "through the college access" process—also providing inspiration and education on steps in the educational pathway for Latino, immigrant students.

4. *Seek information regarding the rights of immigrant youth for higher education access.* First and foremost, educators and counselors must understand the context of immigrant rights to best advise immigrant students. Simply discouraging students from pursuing higher educa-

tion due to a lack of information on the subject may result in higher high school dropout rates at earlier ages. I have seen high schools educate their counselors through unique staff development opportunities that highlight local community leaders and university representatives who are experts on issues related to immigrant youth and access to higher education. As the narrative above describes, students have developed information campaigns, re-educated guidance counselor departments, and provided information to one another about the opportunities that certain colleges and universities provide immigrant youth. If you seek more information regarding the latest immigration legislation and this issue, contact the National Immigration Law Center at www.nilc.org or the National Council of La Raza at www.nclr.org.

5. *Build upon the civic leadership of youth to involve youth, parents, and community with your school.* The DREAM Act movement is an opportunity to engage more families and community members with your school. It provides an opportunity to discuss previous examples of civil rights movements in the United States and the development of leaders from such movements. Likewise, it could bring legal experts, higher education officials, Latino businesses, and others to engage more with your school by providing support to the immigrant students and families. While conventional advice would be to "stay away from controversial topics" at your school, I have seen students become more engaged in their education when the school staff and teachers take a keen interest in this issue on behalf of their students and in support of the student leaders working on changing local and national policy.

Conclusion—Latino Community's High Aspirations for Education Success, Beyond "New Workers" to "Civic Actors" Shaping Their Destiny

Based on survey data, examples from parent educators, and youth leaders in the DREAM Act movement, there is strong evidence that Latino families and Latino youth want more out of education in the United States. Young Latinas, especially, want to feel empowered by the system.

Because many Latino(a) students do not have citzenship they cannot take full advantage of the promise of education in this country. Latino families, according to the examples of the advocates, need more navigation tools through the U.S. system—they want to partner with schools and teachers. As parents seek more assistance from school leaders the interest and motivation by Latino youth and their parents places them as *civic actors* in the education process.

The concept of a "Latino Cultural Citizenship" articulates the positive affirmations that have long existed in the Latino community, despite struggles to be included as legal citizens with rights equal to those of White Americans. According to theorists, "The universality of cultural citizenship aspirations most probably reflects the historical experiences of civil rights and suffrage struggles. In this vein, our (Latino cultural citizenship researchers) found that Latinos are conscious and articulate about their needs to be visible, to be heard, and to belong" (Flores & Benmayor, 1997). Youth leaders and parents in the Latino community are engaged in civic processes and patterns of engagement that exhibit a community "looking forward" and waiting for academic systems that will *modernize* and finally meet the talents and aspirations of Latino youth.

At the beginning of this chapter, a national educational context was set to remind us that we are at a historic moment of reinvestment and reconstruction of education in the United States. Our economic future in the United States depends on how well we will reform education and produce the college graduates necessary for a knowledge-based economy. The Latino youth community, the fastest growing school-aged population, must be at the center of these education policies and practice discussions. Furthermore, the growth of more talent from the Latino community can be drawn directly from how much Latino youth and their parents aspire for partnership with educators, toward educational success, and, ultimately, college and career success.

References

Flores, W. V., & Benmayor, R. (1997). *Latino cultural citizenship: Claiming identity, space, and rights.* Boston, MA: Beacon Press.

Gándara, P. (2010) *The Latino education crisis: Rescuing the American dream.* Retrieved from http://www.wested.org/cs/we/view/rs/1024WestEd

Gonzales, R. G. (2009). Young lives on hold: The college dreams of undocumented students. *College Board Advocacy.* Retrieved from http://professionals.col legeboard.com/profdownload/young-lives-on-hold-college-board.pdf

Kirwan, W. (2009). Can we achieve our national higher education goals? *Trusteeship.* Retrieved from www.usmd.edu/usm/chancellor/speeches/04Feat-Kirwan.pdf

Lopez, M. H. (October 2009). *Latinos and education: Explaining the attainment gap.*

Pew Hispanic Center. Retrieved from http://pewhispanic.org/reports/report .php?ReportID = 115

National Women's Law Center & Mexican American Legal Defense and Educational Fund. (2009). *Listening to Latinas: Barriers to high school graduation.*Retrieved from http://www.nwlc.org/pdf/ListeningtoLatinas.pdf

Pew Hispanic Center. (2009). Between two worlds: How young Latinos come of age in America. *Millenials: A Portrait of Generation Next.* Pew Hispanic Center. Retrieved from http://pewhispanic.org/reports/report.php?ReportID = 117

Rincón, A. (2008). *Undocumented immigrants and higher education: Si se puede!* New York, NY: LFB Scholarly Publishing, LLC.

Suárez-Orozco, C., & Suárez-Orozco, M. M. (2001). *Children of immigration.* Cambridge, MA: Harvard University Press.

Interview, February 2010, Juventino Meza, NAVIGATE leader

Interview, September/October 2010, Alejandra, Minnesota DREAM Act student leader

Interview, February 2010, Rosita Balch, Hennepin County

Interview, February 2010, David Greenberg, Administrative Director, El Colegio Charter School.

QUESTIONS

1. What are some ways Godinez suggests we use families' belief in education to help Latino students in our classrooms? Taking into account culture, language, and varying communities in our cities and towns, suburbs, and rural areas, how can we create a climate of welcome for Latino students and their parents?

2. Godinez gives examples of activist learning with Latino students: creating ways to navigate the college admissions system, supporting students in their communities, engaging in issues that affect them in the areas where they live. What are some ways you can engage the students in your schools, in alliances with students like or unlike them toward the greater good? What does the term Social Justice Education mean to you?

19

I DON'T UNDERSTAND WHY MY AFRICAN AMERICAN STUDENTS ARE NOT ACHIEVING

An Exploration of the Connection Among Personal Power, Teacher Perceptions, and the Academic Engagement of African American Students

Verna Cornelia Price

Recently, while working with a group of teachers from a large urban public school district struggling with student achievement and low standardized test scores, the question emerged, Why are some of the students, particularly African American students, not excelling academically? This question led to others: Why is it that in an age of advanced technology, sophisticated communication systems, and abundant research about education there is still an achievement gap phenomenon between Black and White students, particularly in urban public schools? Could it be that we have been looking for the answer in the wrong places? Could it be that we have complicated the facts and confused the basic tenets of this phenomenon to that place where we can no longer make sense of it? Could it be that we as educators have lost sight of what it really takes to educate children? Or have we bought into the ideals of this phenomenon to the point where we have unconsciously implanted the notion that White students do achieve and Black students cannot achieve into the very fiber of our educational psyche and systems? Do we have a system in which students are underachieving or in which teachers are underachievers? Have we unconsciously created an educational environment where African American students feel as though they are prohibited from achieving? The following concern was expressed by a principal from a large urban public elementary school who participated in a classroom social systems study:

> I really believe that all children have the capacity to learn. But I think that there are environmental things that impact children, such as whether or not they feel good about themselves, whether or not they feel that the people who are trying to teach them are nurturing and caring about them and sincerely enjoy having them in class. And many times, that doesn't have to do with the child's capacity to learn, it just has to do with whether or not they feel welcomed into the learning environment so that they'll put forth their best effort. (Simmons, 1996, p. 10)

This chapter directly addresses the posed questions by exploring the connection among the classroom social system, teacher perceptions of students, and the level of positive personal power displayed by the teacher. In this chapter, I explore what appears to be a missing element in most teacher education and professional development programs: knowledge about the role of personal power in the classroom and how that relates to how teachers perceive their students, create expectations, and interact with students in the classroom/educational setting. The discussion is based on research about effective classroom social systems for African American students and how personal power affects perceptions of self and others (Price, 2002; Simmons, 1996). The goal of this chapter is to challenge us as teachers to think critically about *who* we really are being in our classrooms and *what* messages we are sending our students about our personal power, the learning environment, and their potential to succeed academically. The chapter concludes with strategies for using personal power to influence classroom social systems positively, thereby increasing the academic engagement and achievement of African American students.

Who Are You?

One of my first jobs as a college professor was working with preservice teachers completing their final course work for their teaching licenses. The most compelling part of this job was that moment when I realized that many, not just one or two, of the preservice teachers were clueless about their identity or the reasons that they wished to teach. Most of these teachers had never been asked the critical questions, Who are you? and Why do you wish to teach? When confronted with these questions, many became offended and wished to know what these questions had to do with teaching. Interestingly, these questions have everything to do with teaching, particularly when it comes to teaching African American students. Teachers who are unclear about who they are and what they believe about themselves are destined to place that self-doubt on their students. According to research, when teachers are confident about who they are, understand what makes them excellent teachers, and know that they are called to teach, they create a classroom social system in which students are academically engaged and achieving (Cohen, 1972).

So what does knowing who you are have to do with teaching? Simply stated, knowing who you are naturally leads to understanding a powerful force in you called personal power. Personal power has nothing to do with your position, your credentials, who you know, how many possessions you have (houses, cars, clothes, etc.), your socioeconomic status, your ethnicity, or your culture. On the contrary, personal power is that spiritual internal force that every person is born with that enables him or her to know that he or she can indeed create positive change for himself or herself and others. It is that "knowing in your bones" that "you are called" to make a positive difference in your world and that how you use your power can help or hurt others. Personal power is understanding that you have the ability to *do* something about your life and that by taking specific action steps you can create positive change in your life and those around you. Personal power is a catalyst for change, either positive or negative. Jim Rohn (2004), a noted personal power teacher, coach, and philosopher, said it this way: "The combination of a sound personal philosophy and a positive attitude about ourselves and the world around us gives us an inner strength and a firm resolve that influences all the other areas of our existence" (p. 2). This is very important, because personal power, whether we realize it or not, is always operating and it can either build up or tear down people, structures, or systems. Therefore, first you must understand that you have personal power and then make a conscious decision to use it positively (Price, 2002).

Now, how does personal power relate to you as a teacher? A teacher's perception of, and interactions with, students are directly related to what type of powerful person the teacher chooses to be in his or her classroom.

Will the teacher use his or her personal power to add to, subtract from, divide, or multiply his or her students' academic success? Figure 19.1 briefly describes the four types of powerful people (Price, 2002).

Let's discuss briefly what happens when teachers choose to be Adders to their students and the education profession. When teachers discover their personal power and decide to use it in a positive manner in their profession, with their students and particularly in their classrooms, they will experience most if not all of the following:

- An increased sense of purpose about their "calling" to teach
- An increased passion for living and life
- A greater commitment to the profession and their students

FIGURE 19.1
The Four Types of Powerful People

ADDERS

- Sees that you have potential and is willing to motivate and empower you to succeed by giving you tools to discover your talents and abilities
- Is willing to challenge you to change
- Empowers you through their words
- Makes time for you
- Provides you with opportunities to gain new knowledge, skills and understanding
- Believes in you, your goals and vision
- Empowers you to create a vision and goals for your life.
- Motivates and encourages you to succeed without expecting anything in return.

SUBTRACTERS

- Can see only the worst in life
- Life is filled with "drama"
- Always needs something from you
- Loaded with negative energy, thoughts, and words
- Confidence annihilators
- Seeing others fail makes them feel empowered
- Uses up your time for nonproductive activities and conversation
- Constantly manipulates you to further their negative agenda
- Does not have goals and not interested in yours
- Does not believe in themselves or you

MULTIPLIERS

- Excellent mentors
- Can see you beyond your present circumstance
- Believes in your vision
- Willing to access their resources and networks to help you attain your vision
- Have already succeeded in their arena and don't need you to make them look good
- Focus on your potential and your future
- Create new promotion opportunities for you
- Tells other multipliers about you

DIVIDERS

- Very self-centered
- Seeks to be your only "best friend" very quickly
- Seeks to be the center of your life through control and manipulation
- Wants you to make them look good
- Feeds on your ideas then steals them for their own success
- Isolates you from your Adders and Multipliers
- Over time becomes increasingly abusive both psychologically and/or physically
- Is determined to create chaos at all costs
- Creates an atmosphere of distrust an

- Increased positive energy toward their work and students
- A new level of respect from their students, parents, and colleagues
- Greater levels of influence with students, with parents, and among colleagues
- Enjoyment in teaching and greater energy from their work
- Increased expectations for themselves and students
- Increased levels of personal power
- Greater levels of student academic success in their classrooms

One of the most transformational characteristics of personal power is that when utilized in the classroom it can positively address many of the issues with which teachers typically struggle. For example, one Caucasian middle school teacher recently asked me during a seminar, Can White teachers ever have the power to relate to and effectively teach African American students? White teachers often feel they simply cannot reach students who do not look like them. They doubt their own power Everyone has the same potential to access his or her personal power. Personal power is not bound, lessened, or negated by culture and/or ethnicity. Personal power in the classroom provides teachers, regardless of their color, with a tool that transcends the barriers of race and provides them with the opportunity to empower and motivate their students to learn and achieve. According to Pedro Noguera (2005), a professor from Harvard, in an article about how to engage students of color academically, particularly African American students, "An effective teacher who is able to inspire students by getting to know them can do a great deal to overcome anti-academic tendencies. They can do this by getting students to believe in themselves, to work hard and persist, and to dream, plan for the future and set goals" (p. 3). When a teacher demonstrates that he or she is a powerful Adder, the teacher will gain new levels of trust and integrity in the eyes of his or her students. When students trust that a teacher authentically sees them as important, valuable, and intelligent people, they begin to respect and learn from that teacher, regardless of his or her color.

What Is a Classroom Social System and How Does It Relate to Personal Power?

A social system is an interrelated set of structures and processes that directly affects student achievement while influencing a variety of learning outcomes related to all aspects of student learning. Classroom social systems are often perpetuated consciously and/or unconsciously by the teacher's perceptions of and interactions with students (Cohen, 1986). Educational researchers, such as Scrupski (1975), who have studied school social systems concluded that the classroom is one of the classroom social system's basic substructures where the formal functions of the school and the socialization of cognitive and social competence are met. Classroom social systems are organic structures and processes rooted and grounded in an "invisible/unspoken" sphere of influence and personal power initiated by the classroom teacher. What are these structures and processes? When I discovered the theory behind classroom social systems, it literally revolutionized how I thought about my classroom, my students, and my profession as a teacher. Why? Because the theory not only called into question *what* I was bringing to my classroom but *who* I was being in my classroom.

I remember very clearly as a new fifth/sixth-grade teacher the day when the special education director asked me why my students (many of whom were diagnosed or labeled with conditions such as attention deficit hyperactivity disorder [ADHD], attention deficit disorder [ADD], emotional or behavior disordered [EBD], and learning disabled [LD]) were not coming to the "Stop and Think" room, designed for students who misbehaved. Apparently, many of my students had a history of inappropriate behavior and low academic achievement, so the expectation was that they would continue in this manner even though it was a new school year. I was intrigued by her question and wondered how to respond. At that time, I did not understand social systems and certainly was not aware of the "achievement" dynamic that I had unconsciously created in my classroom through *who* I was being and *what* perceptions I held about my students. I thought for a moment, then gave her a very simple answer, "Because my students are busy learning and doing their schoolwork." Then I walked away, shaking my head.

Years later during the course of pursuing my doctorate degree, I discovered classroom social systems and finally understood the root of the special education director's question. She was asking me about my personal power and how even though I knew the history of my students I could still have high expectations for them and actually teach them so they would achieve academically. She wanted to know how I did it! Classroom social systems are founded on teachers' understanding of *who* they are, *what* they think about themselves and their students, *what* level of confidence they bring to teaching, and *how* they choose to use their personal power with their students. Are they Adders, Subtracters, Multipliers, or Dividers? Personal power combined with perceptions, negative or positive, then serves to form teachers' "reality" about their students' capabilities and ability to succeed academically. When this dynamic is fully actualized, it will directly impact teachers' level of academic expectations for students and becomes the catalyst for teacher-student interactions. These interactions will either empower students to pursue academic excellence or unconsciously encourage students to disengage from school and, ultimately, reject academic achievement (Ross & Jackson, 1991). The theoretical framework in Figure 19.2 illustrates the entire classroom social system dynamic (Simmons, 1996).

The classroom social systems theory was the premise for my dissertation study, *The Impact of Classroom Social Systems on the Academic Achievement of African American Students* (Simmons, 1996). This study involved ten urban public school teachers in grades 4 through 6 across eight different schools who were recommended by their building principals for participation in the study based on the predominant criterion that they were effective teachers of African American students. A diverse group of teachers with varying levels of teaching experience, cultural and ethnic backgrounds, age, and gender were chosen for the study. At least 30 percent of the students in each classroom were African American. The goal of the study was to discover how interactions within classroom social systems influenced academic engagement of African American students. The intention of the study was to explore characteristics

FIGURE 19.2
Classroom Social Systems and Academic Engagement

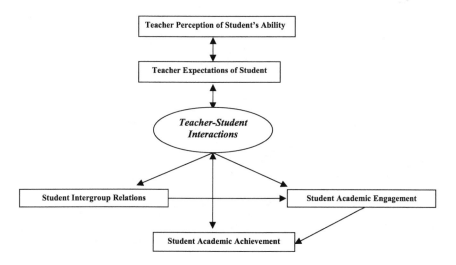

within classroom social systems that could help other teachers increase their effectiveness when teaching African American students. The study, however, resulted in a critical comparison of social systems in which African American students were and were not academically engaged.

The study drew from three bodies of existing research:

1. Current issues, realities, and reasons associated with the lack of academic achievement of African American students such as school dropouts and racial discrimination, particularly Ogbu's (1992) research on why African American students underachieve
2. The sociology of the classroom, particularly Cohen's (1986) research on the social system of the school and learning outcomes, coupled with classroom social systems and their effect on student academic engagement and achievement
3. Research on effective teachers of African American students, specifically Ladson-Billings's (1994) research that discovered specific characteristics of effective teachers of African American students

Three core questions addressed in the research were as follows:

1. How do interactions between the teacher and the African American student relate to academic engagement in the learning process?
2. Are there any specific patterns of teacher-student interactions unique to African American students?
3. What is the role of intergroup (student-to-student) interactions in the engagement of African American students in learning?

A multilevel data-gathering process was used in the study. First, qualitative data were collected from each classroom over the course of two consecutive days using a naturalistic observation method. Second, an observational log with accompanying field notes of classroom events, interactions, and transactions was kept for each classroom. Third, a quantitative observational instrument was constructed to record the amount, type, and characteristics of teacher-student and student-student interactions. Fourth, structured, guided interviews were conducted with each teacher (pre- and postobservation) and each building principal to gather information about their existing perceptions of students, the social system of the school, and that particular classroom social system. Finally, five to six African American students from each class were invited to participate in a confidential, structured small group discussion about their perceptions of and experience within their current classroom social system. The data analysis process included a detailed analysis of each classroom; a cross-site classroom analysis; a comparison of perceptions among the building principal, teachers, and students; and a critical comparison of classroom social systems found to be effective versus ineffective for African American students. The study found that only three of the ten classrooms were social systems in which African American students were consistently engaged in academics.

What Are the Core Characteristics of Teacher-Student Interactions in Classroom Social Systems That Increase the Academic Engagement of African American Students?

The study found that classroom social systems had identifiable characteristics.

It revealed that there are four common types of teacher-student interactions:

1. Academic
   - Related to "what" academic content students are responsible for
   - Connected to the understanding of academic ideas or material
   - Used for teaching a particular subject matter
2. Interpersonal/Complimentary
   - Related to "who" the student is
   - Connected to better understanding the whole student
   - Used to let students know that teachers see them, care about them, and want them to succeed
3. Constructive/Affirmative Discipline
   - Related to helping students understand the "why" of a behavior
   - Connected to clear and known expectations
   - Used to hold students accountable in a fair and equitable manner
4. Punitive Discipline
   - Related to "personal" attacks on students
   - Connected to a reactive communication with students
   - Used to make students feel "less than" their peers and inferior

The most common teacher-student interactions in classroom social systems in which African American students were academically engaged were a combination of academic-interpersonal and/or academic-affirmative discipline.

This finding is very important, because it points to the fact that all of the interactions were based in academics. By contrast, in the seven classrooms found to be ineffective classroom social systems in which African American students were disengaged, the teachers were more likely to focus and base their interactions around discipline, particularly punitive discipline. These interactions in both effective and ineffective classroom social systems were related to *who* the teacher was being, *what* they thought of students, and *how* they treated students.

The following is the profile of teachers in classroom social systems in which African American students were consistently engaged in academics:

Who *Teachers Were Being*
- Respectful—treated students like they were important
- Courteous—used "please," and "thank you" consistently
- Complimentary—noticed the small things about students
- Active listeners—gave students their full attention
- Approachable—laughed easily, appreciated humor, and smiled with students
- Positive in attitude—helped students look on the bright side of the issues
- Positive with energy—helped motivate and inspire their students to learn
- Knowledgeable—knew their content and were motivated to teach it to students

What *Teachers Saw Students As*
- Individuals—appreciated and connected to the uniqueness in each student
- Learners—believed that students could and would achieve
- Accountable—believed that learning was the student's responsibility
- Honorable—believed that each student should be respected and honored
- Successful—facilitated public success of students
- College bound—believed that students would pursue higher education
- Positive—welcomed positive and constructive feedback from students
- Communicators—engaged students in critical dialogue about their academics
- Leaders—provided students with many opportunities to demonstrate leadership

How *Teachers Treated Students*

- Respectfully—listened to students, looked at students, and gave students their time
- As learners—demonstrated the importance of academics
- As intelligent people—engaged in critical dialogue with students
- As important people—valued students as contributors in the educational process
- As cultural people—demonstrated respect and appreciation for cultural diversity
- Responsibly—held students responsible for appropriate behavior
- As academic achievers—clearly stated high academic expectations for students
- As leaders—provided opportunities for students to lead

What about Teacher-Student Interactions in Classroom Social Systems in which the African American Students Were Not Academically Engaged?

As noted earlier, most of the teacher-student interactions were focused around discipline and teachers' perceptions were based on what the students "couldn't" or "wouldn't" do versus what they expected the students to achieve. These teachers demonstrated both open and subtle negative attitudes toward African American students, coupled with negative nonverbal communication such as lack of eye contact, distancing, and refusal to call on them even when they were prepared to engage academically. The teachers were also more likely to relate the students' lack of academic achievement to their "home environment" versus the actual "academic environment" of the school and classroom. For example, many of the teachers when asked about the academic potential of students reported that their African American students don't achieve because they "give up too easily and don't try." On the other hand, when their students were asked about expectations for their teachers, they responded, "We expect our teachers to teach us and to help us try again." Notably, the teachers on average reported that only 32 percent of their students might pursue higher education; however, 100 percent of their students expressed a desire to go to college. Another major characteristic demonstrated by teachers with ineffective classroom social systems was a phenomenon called "scapegoating," in which a teacher will choose one African American student, typically male, and use him as an example to show how much "power" he or she has as a teacher. In this phenomenon, the teacher publicly confronts the African American boy; publicly questions his ability; uses him as a public punitive discipline example to get the class to quiet down and pay attention; and continues this pattern of interactions until the student simply explodes emotionally, becomes a discipline issue, and/or refuses to engage academically. At this point, the teacher then writes him up as a behavior referral and has him removed from the classroom. When the student has been removed, the teacher then chooses another student and the "scapegoating" phenomenon begins again.

The following is a comparative example taken directly from classroom log data in the study that records two different classrooms with two different teachers that demonstrates the impact of teacher-student interactions on academic engagement:

Classroom I—Classroom social system where African American students were academically engaged

The teacher stands in front of the classroom, she asks the whole class a question, an African American boy raises his hand. The teacher calls on the boy, he doesn't know the answer and begins looking it up in his book. The teacher notices that he is trying and leaves the front of the class, walks over to his desk, bends over his shoulder and begins to help the boy locate the answer. The boy finds the answer, shows the teacher, then says the answer out loud to the class. The teacher says "thank you" to the boy, smiles at him and goes back to the front of the classroom.

Classroom II—Classroom social system where African American students were not academically engaged

The classroom teacher sits in front of the class. An African American boy walks up to the teacher with his reading book. The teacher looks at him and says in a loud voice, "Don't you think this book is going to be too hard for you to read?" The boy immediately lowers his head and mumbles "Yeah." The teacher says to him, "I'll listen to you read tomorrow and we'll see." The rest of the class watches the boy walk back to his desk with his head down. The boy slumps down in his desk with the book closed, he sits and stares. He does not read his book. (p. 79)

Both examples clearly illustrate the impact of teacher-student interactions in the classroom social system. Both teachers chose, consciously or unconsciously, to use their personal power to either help or hinder academic progress. The teacher-student interactions in Classroom I demonstrate that this teacher's perceptions of the student are positive and that her expectations are high. This teacher is also comfortable around her students and confident as a teacher. In terms of personal power, this teacher would be considered an Adder. The teacher in Classroom II has a negative perception of the student's academic ability and low expectations for him. The personal power of this teacher is being used to subtract from instead of add to the student's academic engagement. The big question that remains unanswered is, Is the teacher aware of how her use of personal power as a Subtracter is creating a social system that discourages students from achieving? When teachers understand how their own personal power influences their interactions with students, they can begin to change consciously *who* they are being, *what* they think of students, and *how* they treat students.

Now What? How Can You Use Your Personal Power as an Adder to Create Classroom Social Systems in which African American Students Will Be Academically Engaged?

Before concluding with personal power strategies for teachers, it is imperative to note that even though this chapter has focused on African American students, the principles of personal power in the classroom are applicable to all students. The bottom line is that as teachers we all have personal power, and when effectively applied to our teaching and learning, we will find that all of our students will progress to new levels of academic engagement that will ultimately lead to academic achievement.

Personal Power Strategies for Teachers

1. *Understand and learn more about your personal power:* Read as much as you can about personal power, journal about it, talk about it with your colleagues, take a course on it, and attend seminars and listen to tapes.
2. *Reflect on and reevaluate your "calling" as a teacher:* Know why you are teaching and understand your power in the lives of your students.
3. *Learn about how to be a more effective leader in your classroom:* Understand that students are looking for teachers whom they can trust and follow. School is a difficult place for many students, so having a teacher who is also a confident but caring leader is imperative.
4. *Choose to be an Adder to your students and colleagues:* Decide to make a change and then take action steps to realize that change. This is

what personal power is all about. When you decide to add, students will notice and be inspired to become Adders themselves.

5. *Discover the "story" in your students through critical but thoughtful questions, reflective dialogue, and active listening:* Provide opportunities for your students to help you understand their world by having small-group discussions, journal-writing sessions, individual conversations, and classroom community-building activities; attending their community events; talking with their relatives; and visiting and learning about their community.

6. *Decide to change your perceptions of your students:* Begin seeing your students for who they could become. Focus on their potential, not their past failures. Stop talking to other teachers about how "poorly" your students are doing, and begin to "brag" about your students.

7. *Encourage your students to dream and envision their future and then ask them to write it down:* Keep a copy for yourself so that you can use it to remind the students of their dreams when they go through a difficult time.

8. *Create a personal vision for yourself as a teacher and for all of your students:* Who do you wish to be as a teacher? What kind of impact do you wish to have on your students? This can be a collective vision for the class or for each individual student. Keep your vision in a place where you can read it on a regular basis.

9. *Challenge your students to achieve and refuse to let students fail by giving them opportunities to try again:* Clearly and regularly state your academic expectations for students.

10. *Use your words to motivate and encourage students:* Decide to have at least one complimentary/interpersonal interaction with every student, every day. Use words that will create a classroom social system in which students feel empowered and capable of achieving their highest level.

References

Cohen, E. G. (1972). Sociology of the classroom: Setting the conditions for teacher-student interaction. *Review of Educational Research, 42,* 9–24.

Cohen, E. G. (1986). *On the sociology of the classroom: The contributions of the social sciences to educational policy and practice: 1965–1985.* Washington, DC: McCutchan Publishing.

Ladson-Billings, G. (1994). *Dreamkeepers: Successful teachers of African American children.* San Francisco: Jossey-Bass.

Noguera, P. (2005, January/February). How racial identity affects school perform-ance. Harvard Education Letter—Research Online. www.edletter.org.

Ogbu, J. (1992). Adaptation to minority status and impact on school success. *Theory into Practice, 31*(4), 287–295.

Price, V. C. (2002). *The power of people: Four kinds of people who can change your life.* Robbinsdale, MN: JCAMA Publishers.

Rohn, J. (2004). Attitude is everything. Jim Rohn's Weekly E-zine. Available at: ezine@jimrohn.com.

Ross, S. I., & Jackson, J. M. (1991). Teacher expectations for Black males' and Black females' academic achievement. *Personality and Social Psychology Bulletin, 17*(1), 78–82.

Scrupski, A. (1975). The social system of the school. In K. Shimahara & A. Scrupski (Eds.), *Social forces and schooling* (p. 659). New York: McKay.

Simmons, V. C. (1996). *The impact of classroom social systems on the academic achieve-ment of African American students.* Unpublished doctoral dissertation. Minneap-olis: University of Minnesota.

QUESTIONS

1. When you look at the characteristics of successful teachers of African American students, how does your teaching style fit with these? In what ways are these simply good teaching methods for all teachers? How do you think they apply specifically to the African American students you teach?

2. Are we made, as teachers, to believe we have personal power? What keeps us from believing we can be successful with all children?

20

AFRICAN AMERICAN MALE STUDENT-ATHLETES AND WHITE TEACHERS' CLASSROOM INTERACTIONS

Implications for Teachers, Coaches, Counselors, and Administrators

Bruce B. Douglas, Esrom Pitre, and Chance W. Lewis

Since the establishment of the public school system in the United States, course offerings have evolved from the basics of reading, writing, and arithmetic to a more comprehensive academic curriculum. As schools have become more diverse in their curricular offerings, extracurricular activities (e.g., athletics) have become equally as diverse. Athletic activities are extracurricular activities that are most prevalent on public school campuses. High school athletic events serve to help students develop outside of the traditional academic classroom. Silliker (1997) suggests that athletics can provide learning experiences not generally found in a classroom and have been recognized as an important part of a student's school experience. For the student-athlete, athletic activities provide a way for the student to excel and achieve in various sports, which may have a direct impact on the student-athlete's classroom performance. As a by-product, high school athletics also provide an avenue for the student body, particularly non-athletes, to participate as fans and loyal supporters in activities that highlight their school, facilitating a bond between the students and their school. Gerber's

(1996) research found that participation in extracurricular activities developed a positive relationship between achievements in both African American and White students.

High school athletic teams are generally held in high esteem within the school culture. Student-athletes usually receive preferential treatment from teachers, counselors, administrators, and the rest of the student body and are celebrated as the heroes of the school. Players wear special jackets displaying their particular sport and any specific awards they have earned, and on game days, they may dress in similar fashion for the sole purpose of setting themselves apart from the rest of the student body. These student-athletes usually have special meetings with their coaches; eat together before and after games; and are automatically granted certain privileges, such as early release time from school when the team has to travel to another school for a game. On game nights, fans gather; pay entrance fees; and sit collectively in the stands, rooting the team to victory. Finally, when the athletic event is over, the loyal fans celebrate the efforts of these athletes. However, despite this celebration at athletic events, there is an underlying problem in our public schools that is not being addressed adequately: the academic achievement of the African American male student-athlete in the classroom. Frequently, African American student-athletes are asked to provide their best efforts in athletic events but are not asked or required to do the same in the classroom. This means that the people who are hired to help them academically often are the very people who are hurting them.

The Stereotype of the African American Male Student-Athlete

Athletics have always been an avenue for stereotypes, especially for the African American male student-athlete. Stereotyping is the process of imposing characteristics on people based on their perceived group membership. As a society, we develop stereotypes when we are unable or unwilling to obtain all of the information we would need to make fair judgments about people or situations. Stereotyping is often used in association with race and most often leads to feelings of prejudice and discrimination. Stereotypes of African American male student-athletes have been linked historically to theories developed that explain the differences athletically between African American and White athletes (Miller, 1998). Athletics have also been commonly known as one of the very few domains where African Americans are stereotyped as being superior in terms of performance in comparison with their White counterparts. These types of stereotypes are perceived views that racial group affiliation serves as an essential element in athletic success or failure.

The realities of racism and stereotypes for many African American male student-athletes further their feelings of isolation in the classroom. These feelings of isolation can also be regarded as one of the main explanations for the differences in academic performance and social and psychological adjustment of male African American students in the classroom. In many predominately White school environments, African American male student-athletes arrive on campus faced with others' perceptions of them as superior on the athletic field but inferior in the classroom. They usually feel isolated and often experience depression related to direct incidents of racism and discrimination. Frequently, they do not feel fully welcomed on campus other than for the sole purpose of winning an athletic championship for the school. As a focal point of this chapter, it is important to make sure that we get male African American student-athletes to feel that they are important and appreciated. When this happens, they will become more involved and attached to the school, which will result in increased academic achievement.

The African American Male Athlete and Academic Achievement

Concern about male African American student-athletes and their level of academic achievement has been well documented (Benson, 2000; Broh, 2002; Hoberman, 2000; Young & Sowa, 1992). The general perception is that the lack of academic achievement is primarily the fault of African American student-athletes. Unfortunately, this emphasis is shared by many teachers who are responsible for the education of these student-athletes. These teachers usually shift the blame for this lack of academic achievement back to the student-athletes' respective home environments. Although this may have some merit, others believe that these student-athletes' academic underachievement may be caused in part by the way schools are structured to maintain prevailing social and economic order. However, one viewpoint that is missing from this discussion is the perspective of African American student-athletes in relation to their academic achievement.

In public schools, we see evidence to suggest how academically inadequate their teachers have judged these African American male student-athletes to be, but very few studies address their experience in school. Only a few researchers (Adler & Adler, 1991; Person & LeNoir, 1997) have used qualitative research inquiries to discover the experiences and perspectives of male African American student-athletes. Today, more is known about defi-cient test scores and intervention strategies for this group of students than about their experiences in the school setting. From the work of researchers (Fine, 1991; Freeman, 1997), the field of education has learned that listening to student voices has the potential to reveal better solutions to problems in school. What is amazing is that little of this intervention strategy has been applied in the research and discussions of the issue of academic achievement of African American male student-athletes. What would happen if these stu-dents could speak to the education profession? What if the education profes-sion could understand their experiences and perspectives in the school environment? What if educators could understand these students, rather than categorize, judge, and reform them? What would happen if educators just took the time to listen to the student-athlete? Given these prevailing questions, the purpose of this chapter is to express African American male student-athletes' experience in school from their point of view. Their voices must be heard and understood in order to address the problem successfully. In addition, firsthand glimpses of these students' school experience by teach-ers, coaches, counselors, and administrators will provide a solid foundation for determining possible interventions that will lead to increased academic achievement.

Methodology

A qualitative research design utilizing retrospective interviews (Reiff, Gerber, & Ginsberg, 1997) was employed with recent African American male student-athlete graduates from high schools in the Deep South. All students included were typically "star athletes" at their respective high schools. Each student had athletic aspirations beyond high school as well as academic aspi-rations at the college level, selecting a major that would prepare him for gainful employment at the end of his athletic career. Each interview was con-ducted in a face-to-face format and ranged from ninety minutes to more than two hours.

Findings

Four emergent themes characterized the experiences of the African American male student-athlete respondents who were gifted athletically but wanted their teachers and coaches to know them also for being good students aca-demically. These themes were "We Get Big Respect," "Preferential Treatment of Athletes: Giving Good Grades," "Don't Judge Me by My Appearance," and "It's Tough Coming from a Single-Parent Home." Based on these themes, a series of consistent ideas for improving the relationship between African American student-athletes and their teachers, coaches, counselors, and administrators also emerged. The following sections explore the four themes, and at the end of the chapter specific recommendations are provided for teachers, coaches, counselors, and administrators to improve the academic achievement of these student-athletes.

We Get Big Respect

One of the most common themes originating from the experiences of African American male student-athletes was the notion that they are well respected on the high school campus as well as in the community. All the student-athletes interviewed agreed that respect is the biggest reward for being a student-athlete. However, with that respect came other responsibilities, such as being a leader at school and in the community. Some of the student-athletes expressed the feeling of being pressured to be leaders because of their athletic prowess when they really did not wish to be leaders other than in their respective sports. Following are some of the comments that the student-athletes made on the issue of respect and leadership:

> "Well, to me most people respect you more when you're an athlete. . . . Everybody knows you and the bad part is everybody expects you to be a leader and when you don't really wanna be a leader, you just wanna be at school."

> "One of the pros would be respect 'cause if you're an athlete and you're good, everybody gonna give you respect. . . . They kinda look up to you as you're a senior or junior; the freshmen and sophomores look up to you."

> "You get a lot of respect on campus. Everybody try to look at you like you suppose to be the leader on campus."

> "It's pretty cool being an athlete around the community and the school. . . . Everybody know you, everybody like okay they out there handling their business, but when it comes back, the cons, teachers look at you like okay they suppose to be the main ones getting their work but you gotta look at too, in sports and stuff, it's only so much you can maintain and so much you can go through."

These comments clearly paint a picture of African American male student-athletes feeling plenty of pressure to become leaders in situations other than sports. Although the respect and notoriety are things to treasure, these student-athletes emphasized that they are forced to take on leadership roles with which they are not necessarily comfortable.

Preferential Treatment of Athletes: Giving Good Grades

One of the most intriguing themes that emerged from the experiences of African American male student-athletes was the fact that they receive good grades just because they are athletes. For several students, their teachers just gave them the grades required to stay eligible to play sports. Some of the students commented that when the athletic season was in session, it played a key role in whether or not they received a good grade, with very minimal effort in the classroom. Listed next are some of their comments related to this theme:

> "The teachers look up to you but a con is also that some teachers will give you grades and certain things so you could continue to play that sport 'cause you are good so the school can be good and be rated highly."
> "Some teachers give you the grades because they like football or whatever you play and they give you the grade to make it."
> "I think they hold off like whenever your season around, they'll let you go out and let you run errands and they'll run your notes off and stuff like that and you won't have to copy like everybody else in the classroom."
> "I maintained a 3.0 but on maintaining it, most of the time I'll be chillin' in class. I didn't have to do as much in certain classes because I'm a Black athlete or whatever, but I'll still come out with an A or B so I think if they woulda pushed me, maybe I woulda learned more and I coulda did better maybe on my ACT or something like that to achieve more."

These comments indicate that preferential treatment of student-athletes is a fairly common occurrence. Based on these comments, if student-athletes are good on the field or court, the grades will take care of themselves. They document a problem that continues to occur in schools, that may have long-term consequences for the male African American student-athlete.

Don't Judge Me by My Appearance

Some of the African American student-athletes indicated that most teachers perceive them to be something or someone they aren't just because of the clothes they wear. Most of the male student-athletes are from the hip-hop culture, and they try very hard to keep up with the latest fashions. Although they wear their clothes a certain way, they still consider themselves good students and law-abiding citizens in society. However, their appearance usually invites negative stereotypes from teachers, coaches, counselors, administrators, and peers. Following are some of their comments regarding appearance:

> "If you come to class, you probably a good student but you dress different and they might judge you on it. You got baggy pants on, your shirt big or whatever. You ain't trying, you just lazy, you not taking the class serious."
>
> "They [teachers] try to characterize you by the way you look. They might look at you and you might be dressed this way, but you be a whole different person. They try to put you in that category."
>
> "I'll give you an example about the way I dress. I think a teacher would stereotype me as far as how the latest African American styles are. I'm one that will follow a hip-hop style I see on TV and they see people dressed like on the news in trouble, selling drugs, or you see somebody like a drug dealer with rims on his car, loud music and I might have the same thing and they put me in that category with those types of people and I think that's a bad stereotype that a teacher or student or anybody of a older age would give around here."
>
> "I think a lot of teachers see stuff on TV and they might stereotype Black students and think they sell drugs . . . I think and it's a stereotype they put on Black kids."

These comments by the male African American student-athletes indicate that they are generalized by the clothes they wear, the cars they drive, and the music they listen to. Most of the students feel that this is a serious barrier to their success academically. Their teachers see them as part of the criminal element and treat them differently in the classroom because of their perceptions of them.

It's Tough Coming from a Single-Parent Home

The theme of coming from a single-parent home concentrates on external forces that impede success in the classroom for African American male student-athletes. Several of the African American student-athletes came from single-parent homes, headed solely by a female parent. These student-athletes take on many responsibilities that most student-athletes do not encounter. The added pressure and stress of everyday life pays an integral part in whether or not African American student-athletes decide to continue their education beyond high school. Following are some of their comments about coming from a single-parent home:

> "It's kinda hard for us being young athletes in school, it's kinda tough because it's like a lot of responsibility and people wanna work and they trying to play sports and they trying to do school and keep up with your grades and work hard at practice and be to work on time. It's just a lot."

> "For instance, say if you stay with a single parent and you have a younger brother, you gotta make sure right after practice he doing his homework, you gotta do your homework, you gotta make sure the house clean when your mom comes in or whatever. Then you trying to work so you can have money in your pockets."

> "It's tough, single parent environment, younger brother, younger sister, a animal, a pet, it's hard; then chores around the house after doing so much you'll forget about homework sometimes and then other things with the environment and with family, it's just so much a young athlete can take."

> "I mean it's like you gotta be a student, you gotta be an athlete, you gotta do stuff around the house, you gotta be a big brother or big whatever, but then again besides all that you don't have a chance to enjoy your childhood. You have so much responsibility like we're grown before it's time."

These comments describe how difficult it is for African American student-athletes to grow up in a single-parent environment. Most of these student-athletes are compelled to help out around the house and consider this a priority. However, trying to juggle school and family responsibilities often interferes with their academic success. The responsibility is much greater than one can imagine.

Discussion

This chapter has explored several important questions: What are the pros and cons of being an African American male student-athlete in a public high school? Is it difficult for African American student-athletes to excel academically in the classroom? Do White teachers push African American student-athletes to excel academically in the classroom? Do White teachers hold male African American student-athletes to a different academic standard than their classmates? What would African American student-athletes recommend that White teachers do to help them improve their experience in the classroom? Interviews with African American high school athletes who were gifted athletically but wanted their teachers, coaches, counselors, and administrators to know them also for being good students academically revealed four themes: "We Get Big Respect," "Preferential Treatment of Athletes: Giving Good Grades," "Don't Judge Me by My Appearance," and "It's Tough Coming from a Single-Parent Home

Given each of these themes, the field of education has a long way to go in meeting the needs of the male African American student-athlete. Earlier research on African American student-athletes has documented that the field of education has learned that by listening to student voices better solutions to problems that involve student success may be revealed (Fine, 1991; Freeman, 1997). The findings of this chapter's interviews provide solutions to how school officials (teachers, coaches, counselors, and administrators) can improve the academic achievement of male African American student-athletes.

Recommendations for Teachers

To improve the academic achievement of African American student-athletes in our public high schools, teachers, White teachers in particular, must take a more active role than ever before. A review of the literature and the findings of our study indicate that all teachers, especially White teachers, play a vital role in promoting academic achievement in this setting. We recommend that all teachers take the following steps as professionals on the front lines with male African American student-athletes:

1. Hold African American student-athletes to the same academic standard as their peers in the classroom. Preferential treatment only damages African American student-athletes in their academic development.
2. Do not give African American student-athletes good grades just because they are "stars" on the athletic field. Giving good grades sends an underlying message to other students in the class that athletics are more important than academic learning.
3. Increase efforts to push African American student-athletes toward greater academic achievement. Too often, academic achievement is marginalized for the sake of winning championships for the school.
4. Do not judge African American student-athletes solely on their ap-

pearance. Many of these students wish to be as good academically as they are athletically.

Recommendations for Coaches

To increase the academic achievement of male African American student-athletes, coaches must become more involved with other school officials (teachers, counselors, and administrators). Review of the literature and the findings of our study indicate that several recommendations are paramount for coaches:

1. Increase efforts to work with teachers to ensure that African American student-athletes are fulfilling the academic requirements to a satisfactory level. In addition, let teachers know that these athletes are not to be "given" any grades; they must earn their grades just like every other student.
2. Hold a strict rule that if African American student-athletes do not fulfill their academic requirements, they cannot play on the athletic team. This will help these students understand that they are truly student-athletes.
3. Pick up weekly reports from teachers on the academic progress of your athletes. This will ensure that you are always informed about how the student-athlete is progressing in the classroom.

Recommendations for Counselors

Counselors also play a crucial role in the academic achievement of male African American student-athletes. Counselors should be a critical component in the school setting to help these student-athletes understand what they need to do to fulfill their academic requirements. It is recommended that counselors do the following :

1. As early as possible, inform African American student-athletes of the academic requirements for staying eligible to play sports at their respective high schools.
2. As early as possible, inform African American student-athletes about the GPA and standardized test requirements for athletic scholarships at colleges and universities.
3. Inform African American student-athletes about college options even if they do not plan to play sports after high school.

Recommendations for Administrators

To promote the academic achievement of male African American student-athletes, the role of the administrator is especially important. As the top official in the school, it is paramount that the administrator set a standard for all students, especially African American student-athletes. The following recommendations are especially important for administrators in the public high school setting:

1. Stress to teachers, coaches, and counselors that academic achievement is the first priority over any athletic activity. By doing this, you can set the standard for academic excellence in the school setting.
2. Reprimand any teacher found guilty of "giving" grades to African American student-athletes to keep them "eligible" to play sports. These student-athletes should earn their grades like any other student.
3. Require coaches to make sure their athletes meet an academic requirement that is in alignment with the goals of the school.
4. Require that at least one counselor in the school setting be involved with the student-athletes at the school. This will help these students get information on athletic scholarships, academic scholarships, and other pertinent information that will help facilitate their success after high school.

Conclusion

Several key conclusions can be drawn from the research that we have presented. First, there was a powerful sense in each of the themes that the male African-American student-athletes thought they were judged and treated differently because they were student-athletes. They felt they stood out as being different because of their outward appearance. Obviously, they believed their teachers stereotyped them the first day they were introduced. Greater effort is needed to reverse the stereotypes White teachers have of African American student-athletes. School administrators need to become more sensitive to the specific needs of these student-athletes and provide professional development workshops for teachers. As these student-athletes clearly expressed, they are different because of their athletic ability.

Second, the male African American student-athletes expressed a major concern that they received preferential treatment. They believed their teachers had to "give" them grades because they were student-athletes. The student-athletes in this study wished to prove to the teacher that they could also be effective students in the classroom setting.

Finally, there was an incredible notion of "self-reliance" among the students we interviewed. They persisted in spite of all of the difficulties encountered. When the interviews were conducted, nine of the students were high school students and four were freshmen students in college. The four college students received athletic scholarships to participate in various sports. Five of the nine high school athletes received athletic scholarships to attend major universities, and the remaining four high school students received athletic scholarships and academic scholarships.

Teachers, counselors, coaches, and administrators play an important role in students' lives. It is incumbent on these professionals to inform male African American student-athletes of their academic progress, hold strict rules for these student-athletes who do not fulfill their academic requirements, and hold all students to the same academic standard as other peers in the classroom. The principal is the primary leader in most high school settings, and it is his or her job to ensure a quality education for all students. The principal and other administrators must set the standard for the overall academic achievement in the school setting. Teachers and coaches found guilty of "giving" grades or promoting the giving of grades to keep male African American athletes eligible to participate in sports should be reprimanded. In addition, administrators need to make sure coaches, counselors, and teachers focus on the academic achievement of male African American athletes. This is a huge responsibility for administrators and is very important to the community, parents, and student body. School administrators should always remember that "schools reflect the community."

References

Adler, P. A., & Adler, P. (1991). *Backboards and blackboards: College athletes and role engulfment.* New York: Columbia University Press.

Benson, K. F. (2000). Constructing academic inadequacy: African American athletes' stories of schooling. *The Journal of Higher Education, 71*(2), 223–246.

Broh, B. A. (2002). Linking extracurricular programming to academic achievement: Who benefits and why? *Sociology of Education, 75*(1), 69–91.

Fine, M. (1991). *Framing dropouts: Notes on the politics of an urban public high school.* Albany: State University of New York Press.

Freeman, K. (1997). Increasing African Americans' participation in higher education: African American high-school students' perspectives. *Journal of Higher Education, 68*(5), 523–550.

Gerber, S. B. (1996). Extracurricular activities and academic achievement. *Journal of Research and Development in Education, 30*(1), 42–50.

Hoberman, J. (2000). The price of "black dominance." *Society, 37*(3), 49–56.

Miller, P. (1998). The anatomy of scientific racism: Racialist responses to Black athletic achievement. *Journal of Sport History,* 25(1), 119-151.

Person, D., & LeNoir, K. (1997). Retention issues and models for African American athletes. *New Directions for Student Services, 80,* 79–91.

Reiff, H., Gerber, P., & Ginsberg, R. (1997). *Exceeding expectations.* Austin, TX: Pro-Ed.

Silliker, S. A., & Quirk, J. T. (1997). The effect of extracurricular activity participation on the academic performance of male and female high school students. *School Counselor, 44*(4), 288–293.

Young, B. D., & Sowa, C. J. (1992). Predictors of academic success for black student athletes. *Journal of College Student Development, 33*(4), 318–324.

QUESTIONS

1. Given the perceptions of African American athletes by their teachers as good on the field but not good academically, what can be done to change this perception? How is it reinforced in your school? What do Black athletes in your school feel about their own academic records? What are their academic goals, separate from their plans in sports?

2. What are some ways to counter the special treatment, low expectations, and easy grading given athletes in general? What in the lives of African American students might make this even more essential for their future?

PART FOUR

CREATING CLASSROOMS FOR EQUITY, ACTIVISM, AND SOCIAL JUSTICE

21

EDUCATORS SUPPORTING DREAMERS

Becoming an Undocumented Student Ally

William Perez, Susana Munoz, Cynthia Alcantar, and Nancy Guarneros

During the last two decades, the United States has undergone a significant demographic transformation due to immigration. Whereas in 1990 the foreign-born population was less than 20 million, it had nearly doubled to 38 million by 2007—a trend driven primarily by economic push-pull factors. Due to failed immigration policies, among the immigrant population are 12 million undocumented persons with approximately 2.8 million children under 18 years old who were brought to the United States by their parents during childhood (Passel, 2006). Immigrant children currently represent about 20 percent of the student population in school districts across the nation—a figure expected to increase to 30 percent by 2015 (Fix & Passel, 2003).

Being a first-generation college-bound student can be a daunting process, but imagine also being undocumented. For a student, being in this position can be scary, confusing, and frustrating. For an educator, this situation could be an opportunity to support an undocumented student so that she or he can fully reach her or his educational potential. Helping students excel academically is one of the most rewarding aspects of being an educator. It can be particularly fulfilling to help disadvantaged students overcome difficult circumstances, like those faced by undocumented students as they near high school graduation. In this chapter, we highlight some of the most significant challenges undocumented students face to provide educators with concrete strategies to best support this marginalized, and often overlooked, student population. We propose that educators actively commit themselves to becoming undocumented student allies. Being an ally can be rewarding, but it also has its challenges and heartbreaks, as described in the following story recounted by one of the authors, Cynthia:

> As a high school track coach, I mentored a young man who immigrated from Mexico the summer before he started high school. I initially met him when he was a freshman and I was a senior. There was no doubt he was a talented athlete in track and field. As a freshman, he had already made the varsity team and won several major competitions. I mentored him by motivating him to do well in school and begin planning for college. A year after I graduated and returned to coach, I discovered his path to college was not going to be as easy as I thought. All the coaches were confident [that] he had a shot of being recruited by some of the most prestigious universities, so we were all hopeful about his future. Unsurprisingly, he was accepted to several selective public universities based solely on his academic merits. Sadly, he received little guidance from his academic counselors about applying to colleges as an undocumented student. The only educators that knew about his undocumented status were the coaches. All too soon, he realized he was not eligible to receive financial assistance from the universities that had accepted him which limited his options. He had not applied to any private scholarships and had no financial support from his family. Despite the odds, he was determined to get a college education and enrolled at a local community college. We kept in touch throughout his college career. On my way to the local university, I would often see him waiting for the bus and would stop to offer him a ride. He continued running in college and maintained a high GPA. Two years later, he was accepted to the University of California at Los Angeles (UCLA). Since tuition was going to be much higher than at the community college, he emailed everyone he knew asking for donations to help pay his tuition. He unfortunately was not able to raise the money he needed to attend UCLA so he made the difficult choice to return to Mexico and be separated from his family and friends. The day he left the United States lost a valuable and talented individual. Today, he longs to be reunited with his family and return to pursue his deferred American dream.

Before 1982, various school districts across the country tried to bar undocumented children from attending public schools. Undocumented students gained education access as a result of the 1982 Supreme Court case of *Plyler v. Doe*. The Court ruled that undocumented children must be provided with a public education, indicating that denying education to children who cannot affect their own status would impose a lifetime hardship. Presently, however, court-mandated equal access to education ends every year for approximately 65,000 undocumented students when they graduate from high school (Fix & Passel, 2003). After extensive public educational investment, higher education becomes an elusive dream for these students with only about 10 percent enrolling in college (Fortuny, Capps, & Passel, 2007).

Despite the efforts of immigration reform proponents, and the introduction of the Development, Relief, and Education of Alien Minors (DREAM) Act to Congress in 2001 to provide a path to legalization and higher education access for undocumented students who graduate from high school, as of 2010 the DREAM Act has not been passed into law and the future of undocumented students remains uncertain. Beginning in 2001, Texas, followed by California, Illinois, Kansas, Nebraska, New Mexico, New York, Oklahoma, Utah, and Washington took matters into their own hands by passing legislation that allows undocumented students to be eligible for in-state tuition rates. The process, set in motion through the 1982 federal ruling calling for a national guarantee of basic education to all students regardless of immigration status, continues to fuel debates on state policies around postsecondary admission, tuition, and financial aid for undocumented students.

Research on college-eligible undocumented students indicates that they exhibit academic achievement, leadership participation, and civic engagement patterns that are often above that of their U.S.-citizen counterparts (Perez, 2009; Perez, Espinoza, Ramos, Coronado, & Cortes, 2009; Perez, Espinoza, Ramos, Coronado, & Cortes, 2010). More than 90 percent report volunteering and 95 percent participating in extracurricular activities. In those activities, 78 percent held a leadership position such as club president. Undocumented students also exhibit various aspects of psychological resilience, perseverance, and optimism. In addition to responsibilities at home such as taking care of younger siblings, they work various jobs at an average of 13 hours per week during high school, 30 hours per week during college, participate in extracurricular and volunteer activities at very high levels, and still earn high grades in their academically demanding courses. Despite high levels of achievement, community service, leadership experience, and a deep sense of commitment to American society, they remain without legal status, are not considered American, and are not eligible for any type of college financial assistance even though more than 90 percent of the students surveyed aspire to obtain a master's degree or higher. If these qualifications do not warrant access to higher education and legal status, what more can they do?

For most undocumented students, the United States is the only country they know. They have grown up "American," their dominant language is English, yet they face major obstacles in their pursuit of higher education even when they have remarkable academic qualifications. In spite of these challenges, undocumented students exhibit the same type of tenacious optimism, drive, and perseverance that fueled their parents' desire to immigrate to the United States to pursue a better future. Although the Supreme Court mandates undocumented children be accepted as students, immigration policies prohibit them from being accepted as citizens. While Congress continues to debate immigration legislation, an increasing number of undocumented students are graduating from high school with little information about their higher education options. Now more than ever, educators need to familiarize themselves with the struggles of this emerging student population and become more proactive in ensuring their academic success. Schools must pay close attention to the challenges undocumented students face in order to develop efficient strategies to support their achievement and facilitate their transition to college (Dozier, 1995). Based on a review of the literature and our collective research and professional experiences, we have developed the following recommendations for educators.

Ensuring Undocumented Student Success

Chances are that most educators know an undocumented student. They may not know that the student is undocumented because they are usually indistinguishable from U.S.-born children. Nevertheless, life for these students is much more restricted than for any other student group. It is important to learn more about them and how research-proven best practices can enhance their academic success and access to higher education. Undocumented college students report that educators are often unaware of their extenuating circumstances. The embarrassment and anxiety of revealing their immigration status keeps many students from disclosing this information. They fear that educators may not be sympathetic to their situations. Since you may not know who these students are, it is important to create a learning environment that is comfortable, respectful, and welcoming. Also, avoid making assumptions about a student's status based on their race, ethnicity, accent, or appearance.

One of the most important lessons we've learned as educators and researchers is the significance of building rapport with undocumented students in order to help them achieve academic success. Although legally K–12 educators cannot ask a student about their own and their parents' immigration status, there is no law against getting to know students. Once students feel comfortable and know they can trust you, they will confide in you if you make the effort to get to know them as individuals and encourage their educational and career goals. As you develop rapport with students, it is important to be properly informed about the educational options available to undocumented students to avoid the scenario that Cynthia experienced:

> As an academic outreach professional, high school guidance counselors thought of us as the college gurus. One counselor in particular always sought my advice on college admission matters. During the college application season, the counselor asked me if I could advise a student that was in her office asking about where to apply for college. As we walked to the office, she informed me the student was undocumented. The student had a 3.5 GPA, had taken numerous AP classes, and was involved in extracurricular activities. I recommended that the student apply to several private schools that did not have the same financial aid restrictions as public universities and could provide full scholarships if accepted. I could visibly see the mix of confusion and disagreement on her face. After the student left, the counselor told me that she didn't think the student could get in to a private school because her grades were not high enough!

One of the most important things an educator can do is become informed about the options, regulations, and opportunities available to undocumented students. Although there are increasing opportunities, students do not always know where to find them. Being undocumented does not completely close the door to college, but it is often only with the assistance of educators that students can learn how to strategically apply to colleges that offer more financial aid. This often requires that educators go above and beyond the call of duty to help undocumented students as demonstrated by Cynthia:

> When I worked for an academic outreach program, there was a family of five who came to the United States when their children were elementary school age. I met the family when the oldest was a freshman in high school; the middle child was an 8th grader, and the youngest a 6th grader. The parents were highly involved in their children's educations, especially the dad who I would see frequently visiting with the guidance counselor. The students were very polite and eager to listen to advice, asking lots of questions. It was hard to not want to

assist the family in some way. Before the beginning of senior year, the oldest found out that her grandfather who was a legal citizen was unwilling to vouch for the family to finalize their legal residency. As such, she was scared, confused, and nervous. Shortly after I stopped working for the program, I took her and her brother to dinner to talk about what being undocumented would mean when applying to college. We talked about scholarships, extracurricular activities, academic performance, and college recommendations. We made a plan that they would begin searching for private schools that could provide funding and applying for scholarships that didn't require U.S. citizenship.

To maximize your impact as an educator, it is important to consider the variety of ways that information can be disseminated to undocumented students. Have handouts available for students, post some on your office walls or door, and distribute them directly to students. Other ways to circulate information include email, instant messaging, and social networking sites. You can create an email group in your contacts called "Mentees" to send mass emails to your students about newly announced resources and opportunities. In addition to academic and college information, educators may be asked to provide students with ongoing emotional and moral support.

Undocumented Immigrants in the Latino Diaspora

Undocumented students who live in states and cities with large long-standing immigrant communities tend to have more options for support than those that live in places where the immigrant population is new and small. This is the case for undocumented students in many Midwest states whose educational challenges can be much greater. Munoz's (2008) research in a New Latino Diaspora[1] community finds that the educational support and college preparatory assistance undocumented Latina students received came not from school staff, but from outside community members who were involved with nonprofit organizations focused on educational issues. Other support came informally from local college personnel who had developed trusting relationships with the students. In addition to the personal and moral support these students received from community members, a community-based college prep program also served as an important resource. Program staff provided a welcoming environment which made immigrant students comfortable accessing resources such as information about colleges, ACT and SAT exams, and scholarships.

In fact, the undocumented students in Munoz's study received virtually no support at school. They reported experiencing low expectations from teachers and grappled with how to advocate for themselves in the classroom. They felt that the school did not consider them to be college material, and thus never suggested they enroll in college preparatory courses. This trend illustrates the power teachers have to not only validate students as learners but to impact students' college aspirations as well (Rendón, 1994). These findings suggest that undocumented students, particularly those in the Latino Diaspora, need ongoing support from "ally" educators.

Becoming an Undocumented Student Ally

An undocumented student ally is a person who becomes informed and knowledgeable about the rights afforded by law to undocumented students, recognizing that they have a right to access education and should not be the targets of anti-immigrant discrimination. Educator allies recognize that their professional status affords them the power to initiate institutional support and advocate for students to help them meet educational goals. Cynthia's account of the following educator captures the essence of an ally educator:

> *I once visited a school where I met an educator who takes pride in connecting with her students and is the epitome of an educator ally. When you walk into her office she has a large collage of cards, artwork, and photographs made or given to her by her past students to thank her for her dedication and support. She makes it clear to all her students that she is their advocate. She has a sticker on her office door that reads "Support the DREAM Act." Next to the sticker is a flier that displays a scholarship opportunity for undocumented students that she actively fundraises for.*

As Cynthia notes, an ally creates a climate of trust that allows students to reveal their situation at their own pace. An ally does not interrogate the student about their immigration status, does not "out" the student to others, and is committed to maintaining a student's complete confidentiality. An ally also handles a student's emotions with reserve, empathy, and support. An ally discourages others from assuming that immigrants are scapegoats for economic ills or burdens on society, and refuses to tolerate derogatory or anti-immigrant jokes and remarks.

Educator allies must work to educate other community members and educational practitioners. It is important for allies to ensure that they learn accurate information about undocumented students and recognize potential risks and benefits. Allies have the potential to make a difference in the lives of young people who see you speak in support of their group. Allies are also important role models whose actions can influence others to speak and act in support of undocumented students. However, it is important to recognize that others may be intolerant of the undocumented, and allies could become the target of discrimination. As an ally, your politics and morality may be questioned by people who believe that undocumented students should be deported. Because of past negative experiences, undocumented students may not trust you and may question your motivation for helping them.

When a student comes out to you, they share information about their immigration status with the keen awareness of the risks involved; the risk of jeopardizing their relationship with you, the risk of being rejected, and the risk of being denied success in your class or program. Unless you have given some indication of your feelings or beliefs about the undocumented, they may have no way of knowing in advance whether your reaction will be positive or negative. They may feel that you are a person who will be understanding and accepting, and therefore will trust you with very personal information. They may also come out to you because you are in a position to assist them with a concern by providing information or access to resources, or simply because another undocumented student gave them your name.

When a student discloses her or his status to you, you might experience a range of emotions. You may be surprised, unsure of how to help, what to say, or how to find out what to do. You might feel compelled to be supportive and want to help them seek alternatives, or you may feel angry and upset about anti-immigrant sentiments. How you react to their disclosure is critical. It can potentially help or discourage them enough that they will abandon seeking help from you. The more positively the person receives the information, the more comfortable it will make the student. The student may even share their ambivalence about telling you. Do not try to "fix" everything without knowing what could jeopardize a student's immigration status. If you would like more information, ask in an honest and respectful way. If you show a genuine and respectful interest in their situation, they will appreciate it. Do not assume that you know what it means to be undocumented. They may not want you to do anything, as much as they need information or referral. Thank them for trusting you and clarify with them what level of confidentiality they expect from you as they may not want you to tell anyone.[2]

Effective Ally Strategies

Take the initiative to become as knowledgeable as you can about the issues that surround the lives of undocumented students' situations. Assume that the issues of prejudice and discrimination of immigrants are everyone's concern, not just those who are targets of prejudice and discrimination. Inform others that undocumented children who were raised in the United States have a right to an education and that immigration policy changes are under way to provide law abiding, educated young people a pathway to legal residency and naturalization. Continue to work with others to reduce xenophobia and create a welcoming school climate. Get to know undocumented students so that you can honestly write them highly effective letters of recommendation that will help them apply for college admissions and for scholarships to finance their education. Within the spirit of academic standards and legal requirements, become flexible about course and program requirements so that they do not cause barriers for undocumented students' academic success. Finally, graciously accept any gratitude you receive, but do not expect it.

Training Others to Become Allies

Ally training should engage all educators to become informed about the needs and concerns of undocumented students and their families. Ally training should focus on developing strategies to create a welcoming and supportive school environment for undocumented students. Allies can train other educators to help establish a schoolwide network of easily visible allies that can provide comfortable access to trustworthy, knowledgeable, and sensitive people who can give support, information, and assistance to undocumented students in a safe and non-discriminatory environment. Allies can help students respond to instances of discrimination and harassment to inform other educators about the fear and discrimination experienced by students based on their immigrant status. These support structures can help to foster a campus atmosphere that supports the academic success, as well as the personal and social growth, of undocumented students. Once the work of becoming an effective ally is well under way, there are several key areas where undocumented students need the most help.[3]

Assistance Securing Financial Resources

Even when college access is presented as an opportunity for undocumented students, the financial burden of financing tuition and fees becomes a considerable barrier. Until the federal DREAM Act passes, undocumented students are ineligible for federal loans. Thus, students have to take initiative and become creative in locating scholarships and other types of funds to pay for college. A fortunate few are able to secure a sponsor who agrees to pay for all college and living expenses. Often these sponsors do not want to be identified publicly. The majority of undocumented students need assistance finding financial support through private or non-governmental scholarships. The Mexican American Legal Defense and Educational Fund (MALDEF), the University of Southern California Center for Higher Education Policy Analysis, the Tomás Rivera Policy Institute, and the National Council of La Raza (NCLR), have compiled extensive lists of scholarships for which undocumented students are eligible. Counselors and teachers should disseminate these scholarship resources to undocumented students on their campus. In our work we have also learned about a handful and growing number of private colleges that provide full scholarships for undocumented students derived from private donations and unrestricted funds.[4]

Outreach and Recruitment

During high school, it is important to provide information about resources for undocumented students who want to pursue higher education. It is critical to inform them that college is an option even though they are undocumented. Undocumented students need ongoing encouragement and moral support to pursue college. If students live in one of the eleven states that provide in-state resident tuition rates for undocumented students, it is important they are provided with this information as early as middle school. These laws make college more affordable. In these states students are eligible for in-state tuition if they attended a state high school for at least three years or receive the equivalent such as a GED. Sadly, many undocumented students either do not find out about these in-state tuition rate laws or discover them after they have already graduated.

High schools and colleges should collaborate to organize conferences where undocumented students and their families can learn about getting accepted to and navigating college as an undocumented student. Teachers and counselors should encourage undocumented students to take as many Advanced Placement (AP) tests as possible to save money by fulfilling college General Education (GE) requirements. Where available, counselors should advise undocumented students to participate in dual enrollment programs with community colleges to earn college credit without the tuition cost. High school teachers should work with colleges to examine and modify administrative procedures that may inadvertently stigmatize undocumented students. For example, they should ensure that online applications do not exclude undocumented students by requiring a social security number to file an application.

Facilitating Transfer

Community colleges are the gateway to higher education for many undocumented students due to their affordability. Students should be encouraged to complete Transfer Admission Guarantee (TAG) agreements if available. TAG agreements guarantee university admission to well-qualified community colleges transfer students who meet the eligibility requirements and complete the procedure required to obtain a TAG. Counselors should also explain to students the differences between quarter and semester sessions. Transferring to quarter-based schools will often pose hardships to undocumented students since they have to raise money in a shorter time span. Students should also be encouraged to tour campuses to learn more about resources for undocumented students.

Individual and Systematic Strategies to Support Undocumented Students

Teachers and counselors can serve as advisors for undocumented student clubs or help create a campus task force that serves as a "think tank" for fundraising and generating ideas to support undocumented students. On college campuses, the task force could establish a faculty mentoring program since most undocumented students are first-generation college students. Mentors can help students navigate higher education and provide the necessary social support to reduce stress.

As undocumented students select which schools to apply to it is important to help them start building relationships with student support groups at university campuses to help them transition. Many universities, and a growing number of high schools, have created their own DREAMER student groups (the name is a reference to the proposed federal DREAM Act). Encouraging students to join or create an undocumented student support group can help them access different resources and support services to help them adjustment to college life. Getting involved with undocumented student support clubs is particularly valuable because they provide students with peer role models who share critical information about navigating college. Clubs also provide students with a sense of empowerment and official institutional recognition, often serving as a platform for student activism and advocacy.

Broad systematic efforts to support undocumented students have grown substantially in recent years. At some institutions, student organizations have been established to support students, while at other schools academic and student affairs personnel have taken on leadership roles in creating more equitable opportunities. Despite these institutional efforts, support for undocumented students remains inconsistent due to the lack of standardized practices and awareness of the issue. Few education professionals are aware that there is no law that prevents them from assisting students and that they are eligible for most campus support programs, with the exception of select state and federally funded resources (Herrera & Chen, 2010).

A growing number of advocates for undocumented students have begun to share the lessons they have learned in their work to develop campus resources at their home institutions and in collaboration with other practitioners. As a result of discussions between practitioner allies and students, strategic plans have emerged on how to develop more visible and institutionalized support systems to effectively respond to the growing needs of undocumented students. They have organized members of the campus community, including undocumented students themselves, to come together to discuss the challenges they face in their daily lives and what can be done to ensure a smoother college transition. This community becomes a space where institutional leaders and undocumented students engage in dialogue and work collaboratively to create services and programs relevant to student needs. Similar to the strategies proposed in this chapter, Herrera and Chen (2010) note that key strategies on being an effective practitioner ally include raising awareness with the campus community, empowering students by helping them create a safe space where they can meet and support each other, reaching out to students and providing easily accessible information and resources, connecting students to financial support, and developing a network of allies on and off campus to assist students and parents.

Conclusion

There are thousands of undocumented college students who, despite facing numerous social and educational challenges, are determined to go to college. To overcome the barriers they frequently face, undocumented students need friends, family, faculty, and school administrators to support them. If undocumented students do not have the good fortune to meet a caring and supportive teacher or community member, who will encourage, support, and validate them as learners and as potential college students? Teachers and school administrators have the power and privilege to make meaningful change for undocumented immigrant students. Relationship building with an individual who provides caring support and validation is when students begin to see their college potential. Coordinated efforts by the school, community, and university to develop a clear and guided pathway toward college makes the process less ambiguous and daunting for students. By creating an intentional system of academic success and college access, students are able to find information and resources more readily, particularly sources of financial support. Parents also need to be included into this support network so that they can encourage college readiness at home. With the proper financial and moral support, undocumented students can realize their full educational potential.

Among the 11 states that provide in-state tuition to undocumented students, only Texas and New Mexico provide financial aid to undocumented students. The federal DREAM Act (the Development, Relief and Education for Alien Minors Act), a bipartisan bill first introduced in Congress in 2001, is the only viable way that undocumented students can legalize their status. If passed, the DREAM Act will allow 360,000 high school graduates to gain legal status, while an estimated 715,000 children would be potential beneficiaries. As of 2010, however, despite wide public support, the bill has not become law.

The topic of immigration continues to be a contentious one across the United States. For teachers, it is important to understand the complexity of societal perspectives on immigration and the impact it has on students. Educators must be equipped with the appropriate research-based information to properly interpret media images and the public discourse that unjustly criminalizes immigrants, and ultimately impacts students' self-image as learners. School administrators and teachers should learn about the immigrant members of the communities they serve as well as the impartial scientific research literature on schooling and immigrant children.

As thousands of undocumented youths graduate from high school every year (Passel, 2003) and set their sights on college, it is critical for institutional leaders to enact policies and practices that can adequately serve this new emerging student population. A crucial factor for undocumented students is financial support. However, there are many other ways that teachers can assist students, including sponsoring a student organization for discussion, feedback, and support; creating opportunities for students to meet with potential sponsors and allies; working with outside agencies to create internship opportunities for students; and developing a campus climate sensitive to understanding the challenges students face to make the campus a welcoming place for undocumented students. Ultimately, supporting undocumented students is in all of our best interest.

References

Brilliant, J. J. (2000). Issues in counseling immigrant college students. *Community College Journal of Research and Practice, 24*, 577–586.

Dozier, S. B. (1995). Undocumented immigrant students at an urban community college: A demographic and academic profile. *Migration World, 13*(1&2), 20–22.

Fix, M., & Passel, J. S. (2003). *U.S. immigration: Trends and implications for schools.* Washington, DC: The Urban Institute.

Fortuny, K., Capps, R., & Passel, J. S. (2007). *The characteristics of unauthorized immigrants in California, Los Angeles county, and the United States.* Washington, DC: The Urban Institute.

Herrera, A., & Chen, A. (2010). Strategies to support undocumented students. *Transitions, 5*(2), 3–4, 10–11.

Muñoz, S. M. (2008). Understanding issues of college persistence for undocumented Mexican immigrant women from the new Latino diaspora: A case study (Doctoral dissertation). *Dissertation Abstracts International, 69*, 203.

Passel, J. S. (2003). *Further demographic information relating to the DREAM Act.* Washington, D.C.: Urban Institute.

Passel, J. S. (2006). *The size and characteristics of the unauthorized migration population in the U.S.: Estimates based on the March 2005 Current Population Survey.* Washington, DC: Pew Hispanic Center.

Perez, W. (2009). *We are Americans: Undocumented students pursuing the American dream.* Sterling, VA: Stylus Publishing.

Perez, W., Espinoza, R., Ramos, K., Coronado, H., & Cortes, R. (2009). Academic resilience among undocumented Latino students. *Hispanic Journal of Behavioral Sciences, 31*(2), 149–181.

Perez, W., Espinoza, R., Ramos, K., Coronado, H., & Cortes, R. (2010). Civic engagement patterns of undocumented Mexican students. *Journal of Hispanic Higher Education, 9*(3), 245–265.

Rendón, L. I. (1994). Validating culturally diverse students: Toward a new model of learning and student development. *Innovative Higher Education, 19*(1), 33–50.

Endnotes

1. The term *New Latino Diaspora* was coined to describe the influx of Mexican/Latino immigrants settling in communities where little to no Latina/o presence has been established (Hamann, Wothan, & Murillo, 2002).

2. A detailed manual on becoming an undocumented student ally developed by a group of educators and undocumented students can be found at: williamperez phd.com/resources.

3. A detailed manual on training undocumented student allies developed by a group of educators and undocumented students can be found at: williamperezphd .com/resources.

4. Links to scholarship and resource guides can be found at williamperezphd .com/scholarship_guides.

QUESTIONS

1. "Although legally K–12 educators cannot ask a student about their own and their parents' immigration status, there is no law against getting to know students." In the case of undocumented students it may be even more important to get to know them and to support them in their situation. How can not only you personally, but your school, do this? How can you create alliances among staff and students to support these often hard working students?

2. What are some strategies in this chapter for working with colleges to make sure students apply, know about resources, and are successful? What can high schools to do bridge this transfer with their students?

22

PREPARING TEACHERS TO DEVELOP INCLUSIVE COMMUNITIES

Sharon R. Ishii-Jordan

The teacher who made a difference in your life was one who touched you emotionally—whether that took the form of academic prowess, personal concern, or serendipitous relief. It may have been the teacher who enthusiastically delivered the subject information in a way that transported you back in ancient history or who brought life to the rationale behind the geometric theorems or who could read Chaucer or Shakespeare with such dramatic delivery that you were held in reverie and understood the plot and characters. Perhaps it was the teacher who asked how you were doing in your classes, who listened when you needed to share with someone how miserable life was for you at that moment, or who accompanied you to the resource that you needed in order to handle a problem. Even more entertaining might have been the teacher who added comedy or delight or unconventional persona to draw you to school with anticipation.

The question that should be pondered in teacher preparation programs is, Who are these individuals who wish to be educators? It is not uncommon knowledge that there are some fabulous teachers who motivate students to desire, to seek, and to persist. How did these individuals come to this disposition? Certainly preparation programs cannot lay sole claim to the development of such individuals. How driving a force is the desire to be an educator? It is easy to love teaching when one's colleagues are thrilled with their career choice and students learn in spite of barriers. It is much more difficult to be an educator when the environment smacks of despair, hopelessness, and isolation. Yet, in such environments, there are teachers who continue to bring enthusiasm to teaching, learning, and living. How are those teachers able to find comfort, joy, and success in what they do?

Which individuals would be willing to stretch their natural knowledge, skills, and dispositions? Which individuals would be willing to risk comfort for more challenging environments? Those are the individuals who become memorable teachers. Those are the teachers who build inclusive communities for all their students.

Higher-Education Preparation Programs

Before we go too far, we should step back. Before developing such splendid educators, the focus must first be on where teacher candidates are formally prepared and who it is that prepares them. To adequately prepare teachers who can develop inclusive communities in P–12 school settings, preparation programs must themselves examine their contexts of formation. Program evaluation in higher education is imperative if deliberate change is to be made in teacher education, with the underlying premise being that such programs cannot be static in nature. Teacher educators must live and understand "the interconnectedness of the three 'c's' of climate, community, and change" (Christiansen & Ramadevi, 2002, p. 14). They must continually assess and act on necessary program change in relation to the changing climate of local and global communities. This chapter does not endeavor to suggest that all changes in the social, political, or physical environment will warrant change in teacher preparation, but the preparation must enable future teachers to create the type of learning communities that will benefit the students whom they teach. Doyle (2004) promotes three metaphors for preparing administrators that fit with the concept of teacher preparation that is described in this chapter. These metaphors are moral stewardship, community building, and educating. Thomas (1990) sees schools as moral communities because they are indeed social communities. While Doyle's and Thomas's concepts are not congruent, they certainly fall in parallel with the relative beliefs that are promoted herein. Regardless of the terminology, the preparation of any educators (administrators, teachers, support personnel) in developing learning communities will be similar in nature.

Part of the reformation of teacher preparation programs involves tabulating what is known, recognizing what is unknown, having the foresight and courage to search out the unknown questions to realities not in current experience, and acting on the commitment to benefit the inclusive community. Knowledge is neither created nor distributed in a vacuum. The benefit of being in the education field is the impact that social issues (from individuals to cultures to economic and political systems) have on its direction. Education cannot languish but must continually reshape itself.

The building of an inclusive community in education is grounded in both colearning and the sharing of resources and expertise that will enable all members of the community to rise together. Uplifting comes at the cost of additive and subtractive components, and therein rests one of the reasons that change is difficult, yet necessary.

A Changed University

The concept of a colloquium of scholars and learners is the foundation for a university. A student of higher education not only should be prepared for occupational skills, but should be engaged in a breadth of intellectual ideas, be provided with opportunities for reflective thought and discourse, and be exposed to the convergent and divergent aspects of knowledge and perspective. With this base of learning and the ever-dynamic life experiences that a student shares with others, the process of community emerges. The idea of a single field of focus where scholars deliver a single stream of knowledge to learners is no longer valid in a global community. It is incumbent upon future teachers to recognize relationships among different perspectives if they are to teach diverse learners in an inclusive community. Mathematics impacts economics, philosophy impacts science, linguistics impacts politics, and the research in one area of study can turn the tide of research in another. In short, a miscellany of knowledge indeed functions as a community—a dynamic, interwoven entity that shapes the outcomes of living and learning. Therefore, the university setting must be the philosophical and, indeed, the physical model for community building if future educators are to understand how to create inclusive communities in and out of the classroom. Doyle (2004) purported that "inclusion" (the education of all students in a school setting) is the construct by which university preparation programs for school administrators should be designed. Some of the research that she gleaned indicates that the "structures and practices within the preparation programs" do not model the inclusive concept that they preach to students (pp. 368–369). The same can be said of preservice teacher preparation programs. Talking about the importance of building inclusive communities but not modeling them may unintentionally lead future teachers to practice what they saw rather than what they heard.

While the concept of "community" may vary little among different societies or groups of people, the way in which the diverse entities of the community interact and the values that are held will undoubtedly change in the face of domestic and global shifts in power, common technology use, and new knowledge. That is, the culture of any community must undergo change if the community is to thrive. No enclave is ever secure amid large-scale change; disequilibrium compels change in practice or may consequently lead to dissolution.

The field of education is no different. It cannot be responsible for developing educators on its own. All university faculties must provide the higher order development of knowledge and skills that educators will need. However, a conceptual understanding of preparation is requisite.

Conceptual Understanding of Preparation

Within the design of teacher preparation programs should be three embedded motivators for change. There should be a philosophy of teaching that asks, Whom are we responsible for teaching? How should that be done? and Why? In addition, an understanding of changing communities and what that means for teaching should be incorporated. Finally, the program should raise the question, What changes on the horizon will compel society (and the field of education) to alter its mode of operation?

Education is a field in which philosophical ideas buttress knowledge. Without an underlying philosophy, the pursuit of knowledge has no direction or purpose. Debate over the purpose of schooling is dynamic because the societies in which we live change through time, as does the future direction and the means to pursue that direction. With continual research revealing new knowledge in pedagogy, philosophical issues, and physiological effects on learning, the belief about teaching/learning will shift from long-standing philosophies surrounding the what, how, and why of teaching.

Part of any philosophical discussion on teaching must include future trends and possibilities. Without that, we are left teaching in a world that no longer exists. Higher education must prepare educators to teach in a world that projects at least five years into the future. They require an understanding of changing communities, such as what globalization effects impact local populations, and the interactive dynamic when local populations experience shifts. Hence, professors must continually seek knowledge for themselves.

The preparation of teachers is predicated on the qualities that would be evident in teachers who are successful in creating the learning communities that I speak of in this chapter. Schussler (2003) suggested three dimensions that should be evident in a learning community: (1) cognitive, (2) affective, and (3) ideological. Schussler appeals to the notion of academic rigor, interpersonal relationships, and the values or purposes that underlie the first two dimensions. If learning communities are to thrive in schools, teachers must be prepared to expect and maintain academic rigor among students. Schools are, after all, expected to provide young people with the knowledge and skills to prepare them to make contributions to the society in which they live. There must be accountability in developing the "academic" in students. The cognitive dimension in a learning community, however, should not focus solely on the achievement of academic ends, but also on the process of learning.

The affective dimension correlates to the process of learning in that teachers should understand how students learn, be willing to motivate and engage the students in learning, and truly care for students. Schussler (2003) cited numerous examples of research into interpersonal relationships and caring, which she believes are two prominent features of the affective dimension. Although developing relationships with K–12 students is key, teacher preparation programs should also create an awareness of the importance of teachers having positive relationships with other educators and with parents/ families of students, and then provide opportunities for them to witness and practice these relationships in the field.

The third dimension that Schussler imparts as important in developing a learning community is the ideological facet. Without values and shared purpose, the other two dimensions cannot stay the course, and roadblocks will rise to detract the learning community from being successful. Teacher preparation programs must continually tie their own mission and core values into the course work so that future teachers will recognize how purposeful and deliberate ideals are in an institution.

Instructor Self-Examination

The inclusive nature of schooling presupposes the gathering of educators, students, and families of diverse beliefs, life experiences, languages, and resulting dispositions. No amount of external focus on diverse others can ameliorate the challenges that will occur if one does not also understand the impact that one's own life experiences have had on expressions of behavior, thought, and belief. The lens through which all of us interpret the expressions of others is quite powerful and often unconscious.

Like fish unaware of their relationship with water, because of our immersion in the "natural" order of our own developed environment and expressions (e.g., behaviors, communication, unspoken understandings), we are not aware of what is rote in our thinking and acting until it is challenged by unfamiliar expressions of others. Any introductory textbook in education speaks to the Piagetan developmental levels in which we find ourselves when confronted with strangeness. We tend to move toward some level of disorientation and attempt to interpret an unexpected response from someone within the framework of our own cultural and life experiences. It is not until we recognize the lack of personal experiential events with which to mediate the other person's response that we are able to build a new cognitive scaffold around the new life experience.

The solution to this uncomfortable unfamiliarity is to provide teacher candidates with opportunities to add to their life experiences through contact with diverse others, whether the difference is racial, socioeconomic, cognitive, age, or some other construct. Culture is not static: "The more experiences an individual has, the more his or her own culture changes from that of the initial natal environment" (Ishii-Jordan, 1997, p. 28). Mio (1989), in a study of two cultural experiences with graduate college students, found that greater understanding of diverse cultures occurred through a single in-depth experience with one diverse individual rather than through a breadth of knowledge acquired about a diverse group. It would follow, therefore, that relational experiences and skills would be demanded in an environment of greater diversity.

Linton (1936), an anthropologist who studied personalities and cultures, asserted that "culture is essentially a socio-psychological phenomenon . . . carried in the minds of individuals . . . find[ing] expression only through the medium of individuals" (p. 290). Aspects of culture are transmitted, invented, and interpreted through individuals and their life experiences. Therefore, university instructors must be willing to recognize their own personal life histories, their cultures, and the effects of their backgrounds in order to understand the biases, as well as the strengths, that have enabled them both to improve themselves and to impact the lives of others. With an examination and understanding of themselves, the next step is for the educators of educators to extend their own life experiences through contact with diverse others. Only then can instructors provide the opportunities for teacher candidates to engage in extracurricular or embedded course activities involving diverse relationships. Such activities would assist both instructors and teacher candidates in building and working within inclusive communities. It is incumbent upon personnel in higher education to understand that they prepare future educators for the present and future communities in which they will teach, not the communities from which their own experiences arose.

Program Design

Partner Preparation

The preparation of teachers starts with an interested candidate. To that candidate is added the breadth of subject knowledge from a college of arts and sciences; the specialization in pedagogy from an education college or department; and, finally, the practical experience that can only be attained in P–12 schools. This fourfold development of a teacher is the overriding conceptual design.

The P–12 school partnership should provide professors with the opportunity to connect with the current state of schools: to see the present realities, experiment with best practices, and share new knowledge with P–12 practitioners from the larger field of education. It should also be a productive learning environment for pre-practicum and practicum experiences for teacher candidates. Preparing educators for building inclusive communities cannot occur effectively without strong relationships in teaching, learning, and research between P–12 schools and institutes of higher education. This is a partnership that is vital (Christiansen & Ramadevi, 2002; Comer, Haynes, & Joyner, 1996; Goodlad, 1994; Langer, 2004).

Curriculum Content

Subject Knowledge

To prepare future educators for developing inclusive communities, a curriculum is warranted of authentic inquiry, flexible thinking, diverse strategy and skill development, grounded research, broad liberal arts study, and immersive experiences. Skills in communication (interpersonal and technological), convergent and analytical thinking, and practical application must be necessarily incorporated into the curriculum. First, the university curriculum should include opportunities for future teachers to reflect on subject matter theories and discuss their interrelatedness to educational practice. Rather than spoon-feeding information to students, a climate of authentic inquiry should exist that welcomes disagreement in the search for practical reality and future possibility. Second, flexible thinking allows students to begin in one direction and then, given alternate perspectives or new knowledge, to change views. The presentation of material by both professors and teacher candidates should encourage cognitive dissonance, for that is how growth and novel ideas are born.

Third, teacher preparation programs should teach diverse pedagogical strategies and skills that will enable all students to learn from them. The higher-education curriculum methodology should reflect research-based practices in multiple intelligences (Gardner, 1983), so that university students will learn through all their senses. Then they will understand about children learning in the same manner. The mind's recall pivots on the emotion and sensory connection that is attached to the knowledge and experiences gained. The fervent and passionate delivery of a favored professor can cement the shared knowledge into an easily accessible cognitive storage location for the future teacher. When professors teach in such a manner, teacher candidates will teach likewise. The curriculum in the education college or department should help teacher candidates to teach subject area material so that diverse students in a community can learn. Fourth, teaching practices grounded in research give future teachers the support to try approaches that have been proven effective.

Fifth, the acquisition of knowledge and ideas through the broad liberal arts provides teachers with a solid foundation in subject matter. The more knowledge one has in various subjects, the more likely one is able to blend together thematic approaches in teaching. Knowing *how* to teach (methodology) cannot substitute for knowing *what* to teach. In addition, the greater the knowledge one has about topics and ideas, the more able one is to build one community from many backgrounds.

Finally, there should be immersive experiences in working with and understanding diverse student populations, families, and traditions. Future teachers should experience, through guided practica and reflective connections, the frustrations, enjoyment, and challenges of stepping out of their comfort zones and own life experiences to teach P–12 students with different abilities, talents, and motivations. It is in these immersions that the teacher candidate begins to develop the teaching styles, lessons, management supports, and communication skills that highlight her or his own personality, in order to build the inclusive learning community successfully.

Social Knowledge

Subject knowledge must be delivered alongside social knowledge, for teaching cannot exist with only one or the other. Beyond the academic content of the curriculum, it is imperative that future teachers have knowledge about (1) multiple populations of students (e.g., students who have disabilities, who are linguistically/culturally diverse, who are gifted, who are at different socio-economic levels), (2) families, (3) community resources, and (4) advocacy efforts.

Teacher preparation institutes that are involved in accreditation evaluations include in their curriculum the study of multiple populations of students with special considerations. This curriculum content must include not only the knowledge of diverse school-age populations, but the strategies for assisting students in these populations with successful learning and the opportunities to work with the diverse populations in schools. Correa, Hudson, and Hayes (2004) studied the conceptual changes that occurred among education majors at a university in Florida when given a multicultural education course. Given the limitations that they expressed in their study, they still found that positive change occurred among the students in "understanding their responsibilities as teachers to make a difference in the attitude and behaviors of the children they will teach" (p. 338). These researchers felt that concept maps helped the students to reflect more on their views; however, they also found a need for more learning or different activities to move students to a deeper level of understanding.

Building creative classroom communities requires teachers to understand their students in the social relationships that occur or can be promoted in the classroom. In a study assessing the preservice course work that current teachers received in understanding and facilitating social relationships in the classroom, Pavri (2004) found that teachers reported that very little was covered on this topic. The need expressed by the teachers for more information seemed especially critical among those working with elementary-age students.

For inclusive community building to occur, future teachers must continually be reminded of the impact that families have on the partnerships with the schools. Teachers and administrators must respond to students' lives outside the school context, the families from whom they learn, and the neighborhoods in which they live (Langer, 2004). Whether a teacher focuses on building inclusive communities within her or his classroom or becomes involved actively with community building in the larger sense outside the actual school grounds, the connection with families can make or break the initiatives. Rupiper and Marvin (2004) found that more than half of the institutions preparing early childhood special educators have incorporated into their curriculum the content necessary for understanding and working with families. Through their experience in changing schools with disrespectful climates into "communities" of genuine learning, Comer et al. (1996) found that "when adults in their lives show trust, support, positive regard, high expectations, affiliation, and bonding, learning comes naturally" (p. 1). Therefore, the development of school communities that include parents and other community resources in as creative and multiple ways as possible will help develop the whole child.

The current understanding of school and community partnerships includes the innovation of wraparound services whereby students and families can use the school, the community locale where families connect most often, to access the other needs of families (e.g., health, social services, recreation). In wraparound services, the school building is used in partnership with the community to provide information or access to agency representatives who can assist families in meeting their needs. For future teachers to consider innovative ways to build community, knowledge of community and school partnerships is important.

Ford (2004) promotes a paradigm of "the culturally responsive school-community structure" that "would provide meaningful services which improve educational outcomes for multicultural students" through resources that recognize the cultural effects of families (p. 225). Creating classroom environments that are amenable to learning for all students involves the demonstration of caring and communication by educators that is steeped in cultural competence (Gay, 2002). Without the ability to learn about and experience such classroom environments through a teacher preparation program, future teachers are left to punt.

In creating inclusive communities both inside and outside the classroom, teachers must also be willing to work toward social justice. Within societies exist the privileged and the marginalized, and learning communities must embrace both populations. Ford (2004) addresses the need for school-community partnerships to "operate from culturally responsive frameworks" (p. 224). School settings exist with diverse populations of students (e.g., students are from different cultures, speak different languages, and possess different abilities), which makes teacher preparation programs responsible for preparing future teachers to work with these diverse students and advocate for access to education for the marginalized groups in our society. A community cannot exclude from access or contributions those individuals whose traditions or learning needs have not matched the privileges of the majority or norm. Building inclusive communities means using the leadership necessary to advocate for all students. It means becoming an activist to ensure that all students are included in that community.

Relationships with Teacher Candidates

The teacher preparation program's curriculum design suggested in this chapter outlined the subject knowledge and social knowledge that future teachers should acquire. However, as in all personal development, learning occurs more easily when relationships are formed, whether at the P–12 level or the university level. Examination of the construct of "learning communities" (Schussler, 2003) includes the affective dimension. That is, schools as learning communities must not only promote lifelong learning and academic rigor among their members, but also engage the student or "foster each student's sense of connection to the material" (p. 508). Integrated in the idea of engagement is the ability to develop interpersonal relationships and a sense of caring about others. Preservice teaching programs should be stressing the need for future teachers to develop positive and constructive relationships with students, collegiality with other educators, and understanding of parental and family dynamics. If such a disposition is expected of teachers, it surely must be taught and demonstrated by the instructors and professors during the process of preparing teachers. One cannot build community if one does not have the opportunity to practice community, and this is true for both university personnel and university students. Two examples of means by which teacher preparation programs might employ additional connections with their candidates follow.

Retreats

Learning about the teacher candidates in a preparation program cannot fully occur without the ability of instructors and candidates to spend time focusing on the core values of the institution and the affective dimension of a community. The institution's classroom setting is not designed physically or psychologically to engage teacher candidates in a trust-filled and relaxing space. One way to incorporate the ideological and affective dimensions of learning communities into a teacher preparation program is to offer teacher candidates the opportunity to practice interpersonal relationships that tie in with the institution's core values in a retreat setting. Retreats provide the means to engage the teacher candidates in an environment that is not so cognitively structured and construed. Thematic focus on specific institutional core values in relation to building learning communities in P–12 school settings will provide both reflective time and demonstrated practices that the candidates may carry with them. Learning is more solidly embedded when it is experienced and time is provided for reflection.

Informal Bonding

Informal opportunities to share reflections or seek bonding experiences in a teacher preparation program can be brought about in discussions that occur outside the confines of both the classroom and the objectives of a specific course. Graduate students have been known to engage in such experiences after an evening class, during which conversation may be related to some aspects of reflection from a variety of courses, but also may be driven primarily by the sheer pleasure of bonding with members of the class. Topics of discussion are not predetermined but arise as a result of personal experiences that are tied to some aspect of a course's content. Although professors may be involved in this gathering, teacher candidates may choose to meet to develop horizontal interpersonal relationships with each other rather than vertical relationships with the instructor.

Recommendations for Teacher Preparation Programs

Following are recommendations for developing higher-education personnel and improving program design:

Higher-Education Personnel
- Engage in discussion and reflection on (1) the role of education in a society, (2) the effects of social change and technology on changing realities in communities, and (3) the status of inclusive learning communities in their regions.
- Review and revise the teacher preparation curriculum to reflect cognitive, affective, and ideological facets of the current or emerging realities.
- Conduct a self-examination of the cultural norms and biases that have shaped their lives, and determine the changes needed to model positively the development of an inclusive learning community.
- Participate in immersion experiences among unfamiliar cultural populations to gain a greater understanding of differing perspectives.

Program Design
- Develop partnerships with diverse P–12 school communities to provide practicum experiences for teacher candidates and to gain more knowledge of community needs.

- Provide authentic learning experiences for students that will enable authentic inquiry and cognitive dissonance.
- Use and teach diverse pedagogical strategies and assessments.
- Demonstrate the interconnectedness of a breadth of subject matter from diverse perspectives.
- Provide immersive experiences and reflective opportunities as part of teacher candidates' preparation.
- Build social and academic knowledge.
- Provide opportunities for teacher candidates to work with diverse families/parents.
- Design retreats for faculty and teacher candidates to share discussion on the institution's and each other's core values.

Conclusion

How do we find or develop the kinds of memorable teachers who rose to the top in our own school experiences? Some teachers have natural dispositions and skills to work with anyone who comes their way. Some are drawn to serve all students in an inclusive environment. However, more likely than not, each of these teachers has had experiences in their lives that enabled them to learn about and foster the creation of inclusive learning communities. Rather than waiting for the accidental few who will inevitably make their presence known in P–12 school settings, it is the responsibility of teacher preparation programs to incorporate the type of curriculum, environmental context, and immersive reflective experiences that will develop teacher candidates into the architects of inclusive communities in the schools.

The design of teacher preparation programs that model inclusive learning and inclusive communities is not only *essential* to developing teachers—it is *possible* (Blandon, Griffin, Winn, & Pugach, 1997). The collaboration must include redesigned curriculum, shared teaching, program assessment, and willing and enthusiastic higher-education activists who believe in the reform and in the impact it will have on P–12 settings.

Preparing teachers to develop inclusive communities is a calling to act against the tide of traditional norms. Thus, preparation will require doses of inquiry, skill development, methodology, communication ability, and reflective decision making, all of which lead to a social action—the action of bringing all students to the center so that their needs and aspirations can raise the standards by which all members of our society are valued and served. Sirotnik (1990) stresses the building of character in teachers to prepare them. Perhaps that is the ingredient that contributes to developing memorable teachers who create inclusive learning communities.

References

Blandon, L. P., Griffin, C. C., Winn, J. A., & Pugach, M. C. (Eds.). (1997). *Teacher education in transition: Collaborative programs to prepare general and special educators*. Denver: Love.

Christiansen, H., & Ramadevi, S. (Eds.). (2002). *Reeducating the educator: Global perspectives on community building*. Albany: State University of New York Press.

Comer, J. P., Haynes, N. M., & Joyner, E. T. (1996). The school development program. In J. P. Comer, N. M. Haynes, E. T. Joyner, & M. Ben-Avie (Eds.), *Rallying the whole village* (pp. 1–26). New York: Teachers College Press.

Correa, V. I., Hudson, R. F., & Hayes, M. T. (2004). Preparing early childhood special educators to serve culturally and linguistically diverse children and families: Can a multicultural education course make a difference? *Teacher Education and Special Education, 27*, 323–341.

Doyle, L. H. (2004). Inclusion: The unifying thread for fragmented metaphors. *Journal of School Leadership, 14*, 352–377.

Ford, B. A. (2004). Preparing special educators for culturally responsive school-community partnerships. *Teacher Education and Special Education, 27*, 224–230.

Gardner, H. (1983). *Frames of mind: The theory of multiple intelligences*. New York: Basic Books.

Gay, G. (2002). Preparing for culturally responsive teaching. *Journal of Teacher Education, 53*(2), 106–116.

Goodlad, J. I. (1994). *Educational renewal: Better teachers, better schools*. San Francisco: Jossey-Bass.

Ishii-Jordan, S. R. (1997). When behavior differences are not disorders. In A. A. Artiles & G. Zamora-Duran (Eds.), *Reducing disproportionate representation of culturally diverse students in special and gifted education* (pp. 27–46). Reston, VA: The Council for Exceptional Children.

Langer, J. A. (2004). *Getting to excellent: How to create better schools*. New York: Teachers College Press.

Linton, R. (1936). *The study of man*. New York: Appleton-Century.

Mio, J. S. (1989). Experiential involvement as an adjunct to teaching cultural sensitivity. *Journal of Multicultural Counseling and Development, 17*, 38–46.

Pavri, S. (2004). General and special education teachers' preparation needs in providing social support: A needs assessment. *Teacher Education and Special Education, 27*, 433–443.

Rupiper, M., & Marvin, C. (2004). Preparing teachers for family centered services:

A survey of preservice curriculum content. *Teacher Education and Special Education, 27,* 384–395.

Schussler, D. L. (2003). Schools as learning communities: Unpacking the concept. *Journal of School Leadership, 13,* 498–528.

Sirotnik, K. A. (1990). Society, schooling, teaching, and preparing to teach. In J. I. Goodlad, R. Soder, & K. A. Sirotnik (Eds.), *The moral dimensions of teaching* (pp. 296–327). San Francisco: Jossey-Bass.

Thomas, B. R. (1990). The school as a moral learning community. In J. I. Goodlad, R. Soder, & K. A. Sirotnik (Eds.), *The moral dimensions of teaching* (pp. 296–327). San Francisco: Jossey-Bass.

QUESTIONS

1. Considering Ishii-Jordan's suggestions for training teachers, how many of these ideas were part of your own training to be a teacher or a principal, a social worker, or a counselor? How can you begin to fill in the gaps in your own education?

2. How important is it for student teachers to have "immersive experiences" in schools before they run their own classrooms? What do you feel are the things that you simply cannot be taught in a college classroom, but need to learn on the spot, with students themselves? In what ways do these experiences create a self-reflective part to your work?

23

CULTURALLY RESPONSIVE SCHOOL-COMMUNITY PARTNERSHIPS

Strategy for Success

Bridgie A. Ford

A large Midwestern urban school district is in the process of planning a series of school-community focus group meetings. The meetings are designed to address the multifaceted barriers to quality educational services for specific populations of students. Within the last fifteen years, the district's student demographics have changed dramatically from predominately White students of varied economic backgrounds to large numbers of students from ethnically and racially diverse groups, including African Americans, Hispanic Americans, and Asian Americans. Presently, African American youth comprise the highest percentage of multicultural students. Many of these youth reside in low-income neighborhoods. The district dismantled its desegregation structure of busing African American students from predominately Black schools to predominately White schools. The current policy of neighborhood schools for all students has resulted in a resegregation of students along racial and economic lines. The district's superintendent is an African American male. The majority of central and building-level administrators and teachers are White females. Only a few of the district's administrators and teachers live in the neighborhoods surrounding the schools in which they work. The State Department of Education has designated several of the district's schools as being under "academic watch" because of inadequate student performance on statewide achievement tests. Independent investigative activities pinpointed the existence of a disproportionate number of ethnically diverse students (males) in the disability categories of emotional disturbance and mental retardation, as well as the poor reentry rate of these students into general education. Mistrust between school personnel and families is markedly high in the low-performing schools. Many multicultural families and community constituencies have voiced dissatisfaction, asserting that schools are not held accountable for services afforded their children. Seeking better schooling, some parents are opting for charter or religious-affiliated private schools. School personnel cite lack of parental involvement and other out-of-school problems (e.g., poverty) as major causes of negative student outcomes.

The school-community focus group meetings at this district are being instituted as a strategy to emphasize that accountability for effective schools is everyone's business. To this end, public school personnel (central and building-level administrators, certified/licensed staff, and others), parents and other family members, community brokers (local businesses, organizations and agencies, churches and religious groups, and influential individuals), and local university personnel were selectively invited to participate. The meetings are to be conducted at a local community center located in a low-income neighborhood. The center provides a host of services for adults and youth and is highly regarded by constituents and the community at large.

The problems plaguing this Midwestern school district are not distinct; they are evidenced in the public educational systems across the United States. Nationwide, urban, suburban, and rural school districts are under scrutiny to improve achievement of all students. Measurable differences have been attributed to school-community collaborations in the areas of students' grades, attendance, school persistence, behavior, and parental involvement (Banks, 1997; Dryoos, 2002; Hatch, 1998; Sanders, 2001; Wang, Haertel, & Walberg, 1995). Not surprisingly, shared responsibility between schools and communities has been heralded as a major strategy to address the complexity of issues prevalent in today's schools. The national movement toward school-community partnerships underscores the importance of successfully preparing educators (and other school personnel) to work within these collaborative networks.

As illustrated in the example of the Midwestern school district, public school systems are experiencing a rapid increase in enrollment of students from multicultural and bilingual groups. Current student demographic changes necessitate a broad restructuring of school-community partnerships in order to productively attend to the needs of multicultural learners. More than one-third of the students in U.S. public schools are from multicultural and/or bilingual backgrounds. The three fastest growing groups are Hispanic Americans, African Americans, and Southeast Asian Americans (Grossman, 1998). The large population of students from multicultural groups requires that districts embrace school-community partnerships that specifically increase the quality of services for these youth. Doing so demands a culturally responsive framework for school-community action plans that can improve academic success, cultural competence, and critical consciousness (Ford, 2004; Ladson-Billings, 1995).

Through school-community partnerships, teachers are challenged to establish authentic bonds with multicultural students and obtain in-depth knowledge about them by networking within their communities and incorporating relevant experiences and resources into classroom practices. Using this paradigm, a *culturally responsive school-community* structure would (1) provide meaningful services that improve educational outcomes for multicultural youth, (2) utilize significant cultural resources that possess knowledge about multicultural students' experiential backgrounds, and (3) support the resiliency and empowerment of multicultural learners and their families. Unfortunately, public schools (like society in general) have traditionally viewed multicultural communities or economically disadvantaged/disenfranchised communities from a deficit perspective (Ford, 1995, 2002, 2004). Given the importance of school-community partnerships and student outcomes, the fundamental question is, How can educators be prepared to take advantage of *significant* community resources in multicultural neighborhoods? Educators must be equipped with the necessary competencies to help establish and maintain these important partnerships.

This chapter responds to the aforementioned question. It outlines a framework for equipping educators with the competencies required to construct and interact in culturally responsive school-community partnerships. First, I discuss a conceptual view of school-community involvement structures. Second, I delineate specific benefits of culturally responsive school-community partnerships. Finally, I highlight teacher competencies (knowledge, skills, and dispositions) needed to collaborate authentically with multicultural community resources.

Conceptual Frameworks: School-Community Partnerships

Communities play dominant roles in students' educational advancement. Logically, partnerships between schools and communities offer optimal opportunities for the growth of children and youth. Subsequently, infrequent contact in students' communities is documented as a school structure (policy and practice) that negatively affects educational performance and intensifies inequities (Nieto, 1992). School-community involvement in education is not a new phenomenon. Historically, communities have assumed different roles and levels of involvement regarding students' educational attainment For example, historian James Anderson (1988) chronicles the intense struggle of Black ex-slaves to gain universal public schooling for themselves and their children. These pioneering actions served as a foundation for the attainment of today's educational rights of other excluded and/or underserved groups in society, including youth with disabilities. During the 1960s, the ideals and programmatic components embedded in alternative social programs and community empowerment education reflected the centrality of community involvement. However, it was the combination of alarming educational achievement reports during the 1980s (e.g., *A Nation at Risk* [National Commission on Excellence in Education, 1983]), declining fiscal resources in the 1990s, and the spilling over of out-of-school problems (e.g., poverty, inadequate health care) faced by youth that revealed the obvious: schools need help. In other words, schools alone cannot provide children and youth with the resources they need to be competent citizens (Rigsby, 1995; Wang et al., 1995). It becomes fiscally and educationally imperative to institute collaborative models of school-community networks.

As noted by Garcia (1991), public schools are a community affair; they are made up of children from the community surrounding the school and with minor exceptions reflect their human communities. The school's community consists of varied social groups who interact with each other, developing cooperative and interdependent networks of relationships. However, schools are more likely to extend and participate in the critical cooperative and interdependent networks with social groups who are not poor and/or from multicultural backgrounds. Sanders (2001) revealed that when schools engage in school-community partnerships they *underutilize* community partners such as faith-based organizations (e.g., churches), volunteer organizations, community-based organizations (e.g., sororities, fraternities, and neighborhood associations), and individuals in the school community who volunteer their time, energy, and talents. These are essential elements of many multicultural communities. Broadened usage, rather than underutilization, is needed.

Some specialized educators (e.g., special education teachers) often possess certain knowledge of and/or firsthand experiences with public service providers (e.g., medical and mental agencies, social services, and juvenile services). This knowledge, however, usually does not extend to significant resources within multicultural communities. Teacher preparation and district in-service programs have failed to equip teacher trainees and practicing teachers, respectively, with the knowledge, skills, and attitudes required to develop culturally responsive school-community partnerships. If educators are to effectively use school-community partnership as a strategy to positively inform educational outcome for *all* students, including those from multicultural backgrounds, special training must be provided. They must be sufficiently prepared to partner with significant multicultural communities resources (SMCR) in order to improve schooling for multicultural learners (Ford, 2004).

In spite of the historic recommendations advocated within school reform documents and gains made from legislative mandates to promote equitable opportunities and higher academic gains, the educational state of affairs for many multicultural youth remains dismal. Fifty years after the *Brown v. Board of Education* decision, racially and ethnically diverse youth still are not afforded quality schooling (Orfield & Lee, 2004). As indicated in the Midwest school district vignette, many multicultural youth still confront the following issues:

- *Low graduation rates:* In 2001, the high school graduation rate was 75 percent for White students, 53 percent for Hispanic American students, 51 percent for Native American students, and 50 percent for African American students, with lower rates for males within these populations (Orfield & Lee, 2004).
- *Disproportionate representations:* Multicultural and bilingual youth remain overrepresented in special education programs for students with cognitive and/or behavioral difficulties whereas there is limited access to services for learners with gifts and talents (Artiles & Trent, 1994; Cartledge, 2004; Continho & Oswald, 2004; Obiakor & Ford, 2002).
- *Catastrophic conditions in schools:* Presently, twenty-three of the twenty-five largest school systems in the United States are heavily composed of students from multicultural groups. African American and Hispanic students attend schools where two-thirds of the students are African American and Hispanic, which means that most of their classmates are from their own group (Orfield & Lee, 2004). Many of the schools have limited funding and resources, inexperienced or unqualified teachers, lower educational expectations and career op-

tions, nonmotivating instructional techniques and curriculum content, a high teacher turnover rate, and unsafe physical facilities.

- *Inadequate racial ratio of teaching workforce:* There is a substantial decline in the number of teachers and administrators from multicultural backgrounds. In 1996, Wald noted that 86 percent of teachers were White, 10 percent were Black, 2 percent were Latino, and 2 percent fell in the category of "other." Combined with the aforementioned shortages is the dramatic shift toward a female teaching force (68 percent). Ironically, this decline in ethnically and racially diverse teachers is occurring at a time when culturally and linguistically diverse students comprise a large percentage of the student populations in many districts. Additionally, the majority of teachers and administrators do not reside in the communities of the multicultural students they serve. Disconnectedness between schools and multicultural communities is further heightened. Although this shortage of multicultural educators will be a tremendous loss to *all* students, it will be more intensely felt by multicultural students. Historically, multicultural school personnel have served in various critical capacities, such as leaders, role models, mediators, and mentors. The lack of a multicultural teaching workforce means that university and college training programs and school district in-service programs have a daunting task in ensuring that *all* educators (including the current force of White female teachers) be adequately trained.

- *Limited parental/community involvement:* Many multicultural parents have a history of negative experiences with and mistrust of the school. Differences in income, language, dialect, and value and belief systems or insensitivity to religious beliefs impact the involvement of multicultural parents and communities with the school. Consequently, parents are reluctant and/or intimidated about taking advantage of their legal rights (Banks, 1997; Brant, 1998; Cummins, 1986; Harry, 1995). For those parents, a "neutral" mechanism is needed to empower them with information and skills to advocate for their children. SMCR may be used as a strategy to promote increased parental involvement.

All of these problems illustrate the necessity of school-community partnerships. In his classic work, Cummins (1986) concluded that the major reason previous attempts at educational reform have been unsuccessful is that the relationships between teachers and students and between schools and communities have remained essentially unchanged. He emphasized that the required changes needed to involve *personal redefinitions* of the way class-room teachers interact with children and the communities they serve. A comprehensive culturally responsive school-community partnership can serve as a strategy to address authentically the endemic problems confronting multicultural learners. Essential components of this partnership would incorporate *significant* resources from multicultural communities. Therefore, preparing teachers to connect with these resources is fundamental. In accomplishing this, both teacher preparation and district in-service programs must respond to two key questions: How are teacher standards and requirements, paradigms, and practices systemically aligned to reform the professional development of preservice- and in-service-level trainees? How are teacher candidates and/or building-level administrators and practicing teachers equipped with the necessary professional tools (knowledge, skills, and attitudes) to advocate for a culturally responsive school-community partnership model and incorporate it into schools?

Elements of Culturally Responsive School-Community Partnerships

School-community partnerships vary in type and degree. Terms such as *integrated, collaborative, coordinated, school-linked services, community schools, full-service community schools,* and *twenty-first century schools* are used to describe program models that reflect the present school-community movement (Dryfoos, 2002; Rigsby, 1995). This current "linking of resources" paradigm encompasses two interrelated premises. First, as previously stated, schools alone cannot adequately address the multifaceted problems confronted by today's youth. This reality is more pronounced for districts in urban, low-socioeconomic locales where the prevalent problems include poverty; poor health; hunger; physical, mental, or substance abuse; unemployment; and teen pregnancy. These out-of-school, noneducational predicaments serve as barriers to students' academic achievement. Second, there is a need to secure the involvement of significant others (i.e., parents and community leaders), who have a *direct stake* in what happens to youth.

Effective school-community partnerships are beneficial to *all* students. This linkage is especially critical in maximizing educational opportunities for students from multicultural and/or bilingual backgrounds (Ascher, 1987; Banks, 1997; Comer, 1989; Epperson, 1991; Ford, 2002). Epperson (1991) called attention to the need for collaboration among public schools, multicultural communities, and parents as essential for the enhancement and development of youth. Given the persistent negative assumptions afforded multicultural populations and their communities by public organizations (including the school system), precautions should be taken to help ensure that needed services are delivered within a positive and culturally responsive framework. For example, Kemper, Spitler, Williams, and Rainey (1999) interviewed African American adults about the important characteristics and criteria that their youth needed in order to be successful. Nine themes were identified:

1. Healthy self-concept
2. Expectations of success
3. Religion
4. Refraining from obstacles
5. Goals
6. Education
7. Personal characteristics and traits
8. Appropriate behaviors
9. Connectedness

Using these criteria, the investigators examined program offerings of public agencies that provided services for African American youth. They found that, although the agency representatives viewed the nine themes favorably, little explicit information existed about how these criteria were incorporated into their programs. These findings have direct implications for school districts as they create frameworks to meet the challenge of school-community partnerships.

The provision of culturally responsive services must permeate the entire school-community network. To enhance accountability, a *student cultural systems* approach may serve as a framework when instituting the inclusion of SMCR into existing school-community partnerships (Ford, 2002, 2004). This student cultural systems framework places multicultural children at the core of community services to the school by *significant* nonprofit multicultural organizations/agencies. Thus, the student cultural systems approach includes multicultural community involvement activities that embody (1) the student's values, beliefs, affirmations, and socialization that are reflected in the delivery of noneducational and educational offerings to youth and families through the programmatic themes, topics, activities, strategies, materials, communication styles, program location, and parental involvement; and (2) the *significant multicultural* organizations, agencies, clubs, religious groups, and individuals that make up the immediate school community and those "at large" that target youth as a priority. Moll, Amanti, Neff, and Gonzalez (1992) used the term *funds of knowledge* to refer to historically accumulated and culturally developed bodies of knowledge and skills essential for household or individual functioning and well-being. In their work, they focused on preparing teachers to obtain and use household information regarding Mexican and Yaqui families' and communities' funds of knowledge. They concluded that an awareness and incorporation of the student's household and community funds of knowledge can help educators draw on the resources outside the context of the classroom.

As indicated, SMCR include not-for-profit service or social organizations, sororities, fraternities, clubs or agencies, religious groups/churches, and individuals whom local community residents perceive as providing valuable *significant* services (Ford, 1995, 2002). These services may include educational, advocacy, financial, legal, and/or empowerment assistance. SMCR generally offer numerous types of services/programs that may potentially impact the overall well-being of the school as well as the various developmental needs of youth. For example, within many segments of the African American community, the African American church remains an important leadership institution (Billinsley & Caldwell, 1991). It extends a host of outreach programs to support educational (e.g., early childhood and literacy programs) initiatives. Innovative programs that have made efforts to enhance the quality of Latino parent participation include Fiesta Educativa, Say Yes to a Youngster's Future, the MALDEF Parent Leadership Program, and Parent Empowerment Program—Students Included/Padres en Poder-Si (PEP-si) (Dias & Furlong, 1994; Rueda, 1997). In many cities, community resources that target the needs of American Indians may be centralized or confined to a local or regional "Indian center."

Some educators are teaching in "site-based" managed schools wherein the locus of decision making shifts from centralized bureaucracies to more local district and school levels (Cook, Weintraub, & Morse, 1995). Under this organizational arrangement, teachers take on new leadership and collaborative roles and make decisions that impact the entire school. Given the current priority of improving school-community relationships, this is a major decision-making issue. Educators in their new roles must see themselves as advocates for *all* students, including multicultural youth. In advocacy roles, they must *rethink* ways to complement service delivery to these students. Accordingly, they can help facilitate students' participation within SMCR programming activities.

SMCR: Benefits to Multicultural Learners

Specifically, SMCR have the potential of affording numerous benefits to multicultural learners (Banks, 1997; Billinsley & Caldwell, 1991; Brant, 1998; Epperson, 1991; Ford, 2002; Ford & Marino, 1994; Rueda, 1997). These benefits include the following:

- Resilience-enhancing resources through accessible adult role models, mentors, and advocates.
- Reinforcement of school-related skills through academic motivation, tutoring, and test-taking skills.
- Exposure to self-enhancing/affirming activities (e.g., developing values, cultural group identity, and decision-making skills; setting goals; and participating in rites of passage).
- Avenues for sensitivity toward culturally responsive programming through face-to-face encounters among administrators, teachers, and multicultural families and community resource persons.
- A forum for dissemination and collection of information. The need for information is a consistent theme regarding multicultural parents. This need has become increasingly urgent today. Communication remains the key!

Table 23.1 outlines a sample session of an SMCR program for third- to fifth-grade students.

TABLE 23.1
Sample Session of an SMCR Saturday Program for Third- to Fifth-Grade Students Sponsored by Alpha Kappa Alpha Sorority, Inc. *(see Ford, 2002)*

- Icebreaker: large group activity to get youth interacting with each other
- Direct instruction in test-taking and mathematical problem-solving strategies
- Session's guest speaker: African American male author of African American children's literature; interactive presentation/workshop focusing on the theme "follow your dreams"
- Self-affirming chant for the day corresponding to the above theme
- Closure activities: (1) dissemination of student materials and parental information (e.g., program and local information), (2) preview of next program's session, and (3) interactive self-esteem game
- Lunch with significant African American adult program leaders and attending parents/guardians

Preparing Educators for School-Community Partnerships with SMCR

Productive school-community linkages with multicultural communities require (1) the support and commitment of all major stakeholders (e.g., school administrators, certified/licensed school personnel, nonlicensed staff, and the targeted SMCR), and (2) the adequate preparation of school personnel. The combined efforts of a supportive administrator, a designated coordinator, and a committed building-level team are correlates of successful school-community partnerships (Dryfoos, 2002; Jehl, Blank, & McCloud, 2001). To prepare preservice trainees and in-service-level teachers to collaborate productively with SMCR, certain knowledge, skills, and attitudes are vital. Future and practicing teachers must be exposed to enrichment readings, multicultural workshops, firsthand experiences within SMCR, self-reflective activities, and varied systems of communication. The three-phase training model (Ford, 2002, 2004) presented in Table 23.2 can serve as a guide in preparing both preservice and in-service trainees to collaborate with SMCR.

Corresponding Knowledge, Skills, and Attitudes

If SMCR are to be systematically infused within school-community partnerships and used to impact outcomes for multicultural youth, there must be corresponding changes in knowledge, skills, and attitudes of school personnel. Teacher preparation programs and district-level in-service training must offer professional experiences that focus on how to

1. Examine past and current school linkages with SMCR.
2. Communicate with SMCR.
3. Share information about SMCR with other professionals.
4. Share information with parents about relevant SMCR.
5. Incorporate into the classroom environment education that enhances knowledge and skills.
6. Document changes in students' school performance and behavior.
7. Share with other professionals and parents about changes in school performance and behavior.
8. Share with SMCR the impact of programming on students' school behavior.

TABLE 23.2
Three-Phase Model for Preparing Educators for School
Partnerships with SMCR

Phase 1: This deals with reshaping attitudes and personal redefinitions through self-reflective assignments. Self-knowledge is a critical part of the process, because it helps teachers to know their privilege, pride, and prejudice.

Phase 2: This deals with reviewing and refining school-community partnership networks. Specifically, it entails
- Proper examination of roles and responsibilities
- Critical evaluation of historic and existing school-community partnerships with SMCR (e.g., policies, goals, practices, and outcomes)
- Collaborative participation in SMCR youth activities
- Adequate refinement of existing structures and practices that include SMCR
- Innovative creation of a database detailing SMCR
- Concrete determination of SMCR for school-community partnerships
- Consistent construction of varied systems of communication with SMCR

Phase 3: This deals with promoting successful participation of youth within school-SMCR partnering activities. It entails
- Real institution of collaborative procedures with SMCR regarding participation of youth
- Collaborative construction of varied systems for disseminating information about SMCR to parents
- Adequate integration of appropriate SMCR activities in the classroom
- Proper implementation of monitoring systems regarding the impact of SMCR activities on students' school performance

Conclusion

This chapter provides a framework for preparing teachers to establish authentic linkages between schools and SMCR. It emphasizes that *significant* resources from multicultural communities are important elements of a culturally responsive school-community partnership. Teacher preparation programs and school district professional development programs therefore must (1) engage in systematic processes that connect trainees with relevant (significant) resources within the communities of multicultural learners; and (2) equip them with the knowledge, skills, and attitudes to successfully use these strategic resources to advance the educational attainment of multicultural learners. Ultimately, there must be mutual partnership that respects and treats *all* involved as equal stakeholders excited about the future of multicultural children and youth.

References

Abrams, L. S., & Gibbs, J. T. (2000). Planning for school change: School-community collaboration in a full-service elementary school. *Urban Education, 35,* 79–103.

Anderson, J. D. (1988). *The education of Blacks in the south, 1860–1935.* Chapel Hill: University of North Carolina Press.

Artiles, A., & Trent, S. (1994). Over-representation of minority students in special education: A continuing debate. *The Journal of Special Education, 27,* 410–437.

Ascher, C. (1987, December). *Improving the school-home connection for poor and minority urban students* (ERIC/CUE Trends and Issues Series No. 8). New York: Columbia University, Institute for Urban and Minority Education.

Banks, C. A. M. (1997). Parents and teachers: Partners in school reform. In J. A. Banks & C. A. M. Banks (Eds.), *Multicultural education: Issues and perspectives.* Boston: Allyn & Bacon.

Billinsley, A., & Caldwell, C. H. (1991). The church, the family and school in the African-American community. *Journal of Negro Education, 60,* 427–440.

Brant, R. (1998, May). Listen first. *Educational Leadership, 55*(8), 25–30.

Cartledge, G. (2004). Another look at the impact of changing demographics in public education for culturally diverse learners with behavior problems: Implications for teacher preparation: A response to Festus E. Obiakor. In L. M. Bullock & R. A. Gable (Eds.), *Quality personnel preparation in emotional/behavioral disorders: Current perspectives and future directions* (pp. 64–69). Denton: University of North Texas, Institute for Behavioral and Learning Differences.

Comer, J. P. (1989). The school development program: A psychosocial model of school intervention. In G. L. Berry & J. K. Asaman (Eds.), *Black students: Psychosocial issues and academic achievement* (pp. 264–285). Newbury Park, CA: Corwin Press.

Cook, L., Weintraub, F., & Morse, R. H. (1995). Ethical dilemmas in the restructuring of special education. In J. Paul., H. Rosselli, & D. Evans (Eds.), *Integrating school restructuring and special education reform* (pp. 119–139). Fort Worth, TX: Harcourt Brace.

Cummins, J. (1986). Empowering minority students: A framework for intervention. *Harvard Educational Review, 56*(1), 18–35.

Dias, P., & Furlong, M. J. (1994). School counselors as advocates for increased Hispanic parent participation in schools. In D. Pederson & J. Carey (Eds.), *Multicultural counseling in schools: A practical handbook* (pp. 121–156). Boston: Allyn & Bacon.

Dryfoos, J. (2002, January). Full-service community schools: Creating new institutions. *Phi Delta Kappan, 83*, 393–399.

Epperson, A. I. (1991). The community partnership: Operation rescue. *Journal of Negro Education, 60*, 454–458.

Ford, B. A. (1995). African American community involvement processes and special education: Essential networks for effective education. In B. A. Ford, F. E. Obiakor, & J. M. Patton (Eds.), *Effective education of African American exceptional learners: New perspectives* (pp. 235–272). Austin, TX: Pro-Ed.

Ford, B. A. (2002). African American community resources: Essential educational enhancers for African American children and youth. In F. E. Obiakor & B. A. Ford (Eds.), *Creating successful learning environments for African American exceptional learners* (pp. 159–174). Thousand Oaks, CA: Corwin.

Ford, B. A. (2004). Preparing special educators for culturally responsive school-community. *Teacher Education and Special Education 27*, 19–25.

Garcia, R. L. (1991). *Teaching in a pluralistic society: Concepts, models, strategies.* New York: Harper Collins.

Grossman, H. (1998). *Special education in a diverse society.* Boston: Allyn & Bacon.

Harry, B. (1995). African American families. In B. A. Ford, F. E. Obiakor, & J. M. Patton (Eds.), *Effective education of African American exceptional learners: New perspectives* (pp. 211–233). Austin, TX: Pro-Ed.

Hatch, T. (1998). How community contributes to achievement. *Educational Leadership*, 16–19.

Jehl, J., Blank, M., & McCloud, B. (2001). *Education and community building.* Washington, DC: Institute for Educational Leadership.

Kemper, K. A., Spitler, H., Williams, E., & Rainey, C. (1999). Youth service agencies: Promoting success for at-risk African American youth. *Family and Community Health, 22*, 1–15.

Ladson-Billings, G. (1995). But that's just good teaching! The case for culturally relevant pedagogy. *Theory into Practice, 34*, 159–165.

Moll, L. C., Amanti, C., Neff, D., & Gonzalez, N. (1992). Funds of knowledge for teaching using a qualitative approach to connect homes and classrooms. *Theory into Practice, 31*(2), 132–141.

National Commission on Excellence in Education. (1983). *A nation at risk.* Washington, DC: U.S. Department of Education.

Nettles, S. M. (1991). Community contributions to school outcomes of African-American students. *Education and Urban Society, 24*, 132–147.

Obiakor, F. E., & Ford, B. A. (2002). *Creating successful learning environments for African American exceptional learners.* Thousand Oaks, CA: Corwin.

Orfield, G., & Lee, C. (2004). *Brown at 50: King's dream or Plessy's nightmare?* Cambridge, MA: The Civil Rights Project, Harvard University.

Rigsby, L. C. (1995). Introduction: The need for new strategies. In L. C. Rigsby,

M. Reynolds, & M. Wang (Eds.) *School/community connections* (pp. 1–18). San Francisco: Jossey-Bass.

Rueda, R. (1997, January). *Fiesta educativa: A community-based organization.* Paper presented at the Council for Exceptional Children Multicultural Symposium, New Orleans.

Sanders, M. G. (2001). The role of "community" in comprehensive school, family, and community partnership programs. *The Elementary School Journal, 102*(1), 19–34.

Wald, J. L. (1996). *Culturally and linguistically diverse professionals in special education: A demographic analysis.* Reston, VA: National Clearinghouse for Professions in Special Education.

Wang, M. C., Haertel, G. D., & Walberg, H. J. (1995). The effectiveness of collaborative school-linked services. In C. Rigsby, M. Reynolds, & M. Wang (Eds.), *School/community connections* (pp. 283–309). San Francisco: Jossey-Bass.

QUESTIONS

1. Does your school, your classroom, your administration use the cultural backgrounds of students and their communities as assets to build on? How much do the teachers in your school know about the neighborhoods and places from which their students come? Do they have a positive perception of their students' families, neighborhoods, and communities?

2. Do an informal inventory of your school and community resources including churches or mosques, agencies, informal groups, libraries, etc. What do you come up with? If you don't know of any, what does this mean about how your school is reaching out to the communities of its student population? How can this change or be built upon to create successful alliances?

Walking Down the Corridor Is Being in Another Country

Julie G. Landsman

Released from first hour,
students pour into the hallway.
Hands on hips, some shout:
You tol' her you thought I was with her man last night you know that's not true.
Others walk by in orange, blue or purple scarves and veils.
In stairwells young men pray and bow—
        cramp into a space to bend toward Mecca.
White girls put on makeup, spike up their hair with black polished
    fingernails,
        pull at rings in their noses and lips.

A hush of Hmong slips through, gaining volume as girls giggle
after huddling quiet in the corner all during science lab.

Five minutes of hip-hop, earphones curved over heads: the latest Outkast.
One young man takes dreaming steps, tuning into Monk's piano:
        a CD his father gave him in the hope it might calm his son during long
            afternoons.

Someone prays and someone sings and someone cries;
        one quiet, hungry girl who never knows where she is going
        slouches against a corner of the third-floor hallway.

Noise thins,
        teachers pull doors closed in unison, calling to their students as they
            might
        call to their own children on an early evening in November when
        the light has changed and they want to begin dinner.

A boy speaks quickly, Liberian accent,
a girl from Eritrea slaps palms with her friend from the North Side,
Mexican music syncopates from the lunchroom
        where study hall is just beginning.

Silence,

a flat surface of doors.

The young girl who was crying darts into the bathroom.

Women in uniforms patrol with walkie-talkies: crackle from the office
     "Fight in the parking lot"
     voice back,
     "I'm comin', honey, are the cops on their way?"

Hallways stilled: two lovers press up against the lockers on the second floor,
laugh deep into the skin of each other's neck,
keep a lookout. Between glances they touch and touch and touch.
Second bell, they arrange hair and clothes, buttons and lips, drift to class.

After they have gone, silence,
except for a whispered prayer in Somali
as a single delicate boy bends his body toward the eastern sun.

ABOUT THE EDITORS

Julie G. Landsman taught in Minneapolis Public Schools for 25 years. She has also been a visiting professor at Carleton College in Northfield Minnesota, and an adjunct professor at Hamline University and Metro State University in St. Paul. She has published numerous articles in journals such as *Educational Leadership* and *Teachers and Writers Collaborative.* She is the author of *Basic Needs: A Year With Street Kids in a City School*; *A White Teacher Talks About Race*; and *Growing Up White: A Veteran Teacher Reflects on Racism*, all published by Rowman Education. She has also published a behavior guide called *Tips for Creating a Manageable Classroom* with Milkweed Editions. Julie Landsman authored *Welcome to Your Life: Writings for the Heart of Young America*, with David Haynes, also with Milkweed. She also edited *From Darkness to Light, Teens Write About Overcoming Trouble*, with Fairview Press. Julie writes poetry and fiction and recently won the New Letters Prize for her short story, "Suspension." She is currently co-editing a new book for Stylus with Robert Simmons and Steven Grineski with the working title, *Going Deeper: Ideas From the Field for Having Open and Honest Conversations About Race.* Julie is a frequent speaker and consultant around the country and abroad. She can be reached by email at jlandsman@goldengate.net or through her website at jlandsman.com

Chance W. Lewis is the Houston Endowment Inc., Endowed Chair and associate professor of urban education and the co-director of the urban education graduate program in the College of Education at Texas A&M University. Additionally, Dr. Lewis is the co-director of the Center for Urban School Partnerships at Texas A&M University. Dr. Lewis also serves as the deputy director for the Center of African American Research and Policy (CAARP) at the University of Wisconsin-Madison. Dr. Lewis's over 100 publications include over 50 refereed journal articles in some of the leading academic journals in the field of urban education and teacher education. He has also received over $4 million in external research funds to support his research. To date, Dr. Lewis has authored, co-authored, or co-edited four books: *White Teachers/Diverse Classrooms: A Guide for Building Inclusive*

Schools, Eliminating Racism and Promoting High Expectations (Stylus, 2006), *The Dilemmas of Being an African American Male in the New Millennium: Solutions for Life Transformation* (Infinity, 2008); *An Educator's Guide to Working with African American Students: Strategies for Promoting Academic Success* (Infinity, 2008); and *Transforming Teacher Education: What Went Wrong with Teacher Training and How We Can Fix It* (Stylus, 2010). Finally, Dr. Lewis has provided consultative professional development and research services to over 100 school districts and universities across the United States and Canada. Dr. Lewis can be reached by email at chance.lewis@tamu.edu or via his website at http://www.chancewlewis.com.

ABOUT THE AUTHORS

Cynthia Alcantar is an academic coordinator for the Norco Community College Upward Bound Program and an academic advisor for the CGU McNair Scholars Program. She received her MA in Higher Education from Claremont Graduate University. Her research focuses on the role of educators in the educational trajectories and higher education access of first-generation college students.

Kieran D. Coleman of Jennings, Louisiana, serves as principal of Jennings Elementary School. He has been a secondary-school teacher and department chair. He received his BA from the University of Southwestern Louisiana, his MEd from Southern University, and his PhD from Colorado State University. He has done training and consulting in the areas of leadership, community building, and diversity. His email is trugent_louisiana@yahoo.com.

Bruce B. Douglas is a graduate of Colorado State University with a PhD in Education and Human Resource Studies. His scholarly research interests include the academic achievement of African American students, diversity initiatives in organizations, and career advancement opportunities for minorities in organizations. Bruce can be reached at bdouglr@gmail.com.

Stephanie A. Flores-Koulish is an associate professor and director of the Curriculum & Instruction program at Loyola University Maryland. She is a Colombian adoptee, born in the United States, and she is exploring her adopted identity through research and writing. She has also conducted research in critical media literacy education. She can be reached at sfloreskoulish@loyola.edu.

Bridgie A. Ford is a professor in the Department of Curricular and Instructional Studies, The University of Akron, Akron, Ohio. She is the author or co-author of several works in special education and general education journals and books, and of state-level in-service training materials. She serves on several editorial boards. Her work focuses on effective service delivery for African American youth and productive school partnerships with African American (and other culturally diverse) communities. She is the first editor of *Multiple Voices,* the refereed publication of the Division for Culturally and Linguistically Diverse Exceptional Learners, a division of the Council for Exceptional Children. She has conducted numerous professional workshops for school and medical personnel and has presented papers at local, state, regional, national, and international conferences. Her email is alexis2@uakron.edu.

Dorothy F. Garrison-Wade is an assistant professor of Administrative Leadership and Policy Studies in the School of Education and Human Development at the University of Colorado Denver. Dorothy's professional work includes experience in public and private schools as a principal (high school and middle school), assistant principal, counselor, teacher (secondary and postsecondary) and researcher. She is committed to offering high quality instruction that addresses the needs of diverse learners. Dorothy's research interests include access to equitable and fair educational opportunities for individuals regardless of race, disability, gender, or social status; and inclusive leadership. You may write Dorothy at UC Denver, Campus Box 106, P.O. Box 1733364, Denver, CO 80217-3364 or email her at dorothy.garrison-wade @ucdenver.edu.

Jennifer Godinez has been developing educational access programs and initiatives since 1999. As leader of the community-based organization, *La Escuelita,* she developed a comprehensive after-school center and was awarded a federal "Community Technology Center" grant for her involvement in addressing Latino youth achievement issues in Minneapolis, Minnesota. Since 2006, as associate director of the Minnesota Minority Education Partnership, she has developed the Minnesota College Access Network which provides professional development support for college access programs statewide, and she has led technical services for the development of three college access center pathways in Minnesota. Since 2005, she has been founding chair of the Latino Scholarship Fund of Minnesota with the Latino Economic Development Center. Jennifer often does trainings with Latino families, Latino youth organizations and diverse college student populations. She has spoken to audiences regarding access to higher education at the University of Minnesota, St. Cloud State University, College of St. Catherine's, and Hubert H. Humphrey Institute of Public Affairs. Jennifer received her BA in Sociology from Drake University and her Masters in Public Policy from the Hubert H. Humphrey Institute of Public Affairs at the University of Minnesota.

Paul C. Gorski is an assistant professor of Integrative Studies in George Mason University's New Century College, where he teaches classes on poverty and economic justice, educational equity, and environmental justice. He has been an active consultant, presenter, and trainer for twelve years, conducting workshops and providing guidance to schools and community organizations committed to equity and diversity. He created and continues to maintain the Multicultural Pavilion [www.edchange.org/multicultural/index .html], a website focused on critical multicultural education. Paul is actively involved in the International Association for Intercultural Education [www .iaie.org] (IAIE) and is currently serving his second term on its board of directors. He has published three books and more than 40 articles in publications such as *Educational Leadership, Equity and Excellence in Education, Rethinking Schools, Teaching and Teacher Education, Teachers College Record,* and *Teaching Tolerance.* His email is contact@edchange.org.

Justin Grinage is a PhD student at the University of Minnesota (Culture and Teaching). He is also the Advancement Via Individual Determination (AVID) coordinator, AVID teacher, and an English teacher at a high school in the Anoka-Hennepin school district. You may email him at Justin.Grinage @anoka.k12.mn.us.

Nancy Guarneros is a doctoral student at Claremont Graduate University. She received her MA in Social Science and Comparative Education with a focus in Race and Ethnic Studies from UCLA. Her research interests include immigrants, youth in higher education, undocumented communities, Critical Race Theory and Latino Critical Race Theory.

Stephen D. Hancock is an associate professor of Multicultural Education in the Department of Reading and Elementary Education at UNC Charlotte. Dr. Hancock serves as an instructor, researcher, and leader. His primary research interest is sociocultural perspectives in an urban elementary school context, which includes foci on the development of healthy academic relationships and the perceptions and psychology of self and others. In addition, his research interest focuses on intercultural identity in domestic and foreign spaces. He received his BA in English (language concentration in Latin), MA in teaching from Virginia Commonwealth University, and his PhD from The Ohio State University.

Aaron Rudolf Miller Hokanson is a PhD student at the University of Minnesota, studying Culture and Teaching. A former public primary school teacher in Australia, his research and teaching elaborate on his childhood love of *Sesame Street* and *Mr. Rogers*, exposing the educative experiences in personal, emotional connections often involving difference. His work relies on his family, friends, and the folk who share the spaces in which he lives, as it does the academic activists and outlaws who grow in the cracks of ivory towers.

Carolyn L. Holbrook is a writer, educator, and longtime advocate for the healing power of the arts. Her passion for providing grassroots accessibility to the literary arts inspired her to create SASE: The Write Place, a community-based organization for writers. She served as artistic/executive director from 1993–2006, when she spearheaded the organization's merger with Intermedia Arts. Her personal essays have been published widely, most recently in *The Black Body* (Danquah, Seven Stories Press 2009), *Black Renaissance/Renaissance Noire* (New York University, April 2008), and *White Teachers/Diverse Classrooms* (Landsman/Lewis, Stylus, 2006). A chapter of her memoir-in-progress inspired a choral piece composed and performed by the Twin Cities Women's Choir in 2004. She teaches English and creative writing at Hamline University and Minneapolis Community & Technical College. She was named one of "100 People to Watch" by *Mpls/St. Paul* magazine in the year 2000 and won the Minnesota Book Awards Kay Sexton Award in 2010.

Sharon R. Ishii-Jordan is an associate professor and chair of the Education Department at Creighton University. Her professional work has included teaching ESL in Japan, teaching secondary level special education in a public school, teaching in and administrating an education program in a psychiatric hospital setting, and presenting on topics in special education, ESL, and institutional values in online learning. You may contact Dr. Ishii-Jordan at Education Department, Creighton University, 2500 California Plaza, Omaha, NE 68178-0106, or at sij@creighton.edu.

Beverly J. Klug is an associate professor, Department of School Psychology, Literacy, and Special Education, Idaho State University. She has been working in the field of education for over 30 years. She has been involved in the education of ethnically diverse populations throughout this time, especially in the area of literacy development. Dr. Klug is co-author of the book *Widening the Circle: Culturally Relevant Pedagogy for American Indian Children* and has authored and co-authored numerous articles and chapters on related topics. Correspondence concerning this article should be addressed to Beverly J. Klug, College of Education, 921 South 8th Ave., Stop 8059, Pocatello, Idaho 83209-8059. Email: klugbeve@isu.edu.

Gloria Ladson-Billings is the Kellner Family Chair of Urban Education at the University of Wisconsin–Madison. You may write Professor Ladson-Billings at Department of Curriculum & Instruction, 225 N. Mills Street, Madison, WI 53706 or email her at gjladson@wisc.edu.

Ok-Hee Lee is an associate professor in the School of Teaching and Learning at Minnesota State University Moorhead. She was an elementary school teacher in Seoul, Korea, before she came to the United States to pursue her Master's and Doctoral degrees. She received her doctorate from Indiana University at Bloomington, Indiana. Her areas of professional interest include postmodernist perspectives in early childhood education, curriculum and instruction, and teacher education. Her email address is okheelee@mnstate.edu.

Valerie Middleton is currently a professor and the Secondary Professional Teacher Education Program Director at the University of Northern Colorado, teaching and researching in the areas of diversity, exceptionality (special needs), international education, and educational methodology. She holds a BA in Special Education from Illinois State University, an MA in Special Needs from Colorado State University, and a PhD in Teacher Education & Staff Development from Colorado State University. Previously, she taught students in grades K–12 in Chicago area public schools. Contact email is valerie.middleton@unco.edu.

H. Richard Milner IV is associate professor of Education and a founding director of the graduate program Learning, Diversity, and Urban Studies in the Department of Teaching and Learning at Peabody College of Vanderbilt University. Professor Milner is also a faculty affiliate in Social Sciences at Fisk University in Nashville, Tennessee. A former high school teacher, Professor Milner has served as a visiting professor at the University of Texas-Austin and was named a visiting lecturer in the graduate program of education at York University in Toronto, Canada, where he taught in the Language, Culture and Teaching program. His teaching, research, and policy interests concern urban education, teacher education, English education, and the sociology of education. Professor Milner's research and scholarly contributions have been recognized with an Early Career Award from the American Educational Research Association, and the Carl A. Grant

Multicultural Research Award from the National Association for Multicultural Education. His research has appeared in journals such as *Educational Researcher, Journal of Teacher Education, Journal of Public Management and Social Policy, Theory Into Practice,* and *Race, Ethnicity, and Education.* Professor Milner consults with schools and districts concerning diversity and opportunity both domestically and internationally. He can be reached at rich.milner@vanderbilt.edu.

Susana Munoz is a postdoctoral research associate and lecturer in the Department of Educational Leadership and Policy Studies at Iowa State University. Her research interests include college persistence and equity issues for under-represented students, with a special focus on undocumented college students. She received her doctorate in Educational Leadership and Policy Studies from Iowa State University and her Master's degree in Student Affairs and Higher Education from Colorado State University.

William Perez is an associate professor of education at Claremont Graduate University. His research focuses on the social and psychological development of immigrant youth. His most recent work examines the achievement motivation and civic engagement of undocumented students. Before joining CGU, he worked at various research institutes including the RAND Corporation, the Stanford Institute for Higher Education Research, the UCLA Neuropsychiatric Institute, and the Tomas Rivera Policy Institute.

Esrom DuBois Pitre, a former head boys' basketball coach, is a PhD student (educational leadership) at Colorado State University. You may write Esrom at Room 221, School of Education, Colorado State University, Fort Collins, CO 80523 or email him at esrom@cahs.colostate.edu.

Verna Cornelia Price is the founder and president of J. Cameron & Associates, a consulting firm committed to empowering people to excellence through personal power in the workplace and motivational leadership. She is an international educational consultant specializing in the areas of urban education, multicultural education, and service-learning. Dr. Price cofounded the Undergraduate Minor in Leadership at the University of Minnesota, where she is currently an adjunct professor in the College of Education and Human Development. She earned her PhD from the University of Minnesota–Twin Cities in Educational Policy and Administration. Dr. Price is the author of *The Power of People: Four Kinds of People Who Can Change Your Life* and *The Service-Learning Integration Guide*. You may email her at jcameron@jcama.com.

Robert W. Simmons III is an assistant professor in the Department of Teacher Education at Loyola University Maryland in Baltimore, Maryland. You may write Dr. Simmons at Loyola University Maryland, School of Education, 4501 North Charles Street, Baltimore, MD, 21210, or email him at rwsimmons@loyola.edu.

Joseph P. White has enjoyed a distinguished career in the field of psychology and mental health as a teacher, mentor, administrator, clinical supervisor, writer, consultant, and practicing psychologist for the past 49 years. He is currently Professor Emeritus of Psychology and Psychiatry at the University of California, Irvine, where he spent most of his career as a teacher, supervising psychologist, mentor, and director of ethnic studies and cross-cultural programs. Dr. White received his PhD in clinical psychology from Michigan State University in 1961. In 2007, he received an honorary degree, *Doctor of Laws*, from the University of Minnesota, which is the highest award conferred by the University of Minnesota, recognizing individuals who have achieved acknowledged eminence in cultural affairs, in public affairs, or in a field of knowledge and scholarship. In 2008, he was inducted into the San Francisco State University Hall of Fame as Alumnus of the Year. Dr. White is the author of several papers and seven books: *The Psychology of Blacks: An African-American Perspective* (1999, 1990, 1984); *The Troubled Adolescent* (1989); *Black Man Emerging: Facing the Past and Seizing a Future in America* (1999); *Black Fathers: An Invisible Presence in America* (2006); *Building Multicultural Competency: Development, Training, and Practice* (2008). He was a pioneer in the field of Black psychology and is affectionately referred to as the "Godfather" of Black psychology by his students, mentees, and younger colleagues. His seminal article in *Ebony* magazine in 1970, "Toward a Black Psychology," was instrumental in beginning the modern era of African American and ethnic psychology. In addition to his teaching and research, Dr. White has been a practicing psychologist and consultant. He has served as a supervising psychologist and staff affiliate psychologist to five hospitals and three clinical practices in Southern California. He has worked as a consultant with school districts, universities, private organizations, drug prevention programs, and government agencies. Dr. White was appointed to the California State Psychology Licensing Board by Governor Edmund G. Brown, Jr., and served as chairman for three years. He is currently a member of the Board of Trustees of The Menninger Foundation in Houston, Texas.

Kao Kalia Yang is author of *The Latehomecomer: A Hmong Family Memoir*; she is a product of the English Language Learner Programs of St. Paul's public schools. A graduate of Carleton College and Columbia University's MFA program in nonfiction, Yang lectures throughout the country on the significance and beauty of story in constructing life perspective. She is serving as Writer-in-Residence in the English Faculty of the University of Wisconsin-Eau Claire.

experiences of, 25–30
  Black, 47–55, 123–125, 243–254
  Latina, adopted, 173–180
  White females in urban schools, 98
  and identity, 270–273
  interactions with students
    with athletes, 284–296
    and failure of engagement, 279–281
    fostering engagement, characteristics of,
      277–279
    goals for, 282
    types of, 277
  and personal power, 281–282
  and self-reflection, 253
  service learning and, 156–157
  and undocumented students, 299–313
teacher education
  and community partnerships, 335
  conceptual understanding of, 317–318
  culpability of, 42–43
  and cultural literacy, 105–107
  and inclusive communities, 314–328
  program for, 320–324
    recommendations for, 325–326
  self-examination in, 318–320
  SMCR and, 338–339, 340*t*
teen parents
  demographics of, 246
  experiences of, 243, 245–246
Thandeka, 17, 23
Tomás Rivers Policy Institute, 308
tracking, challenging, 120–121
transcultural adoption, 173–180
  definition of, 179n1
transfer, undocumented students and, 309
transformation
  of good intentions, 56–74, 71*t*
  and inclusiveness, 239
  multicultural education and, 81–82, 88
  personal power and, 272–273
  reflection and, 13–14
  teacher education and, 322

unconscious bias, 123–135
  and disinviting schools, 214–216
  effects of, 131–133

undocumented immigrants, 257
  characteristics of, 301–302
  in Latino Diaspora, 304–305
  support for, 299–313
university, reform and, 316–320
University of Southern California Center for
  Higher Education Policy Analysis, 308
urban schools
  context of, 96–97
  versus suburban, 127–129
  White female teachers and, 93–109
urban students
  Black, achievement of, service learning
    and, 149–169
  service learning and, 157–159
  world of, 53

vision statement, 282
Vygotsky, L., 190

"Walking Down the Corridor Is Being in
  Another Country" (Landsman),
  345–346
White(s)
  schools, Black youth educated in, 208–227
  students, 59*t*, 97*t*
  teachers, 1–8
    and Black student-athletes, 284–296
    female, in urban schools, 93–109
    and overcompensation, 219–220
    prevalence of, 58*t*
    White on, 202
White, Joseph, 19, 21, 198–207
White privilege
  approach to, 19–23
  benefits of acknowledging, 19
  and Black youth in White schools, 222
  cost of, 17–19
  definition of, 14–17
  examination of, 11–24, 27–29, 59–60
White shame, 17–19
Winfrey, Oprah, 11
writing, and student voice, 114

Yang, Kao Kalia, 25–27, 29–30
Young, Iris Marion, 127

Also available from Stylus

Teachers As Mentors
Models for Promoting Achievement with Disadvantaged and
Underrepresented Students by Creating Community
Aram Ayalon

The book describes two similar and successful models of youth mentoring used
by two acclaimed urban high schools that have consistently achieved exceptional
graduation rates. Providing a detailed description of their methods—based upon
extensive observation, and interviews with teachers, students, administrators,
and parents—this book makes a major contribution to the debate on how to
reduce the achievement gap.

Using their similar teacher-as-youth mentor and youth advising models, these two inner city schools—
Fenway High School in Boston, Massachusetts; and the Kedma School in Jerusalem—have broken the
cycle of failure for the student populations they serve—children from underrepresented groups living in
poverty in troubled neighborhoods with few resources.

Apart from the potential of these models to narrow the achievement gap, these two schools have a record
of creating a school climate that promotes safety, and reduces the incidence of bullying and violence. At
the heart of both programs is creating community—between departments and functions in the school;
and between teachers, staff, students, and parents. Everyone in the school system should read this book.

Transforming Teacher Education
What Went Wrong with Teacher Training, and How We Can Fix It
Edited by Valerie Hill-Jackson and Chance W. Lewis
Foreword by Peter McLaren

"*Transforming Teacher Education* is provocative, insightful, precise, and vital to
our profession. Those whose lives intersect with teacher education will understand that this 'must read' text does more than merely encourage a transformative moment—it insists that a critical transformation is essential for the very
survival of teacher education. The editors have masterfully assembled the writings of preeminent scholars to crucially examine the profession while constructing a focused vision for the future of teacher education."—*David Whaley*,
Associate Dean and Director of Teacher Education, College of Human Sciences,
Iowa State University

"This volume is the one of most comprehensive and deeply analytical works on teacher preparation to
appear in decades. As a teacher educator, I deeply appreciate this thoughtful and critical examination of
the issues, dilemmas, and trenchant problems of teaching and teacher education in America. This is a
work well worth reading!"—*Peter C. Murrell, Jr.*, *Founding Dean, School of Education, and Professor of*
Educational Psychology , Loyola University Maryland

22883 Quicksilver Drive
Sterling, VA 20166-2102

Subscribe to our e-mail alerts: www.Styluspub.com